praise for *re*

resilient is a memoir of extraordinary power. I .... on every level, pulling you in deeper with every page, until the realization hits: You can't stop reading this harrowing and gorgeous story, and you'll be devastated when it ends. I truly believe *resilient* should be required reading for every person interested in any form of advocacy in our current tumultuous times.

-Lauren Sapala, author of *The INFJ Revolution*

This book is—without a doubt—the bravest and most vulnerable memoir I've ever read. In an age where so many of us feel alone in our personal darkness, this kind of soul sharing is absolutely vital, and Katherine Turner does so with honesty and grace. *resilient* is a teacher of acceptance, tolerance, and understanding, but its most important lesson is this: You are not alone.

-Kayli Baker, writer and editor

In her gripping memoir, *resilient*, Katherine Turner reveals the raw details of her traumatic childhood and youth in such a way that I could not put this book down. Katherine articulately describes her experiences with molestation, sexual assault, rape, neglect, and poverty, bringing you directly alongside her to share in every feeling and emotion. I often had to remind myself that this is no story, but a real-life narrative of events no person should ever have to endure. Katherine attempts to bury her suffering at every opportunity, only for it to manifest in self-harm, suicidal thoughts, self-blame, and impaired decision-making. Though her words are tough to read at times, Katherine reminds us all that we are not alone. As survivors of intense trauma, we are resilient in our many different ways and it certainly does not have to fit the textbook definition. She reminds us that our trauma does not have to define us, but that it is a part of who we are, not to be shamed and brushed under the rug. *resilient* is powerful, life-changing, and will help so many. It will stick with me for the rest of my life.

-Rachael Brooks, author of *Beads: A Memoir about Falling Apart and Putting Yourself Back Together Again*

Reading *resilient* is like falling into a soft, strong embrace halfway through a difficult journey—a journey of unknown length, unknown obstacles, and increasing challenge. Katherine Turner's story—and the brutally-honest manner in which she tells it—comforts readers with the reassurance that they aren't alone. No matter one's scars and pain, *resilient* tells them they can overcome. This is the book loved ones and survivors of loved ones alike need to read. For loved ones, *resilient* describes so clearly what it's like to survive trauma, and for survivors, it tells us that we can, in fact, survive, and we can always begin again.

-Olivia Castetter, editor, author, and activist

Turner's memoir is a gut-wrenching must-read for any sexual trauma survivor. Written with such raw, painstaking detail, you feel every one of her memories come to life. If you're a survivor, you're sure to feel less alone between the pages of this very important read.

-Rebekah Mallory, author of *Train Gone*

Katherine Turner's memoir *resilient* is a very courageous and gripping account of her past, filled with so much more misfortune and atrocities than anyone should ever have to face. Yet, what's most striking about the story is its positive, inspirational message, which Katherine Turner manages to transfer to her readers through her direct, grounded, and pleasant writing style. This book has the ability to change lives—both the lives of people struggling to come to terms with their own traumas and the lives of the people who care about someone with a traumatic past. This testimony should be mandatory reading for anyone who comes into contact with children or adults with traumatic early life experiences. The thoughts, mental associations, and explanations Katherine Turner shares so clearly on paper, are undoubtedly shared by most people who had the rotten luck to fall victim to abuse. Putting largely unconscious thought processes into words is incredibly difficult, which leads to a lot of misconceptions and frustration. This book provides a vital link between people, offering them the words they struggle to form themselves.

-Sanne Vermorgen, author of *Scar Tissue*

Courageous and moving, *resilient* powerfully captures a woman's memories of trauma and abuse throughout her childhood and early adulthood. Told with raw honesty, it's a shocking—but necessary—collection of experiences that show us with clarity where our society is failing, especially in relation to our children. While solving all the problems is no easy task, Katherine Turner shows us that healing one person at a time, at least, has a significant impact on the next generation. *resilient* is a bold and heroic piece, a memoir that will change the way you see poverty, privilege, and survivors.

-Ana Hantt and Josie Baron, authors of the Extraordinary Series and founders of the @30ontheroad project

resilient

a memoir

resilient

foreword by Rachael Brooks

a memoir by
katherine turner

Josha
Publishing

This book is a work of creative nonfiction. It reflects the author's present recollections of experiences over time. Some names and characteristics have been changed, some events compressed or excluded, and some dialogue has been recreated.

First edition: August 2021

Editing by Kayli Baker and Olivia Castetter
Cover design by Murphy Rae
Cover and interior art by Shelly Person
e-book formatting by Jo Harrison

Library of Congress Control Number: 2021909799
Library of Congress Cataloging-in-Publication Data available upon request.

ISBN 978-1-7344230-6-8 (ebook)
ISBN 978-1-7344230-7-5 (paperback)
ISBN 978-1-7344230-8-2 (hardcover)

Josha Publishing, Independent Publisher
www.joshapublishing.com
Haymarket, VA

Printed in the United States of America

a note of caution

this is a memoir about childhood trauma and
the struggle into adulthood as a result of that
trauma; there are descriptions of and
references to physical, sexual, and emotional
abuse, rape, suicide, self-harm, and addiction

table of contents

for my fellow travelers on this journey of
healing from childhood trauma

you are **seen**

you are **worthy**

you are **not alone**

foreword

When I look back on my childhood, it is filled with many happy memories. Not all are happy, but many are. Pool parties with my friends. Soccer games on the weekends. Christmas mornings filled with a sea of gifts under the tree. Hugs and well wishes on the first days of school. Not that I ever took these moments for granted, but I figured this was typical of all childhoods.

In fact, though, it is not.

As a memoir author myself, I understand firsthand the fear that accompanies sharing what is unknown to so many. Through sharing our truth, though, that initial fear evolves into motivation, hope, a renewed sense of self-assurance and control. There is motivation to finish the amazing accomplishment of writing a book. There is hope that your words will have a lasting impact and help others. There is this confidence that builds as you get further along in the process because you are in complete control of how your narrative is presented.

Shortly after the 2019 release of my memoir, *Beads: A Memoir about Falling Apart and Putting Yourself Back Together Again*, I took a pause. My truth was out there: a stranger raped me in his faux taxi cab in the summer of 2008, shortly after I graduated from college. *Beads* details my journey from that moment as a broken victim to becoming a strong survivor, and everything in between. But you never really know how something like this is going to be received beforehand.

And then it was confirmed: my words had helped another.

I began seeing the same name scattered across my social media, liking posts, commenting here and there, a few messages back and forth. One day, I received an email. It was from Katherine Turner. She had finished reading my book and thanked me for everything I was doing for survivors. I cried. I'd always said if I could help just one person in their healing journey, then mission accomplished. And here we were.

Fast forward to present day, and I am now thanking Katherine for everything *she* is doing for survivors. *resilient* reveals a childhood that should never be. It reveals the horrors of abandonment, poverty, abuse, rape, self-harm, and how a young girl navigates through that trauma the best way she knows how. Katherine leaves nothing unsaid as she details the raw truth about what it was like to grow up in a world where no one believed her, resulting in years of self-blame and debilitating guilt. Her strength, however, to push forward, to find her way, is one so incredible that it becomes nearly unbelievable that she has lived to tell of her past.

I read *resilient* in three days. And while I am a writer, I am not much of a reader. I simply could not put it down. Evoking tears of anger, pride and gratitude, solace and empathy, *resilient* resonated with me on the deepest of levels. It reminded me that we are not alone in our fight for survival, our journeys to heal. It reminded me that being resilient does not have to mean everything is fine. It reminded me that there is no timeline for recovery.

resilient is the type of book that will stick with you in the good, the ugly, and the best of ways. Brace yourself, because once you dive in, you won't ever be able to look back.

-*Rachael Brooks*

Rachael Brooks is the author of *Beads*, a speaker, and a victim rights advocate for sexual assault survivors. She currently lives in North Carolina with her husband and two children.

Courage to Fly

Precious one, you gaze with longing at forget-me-not skies while you remain grounded on the earth below, so deeply rooted in your fear.

Fear of rejection, fear of failure, fear of others. Afraid to fall, yet even more afraid to fly. You fear success as much as you fear defeat, and so you tell yourself you are content here on familiar land where it is comfortable and safe. Yet your spirit is a restless wind, a fervent ocean, like a force of nature your heart is wild, free, uncontained.

Beloved, you have been held down for so long now. The weight of all you have carried corrupted your wings until you no longer tried to fly. Worse yet, until you no longer wanted to. And even now, even as you heal, even as you are healed, you are too afraid to once again lift your wings toward skies that long to set you free.

But look at all you have become. See your strength, resilience, power, beauty, determination, fortitude. Now is your time to take flight beloved. The universe is quiet and hushed as it waits with eager anticipation to see you rise, to stand in awe of your creation, just as it did the day you were born.

Everything you need is contained within your valiant spirit. You are light to the darkest of places, salt to the corners of the earth, healing to the wounded, love to the broken-hearted.

Your faith wavers, so fragile in your chest, so unsure, so filled with doubt. Breathe, for you no longer have a spirit of fear, but a spirit of power. Your heart can no longer be contained in your chest, your spirit no longer caged in your body, your wings no longer cast down by your side.

All you need now, beloved, is the courage to fly.

-Kathy Parker

Resilient

Adjective \ri-ˈzil-yənt, -ˈzi-lē-ənt\

1   Returning freely to a previous position, shape, or condition: such as

    a   capable of withstanding shock without permanent deformation or rupture

    b   tending to recover from or adjust easily to misfortune or change

introduction

Resilient. What an upbeat word, right? You read it and think, *Wow, recover easily from misfortune? I want to be resilient!*

Sounds so lovely, doesn't it? And even better, if someone calls you resilient? What a sense of accomplishment that gives you! How proud you are of yourself because resilience is not easy to come by—especially when those words are spoken with such pride from people you look up to, people you trust to guide you in life.

From the day we're born, as we grow and learn, we all develop our own distinctive tastes, our own likes and dislikes unique to the person we are. We all have a favorite food as well as those we avoid at all costs; activities we enjoy as well as those we can't be persuaded to engage in. Most people I've met also have a favorite word and a least-favorite word, and I find it fascinating to learn the *why* behind the words people choose. Knowing what those words are without the story behind them is akin to someone saying "three thousand" and nothing else. *Three thousand what?* Maybe that's the number of seconds that person slept the night before. Or the number of miles they walked on foot in the last five years. Or the number of books they own or coins they've collected or... the list could go on for pages, limited only by your imagination, because the thing is that *you just don't know*. Until they tell you.

As a voracious reader and writer, I love words; every word has its own nuanced meaning and unique context for its ideal usage. And then it has slightly different meanings determined by how it is commonly used in society, which shifts with the passage of time—slang usages that seemingly crop up out of nowhere. Of course, there are even completely different definitions within professional contexts where the word becomes jargon. As a result, I don't personally have a long-standing favorite; it just depends on the day. As I'm writing this, I'm thinking, *I love the word "gobbledygook"—it's so much fun to say!* Though I also love the word *nonsensical* because it always brings to mind one of my favorite books since I was young, *Pride and Prejudice*. And if you asked me tomorrow, I'd probably think of yet another word.

I have no problem identifying the words I *dis*like, however. Despise, even. My long-standing *least*-favorites. I have my more obvious selections—words that seem so common in society today that I absolutely cannot stand. Words that make me cringe and ignite an instant flame of disgust and anger in my soul. Words like *pussy* and *cunt*. Words like *nigger* and *faggot* and *retard*. Pretty much anything derogatory about a person's race or sexual orientation or body parts or mental ability is guaranteed to get under my skin. And I think dislike of these words is common enough that I'll skip the why. But I have one more word to add to this list.

Resilient.

When I was very young, I was like most people—the people who love this word and feel pride when it is used to describe them—but that sentiment disintegrated as the word took on a meaning I never expected, brought with it a weight I was unprepared to bear. As I got older, I started to cringe when I heard someone say it, my stomach tightening and a slight feeling of nausea passing over me as my heart raced. It wasn't long until I began detesting the word, a sentiment I harbored for most of the last twenty-five years.

This book is my why.

ill-equipped

"Addiction is a family disease... the whole family suffers."

-Unknown

I read somewhere once that babies born during certain seasons tend to be drawn to those seasons, to enjoy them; if they're born in the winter, they like the cold winter months, or if they're born in spring, they like the cool spring months. Even if that's true for most, though, it certainly isn't for me. I don't like even going outside in the heat of the summer in Virginia, the state in which I was born at the beginning of August in 1984 to my unwed parents, Kathy and Teddy.

My mom was around thirty when I was born and already had two boys from different dads: James, who was five years old, and Al, who was three years old. I also had an older sister, who would have been quite a bit older than James and from yet a different father, but she'd died years before I was born after my mom left her alone in the bathtub at eight months old to go smoke a joint with the father.

I imagine that, with my mom's combination of both diagnosed and untreated bipolar disorder and schizophrenia (what today would be classified as schizoaffective disorder, bipolar type), my birth after the loss of her firstborn daughter was incredibly difficult. Unfathomably triggering. I can only imagine that she looked at me as a newborn in the hospital and was immediately overwhelmed by both intense joy and bitter sadness.

I wouldn't know this until many years later, but my dad was already divorced at the time, already father to a few children with another woman. I never met any of them, and he never once mentioned them after I was born; I found out when I did entirely by accident. But I was my dad's first

3

girl and he immediately had a soft spot for me. I picture him standing next to my mother in the hospital, eyes watery and a huge smile when I was born.

I would also learn later that my parents had gotten married, and we'd already moved once by the time my younger sister, Laurel, was born fifteen months later. We went on to move two or three times each year until I was five, when we finally stayed in a single home for an entire year.

We never met anyone on our mother's side, something she blamed on the fact that she was married to a black man and all of her children were biracial. But I discovered in adulthood that her story was a fabrication. She'd long since estranged herself from the family that adopted her as a toddler for disapproving of her life choices, a natural progression from her troubled teen years, during which she repeatedly ran away from home. It was when I discovered this information that I found out I also had an aunt on her side; my mother had never once mentioned she had a sister.

I don't remember a time, however, when I didn't know my father's side of the family—a large, raucous, and dominating group who got together often. My Aunt Pauline and my Grandma Virginia (who lived alone since my grandfather had died of liver failure related to severe alcoholism shortly after I was born) opened their homes to the extended family on Sundays. My siblings, dad, and I often spent the afternoons there after church, especially during football season. Summers brought enormous family reunions, aunts and uncles and cousins upon cousins coming out of the woodwork, usually at my grandma's house, which was a little bit larger and had a bit more outdoor space than my Aunt Pauline's tiny urban townhouse.

My brothers, my sister, and I were the only biracial kids on my dad's side of the family, our skin much lighter than everyone else's, my mom the only white person who someone from my dad's family had dared to marry. And while my brothers could pass visually for being black like all our cousins—even with their lighter skin—thanks to having "black hair," my sister and I could not. Our dad insisted we obey our aunts and uncles and cousins and sit on the floor for an hour or more during those family visits while our cousins and aunts roughly braided our hair to look more like theirs.

When our parents were still together, there wasn't a time that my dad didn't work; I don't have memories from a time when my mom *did*. My dad would later explain that my mom tried to work, but she struggled to keep a job. Between her progressively worsening alcoholism, which led to her sneaking small bottles of vodka in her purse and often needing medical attention for alcohol poisoning, and her mental health struggles that led to periodic hospital stays after failed suicide attempts, she was an unreliable employee and was often fired shortly after she started. It became more and more difficult for her to get hired, and eventually, she stopped trying. The burden of financially providing for a family of six ended up squarely on my father's shoulders, as did the need to ensure some level of care for us when our mother was unexpectedly absent because of another stay in the hospital.

When I think back on what my parents were dealing with in their lives while trying to raise children in poverty, neither of them with more than an eighth-grade education, my heart aches for them. I can see clearly how little control they had in their lives, how they were often stuck making impossible decisions, choosing between the lesser of two evils. Neither of them was really equipped for everything life had thrown at them, even without kids in the mix—let alone four of us.

My parents weren't evil. They may have been ill-equipped for the lives they had, but they certainly weren't ill-intentioned. They loved us, and they did what they thought was best at the time, relying on the knowledge and coping mechanisms they knew. I fully recognize that now as an adult, of course, but I even had some subconscious understanding of this when I was young. That recognition and understanding, however, doesn't change what happened or what it was like to live through those things that happened, and it doesn't change how it impacted every person in our family.

uncle tick

"Each day of our lives, we make deposits in the memory banks of our children."
-Charles R. Swindoll

september 1989

On the way to my Aunt Pauline's house after church, I crossed my fingers and leaned forward in the backseat of my dad's Blazer. "Will Uncle Tick be there?" I asked.

"Yeah," my dad responded with a laugh.

My stomach dropped at his response. I didn't know what it was, but I was terrified of my Uncle Tick. I wasn't even sure if he was a real uncle—we called a lot of family friends Aunt and Uncle—but he was often at our family gatherings. When I'd asked what his real name was, my dad had just told me to call him Uncle Tick, and when I'd asked why, my dad had laughed and responded, "Because he's black as a tick!"

While my mom rolled her eyes, my dad always laughed at my intense dislike of Uncle Tick; he said I was just scared of how dark his skin was. It wasn't his skin, though, it was something else about him; he just gave me the heebie-jeebies. I hated seeing him and was already eager to leave, even though we hadn't yet arrived.

As the scenery blurred by, I closed my eyes and thought about the previous day—a perfect afternoon.

I lay on the floor in the living room, chewing on the nipple of the bottle my mom had given me for nap time with a soft kiss on my forehead, while the rich and beautiful sound of her flute filled the air in the house and spilled out the open windows. She continued to play the entire afternoon, the melody floating on the breeze in the backyard until well after quiet time, when my brothers and sister and I were playing tag.

6

She stopped for a while when I started screaming and crying, running out the back door to see what had happened. I rubbed my palm now, sitting in the car, as I remembered the bee Al had talked me into trapping between my palms with a promise that it wouldn't sting me. *I froze when my mom arrived after it stung me, unsure what would happen; when he'd done it the week before, my mom had screamed at him and spanked him with her wooden paddle right there in the yard. Then she'd yelled at me for being stupid enough to keep believing him when he told me I wouldn't get hurt.*

But it was a flute day, and my mom almost never screamed at us or spanked us on days when she was playing the flute. Instead, she sternly told Al to stop telling me to catch bees, that it wasn't funny to hurt his sister, and then carried me inside. She poured peroxide over my sting, and I watched as the little white bubbles fizzed up and then as she patted it dry with a tissue and covered it with a band-aid. It wasn't really hurting anymore at that point; the pain in my hand had all but disappeared by the time we made it in the back door, my mom's arms wrapped around me enough to beat back the painful sensations. Once I was bandaged, I ran back outside, the screen door closing as another soft melody began behind me.

My dad came home from work later, smelling of sweat and cigarette smoke and car grease and that sweetly-scented pink soap stuff he used with thick blue paper towels to clean his hands, a single grocery bag in his grease-stained hands and a broad smile under his thick mustache.

"Go wash your hands," he called to us. He then disappeared into the house and I heard him shout to my mom over the sound of her flute as the door closed behind him, "Kathy! Come on out back!"

We raced inside to the closest bathroom and washed our hands, pushing each other out of the way in our haste to get back outside and see what our dad had brought home for us. He appeared with my mom right behind him a moment later—a matching smile on her face—now with a fistful of spoons in his other hand. He chuckled to himself, obviously enjoying keeping us in suspense, as he took his time to sit down on the stoop in his grease-covered jeans and blue, button-up, short-sleeve shirt with a stitched tag that read "Teddy" on the chest, the armpits and back and most of the chest dark blue with sweat.

Finally he opened the bag and pulled out a half-gallon container of Neapolitan ice cream, my mom's favorite. He handed out spoons and peeled off the lid as he picked up the container again and held it toward my mom to get the first spoonful. After that, it was a free-for-all, spoons diving into

7

the already softening creamy goodness the second they left our mouths; this was a rare treat. As the container ran low, the scooping slowed. My brothers started chasing each other around the backyard, my sister picked up sticks from the grass, and I climbed onto my dad's lap, leaning back against his dirty, sweaty chest as the sun beat down on us.

"Can we do Lite-Brites in the shed?" I asked hopefully when he finished the last bite of ice-cream and set the container back into the plastic bag.

He leaned forward to pull a blue paper towel smeared with black streaks of grease from his back pocket and wiped the sweat that was pouring down the sides of his face from his forehead. "You wanna do that again? It's hot as hell out here—we'll suffocate in that shed."

"Please, Daddy? Pleeeeeeeease? We can leave the door open!"

My dad's chest rumbled with a chuckle as he used an arm to shift me out of the way and pull a pack of cigarettes and a lighter from his chest pocket. I watched every motion, wishing he would hurry and answer me. After a long pull, he bit the cigarette between his teeth and blew the smoke out around it. Without taking the cigarette out of his mouth—so it was waving around as he spoke—he finally answered.

"Sure, just let me finish my cigarette first."

I squealed and jumped up off his lap, running inside to grab the Lite Brite box to play in our toolshed-turned-clubhouse. As soon as I stepped back outside—

My eyes flew open and I was wrenched from my memory when my dad slammed on the car brakes and I lurched forward in my seatbelt.

"What the fuck, Teddy?" my mom snapped.

"Hubcap," my dad responded as he navigated the car over the rumble strip and onto the grassy embankment next to the highway.

Cars flew past us, sounding like the racecars going around the track that my dad liked to watch. Every one that passed made me cringe, remembering the last time we'd gone to a race and snuck through the barbed-wire fence to get in since we couldn't afford "one of those damn expensive tickets," as my dad had said. I'd lifted my head too soon when I was shuffling my body along the dirt under the fence and gotten a barb stuck in my scalp. By the time the race was over, the dirty blue towel from my dad's pocket, which I'd been holding on the top of my head, was mostly soaked with blood. When we'd gotten home, my mom had yelled at my dad for taking me, then spanked me for getting myself hurt doing it. I shivered as a big tractor trailer flew past us, shrinking toward the other side of the car.

8

"Go on," my dad said, glancing into the rearview mirror.

My brothers rolled their eyes and muttered something to each other that I couldn't understand. I knew they didn't like it when my dad stopped the car and made them get out to grab hubcaps, but it was something my dad never passed up; he said every one we found could get him up to a dollar or two and that driving past was "throwing damn money away."

"If you boys don't get your asses out there right now and pick up that damn hubcap without any back talk, I'll pull my belt off and whoop your asses right here on the side of the road!" my dad roared.

I tried to make myself smaller in my seat, even though it was my brothers who were in danger of getting spanked. My dad's belt buckle was the *worst*. It was even worse than my mom's wooden paddle that she'd gotten when she broke her arm the previous year. She'd been drinking that stuff that looked like water but wasn't—the stuff she said made her a klutz—and she'd fallen down the stairs that afternoon. That paddle would leave bruises and welts, but my dad's belt? It not only did those things, but also left blood spots on our clothes and open sores and scabs that hurt for weeks. Although, sometimes my mom's paddle hurt me in other ways.

Like when I'd heard my mom screaming in her room about not finding her scissors and I saw them sitting by the television in the living room where my brothers, sister, and I were all watching cartoons a few weeks before.

I hesitated because my mom had been mad at us for days and had already spanked me once when my sister kept unplugging the television. She'd thought it was me when my brothers started yelling, so she'd come in and spanked me without listening to my brothers telling her it had been my sister doing it. But I thought taking her scissors to her might make her happy again. I grabbed them and ran toward her room, but tripped in the hall and fell, the point of the scissors stabbing me in the palm. My hand was bleeding, and I couldn't stop myself from crying, but I made sure not to make any sound; when my mom was mad, making noise made her even angrier.

As I walked into her room, I used my arm to wipe my tears off my cheeks and sniffled, trying to clear the snot from my nose. "Mommy? I have—"

"What the hell are you doing with my scissors?"

My heart beat harder and my tears fell faster. "They were by the TV and—"

"Why did you take my scissors—you aren't supposed to touch my—"

"I didn't, Mommy, I swear, I—"

9

"Are you bleeding?"

I looked down and a small sob came out. "I'm sorry. I fell and cut myself."

"You know you aren't supposed to run with scissors, and you took my damn scissors from my room. You asked for this, you understand?" she shouted as she grabbed her wooden paddle and started toward me.

I dropped the scissors and started backing away. "No mommy, please, I didn't take—"

"Shut up!" she yelled and reached out for me.

I tried to turn and run, but I wasn't fast enough, and she grabbed my arm. I wailed and begged her not to spank me again—my butt was still so sore from being spanked earlier.

"Stop trying to get away!" she shouted as we wrestled. "You're gonna get it worse the more you fight me, and now you're getting blood on the fucking carpet!"

The fact that she was telling the truth wasn't enough to keep me from trying to get away. I attempted to twist around and under her arm, but all it did was keep my arm pinned behind my back, and the first swing of the paddle hit square on my butt. Even though my pants were still on that time, it hurt so badly I started screaming and twisted harder to get away.

"Stop it!" my mom ordered as she gave my arm a forceful yank.

Sharp pain shot through my upper body and I cried out in agony. My shoulder hurt so bad I couldn't even feel the pain in my butt anymore.

"Oh, shit!" my mom yelled. Then she called my dad home from work and he took me to the hospital; my shoulder was dislocated... again.

The car door opening and slamming behind my brothers as they climbed back into the car startled me from my thoughts.

"Don't slam that damn door!" my dad shouted at them.

They rolled their eyes again as they sat down. "There were two," James said as he pointed to the two hubcaps Al had dropped on the floor.

My dad grinned and nodded, pleased, and changed gears, pulling back onto the highway. As we neared Aunt Pauline's, I started chanting in my mind. *Please don't let him be there. Please don't let him be there. Please don't let him be there.* Maybe if I chanted and prayed hard enough, Uncle Tick wouldn't come or would have left already. When my dad pulled slowly into one of only a few empty parking spaces down the block from my Aunt Pauline's townhouse, I squinted and scanned all the people milling about in front of her house, spilling over the sidewalk and into the street. If he was there, he was probably outside; Aunt Pauline's house was always hot inside from all the cooking and only having one window-mounted air-conditioner. I didn't think I saw him, and relief flooded through me as I climbed out of the car.

Just as I was shutting the car door, it hit me—all the way down the street, I could smell Aunt Pauline's famous fried chicken. My mouth started watering and my stomach grumbling for some spicy, crispy chicken fresh from the grease. I could already taste the peppery green beans that'd be there in a bowl next to the plate of chicken and knew there'd be an entire cooler full of sliced, perfectly-ripe watermelon wedges, the sugary, sticky sweetness helping to cool us off from the sun beating down and making it feel like the tar on the asphalt was going to swallow us whole.

We navigated the slippery piles of watermelon seeds my cousins were still spitting, plopping loudly onto the pavement like tiny black stones, as we hugged and kissed and said hello to everyone on our way into the house to let Aunt Pauline and Uncle Carmichael know we were there. The lightness I felt in my chest because of Uncle Tick's absence deserted me, though, as soon as we stepped in the front door to see him sitting on the worn sofa, leaning forward and staring hard at the television screen.

I forgot about football. Of course he's inside watching the game. I realized what I hadn't noticed sooner, that none of the adult men in the family were outside—only my cousins. My aunts were helping in the kitchen like they usually did, but the men were inside watching football instead of outside downing beer in the shade of a tree.

"Hey Teddy!" another uncle shouted from the sofa.

Everyone's eyes left the screen of the small tv and turned toward us. I slithered back from my dad's side, trying to hide behind him, and slid my hand into my mom's. I knew what my dad was about to do, but since my mom didn't usually come with us, maybe she'd tell me I didn't have to listen this time.

"Hey Adam. Carmichael, Tick..." My dad acknowledged everyone by name as they each raised a hand holding a beer in return.

Uncle Carmichael suddenly shouted at the tv, calling someone a "fucking moron" and telling him how he should have played. I thought I might be off the hook—maybe they'd be too distracted by the game and I could just sneak into the kitchen for a plate of food.

"Go on kids, quick, say hi," my dad said, and my chest deflated.

"Later, Teddy," one of my uncles said, scooting forward to get a few inches closer to the television set.

My brothers were gone in the blink of an eye and my mom turned around with my sister and me to start toward the kitchen, but my dad snagged my hand and pulled me back around.

"She'll be there in a minute, Kathy," he said to my mom. Then, turning and pointing, he said to me, "Look, it's your Uncle Tick, don't you wanna say hi?" He barely got the words out before both he and Uncle Tick exploded with laughter.

My face felt hot and I could tell that I was about to cry. I wanted to run after my mom, but I knew from the previous time I'd hid in a bush that—after he found me—my dad would pull down my pants and spank my bare butt with his belt buckle in front of everyone. My lips started twitching around as I tried not to cry; they always laughed even harder when I did.

Uncle Tick opened his arms wide. "Come on over here and give your uncle a proper hello, little girl," he said with a big grin.

I felt sick and the smell of fried chicken was now turning my stomach as I took a step forward. My breakfast started to come up my throat, but I swallowed hard, the burning making my tears finally spill out of my eyes. No matter what, I couldn't throw up; anytime I did, my mom and dad were disgusted and angry.

"Look at her, crying like I'm something to be afraid of," Uncle Tick laughed.

I knew my dad's laugh was louder than Uncle Tick's, but I could barely hear anything anymore as I forced my feet to shuffle over, forced my arms to lift and hug him. I was dizzy, holding my breath and hoping it would be over by the time I had to breathe in again, but instead, Uncle Tick picked me up and put me on his lap as everyone continued to laugh.

my sister's keeper

"A sister is our first friend and second mother."

-Sunny Gupta

april 1990

My feet stumbled over one another as I ran around the back corner of the house. The ground was soft and soggy, my bare feet sinking into the muddy earth with each step.

"I'm gonna' catch you!" I shouted as I continued to run.

My sister was ahead of me, about to round the corner from the side of the house into the front yard. We were playing tag, but I was bigger than my sister, so I'd given her a head start. Even so, I knew I'd catch her before she made it to the other side of the house. Then for her turn, I would start out running, but then slow down so she could catch me; if I didn't, she'd get upset and not want to play anymore, then my mom and dad would get mad at me.

I giggled as I turned the next corner and the front yard came into view. Laurel was standing in the middle of the front yard watching for me and shrieked when she saw me. Behind her was our driveway with a small fifteen-foot trailer that belonged to my mom, the door open so she could have fresh air. She liked to go in there and paint, sometimes for days at a time. No one else was allowed to go in or we'd get spanked—it was my mom's special place, just for her. I slowed for a moment to see which direction Laurel would go around the trailer; if I went the opposite direction, I'd surprise her when I caught her.

She veered toward the front of the trailer and I picked up my pace. As I ran, I looked up to see Laurel's foot slide under the thick orange extension cord that ran from our house into my mom's trailer so she could have electricity. Time slowed and my heart skipped as I watched—I was too far away to do anything. The cord prevented Laurel from taking another step and I watched helplessly as her body pitched forward toward the open door of the trailer.

After her forehead connected with the corner of the open door, time sped up and then seemed to move faster than normal, like a VHS that was in fast-forward. I shouted for my parents as I ran over to my sister, who was lying on the ground screaming, blood flowing from her forehead. I'd barely had time to ask her if she was okay when my parents were there, hands grabbing my arms to pull me up and fling me out of the way.

I watched over the shoulders of my crouched parents as they frantically inspected my sister and yelled over each other about what to do. My body felt like it was frozen, like my feet had grown into the ground and couldn't move. There was a strange electric feeling in my arms and legs and chest that made me tremble, my heart hurting every time it beat. Was my sister going to be okay? If she wasn't, it was all my fault. I was playing with her and let her get hurt. If it hadn't been for me, she wouldn't be crying and bleeding.

My mind flashed back to a few months earlier, the ripped flesh and gushing blood coming from the underside of my sister's wrist after she'd been chasing me in the basement. I'd decided to run outside to make our game more fun and when she followed me, trying to push open the storm door with her hand as it was flying closed behind me, she'd instead put her hand and part of her arm through it. The doctor who sewed up the deep gashes told my parents that Laurel was lucky because it almost cut her artery, and if that had happened, she would have died before Daddy had a chance to get her to the hospital. My mom and dad had both spanked me when they got back—my mom with her paddle and my dad with his belt buckle—for not keeping my sister safe. I should have known better than to let her chase me when I went out the door.

I'd thought we were okay if we were outside the whole time; I made sure I held the door open for Laurel when she followed me out. But I should have known she would trip on the cord, and I shouldn't have chased her in the front yard. Why hadn't I thought about that before we'd started playing?

"I think she's okay, Kathy," my dad's words floated into my ears over my sister's wailing. "But she needs stitches."

As my dad carried my sister to his Blazer, my mom turned to me and pointed toward the house. "Go inside and wait for us."

I nodded my head and turned, my eyes fixed on the ground immediately in front of my feet as I shuffled inside. I cried for most of the time I waited for them to come back home, alone for hours because my brothers were at friends' houses. My dad had said that Laurel was okay before they left...but what if he was wrong? And it was all my fault. What was wrong with me? Why was I always being so bad? I tried so hard to be good and to take care of my sister like my mom and dad told me to, but I was always getting in trouble anyway. And now my sister was hurt again because of me. The electricity in my body returned and my chest didn't want to move.

I can't do anything right—I hate myself!

Hours later, my parents got home, coming in the front door quietly. My mom carried my sister to our shared bedroom as my dad walked up to me in the living room. He looked tired more than angry; I hoped maybe that meant he wouldn't spank me.

"Go on, pull your pants down," he said as he crossed his arms over his chest.

My eyes immediately filled with tears again, but I nodded, knowing I deserved it for not keeping my sister safe. I stood up, pulled down my pants and my panties to my knees and bent my chest over the sofa, my fists already clenched tight in anticipation. He gave me five whacks with his hand that left welted handprints, but at least it wasn't his belt buckle.

"Okay, you can pull your pants up now. You understand why you were punished, don't you? That you shouldn't have let your sister get hurt?"

I nodded again as I sniffled, my nose losing almost as much snot as my eyes were losing tears, and quickly pulled my pants up over my sore backside. "I'm sorry, Daddy," I cried.

My mom walked in with her paddle right then and I could feel her anger like a cloud that surrounded her.

"You're not done yet, pull those pants back down."

My dad sighed heavily and I froze. "Kathy, she's been punished enough."

"Teddy! We just got back from the fucking hospital because of her. Laurel has stitches in her forehead, and it could have been worse. And it's her fault!"

"I know, Kathy, but I already spanked her," he replied, sounding weary.

"With what?"

My dad took a deep breath, and I could tell he was starting to get pissed off now, his frustration mixing with my mom's.

"With his hand," I offered quietly.

"So just a *hand* for your precious fucking daughter. Tell me, Teddy, if it was one of the boys, would you have used your belt?"

"Goddamn it, Kathy, that's enough!"

"No, fuck you, Teddy—you always go easy on her!"

"And you're always too hard on her! At least she tells the damn truth about what she does—those boys lie about everything!"

The sounds of them screaming started to fade as I stared at the floor by my feet; they were fighting about me again. If it weren't for me, they wouldn't fight. I wanted to curl up into a tight ball and keep squeezing until I got so small that I just disappeared. But if I did that, then my parents would keep yelling at each other and soon my sister would wake up from all the noise. As my tears came faster, I pulled myself out of the quiet, black tunnel I was in and back into the noise around me.

"Mommy! Daddy! Please stop yelling!"

"What the fuck else can I do?" my mom bellowed over my head as if I hadn't spoken.

I took a deep breath and walked between them, putting a hand on each of them. My mom glanced down at me and smacked my hand off her, but never stopped screaming at my dad.

"I said, she's been spanked enough!" my dad's voice boomed.

"It's okay," I said in the moment of silence that followed. "It's my fault. I should be spanked. Mommy can spank me. You guys don't have to fight."

They both stared at me for a moment and then my mom started up again. My dad used an arm to push me out from between them and the fight continued. Under their shouting, I thought I could hear my sister start crying, and I suddenly felt sick to my stomach.

Don't throw up. Don't throw up. Don't throw up.

I chanted the words over and over in my mind as I pressed my hands over my ears and headed to my bedroom to see if my sister was awake, already contemplating how I might calm her down if she was.

june 1990

My mom and dad were going somewhere alone, and my brothers were at friends' houses, so it was going to be just my sister, our babysitter, Lacy, and me for the entire day. Instead of running to her when she walked in the door like I usually did, I stopped, suddenly feeling sad because I was remembering the last time Lacy had babysat us.

We'd gotten happy meals from McDonald's for dinner, and Lacy had fed my pet rabbit, Bunny, some of her fries slathered in ketchup. I'd had Bunny for about a week, and I loved her so much. She had the softest white fur and a cute little nose, and her whiskers tickled me when I was holding her. But after she ate those fries, she started acting funny, and then she threw up all over her cage. I took her out and wiped her off with a washcloth and tried to make her drink water, but she wouldn't drink anything. I tried to make her hop around, but she wouldn't do that, either.

When my mom and dad came home, they said that Bunny was very sick, that I should put her in her cage and say goodbye to her, but I couldn't leave her all alone when she wasn't feeling well. I hoped that maybe if I was holding her and kept telling her how much I loved her, she would get better. I held her for hours, stroking her and whispering to her, drying her fur when my tears fell on her; I didn't stop until I couldn't feel her heartbeat and her body wasn't warm anymore.

I could feel my mouth turning down with my effort not to cry as Lacy scooped up my sister. She looked at me and her smile faded.

"Hey, kiddo. I'm sorry about Bunny," she said.

I sniffled, trying not to cry as I looked at her. I could tell by her face that she was really sorry, and I wasn't mad, anyway. I was just sad. But I didn't want Lacy to be sad, too. "It's okay."

"Maybe we can find another rabbit today," Lacy offered.

I shook my head. "No, that's okay," I said. I knew we didn't have money for another rabbit—my parents had told me so when Bunny died. Besides, I didn't really want another rabbit; I just wanted Bunny. "But where are we going where there are rabbits?"

Lacy's grin returned. "I was thinking we'd go to the fair for the day."

My sister and I could barely contain our excitement and piled into Lacy's car—my sister in the back seat and me in the front with the broken seatbelt, like always. And before we knew it, we were hopping out of the car, each grabbing one of Lacy's hands as we headed toward the entrance.

The place was enormous and filled with people, the incessant bustle and activity and noise overwhelming, and I clung tightly to Lacy's hand.

"Let's start over here and make our way around, okay?" Lacy said as she started walking to the right.

We navigated through a large crowd of people, and when we emerged on the other side, I froze, my arm pulling tight until Lacy realized I'd stopped walking. Straight ahead was a circular fenced enclosure, and inside that enclosure was a tan pony with a blond mane, a little girl about my age sitting on its back as it walked the perimeter of the enclosure. After a moment, I tore my eyes from the scene and looked up at Lacy.

"Can we go over here?"

"Pony rides are really expensive—we can't do that."

"That's okay, I just want to watch—please?"

"Sure, we can watch for a few minutes."

We found an area near a giant tree that was out of the way of the line of kids waiting for their turn, and I plopped down on the ground amongst the tree roots, next to Lacy's feet. The second girl since our arrival was halfway through her turn when my sister got antsy to do something else— she was bored.

"Okay, time to move on," Lacy said gently.

I looked up at her. "Can I stay? Please?"

"But you'll miss out on everything else if you stay here."

"That's okay, I don't care. I want to stay and watch the pony."

Lacy looked around, her face scrunched up. "I don't know..."

"Please? I promise I won't go anywhere. Nowhere. I'll stay right here until you come back. Please, please, *please?*"

She gazed down at me. "You promise you won't go anywhere?"

"I promise!" I jumped up and wrapped my arms around her waist.

"Okay, stay *right here*. Alright?"

"I will! Thank you, thank you!"

Plopping back down on my butt and sitting cross-legged, I went back to watching the other kids take turns sitting on the pony's back and being walked around in a circle. Over and over, I watched and imagined myself as one of the other kids who could afford to have a turn. I wasn't bitter, though—I was used to not being able to afford things. I was simply happy. *I got to see a pony!*

Hours passed quickly; it felt like only moments had gone by when Lacy was back, telling me it was time to go home. Reluctantly, I got to my feet and slid my hand into Lacy's for the trek back to the car. As we walked, I craned my head first to my side, and then behind me, until I could no longer see the pony enclosure at all. Then I daydreamed as we walked, still seeing that magnificent creature in front of me.

"Can I sit up front?" my sister asked as we walked up to the car.

"But I'm bigger," I replied. I was the oldest when it was just the two of us, so that meant I got the front seat.

"Please? You and James and Al always sit up front, I never sit up front!"

I shrugged. "Sure, you can sit up front just this once."

She squealed and climbed into the front seat while I climbed into the back and started dreaming about that pony again. The mental image of me on the pony going around the enclosure instantly dissipated when a loud screech reached my ears and I flew forward, slamming my face into the back of Lacy's seat before everything went black.

I was still in the back of the car, sitting on the seat, disoriented and staring at the bizarre bubble of glass with drippy red splotches in the windshield in front of the front passenger seat, trying to figure out what I was looking at, when hands I didn't recognize reached in and pulled me out of the car. My gaze flitted around at the shattered glass on the ground that crunched under the stranger's feet, the produce that was scattered all over the pavement. I saw the station wagon in front of Lacy's car, the back smashed in and most of the rear window missing. It was then I noticed the flashing lights coming from an ambulance parked close by and realized the stranger carrying me was a paramedic.

"What's your name, honey?" the strange voice asked me.

"Where's my sister?" I asked.

"The little girl who was in the front is your sister?"

"Where is she?" I screamed.

I twisted around, searching, and looked at Lacy's car again, suddenly realizing that the bubble I'd been staring at was from my sister's head, that the drippy red splotches must have been her blood. My eyes found the emergency responders laying her limp body on a stretcher and I realized the blood on the glass was nothing compared to what I saw coating and oozing from her face and mouth now.

I became hysterical, screaming and begging the paramedics to tell me if my sister was okay, but they wouldn't answer me, remaining silent as if I wasn't speaking. I wanted to look, to check on her myself, but I was restrained on a stretcher of my own by now, my head and arms and legs immobilized. All I could do was stare from the corner of my eye at all the blood and my sister's uncanny stillness. I was so sure she was dead. And it was all my fault; I'd let her sit in the front seat.

It should have been me.

At the hospital, I was told my sister had survived and that she would be okay. She would be in the hospital for a while; she needed surgery to remove a tooth that had been pushed to the middle of her mouth, had a broken collar bone, and may need a skin graft on her forehead, but she had survived.

I cried into her still-unconscious side when I was allowed to see her, her body so small in the hospital bed, her head wrapped in white gauze, her face strangely swollen. Relief that she was alive and guilt that she was hurt were so strong that I felt sick deep in my belly with each exhale. I promised her silently that I would do a better job of protecting her from then on, that I wouldn't let her get hurt again. I told her how sorry I was that she was hurt, because if I'd sat up front like I always did, she never would have been there. Instead, it would have been me in pain, bleeding and with broken bones.

It *should* have been me—and it was all my fault.

predictability

"Children everywhere need stability and certainty."

-Elaine Bainard

december 1990

I rubbed my eyes sleepily and yawned as I tromped down the stairs one at a time. My brothers had just woken my sister and me, then tore out of our room. About halfway down the stairs, I could no longer see the glow the night light in the hall gave off and there was complete darkness ahead of me. James and Al were laughing and snickering, and the sound of wrapping paper reached my ears, so I knew they were downstairs and around the corner from me. And yet, I stood rooted a few stairs down, staring into the blackness ahead of me, my heart racing.

People from the movies my brothers liked watching started flashing through my mind: *A Nightmare on Elm Street, Friday the 13th, Dolls,* and *Child's Play.* What if Freddy Krueger was at the bottom waiting for me with his knives for fingers? What if he grabbed me when I took the next step? Maybe Jason was down there in his mask with that machete. And behind them, would Chucky—with his evil smile—be leading all those dolls that came to life and the hand that could move on its own?

My chest caved in and I couldn't move, couldn't breathe, couldn't blink—if I closed my eyes, they could get me in that split second. The sound of my heart beating and my blood rushing in my ears was like an ocean in my head, and I felt hot all over my body. I lifted my foot and started to put it on the step behind me, but I bumped into something and screamed.

"What's wrong?" my dad asked as he reached under my arms and picked me up.

I wrapped myself around him as tightly as I could and cried with relief that it was my dad and not someone who wanted to kill me.

"What's going on, Katherine?" he persisted.

I told him between hiccupping sobs about being afraid of Jason and Freddy and Chucky and all those dolls being in the darkness at the bottom of the stairs. My dad laughed and reached around the corner into the hall to turn on the stairwell light.

"There's nothing there, see?" he said, still laughing.

I felt stupid for being laughed at, but it couldn't compare to the relief I had that my dad was there. It didn't matter what he said, I knew they were down there in the dark and he just scared them away. My heart was gradually slowing when we arrived in the living room where my brothers were still picking up presents and shaking them.

"Get off those damn presents or I'll whoop your asses," my dad warned, setting me down on the floor. "You should stop watching those movies with your sister. She's scared that all those bad guys are real and out to get her," he chuckled.

My face felt hot and tight as my brothers started laughing so hard that they doubled over and slapped their knees.

"You're such a baby, sis! Look, we'll watch them again and you'll see they're actually funny—they're not scary at all."

I didn't want to watch those movies again—*ever*. And I was about to tell them that when my mom rounded the corner with my sister in her arms and a smile on her face. The fear and embarrassment melted away as I watched my mom walk into the room, which now seemed brighter because she was smiling.

It's going to be a flute day, I just know it! And what better day for a flute day than Christmas!

We sat down and opened our presents rapid-fire while my parents watched from the sofa, drinking coffee and smoking cigarettes. It was the most presents we'd ever gotten for Christmas—the most presents we'd ever seen under a tree!—and the excitement drove us to open all of them without having first spent time thinking about what we'd received. When all was done, I wanted to jump up and down and twirl and scream. I'd gotten everything I'd wanted for Christmas and then some: my own enormous coloring book, my very own pack of brand-new crayons, a Walkman, and two cassette tapes of my favorite bands, MC Hammer and Vanilla Ice.

Most of the day passed by while I sat at the bottom of the carpeted stairs, listening to my new tapes on my Walkman—often pausing to use the rewind button to replay my favorite songs ("Ice Ice Baby" and "Hammertime"), coloring page after page in my thick coloring book, grinning wider than I ever had.

march 1991

Our neighbor, Miss Lisa, was a black woman about my grandmother's age, her tight curls gray with a few threads of black, rather than black with threads of gray, like my dad's. She always wore a housecoat and smelled like cocoa butter, and she was *always* smiling when she saw us.

"Hi, Miss Lisa," I said as I stepped onto the curb in front of my house. "Where's Laurel?"

"Hi there. She's taking a nap inside. How was school today?" she asked as she turned toward her house.

"Good. We got new books from the library today."

"Ooooh, I hope not the same books I've got downstairs for you."

I stopped walking and looked up at her. "For me?"

"Mm-hmm. For you."

"All mine?"

"Well," she laughed, "kind of. They're for you to read when you come over so you aren't watching those cartoons all the time."

"Yes!" I shouted. I couldn't wait to get inside and see what books were there for me to read.

"Have you been writing anything else?" she asked.

That was a question I got from her every time I saw her since the previous year, when I'd gone with my dad to the little Italian restaurant down the road from our house to get a pizza.

The restaurant had a sign in the window, saying everyone under age ten could write about why they thought their mom's lasagna was the best, and whoever wrote the best essay would win Mother's Day dinner for their mom, including a vase with a rose she could take home. I felt like the contest was made for me because my mom made the best lasagna in the whole world.

I asked the man behind the counter for a pencil and a piece of paper and sat down at a table while we waited for our pizza. I filled the entire paper talking about my mom's lasagna. I told them how many layers it

*had—eight—and how many cheeses she used—six—and the color the top
was when it came out of the oven—golden brown, not too dark and not too
light—and how it melted in my mouth when I took a bite and what it tasted
like—heaven—and how I had never eaten her lasagna without smiling
because it was like eating happiness.*

*I couldn't believe it when I found out I won the contest, and neither
could my mom. I'd never seen such a big smile on her face as when we took
her out for her fancy dinner and the waiter brought her a rose and presented
her with it. She even cried, but she promised it was a happy cry.*

"I have to write sentences my teacher tells me to," I responded.
"Where's mommy today?" She'd been really sad and angry lately, not happy
like she was when she had that dinner.

"She's not feeling well, honey."

"She's at the hospital again?"

"For a few days."

"Did she break some bones?"

"Not this time, honey, she's just sick."

I nodded. I knew what she meant. Sometimes my mom was in the
hospital because she fell and broke a bone after she drank the clear stuff
that made her a klutz, and sometimes she was there because she was just
so sad that she needed doctors to help her not be sad anymore. But it
sounded like this time was because she had so much of that clear stuff that
it made her feel really sick and she needed the doctors to help her feel
better again. It was always one of those reasons when Miss Lisa was
waiting for me to get off the bus.

april 1991

My heart raced as I watched cartoons with my brothers and my sister, the
sounds of my parents fighting rivaling the volume of the television. I kept
glancing toward the hall that led to where they were in their bedroom,
unable to focus on what was on the screen.

"Maybe we should go do something," I suggested quietly.

"And get our asses whooped? No thanks," James said, his eyes still
glued to the television.

"It's not our business, sis, leave them alone," Al added, looking at me.

"But they're fighting."

"Seriously, sis, leave them alone."

"But someone has to do something," I muttered, my heart rate increasing as I got to my feet.

"You always go in there. Does it fix anything?" Al persisted.

"No," I said, looking down at my feet. "But maybe this time—"

"Exactly, no. It's their shit, not yours."

"But they're always fighting!" I shouted back. I didn't add what I was thinking—that it almost always ended up being about me, so it *was* my job to fix it.

Al shrugged his shoulders and looked back to cartoons. "It's your own fault if you get your ass whooped for going in there."

"I know," I murmured as I turned and started down the hall, the sound of the cartoons fading into the background as the shouts from my parents grew louder.

As I walked, my chest rose and fell noticeably, and it was getting harder to breathe. Walking between my parents when they were angry was so scary, but someone had to do it. And it was my fault they fought, so it should be me. The back of my mouth felt really full of spit, but when I swallowed, the front of my mouth was strangely dry, and my tongue seemed to stick to the backs of my teeth. As it finally peeled off, I felt it: the unmistakable movement and sensation of a loose tooth.

Oh no, I thought, freezing in the hall. I'd thought if I prayed hard enough that I wouldn't get any more loose teeth. It had irritated both Mom and Dad when I had played with my first loose tooth with my tongue. Dad had gotten his pliers with the blue handles from his toolbox and told me to open my mouth and be still. I'd promised I wouldn't play with my tooth anymore, but it didn't matter—it was too late. He and Mommy had promised me it wouldn't hurt at all. I'd opened my mouth and could taste the metal and grease when the pliers touched my tongue just before he'd yanked out my tooth.

There'd been so much blood, and I'd stood over the sink crying for such a long time, then spent the rest of the evening with a wad of toilet paper in my mouth to stop the bleeding. Something similar happened after the second tooth. I'd risked getting spanked rather than opening my mouth for the pliers with that one. My dad had instead suggested he tie his fishing line around my tooth and tie the other end to a doorknob and slam the door, but I think it was my brothers' idea because they were laughing and giddy about it. I hadn't wanted to do that either, but my dad told me to choose that or the pliers, so I'd chosen the door. It had hurt just as much as the pliers had, though, so I'd started praying every night when I went to bed that I wouldn't ever get another loose tooth. But there I was, walking in to try to break up my parents' fighting, and I had another loose tooth. I must not have prayed hard enough or the right way. I must have done it wrong, just like all my praying for my parents to stop fighting must have been done wrong because they kept fighting anyway.

Why can't I do anything right?

may 1991

I was alone, running in a parking garage. I could hear the voices and see the shadows of those who were chasing me. Without looking, I knew they carried chainsaws and baseball bats and machetes, some of them wore masks, some had knives for fingers. There were dolls with red glowing eyes and limbs that moved without the bodies they'd been severed from, and none of them could be stopped. I ran through a door to find myself at the opening to five different stairwells, some going up and some going down. I chose one and started running, trying not to trip over my own feet.

The stairwell turned into a spiral that circled down and I kept descending as quickly as I could. I could hear the feet and moans of those chasing me, but I couldn't tell if they were in the same stairwell I was or not, so I just kept running. I ran for hours; my legs were tired and didn't want to keep working, but I could still hear the sounds of others close by. I stopped long enough to peer over the railing and look down. The staircase continued to spiral beyond anything I could see, disappearing into a black hole. Flipping my head up, I saw the creatures closing in on me.

Pulling my head back in, I started down the stairwell again, but I was moving more slowly, my legs burning and heavy. I could feel the hot breath of my pursuers on the back of my neck and my whole body prickled with awareness and dread. I didn't want to look, but I couldn't stop myself from turning my head. Just as I did, I felt an iciness grip my chest and—

My eyes shot open in the dark and my hands immediately clutched my chest. *I can't breathe. I can't breathe. I can't breathe.* I tried to make my lungs open to allow more air to come in, but it felt like there was something crushing my chest and my whole body was filled with an electricity that hurt. I could hear my sister's steady breathing a few feet away and tried to reason with myself that I was safe and it was just a dream. But with every second that passed, I knew all those creatures were getting closer to

26

finding me, and if I didn't run soon, they'd come out from under my bed and kill me.

With a sob, I leapt from my bed as far across the room as I could and ran out the door, turning toward my parents' room. As I ran, I saw a glow coming from the downstairs and knew my parents were still up watching television. Passing their door, I started down the stairs, but stopped about halfway when I looked over and saw the television screen. There was a naked woman and a naked man. My face started burning, electricity flooding my body all over again as my stomach started churning. Quickly, I looked away, but my eyes landed instead on my parents on the sofa, sitting next to each other, naked. They were both looking at the screen, but they weren't wearing any clothes and my mom's hand was between my dad's legs.

My eyes widened and I was frozen for a moment as my heart pounded painfully in my chest. I felt like I was doing something wrong because I saw them, even though I didn't understand what they were doing. I only knew that I couldn't go downstairs because this wasn't the first time. The first time I'd had a nightmare and found my parents watching naked people, I'd gone down anyway and been spanked and sent back to bed and told never to leave my room after bedtime again. I glanced over my shoulder toward my bedroom door; I couldn't go back in that room until all those creatures were gone, and I just knew they were waiting under my bed for me to return.

As quietly as I could, I crept down a few more steps so that when I sat down on a stair, there was light from the television flowing behind me; I couldn't leave my back in the dark or the creatures might get me and drag me back to my room. With my body mashed against the railing to be as close to my mom and dad as I could get, I leaned my head on the bars and stared at the far wall, at the shifting light from the tv that assured me I was in the light where I couldn't be reached by the creatures until I dozed off.

and now for something completely different

"We think sometimes that poverty is only being hungry and homeless. The poverty of being unwanted, unloved and uncared for is the greatest poverty."

-Mother Teresa

early june 1991

My feet bounced from where I was perched on the edge of the bus seat, my legs barely long enough for them to reach the floor. I glanced around quickly and confirmed my brothers weren't on the bus with me and shrugged to myself; they often went home with friends and it was the last day of school, so they might have even skipped.

The last day! I felt a pang of sadness over the end of the school year, that I would have months until I could go back and start second grade; I loved school. There were so many cool things I learned from my teachers, and I loved to make them proud of me when I showed them my progress. I got to spend time in the school library, where I could always find a new book to read that week.

As quickly as it arrived, however, the sadness was gone; the end of the school year meant summertime, and summertime meant extra time with my mom. Ever since I started going to school, I missed her when I was gone, even her angry moods. And when she had flute days, I could spend the whole day with her, instead of leaving for school knowing I was missing precious hours where she was happy.

As the bus slowed to a stop, my excitement spilled over and I jumped out of my seat, running to the front. I bounced up and down as I stood there waiting impatiently for the bus driver to open the door. As soon as I could,

I rushed down the steps and flew around the front of the bus toward the other side of the street, the joy of the coming summer enhanced by the bright sunshine and blue skies overhead and positively bursting out of the wide grin stretched across my face.

By the time I reached the curb in front of my house, I was barely shuffling forward, my smile was long forgotten, and I felt sick to my stomach. Something was wrong.

Something was *very* wrong.

My dad was sitting on our front stoop. In all my memories, there wasn't a single one of my dad being home when school let out; not in my two years of school, and not prior to that when my brothers were the only ones in school. We all knew my dad's job didn't let him leave that early, and if something happened that my mom couldn't be there, it was Miss Lisa waiting for us.

"Where's mommy?" I squeaked out around my suddenly very upset stomach. *Don't throw up.*

"She's gone," my dad replied soberly, his face expressionless.

"When is she coming home?"

"She isn't."

"What do you mean?"

"I told you, she's gone."

"Where's Laurel? And what about James and Al?"

"They're gone, too."

"Where are they?"

"I don't know. With your mother."

"When are they coming back?"

"I told you, they aren't."

"But why did they leave?"

"Because she doesn't love us anymore!" he shouted.

By then, I was aware my dad was getting irritated with me, but I could also tell that he was upset. I wanted to hug him, but I wasn't sure if he was already angry enough that he would pull off his belt and spank me if I did. I stood there for a long time, staring at his face, undecided, while he stared at the ground in silence.

early july 1991

"You're a little liar," my Aunt Pauline snarled at me.

I'd just told her that my older cousin Belinda—Aunt Pauline's daughter—had held a pillow over my head while I couldn't breathe and then called me a bitch. We'd been living with Aunt Pauline for a few weeks, and every day, Belinda was meaner and meaner to me.

"No, I'm not!" I fired back.

"Yes, you are," Belinda said. "I would never do that, Mom!"

"Yes, you did," I said.

Aunt Pauline's hand darted out and the back of it connected with my face, making my head snap to the side. "My daughter would never do something like that, and she would never lie to me. She knows better. Which means you're a little liar."

No, I'm not! I screamed in my mind as tears spilled over my eyes and the metallic tang of blood reached my tongue from where my teeth had cut into my cheek. She smacked me almost every day, but the last few days, the smacks were harder, and my mouth kept bleeding.

I turned around to face the living room where my dad was sitting on the sofa, watching television; surely he would tell Aunt Pauline that I wasn't a liar and she shouldn't have smacked me.

"Daddy," I started tearfully, "I didn't—"

"Hush," he said harshly, glaring at me for a moment, then turning back to the television.

"But daddy—"

"I said, *hush.*"

"But—"

"That's enough!" he boomed, turning to me again. He didn't say another word, but I could tell from his eyes that he was going to spank me if I spoke again. My chest started hurting and I wanted to tell him that I hated him, but I knew better. Instead, I turned and ran to the bathroom, where I sat on the floor and cried into my hands.

late july 1991

My dad and I had been living with my Uncle Adam, Aunt Sissy, and their kids for about a week. My dad had said we couldn't stay with my Aunt Pauline any longer as if it was a sad thing, but I was so happy to leave. My

Aunt Pauline used to be my favorite person in the family other than Grandma Virginia, but now I hated her and my cousin Belinda. I hoped I never saw them again.

Uncle Adam gave us instructions to leave him, my other aunts and uncles, and my dad alone. "You kids go on and play, you hear? Don't get into trouble and don't you dare come bother us while we have a few minutes of peace from you little shitheads, or we'll tan all your damn hides, you hear?"

Most of my cousins scattered, gone within seconds, but I didn't have any cousins my age or any friends yet, so I meandered to the living room as the kitchen door shut and the sounds of laughter and glass bottles clanking against each other and the table followed me. Aunt Sissy and Uncle Adam's youngest kid, Terrence, was thirteen; he was already in the living room and sitting in the recliner in the small room with *Looney Toons* on. I sat on the floor between him and the television and started watching.

After a while, Terrence invited me up to share the recliner, so I hopped up to join him. As I climbed up, he helped me turn back around to face the television and situated me on his lap as I lost myself watching Bugs Bunny and Elmer Fudd. At some point, as the cartoons continued, Terrence wrapped an arm around me and pulled me back so I was lying back on his chest. I didn't really want to be lying down because I couldn't see very well, but I didn't want him to make me sit on the hard floor again, so I stretched my neck up so I could curve my head forward over his forearm.

The cartoons disappeared from the screen without warning as Terrence changed the channel; suddenly the screen was filled with naked bodies writhing around on top of each other. My face burned and my stomach turned like they did on those nights I found my mom and dad watching stuff like that. I told him I didn't want to watch that channel and asked him to put the cartoons back on.

"Shhhh," he shushed harshly into my ear, otherwise ignoring me.

My discomfort grew as he began to shift around, still holding me back against his chest.

"Let me go," I said. "I don't wanna watch tv anymore. I wanna go outside and play."

He didn't respond to me; instead, he began running his free hand between my legs, back and forth, as his hips shifted underneath me. I felt something hard now pressing into my butt and he moved my body around on top of it.

31

I didn't understand what was happening, but I definitely didn't like it. And I didn't like that he wouldn't listen to me, that I couldn't move, and that he wouldn't stop touching me in my private area. Tears burned my eyes and my jaw trembled like it always did before I started crying. As the first tears fell, I told him I was going to tell on him if he didn't let me go.

"You go in there, you'll get your ass whooped by every one of the grown-ups. And I'll tell them you're lying anyway. You know they'll believe me over you."

I hated him for saying it, and I also knew he was right. I'd get spanked because everyone thought I was a liar. I cried harder while Terrence continued to rub between my legs with one of his hands as his other arm kept me pinned against him, the thing under my butt pushing against me even harder. His breath became choppy just behind my head and I could feel the little puffs of air shifting my hair around every time he breathed out. My stomach churned and I felt sick, like I might throw up, and I tried to swallow hard; I couldn't throw up. I'd definitely get in trouble if I threw up.

Terrence's arm squeezed around me so tightly I couldn't take a breath, and I started fighting against him so I could breathe again. After a moment, his arm loosened, and his body stopped moving underneath mine. I breathed in as hard as I could, trying to catch my breath.

"If you tell anyone," he panted into my ear, his chest heaving under my back, "I'll beat the shit out of you, got it? *Anyone*, especially your dad, and you'll regret it."

I nodded in agreement and he finally moved his arm off me. I flew off the recliner and ran out the front door.

Later that night, I was sitting alone with my dad on the porch and I decided to tell him what Terrence had done to me. I was afraid he would do it again or hurt me even if I didn't tell on him, and I was sure my dad would protect me. Despite what had happened when we lived at Aunt Pauline's house, and despite what Terrence said about no one believing me, I was certain my dad would believe me and protect me. Scared of being overheard the entire time I spoke, I whispered to my dad everything that had happened while he and my aunts and uncles had been drinking in the kitchen.

When I finished, he yelled at me. He accused me of lying and said that I was never to tell another soul. I swore to him that I was telling the truth, tears pouring down my cheeks as I begged him to believe me, but he didn't. He insisted I was lying, that I was making the story up as he grew angrier and angrier. He demanded that I promise I'd never tell anyone else. Stifling my cries so he wouldn't decide to slide his belt off and spank me, I nodded my head.

"Okay, daddy. I promise."

the birth of a love affair

"Severe early childhood trauma creates a child with equally intense coping mechanisms—these children are often seen as 'mature for their age' or 'old souls.' While maybe true, it often reflects the fact that their innocence was taken away at an early age and they are in survival mode."

-Azia Archer

early august 1991

"Wake up, it's almost time to go," my dad's voice broke into my sleep.

I yawned and stretched and rubbed my eyes—I'd had another nightmare. I had them almost every night, but my dad didn't like me to wake him up because it would make him too tired for work the next day, so I sometimes just didn't go back to sleep. I had different nightmares now that were just as bad as the ones I used to have.

In my new nightmares, my dad and I would be holding hands and walking around at a fair after dark when some men would start shouting. My dad would let go of my hand and start running. I'd run after him, but I wouldn't be able to keep up with him. He would get further away in front of me and the men chasing us would get closer. I'd scream for my daddy, but he would keep running. I could hear the men's feet hitting the ground and their laughs as they got closer to me until suddenly arms would grab me and one of them would say, "Gotcha!" Once they grabbed me, I couldn't scream anymore and I couldn't even see my dad. I didn't know what the men were going to do, but I knew they wanted to hurt me. One would hold me, and the others would start grabbing my clothes and pulling them off. That's when I always woke up crying. And I was too scared to close my eyes again—every time I closed them, I could see everything happening again.

"Come on, hurry up. I need to leave," my dad urged me, grabbing his keys and wallet.

I pulled on my only pair of shoes quickly and was done before my dad had even bent down to put his on. While I waited, I wriggled my toes and watched them peek through the holes in the top of my tennis shoes, like I was playing peek-a-boo with myself. I giggled at the thought of playing with my toes.

"What are you laughin' at?" my dad asked as he straightened up.

"Look at my toes," I giggled. "They're playing peek-a-boo with me."

He looked down at my feet, but he didn't laugh. Instead, he let out a heavy sigh.

"I gotta leave. Let's go," he said more quietly, ushering me out the front door and locking it behind us.

We'd been living in this apartment just the two of us for two weeks, but my dad told me we wouldn't be there for long. And while I missed my dad because he was gone all day every single day, we had a routine, and I got to see him every morning and every night. And at least I didn't have to spend all day with Belinda or Terrence, even if I did spend every day alone.

"I'll be back around dark. Don't get into trouble," he said as we reached his Blazer.

"Okay, Daddy," I responded.

He placed a quick kiss on my forehead. "Love you."

"Love you, too, Daddy."

I stood on the sidewalk in front of the apartment building and waved until I couldn't see him anymore, just like I did every morning. And then I started my trek to the local library a ways down the road since I didn't have a way to get back into the apartment until my dad came back.

I absolutely loved the library. I was enthralled by the sheer number of book spines, how much there was to learn, how many fantastical stories there were to read. I sometimes tried to figure out how long it would take one person to read them all because I knew I wanted to, but I wasn't sure if I could live that long.

On the way to the library, I wandered around all the playgrounds and apartment buildings. At one playground, I saw some kids—the same kids I saw there almost every day—and I pretended I was part of their group, imagining I was playing their games with them, but I kept my distance. The one time I'd tried to play and make friends the first day my dad left, no one would play with me because I smelled really bad. They made fun of me, asking me if I knew how to take a bath and what soap was, and laughed at the holes in my clothes. They made jokes about how I'd probably never been to a dentist because my teeth looked so dirty and asked me if I even owned a toothbrush. I told them I did, but I'd lost it when my dad and I moved to my Aunt Pauline's house, and I'd never been to a dentist. I'd spent the rest of that day crying by the door to our apartment, and the next day I'd found the library.

When I got bored pretending I was playing with the other kids, I moved on, walking in the direction of the library. As I walked, I zigzagged around buildings to look at the trees. I studied the shapes of their leaves and the vein patterns and tried to make out shapes in the grooves in the bark on their trunks. I pretended I could see the entire root when I looked at the lumpiness of the surrounding ground. That day, it was sunny, and I stood behind the branches in the sun-dappled shade. With the soft breeze, the light shifted around and shimmered and I felt like I was a princess in one of the fairy tales I used to watch on T.V. when we had one. Closing my eyes, I pretended I was standing perched on the top of a castle.

After a few minutes, my eyes didn't want to stay closed against the bright sunshine any longer, so I opened them and resumed my trek to the library. As soon as I opened the front door and walked in, I could smell all the books. *I bet I could keep my eyes closed all day and know when I was in a library because of the smell.* With a deep breath through my nose, my muscles relaxed, and my body felt a little heavier and sleepier like it did every time I stepped into the library.

I got in line to the front desk behind several others to wait my turn to speak to the librarian. She always told me she couldn't believe how well I could read and how many words I knew, and it made me feel really proud and happy when she said those things. She also always had some suggestions for me to read that day, so I liked to talk to her first thing when I arrived. When I picked everything myself, I would accidentally spend hours walking around and touching all the books as I read their spines, trying to pick out which ones I should read—it was so hard to decide because I wanted to read them all. But when she picked some for me, it made it easier for me to pick more once I finished those.

I wondered what she'd have picked out for me that day. My favorites were fantastical stories that weren't real, where the main characters prevailed over the roadblocks from others and that they'd unwittingly given themselves. I'd lose myself in the pages, imagining I was in them. I'd cry thousands of fat, salty tears when something sad happened, and I'd get really mad with my jaw clenched and hands fisted when they were wronged. Some of the stories were all happy; they had happy families where the mommy and daddy were together and no one got spanked. When I read those, I'd daydream my family was like that and I'd remember those daydreams when my nightmares woke me up. But I didn't like reading too many stories like that—I liked stories that made me really sad first because it was easier to pretend I was in those.

As I waited, I studied the back of the person in front of me and suddenly realized he only had one leg. There was a crutch under each arm of his camouflage jacket, one leg from his hip to the floor—a scuffed white tennis shoe on that foot—and the other stopped just above where a knee would be. I stared for a moment, trying to imagine what might have happened to that leg. Al had lost almost half of his middle finger when James slammed a door on his hand when I was a baby, and the doctors couldn't put it back on. *Could a door do that to a leg?*

The man suddenly flipped his head around, searching behind me. I turned quickly in search of what he saw, but I didn't see anyone and looked back at the man. He looked younger than my dad because I didn't see as many wrinkles on his face or any gray in his brown hair. His skin was much lighter than my dad's, pale and creamy, and his face was covered in scruffy hair. I studied his face in that moment before his gaze fell and landed on me, catching me staring at him. His light brown eyes were hard when they connected with mine, but then they softened quickly.

We stared at each other, but I felt like the strange man was my friend and I had an urge to talk to him. His eyes looked sad like my mom's did on the days that weren't flute days, and I wondered what happened to make him so sad. *Would a hug cheer him up?* I was too scared to hug a stranger, though, and I didn't really like hugging most people, anyway—especially boys. He grinned at me as if we were sharing a joke that was a secret between us, and I couldn't help grinning back at him. The librarian called him up to her desk and he turned and stepped up to talk to her.

A few minutes later, he nodded at me as he passed on his way out, smiling broadly as he went, and I was glad he didn't look so sad now. Maybe he loved books as much as I did and talking to the nice librarian lady cheered him up the way it always cheered me up. Either way, I liked that he was smiling when he walked past, and I hoped I'd see him the next day, too.

"Well, hello there," the librarian called to me with a bright smile.

I walked up to her desk, smiling back, butterflies fluttering in my stomach in anticipation of what books she might have picked out for me. "Hi," I replied.

"Are you up for a challenge today?" she asked, tilting her head and raising her eyebrows as she looked at me over the top of her glasses.

I giggled. "Yes!"

"I thought you might be," she replied with a smile. "These will take a bit longer to read, so I went ahead and pulled them off the shelves for you. Pick whichever you'd like and I'll put the others back later."

Grinning, I reached forward and turned the stack of books she was sliding in my direction so I could read the spines. *Matilda* by Roald Dahl, *Mrs. Frisby and the Rats of NIMH* by Robert C. O'Brien, *A Wrinkle in Time* by Madeleine L'Engle, *The Lion, the Witch, and the Wardrobe* by C.S. Lewis, *The Borrowers* by Mary Norton, and *Harriet the Spy* by Louise Fitzhugh. I read the spines a second time, then lifted the books one by one to look at the covers. After close inspection, I narrowed it down to two: *Matilda* and *A Wrinkle in Time*. I flipped through the pages and couldn't decide.

"Which one do you think I should read?" I asked, looking up at the librarian.

Her smile broadened and she wriggled her eyebrows. "Well, those two were my top picks for you, but they're very different stories. I think you would enjoy both. One will be a much bigger challenge to read than the other, too."

"Which one's easier?" I asked.

"*Matilda.*"

"Okay, I'll read *A Wrinkle in Time*, then."

"I thought you might say that," she replied, lifting the book to place it into my hands.

I grinned back at her. "Thank you."

"You're very welcome. Enjoy."

I hugged the book to my chest and—still grinning—went in search of a cozy corner where I could read quietly without being disturbed or getting in anyone's way. Snuggled near a window, the bookshelves serving as a backrest, I ran my hand over the cover and looked out the window for a moment. The sun was shining, I had a new book in my hands, and I'd made a friend. Could the day get any better?

welcome to the mountain state

"Family is more than blood."

-Cassandra Clare

mid-august 1991

Hot, humid summer air assaulted my face, which rested on the car door in the open window. It felt like we'd been driving for forever, but I knew better than to ask my dad how much longer until we arrived, no matter how desperately I wanted to know. He'd already grumbled about our destination being "in the middle of nowhere." I wished we could just hurry up—he was taking me to visit my mom, my sister, and my brothers. It would be the first time I'd seen them since I'd left for the last day of school two months ago.

The air whipping into my face tapered off as my dad exited the highway and came to a stop at the traffic light. I closed my eyes and imagined what it was going to be like to see my mom and my siblings again, what the reunion would be like. I imagined they were as excited and happy as I was, as impatient as I felt for my arrival. My mom would be smiling because it would be a flute day and she'd wrap her arms around me in a bear hug while my siblings hugged me from behind. It would be absolutely perfect.

Soon, my dad turned off the main road again onto a much smaller side road through thick woods. I wasn't sure where we were; my dad had just said my mom was living in West Virginia. I sat up a few minutes later when my dad turned yet again, this time onto a bumpy dirt trail that I'd barely noticed. As we drove slowly, I leaned into the center toward my dad so the vines and tree branches that reached in through the open window wouldn't scratch me. It felt like we were going to be swallowed by the forest and I forgot my excitement for a moment, instead feeling scared of the density of the growth around us.

After what felt like hours, I could see there was something up ahead. As we inched closer, I could see a small clearing in the brush, and in the middle sat a trailer. My heart skipped with excitement as my eyes searched and found my two brothers and my sister running around and chasing some small animals I couldn't quite identify.

"What are they chasing, Daddy?" I asked.

"It looks like puppies."

"Puppies?" I screeched. We'd never had a dog, but we used to have neighbors who did, and I always loved it when I was allowed to pet them.

My dad chuckled. "Yeah. Puppies."

Before my dad had even completely stopped his Blazer, I was scrambling for the door handle and flung myself out of the car. "Guys! I'm here!"

My sister came running and barreled into me as I wrapped my arms around her. While I held her, my eyes started burning with tears.

"We got puppies!" she said as she pulled away.

I looked at the puppies again and then ran over to Al and flung my arms around him.

"Hey sis, I missed you," he said as he hugged me back.

"I missed you guys, too," I replied.

A moment later, I ran over to James, wrapping my arms around his waist; he was practically twice my height.

"Hey, Miss Piggy's back," he said with a snort.

I pulled back and used my hands to shove him away from me as he laughed. "That's not funny," I said. I hated when they called me names like Miss Piggy and Fatso; I couldn't help that I was chubby like my parents while they were all really skinny.

"I'm just kidding, Fatso—I mean, *sis*," he snickered.

My eyes stung with more tears, but this time because I was upset.

"Knock that shit off," my dad called from where he was standing near his Blazer with my sister in his arms.

Just then, the trailer door opened, and a strange woman walked out. She was white like my mom, with thick, dirty blonde hair in a long bowl cut. Her eyes lit up when they landed on me and she smiled broadly.

"You must be Katherine," she said. "I've heard a lot about you. I'm Linda."

"Hi, Linda," I replied, unsure what to do. She seemed really nice and like she was excited to see me, but I was expecting to see my mom.

"Linda. Where's Kathy?" my dad asked, his voice tense like it was when he was angry. My body froze, recognizing his tone as the one he used when he was about to spank us, and that electric feeling zapped through me all the way to my fingers and toes.

"Teddy," the woman responded, her face hardening as she looked at my dad. "She's inside. She was taking a nap, but she's getting up now."

Tense silence followed as they stared at each other and my body started feeling heavy. Something slammed into my shins and I jumped, my heart racing in my chest, though I felt stupid for getting so scared when I looked down and realized it was one of the puppies. *How could I forget there were puppies?* I squatted down and the puppy jumped onto my knees and barreled into my face, its little tongue licking me all over. I fell backward onto my butt, giggling as it continued to jump around on me.

"What's its name?" I asked between giggles.

"Haven't named 'em yet," Linda replied. "I just found them this morning. I saw some asshole dragging them to the creek in a bag."

"Why would they do that?" I asked.

"To kill them," she replied soberly.

My heart dropped and my chest felt tight. *How could someone want to kill a puppy?* I wrapped my arms around the bundle of tan fur frolicking in my lap and hugged it. "I won't let anything happen to you," I whispered as its little pink tongue darted out and licked my nose again, coaxing a smile from me as my chest loosened.

The trailer door opened, and I looked up to see my mom coming outside.

"Mommy!" I shrieked, untangling my limbs from the puppy's and launching myself in her direction.

"Oof," she said as I slammed into her.

"Mommy! I missed you!" I cried into her waist.

Her arms circled me and squeezed me into her. "I missed you, too, honey. It's so good to see you."

*****

Shortly after my dad left, my mom and Linda told us to go explore with the puppies for a while. They needed to go into town to exchange some of their food stamps for cash and get some groceries. After they left, the four us began meandering down the trail the vehicles had driven along. Two of the three puppies were running up ahead of us with my sister chasing them and the third was limp, happily sleeping in my arms.

"Does Linda live here, too?" I asked.

James snorted and Al laughed.

"What? Why's that a funny question?" I persisted.

James picked up his pace. "I'm going to catch up with Laurel," he said.

"She's mom's girlfriend, of course she lives with us," Al said a moment later.

"Oh," I said. "Her girlfriend? I didn't know she had a girlfriend. But Mommy and Daddy are married."

Al laughed again. "Didn't your dad tell you anything?"

"He's your dad, too."

"No, he's not. He's *your* dad."

"He just said that Mommy left and took you guys with her." I didn't tell my brother, but I still heard the rest of what my dad had told me. *Because she doesn't love us anymore.*

"She left him for her girlfriend. For Linda."

"Oh." I didn't know what else to say. I'd never known my mom had a girlfriend and I'd never met Linda. "Well, she seems really nice."

Al shrugged. "She's nicer than mom." After a moment, he added, "And your dad."

"Don't say mean things about Mommy and Daddy!"

"Shut up," Al replied, jogging ahead and leaving me trailing behind with the sleepy puppy in my arms.

I walked faster, not wanting to get too far behind in case the woods decided to swallow me like they tried to do to my dad's Blazer, but froze a few minutes later. Standing stock still, I tried to listen over the suddenly loud pounding of my heart; maybe I'd imagined it. But I knew I hadn't when I heard it again.

"Guys!" I called, looking around me frantically, my head whipping in every direction to figure out where the sound was coming from.

"What?" Al called back.

"I hear something!"

"Yeah, you're in the woods, there are lots of bugs and animals," James called back without stopping.

"No, I'm serious!" I shouted, starting to panic as tears stung my eyes. "I think someone is throwing away a baby like Linda said they did with the puppies."

"What, sis? What are you talking about?" James asked.

"I hear a baby!" I shouted.

"A baby?" Al asked as James called out to my sister to stop and wait. They both turned and started walking back toward where I was standing still.

"Yes," I said, my head still whipping around. "A baby."

"Like a baby crying?" James asked.

"No. I hear a baby toy. Like a rattle thing." James and Al both froze about ten or fifteen feet away from me. "I'm not sure if—"

"Shut up!" James shouted. "I can't hear!"

A few long seconds passed while I listened to the rattling sound and wondered why they were just standing there the way they were. "Can you guys hear—"

"Sis! I said SHUT UP!"

"Why?" I yelled back, mad that James kept telling me to shut up.

"That's not a baby, it's a rattlesnake," Al said. "Don't move."

"What?" I asked, but this time my voice was really quiet. That electricity feeling was in my body again and the puppy felt really heavy in my arms. I forced myself to pull it in closer so I wouldn't drop it.

James and Al ignored me, both of them looking around slowly for a moment and then whispering to each other.

"Okay, sis," James said quietly. "You need to toss the puppy over there"—he pointed to my left—"and then run to us, okay?"

I shook my head no. "I'm not putting the puppy down."

"Sis, listen to me. You have to. There's a fucking rattlesnake over there. It's better if it bites the puppy than if it bites you."

I shook my head again. "No. I'll run, but the puppy is coming with me. I'd rather the snake bite me." I raised my arms a few inches. "It's just a baby."

"That snake is going to bite you," James said.

"She might make it," Al said, turning to James. "Okay, sis, run as hard as you can, okay?"

I nodded in understanding.

"Okay," Al said. "On three. One... two... three!"

I ran with everything I had, holding on to the puppy as tight as my arms could manage, following my brothers as they turned and ran when I neared them. After a moment, they slowed down, and I slowed behind them. We reached my sister who was staring at us, wide-eyed, but didn't say anything. The other puppies ran up to my legs, yipping to play, and the puppy in my arms started squirming to get down. Shaking, I bent over and placed the puppy on the ground.

"That was close," Al said to James and they both started laughing.

"Yeah, it was," James agreed.

"Dude, sis, you outran a rattlesnake," Al said. "You're a badass." He burst into laughter again with James. "Who would've guessed your tubby little body could move that fast?"

I started to smile, but the edges of my mouth turned down instead. I sat down on the ground as my legs started shaking and cried into my bent knees as my brothers laughed next to me, wishing my mom or dad was there to hold me. I was so relieved and still really scared, and I was so sick of my brothers being mean to me. Really, I just wanted a hug from them.

*****

It was hotter than the last few days, and the heat made us stinky. All of us—even my sister—had been sweating since the middle of the night, the air swelteringly hot and humid. My brothers, Linda, and I were sitting next to some downed logs along the edge of the creek near where Linda had found the puppies. My sister and my mom were napping in the trailer.

"You have to lick the edge of the paper, but you can't use too much spit or it will fall apart," Linda said. "Like this." She licked the cigarette paper gently with the tip of her tongue. "See? Just enough that it sticks when you press it down. And now we have a finished homemade cigarette."

I nodded. "I'm ready to try by myself."

I watched my brothers and Linda for a moment as they each made another cigarette, just to make sure I remembered all the steps, then carefully peeled a cigarette paper from the stack and laid it on the small paper towel I had to work on. Reaching over to the baggie filled with tobacco, I grabbed a small pinch.

"Not quite enough," Linda said quietly in her raspy voice.

I glanced at her, but she was still focused on her own task. *How did she know?* I dropped the pinch I had back into the baggie and tried again, a little more between my fingers this time.

"Good," she murmured.

I carefully released the pinch of tobacco onto the small cigarette paper, using my fingertip to spread it around the way Linda had shown me. I glanced up at her and she nodded her head approvingly.

"Remember, don't roll it too loosely or everything will fall out."

44

"I got it," I said.

I focused on rolling the cigarette exactly how she'd shown me until just a tiny lip of the paper was sticking up. Using both hands, I very gently lifted the cigarette to my mouth and used the tip of my tongue to lick the edge of the paper and then pressed it down. It stuck to itself, but the paper was a little wet and see-through where I'd licked it.

"Not bad," Linda said. "A little too much spit, but not bad."

"Way to go, sis," James said. "Your first cigarette. It only took you as long as it took me to make five."

I glared at James as he and Al laughed. I didn't understand why he was always so mean to me. But I'd show him; I'd practice every day until I could make cigarettes faster than he could. Without saying anything, I looked back down and reached for the next cigarette paper.

It felt like only moments rather than hours had passed when I noticed the sun was getting low in the sky and Linda told us we needed to head back to the trailer. I had a large stack of finished cigarettes next to me and I was proud of what I'd done, even though my stack was smaller than everyone else's. If it wasn't time to leave, I would have done more; I liked making the cigarettes, doing the same thing over and over. Everyone was quiet and seemed to be content, there was no yelling, and I didn't feel scared or have that electricity in my body. I liked being around Linda, who treated us all like we were her kids, but without all the yelling my parents did. She intervened when my mom got really angry and stopped our mom from spanking us as much as she used to do.

And once I didn't have to concentrate so hard, I could hear all the insects around us out there, the water running over the rocks and sticks in the creek next to us. There were birds flitting around, chirping, having a beautiful conversation with each other. The trees towering over us provided shade and rustled gently when there was a breeze. Everything was so peaceful that I felt more relaxed than I remembered ever feeling before, and I never wanted anything to change.

living a fairy tale

"Peace is the beauty of life. It is sunshine. It is the smile of a child, the togetherness of a family."

-Menacheim Begin

mid-september 1991

It was a warm afternoon one Saturday after the start of second grade. While I'd been in West Virginia with my mom, my dad had found a job that gave him enough money to rent a small white house with a detached garage on a corner lot. My mom, my brothers, and my sister had all moved in with us just prior to the start of the school year. At the moment, my mom and my sister were taking a nap and my brothers were out somewhere with friends. But I wasn't tired, and I didn't have any friends, so I'd meandered outside to where my dad was methodically balancing lengths of two-by-fours on sawhorses and sawing them in half with a handsaw.

"Daddy?" I asked. "Can I help?"

"Sure. Stand over there on the other side of that sawhorse and hold that board down. Keep it still while I'm sawing, and don't let it fall, you hear?"

"Okay."

I walked around the sawhorse and used both of my hands to hold down the board as my dad's saw started moving back and forth, back and forth. I was mesmerized by the fine sawdust floating down and piling up on the driveway between the sawhorses, sometimes scattering and creating patterns on the asphalt when a stray breeze passed by. The sound of the teeth of the saw cutting into the wood was rhythmic and relaxing, and the aroma of freshly-cut wood filled my nostrils.

I heard a car engine and glanced over my shoulder to see who was there, but it was just a car driving past our house. I'd thought for a moment that maybe it was Linda. I hadn't seen her since I stayed with them in West Virginia and I liked her. Though, I figured if she was around, then my mom and dad wouldn't be back together, so it was probably better if she wasn't there. But I wondered if she was lonely now that my mom and siblings had come to live with my dad and me.

After we'd created a big pile of cut boards and an even bigger pile of sawdust, my dad pulled a blue towel from his back pocket and mopped the sweat from his brow and temples. I watched as he stuffed the towel back into his pocket and pulled out a cigarette. The butts of the cigarettes were always dry and stiff when they came out of the pack, but within moments, it would be crushed up and soggy from my dad gnawing on it between his teeth; he rarely took the cigarette out of his mouth until it was time to put it out. It was gross and I felt a little bad for that cigarette butt. But I would sit there and watch him chew on that cigarette butt all day if I could hang out with my dad. I hoped whatever he did for work now—he wouldn't talk to me about it the same way he used to about his job working on cars—he never stopped. My dad had never been home as much as he was now; I got to see him *before* dinner almost every day, and he let me help him do things around the house.

"Whatcha' smiling about over there?" my dad asked, his voice light.

"Thank you for letting me help you," I replied. "I like helping you."

"I like it, too," he replied, his cigarette bobbing up and down in between his lips as he spoke.

I sat down and used my finger to draw designs in the sawdust while my dad finished his cigarette. After he'd tossed the butt on the driveway and ground it out with his boot, he reached over the for the next plank of wood and I jumped up, ready to help.

"We'll do a few more, and then I want you to go in and get your mom and your sister up."

"Okay, Daddy."

"I've decided we're going out to eat tonight."

"Really?"

"Yeah. Somewhere special. It's mine and your mom's anniversary, so I'm going to take us out."

"Where are we going?"

"Your mom's favorite place."

"Chesapeake Seafood House?" I asked excitedly.

He nodded. "Don't tell your mom that's where we're going."

I squealed and clapped my hands together. "I won't, I promise."

*****

I couldn't believe how full I was—I was so *stuffed* that my seatbelt felt too tight on my belly. I thought back to all the food we'd had at dinner and again marveled at how much I'd managed to eat. I hadn't even known they would let you *order* that much food! We'd had lobster—my mom's absolute favorite food—and steamed shrimp and fried shrimp and hush puppies and rice and broccoli and soda as our parents sipped wine. We'd all eaten until we were so full that we couldn't eat another bite, and still there was food left on the table. Then my dad had given us each some money from his pocket and told us to go play with the arcade games while he and my mom drank another bottle of wine.

It had felt like we were living a different life; it felt like all those times we'd been hungry and had to share everything, all those times my parents were screaming at each other and spanking us had been bad dreams. My mom and dad had barely yelled or spanked us since my mom had moved in—they were both always smiling now.

The windows were down, warm and humid air blowing through the car as my dad navigated through the streets to get us home from our fancy dinner out. The sun was setting, twilight beginning to blanket the area. I could hear my mom humming to herself in the front seat every time we slowed for a stop sign or red light and couldn't keep from grinning.

"Teddy?" my mom asked softly at one red light, her eyes closed and her head moving gently from side to side as she hummed.

"Yes, Kathy?"

"I wanna dance."

When we got home a little while later, my dad told us all to go up to the little room on the top floor and that he'd be there in a minute. The room was tiny, hot, and stuffy, but it was completely bare, no furniture or rugs on the wood floors. We opened the single small window to let in some fresh air, and my brothers, sister, and I huddled together against the far wall once my dad arrived with a small portable stereo he set down by the stairs.

My parents danced to *Achy Breaky Heart* by Billy Ray Cyrus blaring from that stereo. Every few songs on that cassette tape, my dad would rewind it back to that song and push play again as my mom watched with a smile, her eyes soft and twinkling—it was her favorite song.

"Look at that grin on Mom's face," Al whispered to James over my head. I was sitting in his lap and leaning back against him while my sister was in James' lap, leaning against him in the same way.

"I know. I think we're going to stay," he replied.

I nodded in agreement. "We're finally back together. Mommy and Daddy never fight any more."

Tipping my head back as far as I could, I looked out the window at the few stars visible twinkling in the sky, tuning out the continued whispering between James and Al, instead focusing on the music. It was too hot to be sitting so close to someone in that room, but sweaty skin wasn't enough to make me want to move; listening to my mom's favorite song and my parents' soft giggling, smelling the familiar mixture of sweat and sawdust and cigarette smoke, feeling the unmistakable warmth of my brother's presence behind me, assuring me I wasn't alone anymore, was wonderful. The sense of being loved and having my family together felt like it was exploding inside me. I grinned up at the stars in the sky and felt gratitude that my wishes on shooting stars and prayers to God with my hands squeezed tight hadn't been in vain. My parents were happy, and things were better for our family than they'd ever been, and that made *me* happy and buoyed my spirit with hope for the future.

an exceptionally shitty week

"A child's innocence is the one gift that, once stolen, can never be replaced."
-Jaeda DeWalt

october 1991

My parents had started fighting a few days after we'd gone to Chesapeake
Seafood House. Every day, the fighting got worse and worse until my mom
had said she was leaving. My dad had followed her over to Linda's
apartment, my brothers and sister and me in tow.

"Fuck you, Teddy!" my mom screamed.

"This is fucking bullshit, Kathy!" my dad screamed back.

Linda had been trying to mediate for over an hour, to get both my mom
and my dad to stop yelling, but they just screamed at her, too. They were
standing in the kitchen behind the living room, and Linda had turned on
cartoons for us to watch, the volume of the television as high as it would
go. My brothers and sister were sitting a few feet from the screen, intently
focused on the animation, but I was standing next to Linda at the threshold
between the two rooms.

I had tried to help as well, but both of my parents had ignored me,
simply using a hand to push me away from them. Linda now had a hand
resting on my shoulder, which she squeezed every time I started to step
forward—I knew it meant she wanted me to stay out of it. My body was
buzzing with that electricity again as my parents got louder and louder,
their faces so close as they screamed that their noses were nearly touching.

"Fuck this!" my dad shouted, turning this time. In a few quick steps,
he'd reached the door, and then he was gone, the walls shaking from how
hard the door had slammed.

With the absence of yelling, there was an eerie silence thickening the air around the sounds of the cartoons coming from the television, and everyone was still for a moment. Suddenly, I realized that my dad had left, and he might never come back. Reaching up, I pushed Linda's hand off my shoulder and took off through the apartment door after him.

"Daddy! Daddy! Wait!" I called as I ran. Once I burst out of the building into the dark night air outside, I could just barely see him and shouted again. "Daddy! Don't leave me!"

He ignored me as he continued rushing away from the building. I struggled to keep up, running as fast as I could, until I finally stopped trying. I slowed to a stop and watched his body shrinking as the distance between us grew. My tears came pouring out as I watched and begged him in a whisper not to leave, to just come back.

Then, I realized he had to at least walk back past me because the parking lot for the apartment was behind me and in front of us was a highway; there was nowhere else for him to go. *He must just be taking a walk to calm down.*

It dawned on me, however, as he took his first step onto the asphalt shoulder, that I was wrong, and my body flooded with electricity, my heart racing. I screamed as my legs started up again, pumping with every ounce of effort I had to get to him. I was nearing the asphalt shoulder when my body was suddenly swept upwards, nothing but air under my feet, and I turned my head to see it was Linda who'd grabbed me and prevented me from following my dad onto the highway. I flung my arms and legs in every direction, trying desperately to get down as my dad stepped into traffic.

I continued to scream while headlights danced into different directions, the sound drowned out by tires screeching across pavement as the cars slammed on their brakes and jerked their wheels to the side in a bid to avoid hitting my dad and each other. While many of the cars plowed into one another, the crunch of metal crashing into metal and glass shattering overtaking the screeching of the tires on the pavement, they all managed to avoid hitting my dad.

I could feel some of the tension leave Linda's body, mine sliding down several inches in her arms as she released a harsh breath and started walking back toward the apartment building. I screamed over her shoulder for my dad, watching helplessly as he sat down right there where he was standing in the middle of the lane and put his head into his hands. I gave up when we were about halfway back, burying my face into Linda's neck as I cried. She stopped just outside the door into the building and held me, the tightening of her arms making it harder to breathe but easier to stop crying.

"He'll be okay," she said when I pulled back to wipe my face.

I nodded and she carried me into the building and back into the apartment. When we walked through the door, my siblings were all still in the living area watching cartoons, but I noticed immediately that my mom was absent.

"Where's Mommy?" I asked as Linda set me down.

"Leave her be," Linda replied. "She's upset and doesn't want to be bothered. It's better to just leave her alone right now."

I knew Linda was right, that my mom would likely spank me for bothering her when she wanted to be left alone, but I kept seeing my dad walking onto the highway and all those cars around him; I desperately wanted to hug my mom. Ignoring Linda, I looked in the bedroom, but my mom wasn't there. I closed the door and turned to the bathroom across the hall, opening the door and barging in.

I stopped just inside the doorway, frozen. I didn't think I was making any sound, but based on how quickly Linda appeared, I must have started screaming. I was still holding the doorknob when Linda swept me up, dislodging my hand and whisking me away before she grabbed the phone off the wall and called 9-1-1. It didn't matter that she'd removed me so quickly, though; the image had already been seared into my brain: my mom, unmoving in a bathtub full of bloody water after slitting her wrists.

I was still using my hands to rub my eye sockets, trying to get rid of the last images I had of my parents, when the emergency responders arrived. As soon as they came in, Linda ushered my brothers and sister and me outside, telling us we were going for a walk for a while. We walked all around her apartment building and the other buildings next to hers, creating figure eights and other loop-de-loop patterns with the paths we took as Linda pointed out the few stars we could see and talked about the ones we couldn't see.

After a while, I started to get the feeling that something or someone was following me where I trailed in the back of the group; I liked being able to see everyone, so I knew they were all still there. I turned to look behind me, but there was no one I could see. Shaking my head, I turned to face forward again and continued walking, but the feeling got stronger. Flipping around every few minutes, I was sure I would see what was giving me that eerie feeling of being watched and followed, my flesh raised with goosebumps and my heart beating really fast in my chest. But I never saw anything except a few feet of darkness before the blackness of the moonless night swallowed everything else. My legs started to feel unsteady and I was having a hard time breathing, my body filled with that electricity feeling again. I was sure if I didn't keep my eyes trained behind me that something was going to reach out and grab me and I'd silently disappear into the blackness behind us. Giving up on being in the back so I could see everyone, I ran around my brothers up to the front where Linda was carrying my sister on one hip and slid my hand into her free one. With her holding my hand and my brothers at my back, my heart finally started to slow.

*****

"Katherine. Do you want to live with me or with your dad?" my mom asked, turning toward me.

She'd survived slitting her wrists a little less than a week before and had just gotten out of the hospital. My dad had brought us all with him to Linda's apartment so he could talk to her, and after some yelling, they'd agreed they weren't going to stay together. And then they'd agreed that my brothers and sister would all stay with my mom again. But then they'd started arguing about who *I* would live with now.

"I want both of you," I said, my eyes filling with tears.

"You can't have both of us," my dad chimed in. "Now choose."

My tears spilled over my lower lids, sliding down my cheeks and leaving hot trails behind. "I can't choose."

"You have to," my mom said.

"Please," I whispered, staring at the floor. "I can't."

"God damn it, Katherine, just fucking choose!" my mom shouted.

I mashed the heels of my hands into my eye sockets and sobbed instead of answering, but my mom yanked my hands down.

"Hurry up!" she shouted. "You need to choose *now*. We don't have all fucking night."

I shook my head. "I can't."

"It's not an option, Katherine. Just pick someone. Pick whoever you love more."

My chest felt like it was being pinched and even more tears came out of my eyes. I loved them equally; I didn't love one more than the other. "Please," I begged. "You pick. I can't. I love both of you."

"You heard your mom, Katherine," my dad said, his voice assuring me he was getting close to spanking me if I didn't do what he said. "You need to choose whoever you love the most."

"You always love someone better than everyone else, so just pick that person already," my mom added, her jaw clenched with frustration.

I loved my parents the same, no matter what my mom said about us loving someone best, so I couldn't make a decision that way, but I had to make a decision or they would both spank me soon. *Well, Mommy is getting three of us already,* I thought. *If I live with her, too, then Daddy won't have anyone and he'll be lonely.* I looked over at my brothers and sister in the living area watching cartoons and felt like I couldn't breathe for a moment. *What if I never see them again?* As much as we all fought when we lived together, it was so much less lonely than when I lived by myself with my dad.

Turning back toward my parents, I realized if there was a chance I'd never see my siblings again if I chose my dad, that meant there was a chance I'd never see my mom again either. But if I chose my mom, then I might never see my dad again. But if I never saw him again, that would mean he never saw any of us again. And then he'd be so lonely—I couldn't let him be lonely.

I knew that my mom and my brothers and my sister would all think I didn't love them as much as I loved my dad, even if I swore to them it wasn't true, and that it wouldn't matter what I said about why I made that decision. *I love you guys just as much,* I said silently in their direction. Then I looked up at my parents through my tears.

"I'll live with Daddy."

unkept promises

"Promise a child ONLY what you can fulfill. Because a broken promise breaks the child from the inside."

-Dr. Preethi Tewari

mid-june 1992

I glanced over my shoulder and grinned at my sister. She'd come to live with my dad and me a few months before; my dad had just announced one day that she was coming.

"Really?" I asked, a flutter of excitement in my chest at the possibility. I hadn't seen my mom or my siblings or Linda since the night I chose to live with my dad.

"Really."

"When?"

"Right now. That's where we're going. To pick her up."

I squealed in excitement. "Are James and Al coming to visit, too?"

"No. And it's not a visit. Your sister is going to live with us."

"Forever?"

"No, not forever. But I don't know how long."

"And James and Al are staying with Mommy?"

He glanced over at me quickly and then back to the road. "No," he replied. Then sighed. "Your mom is going to rehab to get—"

"What's rehab?" I interrupted him.

"It's like a special hospital for people who are addicted to things like drugs and alcohol."

"Oh. For how long?"

"As long as it takes. They'll help her. While she's in there, though, your sister is going to live with us."

"Where are James and Al going to live?"

"They're going into foster care."

"What's that? And why can't they live with us?"

"I can't take care of all of you," he replied, turning onto a side street. "So social services is putting them into a foster home. They'll live with another family until your mom is done with rehab, then she can get them back and your sister will go back to live with her, then it'll be us again."

"Can I see my brothers before they go?"

"No—they're already gone. You can see them when your mom gets them back."

I nodded and looked out the car window, watching the buildings and trees as we drove across town. I really hope Mommy finishes rehab, I thought.

My sister smiled back at me from the back seat of my dad's Blazer, but she looked more scared than excited to me. Our dad was driving us to spend the weekend with our mom. Laurel hadn't seen her since my dad picked her up to live with us, and I hadn't seen her since the night I chose to live with my dad. She'd left rehab without finishing the program, so my brothers were still in foster care somewhere, and my dad said social services had told him that my sister couldn't live with our mom again until she finished the program. But now we were going to see her for an entire weekend!

The Blazer eventually turned off the main road into a large trailer park next to a shopping center. My dad drove slowly, glancing down at a piece of paper in his hand a few times as he navigated through what felt like a maze of trailers in different sizes and myriad states of disrepair. After one turn, I saw my mom's dingy fifteen-foot trailer up ahead, which was the smallest and dirtiest trailer I'd seen so far.

My dad stopped in front of the trailer, the crunching of the gravel dissipating and finally disappearing entirely. As I opened my car door, eager to see my mom, the trailer door opened and Linda stepped outside, a broad grin on her face and her arms open wide. A moment after I ran into her arms, my sister's body slammed into mine from behind. My dad called from the driver's seat that he'd be back on Sunday. Linda nodded at him and Laurel and I shouted that we loved him as he pulled away.

"Where's mommy?" I asked.

"She's inside, taking a nap," Linda said. And then she explained to us that she and my mom didn't have running water, so we had to use the jugs of water sitting outside for drinking or if our hands were really dirty and needed washing. She also explained that it was pretty hot inside because they didn't have electricity for a while either; Linda had lost her job and hadn't been able to find a new one yet, so all the utilities running to the trailer had been cut off. We listened and said okay, but we didn't really care—we just wanted to see our mom.

By the end of the weekend, my sister and I were ready to see our dad again; we'd missed him, and we were hungry because there had only been a little bit of food to eat all weekend. I was worried he might not remember which trailer we were in since he'd only been there once, so I sat outside with my sister to wait. Sunday morning turned into Sunday afternoon, the hours crawling by as the sun tracked across the sky. As evening set in, our mom called us inside the trailer.

"Your dad decided you guys could stay a whole week!" she said. "Isn't that great?"

"Really?" I asked.

"Really! He said he misses you both and will be back to get you next Sunday."

Although I still missed my dad, I was overjoyed that I'd get to spend a whole entire week more with my mom—maybe she'd even have a flute day while we were there.

early july 1992

"Mommy's going to get better, okay?" my mom said to my sister and me with her eyes full of tears. We'd been living with her for about a month; our dad had never come back to get us.

I didn't like that my mom was upset, and I hugged her. "It's okay, Mommy."

She cried for a moment and then responded. "No, it's not okay. I need to get better so I can take care of you girls. I'm not going to drink anymore, okay? I promise."

"Okay, Mommy."

"I promise," she said sternly, using her hands to lift first my face, and then my sister's, to look into our eyes, hers serious. "I. Promise."

I believed her—my mom didn't promise things very often. She and Linda explained that it was going to be really hard and that my mom would be angrier than ever for a while, that we should be on our best behavior and go play somewhere during the day. My sister and I nodded and agreed.

They were right, too. She *was* angry, yelling at all of us constantly for a few days. Laurel and I went out as soon as we woke up and didn't come back until dark every day. But a few days later, it was so hot, and we got so thirsty that we had to go back to the trailer in the afternoon to get something to drink. I told my sister to wait outside so if Mommy was angry, she would only spank me, and I opened the door as quietly as I could. When I peered in, I could see my mom sleeping on the floor and my heart sank; she'd been drinking.

No! I thought. *She hasn't. She promised. She must just be tired after yelling so much. She's taking a real nap. I'll be quiet so I don't wake her up.*

I tip-toed over to the glass of clear liquid on the tiny table, sure it was water since my mom wasn't drinking anymore. Deciding to have a quick drink before taking the glass outside to share with my sister, I put the glass to my lips and took a gulp. When the liquid was about halfway down my throat, I started choking and it all came up, spewing out of my mouth all over the inside of the trailer, all over my mom's sleeping body.

It wasn't water.

mid-july 1992

My body was flooding with electricity and the nauseous feeling in the pit of my stomach almost overpowered the pain from being so hungry as my sister and I trudged next door to the shopping center. Our mom was in a deep sleep that Linda called "napping," but after listening to them fight, I realized our mom was actually passed out—something that happened after she drank too much of the not-water, which I'd also learned was called "vodka." Linda had left when it was still dark outside to go look for work, and it was another day we didn't have any food. If it was just me, I'd go back to the trailer and be hungry because I *hated* what we were about to do. But I glanced back and saw the tears in my sister's eyes and knew I had to do it anyway. For her. I grabbed her hand and smiled at her.

"Come on, we'll get food this time."

A few times a week, my sister and I would try to sneak through the doors of the nearby Subway when the workers weren't paying attention, usually trailing behind someone else. We'd slide quietly into an empty booth, hoping to be unnoticed, our mouths flooding with saliva at the heavenly smell of toasting bread, which wafted down to us a few storefronts away when someone opened the door to exit. I stopped walking for a moment and closed my eyes. *If I inhale the smell long enough, can I trick my belly into feeling full?* I wondered.

That would be so much better than sitting in the booth and watching other people with money eat, knowing it bothered them that we couldn't stop staring. I tried to imagine what it was like to be one of them, what their lives must be like if they could afford to buy food at Subway. We'd cross our grubby fingers as we waited that they would be too full to finish and would leave their food scraps on the table; then we could run over and snatch them up once they had left, before the workers had a chance to clear off the scraps and garbage. Those days weren't that bad.

The other days were—the ones when people would glare at us for being there, sometimes sniffing the air loudly while they looked at us. I already knew we smelled bad, but we couldn't help it; we didn't have water for taking a bath. I felt shame wash over me when they did that, but we were *so* hungry... Those were also the people who—looking directly at us— would walk over to the trash can and throw away the rest of their food as they left, saying something to the workers, who would then come chase us out the door, shouting after us to never come back. I felt like we were criminals or filthy scum who didn't deserve to be alive, and like I was somehow responsible for us having to seek out other people's unwanted scraps in order to eat. And then I felt like a failure for not being able to feed my sister. No matter how hard I tried, though, I couldn't figure out how to make things any better for us.

Flashing my sister another fake smile, I squeezed her hand a little harder and marched up to the front door. Reaching up and grabbing the handle, I pulled the door open and held it for my sister to walk in. One of the workers behind the counter—a woman with a round face and soft brown eyes—looked directly at me as I followed my sister inside and I froze. She stared at me for a moment, then looked back to the customer in front of her and asked the man a question.

That was close. I ushered my sister quickly into a booth out of direct line of sight from the counter and we slid in to start our watch for scraps. There was a long line of customers, but one after another, almost every one of them carried their food back out the door instead of sitting down. Each person that left pulled my heart down a little further; I knew it meant we were that much less likely to eat something. Holding my sister's hand tightly, my eyes flipped back and forth between the only two tables with customers eating as we waited for them to finish. It felt like hours passed with us waiting, and then when they finally left, there wasn't even a single bite left on their wrappers.

My sister and I shrank down in the booth when another worker came out from behind the counter to clean tables, my fingers crossed they'd forgotten we were there and wouldn't see us. He finished with the tables and headed back behind the counter, but then I saw the woman heading in our direction, her eyes fixed on me again. I knew we should get up and run, but that electricity was in my body again and my legs wouldn't work. All I could do was turn my body to shield my sister and wait for whatever was about to happen.

The woman stopped in front of me and pointed to the back corner of the store. "There's a bathroom back there. Go wash your hands. Both of you."

I stared back at her, not moving and not responding, trying to figure out why she wasn't yelling at us to leave.

"Go on, it's okay. Go clean up," she said again, smiling at me.

Carefully, I slid out of the booth, pulling my sister behind me, and we ran to the back of the store into the bathroom. After we'd washed our hands, we walked back out and I saw the woman sitting on the opposite side of the booth we'd been in moments before. As we neared, I could see there was food and soda on the table.

"We don't have any money," I said as we walked up to the booth, my eyes glued to the food.

"I know," she replied. "I also know you're hungry."

I looked up from the food into her face. She was smiling, but her eyes looked sad instead of happy. In fact, she looked like she was about to cry.

She stood up suddenly. "Sit, eat. Take your time. This is all for you and there's no rush." And then she turned and walked away.

I looked back down at the table. There was an enormous sub with chicken and lettuce and tomatoes and cheese, a bag of potato chips, and a big cup of soda with a straw in it. I turned back to my sister, a genuine grin on my face. "It's a feast!"

It felt like we were royalty as we sat there in that booth sharing the meal the lady had given us. I ate quickly, and when I was done, my belly was so full that it hurt. The last time my belly felt like that had been when my dad took us all to Chesapeake Seafood House the night my parents danced in the attic. I closed my eyes as I leaned back against the booth next to my sister, listening to the sounds of the sub wrapper crinkling as she continued to eat her half more slowly.

It was such a wonderful feeling to not be hungry that I had an urge to giggle. But I also knew it wouldn't last and I didn't know how long it would be until we were full again. I missed knowing I'd have food at least once a day; I missed being able to take a bath. And I really missed my dad. I hoped he was okay, but I was sure something must have happened to him. Why else wouldn't he have come back to get us like he said he would? My chest tightened and my eyes filled with tears. I opened my eyelids as wide as I could and stared at the ceiling, willing myself to stop thinking about those things—I didn't want to cry in front of my sister and make her sad, too.

shades of absence

"Indifference and neglect often do much more damage than outright dislike."

-J.K. Rowling

august 1992

From the back seat of my dad's Blazer, I stared at him from behind, trying to sort out what I was feeling. He'd shown up unexpectedly at my mom's trailer about an hour earlier. Laurel and I had been making rock piles outside when his car came to a stop in front of us. It had taken a moment to realize it was my dad, then my sister and I squealed and ran over to him. Mom and Linda had come out of the trailer, my mom with her glass of vodka in her hand, as surprised as my sister and I were.

My mom and dad had started arguing and Linda had grabbed a hand from each of us and taken us on a walk around the trailer park. When we got back to the trailer, my mom was sitting on the steps and my dad was waiting in the car.

"You guys are gonna go visit your dad for a few hours, okay?" my mom said.

I'd squealed and clapped my hands together in excitement. "Okay, Mommy!"

Linda opened the back door for us; although I always sat in the front, I wanted to stay close to my sister this time and climbed into the back with her. And then, as soon as we pulled onto the main road from the trailer park, I'd gotten that electricity in my body again and just wanted to go back to the trailer with my mom. I missed my dad, but I was angry at him and didn't want to see him, either—he hadn't even said he was sorry for not coming back or given us an explanation for why he was gone for so long. And I was afraid that we would never see my mom again. They said it was only for a few hours, but we were only supposed to see my mom for a few days and that was months ago.

My dad went through a McDonald's drive-through and got us Happy Meals, then drove to a nearby motel and parked. He hopped out and ushered us inside a tiny room covered in dirt and cigarettes butts and ashes. There were a few other men inside on the bed, but they stood up when we walked in and headed into the bathroom. After telling us to get up on the bed, my dad switched on the television and found some cartoons, then handed us our happy meals.

"Eat your burgers and don't move off the bed," he said.

"Okay," I said.

"You do and I'll whoop your ass."

"Yes, Daddy," I replied, watching him disappear into the bathroom after the other men.

Within moments, my food was gone, though my sister was still slowly eating hers. I never understood how she could eat so slowly when we were so hungry. Balling up the wrappers and the Happy Meal bag and moving them to the nightstand, I got comfortable on my belly with my head in hands, ignoring the muted thumps and loud laughter coming from the bathroom and focusing on Bugs Bunny. By the time that cartoon episode was over, though, I smelled something strange coming from the bathroom, mixing with the smell of stale cigarette smoke and old cigarette butts, and scrunched up my nose. *Ew.* The stronger the smell got, the more distracted I was; it was really stinky, like burning plastic, and was making my stomach upset.

By the time my dad came out of the bathroom, telling us it was time to leave, I'd lost count of how many episodes of *Looney Tunes* we'd watched and was long past ready to go back to my mom.

*****

I had turned eight the week before, and though my mom had promised me she would stop drinking as her present to me, it had only lasted a day, and then she had another bottle of vodka.

"Give me what you have so I can give it to your mom," Linda said as we walked back to our trailer.

I wonder if she saw everything, I thought as my hand fished around in my pocket.

Linda hadn't been able to find a job yet, so we went with her to the parking lot in the shopping center a few days a week to beg for money from the grocery store customers. Mostly people just passed by us, although some skirted wide circles as if coming too close would make them sick. When that happened, I felt like we were rabid stray animals, but I almost preferred that over the ones who walked into us as if we weren't there at all. But some people, like the nice man and woman today, would go out of their way to walk over and give us a little money from their pockets, though they looked almost as hungry and dirty as we were.

Linda always took everything we got once we started back to the trailer and then would give everything to my mom to figure out how to divide. Despite my mom's promises and—I believe—good intentions, she only bought vodka with that money. I'd started hiding some of it so I could sneak over to the store and buy a can of vegetables for my sister and me to eat. I would stand in the canned vegetable aisle with my few coins clutched in my fist and read every price label and every sign advertising a sale or special deal.

Linda was waiting with her hand out and I carefully left behind what I thought might be a quarter and couple of dimes as I pulled my hand out of my pocket. "Here you go," I said, dropping the last few coins into her palm. Crossing my fingers that she hadn't been counting as people gave me money, I started walking again.

"That's not everything," she called after me. "Check your pocket again."

My heart skipped and I got that same electricity feeling I always did when I was about to be spanked. Linda had never spanked me, but I was always afraid she would. Digging in my pocket again, trying to make it look like I was searching, I pulled my hand out with the rest of the coins.

"Sorry," I mumbled, feeling guilty for the lie I was about to tell. "I missed these by accident." Dropping the coins in her hand, I turned and started walking again. *We'll have to go to Billy and Sue's trailer today.*

Billy and Sue were brother and sister, and their trailer was the biggest one in the trailer park. Most of the kids ended up playing there and their parents sometimes fed us. They were the most popular kids in the trailer park, and they were bullies, leading the rest of the kids to pick on my sister and me for being so poor and dirty, for me being chubby and my sister skinny, and their parents always made comments to us about my mom and Linda being "worthless lesbians"; still, I took my sister over there so we could eat.

*****

"You're so skinny, you could be in a concentration camp!" Billy shouted at my sister. Every one of the twelve or fifteen other kids—mostly older than my sister and me—laughed. We were all squeezed into a small bedroom in Billy and Sue's trailer, kids spilling into the hallway.

"Leave her alone!" I shouted back, glancing over to my sister. We usually stuck together, but this time we'd gotten separated; she was on the side of the room by the door and I was on the opposite side. Normally, I'd grab her hand and we'd leave at this point, but I was stuck on the far side of that crowd, so I had to draw the attention from her instead.

"Shut up, fatso!" he yelled, the other kids joining in to form a chorus of name-calling.

I shouted over them for my sister to leave and then crossed my arms in front of me as they started making jokes about me giving my fat to my twiggy sister. No way I was going to let them treat my sister that way.

"No," I said loudly, though my heart was racing. "I won't shut up. Leave my sister alone."

The first kid shoved me in the chest—hard. I stumbled backward, coming to a sudden halt, then slamming forward when a kid who'd been behind me shoved me in the back. I screamed for help as I fell to the floor in a blur of feet and hands. My hands moved to cover my face and someone's foot stomped on me so hard I couldn't breathe as another's kicked me in the back of my head. I started to come out of my myself; I could feel my body jerking around as they hit me, but I couldn't feel the pain from their strikes anymore. Instead, all my senses became fuzzy, then everything was black.

When I opened my eyes again, all the kids were standing around me, watching and laughing. They allowed me to get to my feet, making fun of me for not holding my own against them. As I made my way through the crowd, they kicked out to trip me, shoved me in the back as I passed, and called me a "cry baby" for the tears tracking down my cheeks out of my control.

My sister was still there, standing on the back side of the crowd now, and I called for her to come on, that we were going home, but she didn't move. Her face was sad when she looked at me, but she didn't say a word or budge to follow me. I felt betrayed after what had just happened to me for sticking up for her and trying to protect her, and my silent tears morphed into loud, uncontrollable sobs. The adults in the front barely even glanced in my direction as I passed them to exit the trailer.

I whimpered for my mom through my sobs as I opened our trailer door but was met with silence; my mom was passed out. Though I knew it wouldn't make any difference, that only the passage of time would bring a change in her state, I wailed for her to wake up as I desperately shook her, wishing just this once that I'd be wrong. Eventually I gave up, huddling into a ball on the floor and pulling her limp arm around me where I sat and cried myself to sleep.

elmer

"Childhood should be carefree, playing in the sun: not living a nightmare in the darkness of the soul."

-Dave Pelzer

september 1992

I yawned as I trailed behind my mom, holding my sister's hand. It was late and dark and I was tired; I just wanted to go to sleep. The night before, I'd been woken up by shouting—my mom and Linda were in an argument with someone else from the trailer park. Linda was holding on to this thing that looked like what boys went pee out of and it flopped around as she shook it; she and my mom kept saying it was their dildo, while the other person shouted it was theirs, that my mom and Linda had stolen it. I sat down on the steps and watched the weird thing bob around as they screamed at each other until a police car arrived, their blue lights flashing, and a police officer got out and made them all stop yelling. It felt like I'd just fallen back to sleep when the sun came up that morning. But instead of letting us go to bed, Mom wanted to go to her friend's trailer for a while and we had to go with her. As we walked, I glanced to my left in the direction of the trailer I'd rather be going to if we had to go somewhere: Wesley-Wanda's trailer.

Wesley-Wanda was my mom and Linda's friend, and we went there a lot until the previous week. My mom got upset with me calling her Wesley-Wanda, but Wesley-Wanda didn't mind and smiled at me when I said it. During the day, she was Wesley, a man who dressed in man's clothes, kind of like the clothes Linda wore. She said she had no choice because that's how she was born, but that inside her body, she was a woman. In the evenings when she got home from work, she put on dresses, make-up, and a wig and was Wanda, a woman. Sometimes I mixed up which name to use when, so I just started saying Wesley-Wanda. She thought it was funny and cute and didn't mind, but my mom thought I should try harder to remember.

We always had fun at Wesley-Wanda's trailer. My mom and Linda would smoke and drink, but my mom usually stayed awake there. They all talked and laughed, and Wesley-Wanda would play fun songs and dance to them with my sister and me. Sometimes we even had dinner there, too, and stayed until really late at night. But Wesley-Wanda never came back after work about a week ago. My mom and Linda said they didn't know why, but I wondered if it was because the other people in the trailer park were so mean about her being stuck in a man's body.

I sighed and turned back in the direction we were walking, toward Elmer's trailer. My mom and Linda had talked about Elmer, but my sister and I had never gone to his trailer or met him. Earlier, I'd heard my mom and Linda arguing about going, but my mom insisted because Elmer had liquor. I think Linda didn't want my mom to go because she would probably wind up sleeping there all night, but she ended up agreeing with my mom like she always did and said she'd meet us there. *Maybe he'll give us some food,* I thought.

As soon as we got there, my mom introduced us to Elmer, who looked like he was a lot older than my mom, and they turned on the television in his living room. With cartoons going, my sister was sleeping under a blanket near my mom's feet within a few minutes, but my heart was beating too fast to sleep; I didn't like going to new places. I sat down on the floor, Elmer on the sofa and my mom on a recliner behind me. At first, they talked and laughed some, the sound of glass clinking as they refilled their glasses with vodka over and over. They smoked cigarette after cigarette, using the ones that were still lit to light the next ones before putting out spent butts into overflowing ashtrays, and the smoke slowly filled the room until there was a thick haze in every direction. With the smoke hanging heavily in the air, the television seemed to glow creepily. After a while, I stood up because my butt was numb, hoping my mom would decide we could go back to our own trailer soon.

It had been quiet for some time, aside from the low hum from the television, when Elmer called my name—just loud enough for me to hear it. I turned my head in his direction and he beckoned for me to come toward him. I shook my head slightly as I felt lead begin to fill my feet, like sand pouring from top to bottom in an hourglass.

"Come on over here," he said, continuing to beckon me over with his hand.

I glanced over to where my mom was and called out for her. "Mommy?"

She didn't stir; she was completely passed out. I knew from experience that I could shake her or even roll her off the chair and it wouldn't matter— she would be out for hours. My eyes darted back to Elmer and he smiled at me.

"It's okay. Just come over here," he said softly.

His eyes were dark and intense, the shadows shifting rapidly around his face as the light coming from the television brightened and darkened with the ever-changing images on the screen. The shifting shadows changed his smile from friendly to sinister and back again, and my body started to fill with electricity as I felt sick to my stomach. *Don't throw up.*

I didn't want to move from where I stood, but I was afraid of refusing and getting in trouble with my mom after she woke up for being rude to her friend. I stood rooted in indecision, wishing desperately that my mom would suddenly wake up.

"Mommy?" I called again, the leaden sand filling my knees and reaching my thighs.

"Shhh, you don't want to wake her up," Elmer responded. "Let her sleep. Just come on over here, now, like a good girl."

I shuffled slowly over, stopping a few feet away from him. I stared at my toes and noticed my stomach fluttering more violently. I hoped I wouldn't get sick in my mom's friend's trailer—my mom would definitely spank me if I did.

"Good girl," he praised in a murmur as he reached out and wrapped his fingers around my forearm.

Pulling gently but firmly, he twisted me around so my back was toward him and I was facing the television again. A woodenness invaded my body, my muscles and joints stiffening as he wrapped a hand around each of my hips and pulled me backward until my butt and back were mashed against him. The television lights flickered through the haze in the room, casting eerie shadows on the wall, as I waited for time to pass, wishing he would let me go soon.

One of his hands gently skimmed up under my shirt and across my chest, his palms rubbing circles over my nipples. His other hand slid across my hip and down my abdomen, his fingers slipping under the waistband of first my pants, and then my panties. His fingertips rubbed vigorously against me, up and down, each pass exploring further down until his fingers began poking painfully inside me.

I tried to focus on the shifting images on the television to distract myself as I waited for him to finish with me, but his breath—increasingly heavy—was louder than the low volume of the television, and the bursts of hot air on the back of my head and neck every time he exhaled were keeping me tethered to what was happening to me.

I stared ahead, perfectly still, my eyes wide and unblinking, my body stiff, screaming inside my head for my mom to wake up.

*****

Elmer had passed out like my mom, and I was sitting on the floor in front of the television when Linda arrived. I had my arms wrapped around my shins as tightly as I could and my forehead pressed hard into my knees as I cried, my shoulders shaking. I looked up when I heard the trailer door open, my heart skipping, not sure who was there, until I saw Linda's face. She squinted and looked around in silence, taking everything in for a moment. Then, she walked over and squatted down in front of me.

"What's wrong?" she asked, her brow furrowed.

I shook my head and let out an unexpected sob, clapping my hand over my mouth when I did; I didn't want to wake anyone up.

"What's wrong?" she asked again, her voice more demanding.

When I shook my head in response again, she picked me up off the floor and carried me outside, closing the door behind her quietly.

"Katherine, tell me what happened," she said. "I know something did because you're crying. You need to tell me."

I stared at her. I was sure my mom would be so mad at me and would spank me if she found out; I didn't want that to happen. And my dad had made me promise not to tell anyone about Terrence—wasn't this the same thing? "I don't want to get in trouble," I whispered through my tears.

"I promise you, whatever happened, you won't get in trouble or be spanked. But you have to tell me why you're crying."

I buried my face in her neck and told her how Elmer had touched me while my mom was passed out.

"Goddamn it, Kathy!" she shouted through gritted teeth. Then she set me down next to the trailer steps in the dark. "Don't move. I'm getting your sister."

70

She disappeared inside the trailer, letting the door slam this time, and reappeared a moment later with my sister in one arm. She grabbed my hand with her free one and walked us back to our trailer. After gently laying my still-sound-asleep sister down, she sat and I climbed into her lap, where I stayed as I cried in the comfort of her arms until I fell asleep.

*****

The sky hadn't even begun to lighten for the next day when I woke to the trailer door closing. I'd fallen asleep on Linda, who was sitting on the floor, and she shifted me gently off her lap as she stood.

"We need to talk, Kathy," she said, angrily pointing to the door my mom had just come in.

My mom rubbed her temples. "I need a drink first."

"NO!" Linda shouted. "We need to *talk* first."

My mom turned and Linda followed her outside the trailer, the door slamming behind her. I heard Linda start yelling at my mom and pulled my knees into my chest, squeezed my eyes shut, and pressed my hands over my ears to block the sound. I wanted to pretend like we'd never gone over to Elmer's trailer. And I didn't want my mom and Linda to fight like my mom and dad used to, especially because it was about me again.

My eyes flew open when the trailer door slammed into the wall. My mom came barreling in, her face red and her eyes hard. She looked like she did the day she'd spanked me so hard that she broke her paddle, and I shrunk backward. *I never should have told Linda,* I thought as I waited for her to grab my arm and pull me around to be punished.

But she didn't. She just stood there and stared at me for a minute, breathing hard. The longer she stood, the less she looked angry at me and the more she looked sad. I knew I was right when she reached up with her hand to wipe away tears that spilled over. Suddenly, she sat next to me.

"I need you to tell Mommy everything that happened," she said, her voice much quieter than I expected it to be.

"You're not mad?" I whispered.

"I am, but not at you, honey," she said gently.

Had she ever talked to me like that before? "Are you going to spank me?" I asked, my voice still in a whisper.

Her voice broke as she responded. "No, honey." She swallowed. "Can you tell me everything that happened?"

I'd already told Linda; I didn't want to talk about it again. But when I told her that, my mom told me I needed to tell her in my own words. I squeezed my arms around my legs and found a dirty spot on the wall a couple of feet in front of me and stared at that as I recited everything that happened after she'd passed out. I wanted to go outside when I was done; it felt like the trailer was getting smaller and I was having trouble breathing. Not only that, but my stomach was really upset, and I knew if I threw up inside, I'd get in trouble. But I froze when I looked at my mom; I couldn't move. I'd never seen her face like it was. Her jaw was clenched, but her lips were open like she was going to talk, though they were trembling. Her face was red and hard like when she was angry, but there were tears falling down her cheeks.

"Has this happened before?" she asked.

I figured she meant with Elmer, but I'd just met him the previous night. "No, he's never done that before," I said quietly.

"Not just him, but with anyone else?" she persisted.

My body froze and my heart skipped as I stared at her. My daddy made me promise not to tell anyone about Terrence, but I didn't want to lie to my mom, either. But no matter what, I had to be dishonest; either break my promise to my dad or lie to my mom, and I didn't know what to do, so I just stared at her as I watched her eyes widen.

"Who?" she demanded, angry.

"I can't tell you," I said quietly, looking down at my knees.

"Yes, you can. It's okay," she replied more gently.

I shook my head. "No, I can't. I promised."

"You promised? Who did you promise?"

"Daddy."

"Something happened and Teddy made you promise not to tell me?" she shouted, her eyes wide in shock.

"He made me promise not to tell *anyone*. He said I was lying."

"I don't give a shit what your dad told you, you need to tell me, right now, what happened?"

And because I didn't want to keep the secret anymore, I opened my mouth and told her about Terrence, too, silently apologizing to my dad the entire time for breaking my promise to him.

When I finished speaking, my mom flew into a kind of rage I'd never seen. She screamed and called my dad words I'd never even heard before and said she was going to "fucking kill that son of a bitch." She walked out of the trailer and slammed the door, then came back in moments later, slamming it again. Linda tried to calm her down and she attacked her, screaming at her and punching and slapping her. No matter what she did, though, Linda never hit her back. She sometimes yelled at her, but she just let my mom hit her.

After a while, my mom and Linda both left, their voices trailing off away from the trailer. I scooted closer to where my sister was still lying on the floor, her eyes wide in fear. I whispered that it was okay, that she could go back to sleep, smiling so she would believe me, then I rubbed her back until her eyes got heavy and closed again.

It wasn't long after my sister fell back to sleep that my mom and Linda returned to the trailer. My mom was shouting obscenities outside the trailer, but Linda came inside and spoke softly to me.

"We called the police and they're on their way. When they get here, your mom and I will talk to them, but you might have to as well. If they want to talk to you, you *have* to talk to them, do you understand? You have to answer their questions, and you need to tell the truth."

I nodded as I looked at her face. She smiled at me, but I could tell she didn't mean the smile because her eyes looked unhappy. She grabbed my hand, and I followed her outside to wait with her and my mom. I sat on the steps into the trailer, Linda leaning back against the trailer next to me, and my mom paced. Every once in a while, she'd shout something about needing a drink, but she never got one. When she made a comment about needing to be there to talk to the police, I realized she wasn't getting a drink because she didn't want to pass out.

But she wouldn't have been pacing around so unhappy, sweating and talking about how hot it was, wouldn't have been so angry, if it weren't for me. It was my fault she was miserable, and I wished there was some way I could fix it. I shrunk down on the trailer steps as small as I could be while we waited for the police, feeling like an inconvenience, and like everyone would be happier if I didn't exist.

whispers of change

early october 1992

"Leave the umbrella here," Linda said as I was opening it in front of our trailer.

We'd found an umbrella in a dumpster a few weeks prior. The metal rods were sticking through in a few spots, but it worked better than having nothing; we didn't have rain jackets.

"Why?" I asked, not yet closing it back up, moving my arm a few inches further from my body to make sure it was completely over my sister's head. It was raining. And cold. And we were headed to the parking lot in front of the grocery store to beg for money.

"If we have an umbrella, no one will give us any money. Leave it here."

I stared back at Linda for a moment, angry that we had to leave the umbrella at the trailer, angry that we had to go out and beg in the cold rain at all.

After closing the umbrella and tossing it inside the trailer, my sister and I trailed behind Linda in silence aside from the sound of the pouring rain. Long before we reached the parking lot, we were all soaked and shaking with cold. As we walked across the asphalt to our destination, Linda spoke again.

"Whenever someone comes close, make sure you cough."

"Why?" I asked, feeling combative.

Linda glanced back at me, her expression betraying irritation and a little surprise—I never back-talked or questioned what I was told to do. "Because it will make you look like you're sick. And if you're sick and wet and cold, you'll look pathetic enough that people will be more likely to give you money. And you know we need the money."

Yes, I know we do, I thought. *But it's just going to buy vodka for Mommy; it's not like she'll ever buy us food.* I glared at the back of Linda's head as we walked, my body filling with hatred. I hated her and I hated my mom because I knew the money would just help my mom stay passed out all the time. I hated my dad for abandoning my sister and me, leaving us there where we were so hungry that we had to beg on the streets. And I hated myself because I knew I would do what I was told, which meant I was about to be dishonest to people who were going to help us. *Besides, aren't we pathetic enough already?*

If it hadn't been for my sister, I might have just run away until Monday. Then I wouldn't have to beg, and I wouldn't get spanked by my mom for not begging. On Monday, I would be in school, where it would be dry and warm and there were books and my really nice teachers who brought my sister and me snacks in the mornings and bought us lunch every day and always smiled at us. I wouldn't mind being hungry all weekend with Monday to look forward to at the end of it. But when I glanced at my little sister, shivering in the cold, I knew I had to just do what I was told.

Maybe the rain will keep Linda distracted and I can hide some money for peas.

november 1992

My mom glared at the two women standing outside our trailer and then looked at my sister and me. "Don't talk to them," she said.

"Ma'am, we need to talk to your daughters without you here if you're going to say things like that."

My mom glared back at them and then walked into the trailer, slamming the door behind her. The two ladies looked down at my sister and me, smiling. They didn't seem to be bothered by my mom's outburst, but my heart was racing, and I had electricity in my body again.

"Hi, sweetie," one of the ladies said. "Would you like to go for a walk?"

I shook my head, not comfortable going somewhere with them.

"Okay," she replied, smiling. "How about we just sit out here and talk, then?"

I sat down on a cinderblock near the front of the trailer and she remained standing in front of me. My sister and the other lady walked to the other end of the trailer and I shifted to another cinderblock so I could still see my sister; I still wasn't sure what the ladies wanted.

She started by asking me about school, and soon I was talking without her having to ask questions. I told her about my favorite books and games at school, the things I'd been learning, about my teacher and all the teachers I'd ever had, and which ones were my favorites. I told her about my teacher buying me lunch and bringing me food in the mornings, and when she asked what we ate on the weekends and in the evenings, I told her about begging in the parking lot and whispered that I tried to hide some money to buy canned vegetables.

When she asked about our friends, I told her we didn't have any, that the closest thing was the other kids in the trailer park, and told her about how they were mean to us and about when they beat me up earlier that year. She asked about Linda and I told her about how Linda tried to find jobs but couldn't, how she was the one who took us to beg because my mom slept a lot, how Linda didn't yell at us much and never spanked us like our mom did. When she asked how often we got spanked, I told her it used to be much more often when my parents were together. I told her about my dad and spanking us with his belt and how much I missed him but that we didn't know where he was, that he was supposed to come back and get us, but he never did.

She asked questions and I answered them without thinking, encouraged by her soft and warm smile, her kind eyes. She never raised her voice or sounded shocked or angry and it made it so easy to talk to her. She laughed with me when I told her funny things, like how Linda wore men's underwear, and touched my hand gently when I told her things that made my eyes fill with tears. And when I told her about my dreams—the scary ones where men were chasing me and touching me and wanted to kill me—she told me I was stronger and braver than I thought, that in my dream I should turn around and stand tall and tell them to leave me alone.

Eventually, it was time for the ladies to go, but I didn't want them to leave. I liked having them there. They promised to come back soon, but I didn't believe them. Why would they want to talk to me again?

*****

"Hi girls!" the ladies greeted us.

It had been a couple of weeks since we'd last seen them, but there they were again, just like they promised. And not only that, but it was my sister's seventh birthday, and they brought her a present and a cupcake. My mom had glared at them when they showed up, but she hadn't said anything; instead, she went back into the trailer and slammed the door behind her, just like last time.

They talked to us about Christmas and said they would bring us a present when they came back. They asked us more questions about our life, and I hesitated before I answered this time; my mom had been so angry about them coming and had yelled at me for telling them so much about us, but I didn't understand why. The ladies were so nice to us. And I really liked talking to someone; I had so many thoughts that I never said out loud because no one ever wanted to talk to me.

car ride to the unknown

"The road to hell is paved with good intentions."

-Henry G. Bohn

early january 1993

I heard my name over the intercom system telling me to report to the principal's office, and my stomach clenched as I stared at the little speaker by the ceiling in the corner of the classroom. *I heard wrong. They don't want me,* I thought. I'd never done anything wrong at school, I'd never gotten into any kind of trouble—why would I be called to the principal's office?

I turned to look at Miss Peterson and she smiled at me, nodding her head. "It's okay."

"Am I in trouble, Miss Peterson?" I asked.

"No, sweetie, you aren't in trouble."

"But they called my name."

"Yep, they did. You have to go, but I promise you aren't in trouble. Take your jacket and your backpack with you."

I knew right then that something wasn't right, but I didn't know what it could be. What had I done wrong? I got the coat and backpack she'd given me from the back of the classroom and headed toward the door. Miss Peterson didn't say anything else, but I saw that her eyes had tears, even though she smiled at me encouragingly.

As the secretary swung the door to the principal's office open, I entered with my heart racing and stopped short. My sister was in the office, seated in a chair opposite the principal. The same feelings I had that day when I got off the bus to find my dad sitting on the front stoop of the house swept over me. *Something really bad happened, I know it.*

"Come in and sit down, Katherine," the principal said with a kind voice.

I shook my head, more in disbelief than refusal. *This isn't happening. Whatever it is, it isn't happening. I must be dreaming. Come on, wake up! Wake up!*

My eyes darted around frantically, searching for some clue to what might be about to unfold, and landed on another person I hadn't noticed. A woman I'd never seen was sitting against a wall and I stared at her, trying to figure out who she could be, until the principal told me again to sit down. I shuffled slowly to the chair next to my sister and sat, afraid I'd get in trouble if I didn't, and finally tore my eyes from the unfamiliar woman. The principal started by explaining that the woman I didn't recognize was from the Department of Social Services and that she was now going to take us to live in a different home, but the rest of his words faded away. I could see his lips moving, but there was no sound over that of my own breath and racing heart.

I grasped at anything I could think of to at least delay what was about to happen, begging to at least be able to say good-bye to our mom—she would be so confused and upset when we didn't return from school.

"She knows you're not coming back," the woman said. "I was in your trailer this morning. She cooperated with us and gave us your belongings."

The words were so matter-of-fact, so emotionless. *Cooperated? My mom cooperated with this lady? So, she's letting her take us away? How is that possible? She would never do that!*

I stared at the floor as my mind raced to make sense of the words I'd just heard. I thought back to the really nice women who'd come to see my sister and me a few times. I was pretty sure when we met them they'd said they were also from the Department of Social Services. Suddenly, I heard my mom's voice telling me not to talk to them, yelling at me after that first visit for not having listened to her. She had told me not to answer their questions, but I had anyway. They were so nice, and they'd promised I wouldn't get in trouble, that no one would be upset if I always told the truth. But was that why we were being taken from our mom now?

This is all my fault.

Coldness spread over and through me as I gripped my sister's hand tight and stood. We were ushered out of the school by the woman from Social Services, our small backpacks placed into her trunk alongside a single—mostly empty—black garbage bag that contained the few items of clothing my sister and I owned.

The strange woman's car pulled away from the school and we initially drove in silence aside from the sound of the tires rolling over the asphalt as we sped down the highway, the miles passing us by under the car. There were no assurances, no words of comfort, no descriptions of where we were headed.

After maybe an hour, my sister and I both began to cry. It started quietly, with an errant tear falling down our cheeks and an occasional whimper, evolving over long, painful minutes into noisy, snot-filled, gut-wrenching sobs.

"Why are you crying?" the woman asked.

I responded honestly, telling her that I didn't want to leave my mommy. I explained that things weren't really all that bad and begged again to at least be able to say goodbye to her.

"Stop crying!" she shouted, her voice reverberating off the interior walls of the car. Her bellow was unexpected and my heart skipped, my body tingling as I squeezed my sister's hand. "You might as well quit crying now," she continued. "You're never going to see her again—you're never going to see either of your parents again, got it? *Ever*. Just accept it now and get used to it. There's no point in crying about it."

As I sat there, trying to stop crying, I hated the woman driving us away from our mom. I hated the women I felt had tricked me into talking to them. And I hated myself most of all, drowning in guilt, because if I hadn't talked to those two ladies, we wouldn't have been trapped in that stranger's car heading away from the only life we'd ever known without even saying good-bye.

welcome to the farm

"History will judge us by the difference we make in the everyday lives of children."
-Nelson Mandela

early january 1993

My cheeks were still wet with the tears I couldn't keep from spilling over when the social worker slowed to exit the highway. We'd passed miles and miles of forest and crop fields and small houses with big red barns and tall silos on the properties. There was an apple orchard on the far side of the highway as we exited, along with a huge banner advertising the county fair eight months away.

To the left, I could see a row of fast-food restaurants, but the car turned to the right toward more trees and fewer houses. In every direction, I could see rolling mountaintops; we were in a huge valley. Houses were sparse, interspersed with more forests and farmland dotted with cows, especially after the next right turn onto a smaller road that didn't even have the lines painted on it. After only a few miles of gently-winding road and a few low, rolling hills, the car slowed for another right-hand turn, this time onto gravel. Up ahead, we could see a small white house if we stayed to the right, but we stayed to the left, following the gravel road slowly into a grove of trees.

We moved at a crawl, the crunch of the gravel loud under the tires, as we wound along the driveway through the dense trees that created a tunnel. Suddenly, the road plunged downward at a steep angle, and moments later, pitched upward again. And then I had my first glance of our destination, which looked like a painting from an old frontier storybook.

Right in front of us was a log farmhouse made of rough-to-the-touch rectangular logs filled with what looked like concrete between the logs, red window frames and a red front door. The house was situated near the bottom of a miniature valley of its own; from that point, you had to climb uphill to just about anywhere else on the extensive property.

The social worker parked her car in a flat area to the right of the house where a small, old, white pick-up truck was parked, though the gravel drive also continued up to the left and disappeared near a massive dilapidated barn that was struggling to keep up the few walls that still stood. My sister and I climbed out, holding hands, as a lady emerged from the house, smiling warmly, flanked by two dogs. The social worker introduced us to the woman as we bent to pet the friendly canines who licked us and wagged their tails excitedly, explaining that she would be our foster mom.

"Nice to meet you, Miss Geoffries," I said.

"Call me Jean, sweetie," our new foster mom said with a smile. "The black and white dog is Princess, and the brown and white dog is Sunny. There's also an orange cat around here somewhere—her name is Molly—and a tabby named Juno. There are lots of animals all around here, if you girls want to take a walk around and look while I talk to your social worker."

My sister and I wandered around, the dogs darting off to sniff patches of ground and chase things we didn't see. The first building we came to was a chicken coop where we heard real live chickens clucking and squawking as we smelled fresh chicken poop for the first time. The chickens were so much smaller than the ones we saw on *Looney Toons*. Weaving between the coop and the house, we saw a fenced area with goats the size of large dogs, eyeing us as they milled around their enclosure. They were cute and looked soft, but we didn't know if they would bite us, so we kept our distance.

As we passed the goats on our left, we could see raised garden beds on our right, not much aside from dirt in them right then in the middle of winter, and soon passed by a patch of dead corn stalks and leafless trees and bushes. Emerging from the dormant growth in the garden, we were suddenly standing on the gravel drive where it passed in front of the imposing barn. The structure was nothing short of enormous—it was easily two or three times the size of the house—dark brown wood siding for walls, but generally missing the two long walls above the ground level; it looked like it might collapse sometime soon.

Below the level where the walls were in disrepair was a pen filled with tiny animals running around. We walked up closer to the metal fencing enclosing the area to realize they were pigs, but they weren't huge and pink like the ones on television; they were small and black with sparse tufts of hair. One pig was larger than the others—the mama, we realized—and the others that were squealing and running around and tumbling over each other so quickly we couldn't count them were only babies. Piglets. We grinned at each other and kneeled down, the possible dangers forgotten as we reached our hands through the fencing, desperately wanting to touch one. I forgot for long moments why we were there as we giggled at the clumsy, tubby little black pigs frolicking around each other.

Eventually, we tore ourselves from the pigs and followed the gravel drive to the right as it looped up around behind the barn. As the drive curved around to the back of the building, there was a steep embankment on the right with what looked like bright orange dirt. Lifting my hand, I pointed at it.

"It's orange," I said to my sister. "We've never seen orange dirt before."

We climbed up the embankment and peered over the fencing there at sizable sheep that largely ignored us, their fleeces gray. As one walked closer to the fence, I realized it wasn't gray after all, just really dirty. I remembered the sheep I'd seen in cartoons; they all had bright white hair, and sometimes people would make sweaters with it. But as I looked at those dirty, fluffy sheep, I didn't understand how that was even possible.

Once we'd meandered back to the house, our foster mom gave us a tour. Near where the cars were parked, there was a room that could only be accessed from the outside where our foster mom said she saw therapy clients, and next to that, a root cellar where she started plants for the garden. Climbing a few steps from the outside led to a breezeway, and to the right—above the root cellar and the therapy room—was a small apartment. She said her parents lived in Florida but spent the summers there. We turned left, which brought us into a kitchen unlike any I'd ever seen, even on T.V.

The ceiling was tall—the lower part as tall as the ceiling in the next room which you had to climb several steps to get into—and the highest part was another story high. The flat area forming the lower part of the ceiling had enormous pots and pans as well as empty glass jars stored on it. To the right was a small table with two chairs pushed up against a wall with a few built-in shelves that were overflowing with cookbooks. After that, the stairs led into the next part of the house, followed by a refrigerator. Straight ahead against the far wall were some cabinets and a sink with a window over it. But the thing that drew my eye was on my left—it was white and pale teal and kind of looked like a stove, but not one I'd ever seen.

"It's a wood-burning stove," the lady said, noticing my stare. "You can cook on the top and bake inside like you would any other stove, but it's heated with a wood fire. See, over here?" She opened one of the many little doors on the front. "You make the fire in here."

I nodded slowly and tore my eyes away. "Okay."

We followed her up the stairs into the next part of the house. We were immediately in a dining area with a table and chairs, followed by a small couch and a chair facing a compact cabinet holding an old television and VCR. On the left was a doorway into a very small room only large enough for a chair and then a bathroom. The floor of the small room had a cut-out in the wood with a metal ring, and she showed us that when you pulled on the ring, part of the floor lifted up.

"Down there's the cellar. It's an old dirt cellar, so it's a little muddy and there aren't any lights. Would you like to look?"

I froze, my vision narrowing and my heart racing as I looked into the hole created by my foster mom holding up the chunk of floor. *Please shut it. Please shut it,* I thought over and over. The last time I'd been in a cellar was my Grandma Virginia's cellar that first summer after my mom left.

She was moving out of her house and my dad and I were helping her. He sent me to grab some boxes out of her dirt cellar, which you got to through a wooden door in the ground outside the house. I climbed down the wooden stairs and stepped onto the packed earth, looking around the musty and shadowy space, lit only by a single bulb in the center of the low wood-plank ceiling; the only way to turn the light on or off was by pulling the chain that dangled next to the bulb.

I walked to the far side of the room to grab a box, weaving around the old pots and pans and large utensils hanging from hooks in the ceiling. Bending, my hands were just touching the cardboard when the light went out, plunging the area into complete darkness.

"Daddy!" I screamed out, panicked as my body flooded with electricity and nausea.

The only response was the sudden ear-splitting clang of pots and pans banging into each other. I screamed and ran, terrified, in the direction of the dimly lit top steps, a pan sailing past my face and slamming into the wall just as I reached the bottom stair. Flying up the steps, I burst into the overcast day, not slowing down until I'd reached my dad's Blazer. By the time my dad arrived a moment later, a box in his hands to put into the back of his car, my legs had collapsed; I was on the ground sobbing and shaking. Through my panic and sobs, I told my dad what had happened, though he only laughed at me and told me what I'd said was impossible.

I realized my foster mom was watching my face expectantly and I managed to shake my head, though my body was filled with that electricity all over again. "No, thank you," I said quietly, pulling my hand from my sister's and wrapping my arms tightly around myself.

Turning, we followed her through the living area, past the black wood stove, which she explained provided most of the house's heat. Along the adjacent wall was a door to a back porch where she showed us stacks of wood for bringing inside, on the left was the front door, and behind that—in the same wall as the stove—was another door. This one was made of wood planks and had a small metal latch that my foster mom lifted to reveal a narrow, steep, dark, and curving wooden staircase. Emerging onto the second floor, there was a landing large enough for the twin bed it held, and behind that was the expansive bathroom with an old clawfoot tub, a small sink, and a toilet unlike any I'd ever seen. I craned my head back to study the tank near the ceiling, a long pipe leading from the tank to the rest of the toilet.

"You see that chain?" my new foster mom asked, pointing to a long chain hanging from where the flush handle was. "You pull on that to flush. And we have a septic here, so don't use a lot of toilet paper."

I nodded at her and then glanced at my sister to see if she was as fascinated as I was by the strange-looking toilet. She was still staring up at the tank and I smiled. *She is,* I thought. *Man, I can't wait to flush this thing.*

With the bathroom in front of us, there was another doorway to the left that led into a small room with a table and chair, and to the right inside that room was my foster mom's bedroom, just large enough for her queen-sized bed and a small nightstand and boasting a couple of windows. Back on the landing, directly over the stairs we'd already climbed was another wooden door with a small metal latch, nearly identical to the one on the first floor. My foster mom lifted the latch and opened the door.

"And up here is you girls' bedroom," she said.

Like the other one, this staircase was curved, narrow, and steep, but it was shorter and brighter than the first one. I understood why when we emerged from the staircase into an expansive room—easily twice the size of the trailer we'd lived in with our mom and Linda, maybe even bigger. I couldn't believe it was our bedroom with all that space. Looking down the length of the room from the top of the stairs, it almost felt like a tunnel with the angled ceiling, except that there was a window at my back, a window on the wall at the other end, and windows in the small alcove along the exterior wall to my left. Along the wall to the right were two twin-sized beds a few feet apart from one another and a small nightstand between them.

"Look over there," my foster mom said, pointing toward the alcove. "I pulled some things out for you girls if you'd like to color while we finish talking."

"Thank you," I said quietly.

"Make yourselves at home," she added, and then she and the social worker started back down the stairs.

Releasing my sister's hand, I walked around the room, though I was drawn to the alcove with the small table holding a stack of blank white paper and a Ziploc bag of colored pencils. I kept finding myself standing in front of the table and staring at the art supplies. Forcing my eyes up, I looked out the two windows over the table and realized you could see a lot of the farm from there; I could see the goats milling around, the raised beds in the garden, a gazebo we hadn't noticed earlier, as well as another tiny building that looked only large enough for one or two people to stand in it. To the right, over the top of the apartment, I could see a pond that was frozen over, and all of it to a background of hilly forest. The view was captivating and I simply stood for a few moments, taking it in.

Laurel sat down and started drawing on a piece of paper and I resumed circling the room, deciding I'd take the bed closest to the stairs; I wanted to be between my sister and anyone who might come in. I sat on the firm bed and touched the bedspread, which was a dense, heavy, scratchy fabric. It certainly wasn't soft, but I figured it would be warm. Pulling back the edge of the bedspread revealed sheets that felt the opposite: incredibly soft flannel in a yellow-beige color with little flowers. I wanted to pull back all the bedding and climb in, but I carefully laid the bedspread back the way it was instead.

*****

"Girls, this is my friend, Martin. He and I built this house together," my foster mom said as we were about to begin dinner that first night. "Martin, this is Laurel." She paused while he said hello to my sister, who quietly responded. "And this is Katherine."

"Hi, Katherine. You're just built like a brick shithouse, aren't ya?" he asked with a chuckle.

I wrinkled my nose and my brow as my foster mom hissed something at him; I'd never heard of a brick shithouse and wasn't sure what it meant. *I wonder if there's a dictionary I can use to look it up?*

"What grades are you in?" Martin asked us, kicking off over an hour of him and my foster mom asking questions as my sister and (more often) I responded. I wasn't used to people asking me questions and wanting me to respond; soon, I was talking animatedly without prompting.

After dinner, Martin left, and the three of us sat in the living room near the wood stove once my sister and I had bathed in the big clawfoot tub upstairs. My foster mom made us each a cup of Sleepytime tea—her favorite, she'd said—that came out of a small, old green tin with rusty rolled edges and a bear on the front.

"What's on his head?" I asked.

"That's called a stocking cap," she replied.

I nodded, gazing at the bear. It was sitting in a rocking chair holding a mug of tea, a fire burning merrily in a fireplace next to it. Inhaling the aroma of the tea, I could imagine being in the scene with the bear; I imagined it was the epitome of comfort and happiness. I wanted to run my fingers over the bear on the tin, but I was too afraid to ask if I could.

While we sipped our tea, Jean read a few books to us, though I wasn't really listening; I'd discovered that if I flung a few droplets of tea from the tips of my fingers onto the top of the wood stove that they beaded up with popping sounds, making these little white balls that skittered across the top of the stove, sometimes bouncing off the cast iron pot of water that steamed, until they evaporated. Watching those little white balls jump around and slide and hearing the hiss and pop was oddly mesmerizing, and I watched with my eyes wide and unblinking, the other sounds around me, the walls to my sides, all of it fading away until it was just the water on the top of the wood stove and me.

I did interrupt occasionally to ask what a word meant, though, the unfamiliar string of letters standing out to my ears and getting my attention.

"You like to read?" my new foster mom asked.

I nodded. "Yes."

"Reading is so wonderful, isn't it?" She smiled, then explained to me what the word meant. "We'll go to the Green Valley Book Fair when it's open soon and maybe we'll get you your own dictionary while we're there."

My heart skipped with excitement when I heard her words. *Book Fair? My own dictionary?*

Once the stories and tea were finished, our foster mom used what I could only describe as an oversized oven mitt to pull off square stones that looked like they came from a patio and shimmy them—one at a time—into quilted cloth bags with flaps.

"These will warm your bed up for you," she explained. "But you have to be careful to not touch the stones themselves or you'll get very badly burned. Watch out because there are some thin spots and holes in the bags. Each of you pick one and we'll head up."

Laurel and I each grabbed a quilted stone and followed Jean upstairs to our new room. She handed us each a pair of huge heavy socks after showing us how to slide the stones between the sheets.

"These are wool socks to keep your feet warm tonight. They're mine, but we'll get you girls some this week. This blanket is wool and will be toasty warm with the sheets and the stone and the socks. Go on, climb in before you get cold."

She tucked the cold blankets around our shivering bodies in nothing but underwear and one of her t-shirts, assuring us the sheets would be warm very soon, and with a last reminder to keep our toes off the stones unless we wanted to burn them, she headed down the stairs, turning off the light as she went.

Soon, the sounds of my sister sleeping filled the air, but I was wide awake, staring into the darkness of the strange room, missing my mom and wondering why we'd been taken away from her. Was it because I'd told her about what her friend had done to me? The more I thought about it, the more I was sure our separation from our mom was my fault. Why couldn't I have just kept it to myself?

I slid out from between the covers into the cold air of the room, tip-toed over to the alcove, grabbed a few of the colored pencils I'd seen earlier, and then was back under my sheets and heavy blanket. My ears strained to make out sounds in the oddly loud silence, wanting to make sure I hadn't woken my sister or my foster mom. When I was certain they were still sleeping, I reached down, pulled my panties to the side, and shoved the pencils inside myself as hard as I could.

The scraping was excruciating, and I cried, biting my forearm to stifle any sound as my other hand held the pencils still inside me. *You deserve this,* I told myself. After a few moments, the sharpness of the pain started to fade, taking on a more manageable dull quality, but I felt like I hadn't punished myself enough yet, so I pushed harder until I couldn't get the pencils to move any further. It was difficult to hold them in place hard enough, so I tucked the opposite ends into the crotch of my panties and used my hands to grab my waistband and pull.

As I held those pencils painfully inside, I squeezed my eyes shut and saw the men in my nightmares, their faces blurry as they hovered over me, breathing heavily, and I knew they were driving what was happening to me, they were causing me the pain I felt. I sobbed until I had no more tears, occasionally pulling harder on my waistband to send a new ripple of pain through my body and detract from the images behind my eyelids. As my cheeks began to dry and my chest ached with each breath, I pulled the pencils out of me, slid my hand into the bottom of my pillowcase and pushed them all the way to the end, knowing I would use them again. Exhausted from crying, I finally dozed off.

*****

I was running as fast I could, screaming for my dad as he disappeared ahead of me, knowing the men chasing behind me were only moments from grabbing me, when I was startled awake by a presence. My eyes flew open, my breathing hard and fast and my body covered with sweat. For a moment, I was paralyzed and couldn't even turn my head to the side to see what was there, too afraid of what I might find. My jaw trembling, I finally turned to find my sister standing next to my bed, staring at me.

"Laurel?"

"I'm scared," she whispered.

I scooted away from her on my bed, lifting my covers. She climbed in silently and I reached over her to tuck the covers around her small body. Once I laid back down, I grabbed her hand with mine.

"There's nothing to be scared of," I started, willing my voice to sound steady and convincing even though I was still trying to catch my breath from my own nightmare. "We're in a nice home with a nice lady."

"I want Mommy and Linda."

"I know. Me, too. But right now, we're here. And we have our own beds! And they're so big we can both fit on one. And our own room, and paper and pencils just for us. And we ate a big dinner and took a bath."

"I'm still scared."

I was quiet for a moment, trying to think of something else to distract her from being scared. "Just think about really happy and beautiful things, okay? Like love and peace and happiness and rainbows and butterflies."

"Can you say them again?" she asked.

"Sure."

And I did. I said them again and again and again until the words were hard to say because they didn't make sense anymore and I could hear her sleeping. Then I closed my eyes and conjured images to represent the words behind my eyelids until I fell asleep again.

echoes from the past

"Trauma is perhaps the most avoided, ignored, belittled, denied, misunderstood, and untreated cause of human suffering."

-Peter A. Levine

late february 1993

My head shook resolutely from side to so side as I stared through the table in front of me, the stark white walls and unfamiliar faces around me nothing more than a swirled blur in my periphery. I was wishing as hard as I could that I could disappear; I couldn't do what those blurry faces were telling me to do. They didn't seem to understand, though, and talked over each other as they tried to find different ways to convince me that I had to do it. Under the table, my clasped fingers tightened as my knees squeezed together harder. *Maybe I can make myself so small that they forget I'm here?*

I was sitting in an unfamiliar room in a courthouse, one filled with strangers. The most familiar person there was my foster mother, a woman I'd only known a few weeks. There was also the new social worker who'd been assigned to mine and my sister's case. A victim rights advocate. A lawyer. And I couldn't remember who the last couple of people said they were.

They didn't understand that I'd barely even told Linda and my mom what happened, didn't understand what it had felt like watching my mom wait for the police. Listening to her rage about Elmer and my dad as she shook and sweat. I'd already made things worse for everyone and was responsible for my sister and me being sent away from my mom; I didn't want to tell anyone ever again. I just wanted to forget it had happened, stop feeling so guilty because I didn't know what to do to fix everything I'd done wrong and messed up for my sister and my mom and my dad.

And now, I was sitting in this cold, white, strange room filled with people I'd never met who kept insisting that I do what he did to me to this innocent, unsuspecting, pristine teddy bear. It was brand new, so clean. And *I* was filthy. I'd never owned something like that—a new and soft and beautiful stuffed animal. I couldn't do those things to it, touch it that way. I knew it wouldn't like it because I hadn't liked it when it happened to me. *Why can't these people understand that?*

But I had to show them what he had done, touch the bear the way he had touched me, they'd said. It was the only way they could prosecute him, they explained. But what did I care about prosecution? I just didn't want to think about him or what he'd done ever again. And I really, *really* didn't want to hurt the defenseless teddy bear.

"You have to show us, sweetie, so we can make sure he never does it to another little girl like you ever again, okay?"

I nodded, the strange lady's voice piercing through me. *It could happen to someone else?* That thought hadn't occurred to me; I'd just thought it was only me. *I can't let him do that to someone else; I have to protect them. And this is what I have to do to protect them. I have to do this. I have to.*

My hands felt like they were stuck together as I tried to loosen my fingers and separate them. They shook as I slowly raised them up over the table and reached for the bear, pressing my legs together so hard the insides of my knees hurt. *Don't throw up. Don't throw up. Don't throw up,* I chanted as my nausea worsened. The skin on my face felt like it was too tight for me to blink anymore and I could feel my entire body sweating. *I don't want to do this,* I thought, my hands pausing. *But I have to.* With my elbows resting on the table, I gently grasped the teddy bear and started to slide my hand over its front.

"Show us where you were with the bear," one of the other strangers said gently. "Put the bear where you were. And then touch it like you were touched. Okay? Pretend like you're him."

My chest felt like someone was squeezing it so hard my bones were going to break—I couldn't pretend like I was Elmer. I couldn't do that. I didn't *want* to be like him. I stared back at the woman who'd been holding the bear out to me as I felt my eyes burn with tears.

She nodded her head. "We need you to do that, okay?"

I hate you. I hate you. I hate you. I hate all of you! I looked down at my hands, the bear blurry through the tears I was trying to hold back. *And I'm so sorry. I know you're going to hate me for this.*

Turning in my chair, I set the bear down on my knee. Everyone's eyes shifted and stared down at where my hands held the unsuspecting stuffed animal, the synthetic fur so soft under my fingertips. My first tears escaped and burned the skin on my cheeks as they fell. *I can't do this. I can't. But I have to do it anyway. I can't let someone else feel like me.*

I squeezed my eyelids shut as hard and tight as I possibly could, so hard it hurt. *I'm sorry. I'm so sorry.* I chanted the apology in my mind with every breath as I fought to keep the oatmeal I'd had for breakfast in my stomach. I imagined a black, empty hole inside my chest where it hurt the most, right over my heart, and started stuffing myself into it. In my mind, I could see my organs—my stomach and my intestines and my bladder—and my feelings all being sucked into the hole and disappearing until there was nothing under my skin except my bones.

A few more errant tears escaped as I listened to the sound of pens scratching across paper to the background of my heavy breathing in the otherwise silent room while I became Elmer and touched that bear the way I'd been touched. I used my fingers to press hard enough between its legs that an indentation formed; the best I could do since there was no hole there to push my fingers into the way Elmer had done to me.

When I was done, I flung the bear on the table. I couldn't stop touching it fast enough; I never wanted to touch it ever again. I didn't turn to face the table because I couldn't even look at it. I didn't *deserve* to look at it after the way I'd just finished touching it.

"Are you okay, sweetie?" another stranger in the room asked.

There was that word again: *sweetie.* It seemed everyone in the room was calling me that, but why? I wasn't a sweetie, not after what I'd just done to that poor bear.

I'm so sorry—so, so sorry, I silently apologized to the bear again.

"Sweetie?" that stranger asked again.

I nodded quickly. "I'm fine."

*****

"Would you like to get something to eat on the way home?" my foster mom asked once we were allowed to leave the courthouse. "We can get a late lunch? Maybe a hamburger? And we could get a milkshake after?"

I shook my head from side to side, just the thought of food making my stomach churn. "No, thank you. I'm not hungry."

"Are you sure, honey? You haven't eaten anything since breakfast."

I nodded; I was sure. I didn't know if I'd ever want to eat again. I couldn't imagine sitting down and having food after what I'd done to the bear. It was quiet as we walked the rest of the way to the parking lot. We got into the used car my foster mom bought a few days after my sister and I arrived, and I buckled my seat belt.

"I still can't believe your mom didn't recognize you," she said, looking over at me.

My heart skipped as her voice faded out, my mind flashing back in time. Before we went into the room with the strangers, my foster mom and I had gone to the bathroom. We were washing our hands when another woman came out of a stall. She'd looked sad and tired and really sick. She was bony everywhere—even skinnier than my sister—and her cheeks were falling in. She had a haircut kind of like my new pixie cut, except even shorter. I'd thought she looked familiar, but had shrugged it off, sure I was wrong. She'd stared at me but turned away a moment later, and then my foster mom and I walked out of the bathroom.

When I'd discovered I had seen my mom and neither of us recognized the other, I was furious with myself. Even if she was suddenly skinny when she'd always been plump, even if her long, stringy, curly brown hair was suddenly no longer than my fingernail was tall, even if she looked completely different from the last time I'd seen her, I should have known she was *my mom*.

"I can't believe I didn't recognize *her*," I said angrily.

"Well, she looked very different from what you said she looked like the last time you saw her."

I turned and glared at my foster mom; I was angry with her for defending me. I didn't deserve to be defended. I didn't even recognize my own mom! "I should have known it was her," I said as I fought back tears.

She was quiet for a moment and I could feel her eyes on me, even though I was staring out my window away from her. "Your mom obviously loves you. She loves you enough that she made it here today. From what you girls and your social worker have told me, that's a really big deal. It wasn't easy for her. But she did it because she loves you."

I heard her words, but how could that be possible? I was responsible for not being with my mom anymore, I was the reason she even had to come to the courthouse, and *then* I didn't even recognize her! And she didn't know what I did to that bear... Even if she did love me, she wouldn't if she ever found out what I'd done. But how could she love me when she'd let that social worker lady take us away? My lips turned down and I knew I was going to cry at any second. Clenching my jaw so tightly my teeth ached, I willed the tears back.

"Are you okay?" she asked me again.

"Yeah, I'm fine," I said, still staring out the window.

"You girls constantly amaze me. I can't believe how resilient you are."

*****

"Leave me alone!" I shouted at my sister. She was following me around wanting to play, but I felt so angry at everything and everyone and just wanted to be left alone. "I don't want to play with you!"

She dropped the Barbies in her hands—her most prized possessions since our foster mom had given them to her—and ran down the stairs out of our room, crying. Part of me felt guilty for hurting her feelings. Another part of me wanted to follow her and yell at her and make her cry even more. My eyes shifted from where they'd been staring at the top of the stairs Laurel had disappeared down and landed on her barbies.

Why does she like those things?

I *hated* Barbies and dolls. I sat up on my bed and slid down to my feet. Walking over to the top of the stairs, I picked them up by their hair and stared at them for a moment as blinding rage filled my body. Turning, the idea still forming in my mind as I went, I walked over to the little table in the alcove, dropped the Barbies unceremoniously onto it, and grabbed the scissors from the little cup at the corner. Grabbing one of the Barbies with brown hair like mine by its hair using my left hand, I held it dangling in front of my face.

I. Hate. You.

And then I used my right hand to hack off her hair as close to her scalp as I could.

*****

I pulled the pencils out of me, angry—they weren't helping tonight. I kept replaying in my mind everything I'd done to the teddy bear that morning, hearing the words "pretend like you're him" on repeat. I'd done what I was told, but I felt like I should have said no, like I should have stuck up for

95

that poor bear. But then I wouldn't be saving other little girls. Why did I have to hurt the bear to help other people? *It's not fair!*

One at a time, I held each of those three colored pencils in my hands and pushed with all my might until I'd snapped them in half. Then, one by one, I shoved the jagged, broken ends of all six colored pencil halves inside myself. The pain was so much worse this way and I could no longer keep straight in my mind what the bear looked like as I cried from the pain, and from the relief that I couldn't see what I'd done anymore. As I pulled on the band of my panties to shove the pencil halves in further, I wondered if pencil pieces would break off and get stuck inside me. If they did, what would happen? Would I get sick? Or I would get sent back to my mom?

Maybe it will kill me? That would be okay.

gifts of solitude

"Life is brutal, but it's also beautiful. Life is Brutiful."

-Glennon Doyle

march 1993

"Out you go. And don't forget the present," my foster mom said with a smile as we pulled up in front of a large two-story white house with a sprawling wraparound porch.

I glanced at her, not wanting to get out of the car. My heart was pounding in my chest and I felt really sick to my stomach. I could see so many of my classmates running around and laughing and it made me want to shrink down in my seat instead of get out of the car to go into the birthday party. The first time Diedre had even talked to me was when she gave me an invitation to her birthday party, and then my foster mom insisted that I go and make some friends. I grabbed the bag with tissue paper poking out of the top in one hand and slowly opened my car door with the other.

"I'll be back in a few hours to pick you up," my foster mom said as I got out of the car. "Have fun, honey."

Nodding, I looked at my sister sitting in the back seat. Her eyes were wide, and her face was solemn; she looked scared. And I understood because I felt it, too. Would we see each other again? I forced a smile when my foster mom began to pull away from the curb. As the car shrunk into the distance down the street, the sounds of my classmates laughing and shrieking started to filter in and I slowly turned around as I stared at the bag in my hand; I'd never been given something that looked like that. I'd never even had a birthday party of my own. Even if I had, I wouldn't have invited anyone because I'd never had any friends. But all these kids knew each other and were friends, except for me. The electricity flooded my body as I tried to make myself step away from the curb and I felt tears sting my eyes. *I don't belong here.*

Two boys suddenly flew past, chasing each other across the front of the porch and disappearing around the side. My stomach dropped even further; one of them was the boy who had called me names on my third day of school. On the way back to our classroom from the lunchroom, he'd called out to me loudly, getting everyone's attention. I'd frozen when he'd singled me out, the same electricity engulfing me, deafening as it moved through my body and made my ears buzz.

"NIGGER!" he'd shouted so loud it echoed as he'd pointed at me.

My skin had suddenly felt really tight and hot, like it could at any moment catch on fire, and I'd wished I could disappear into nothingness as the word rolled around in my mind, echoed in my ears. I wanted to be invisible, out from under the eyes of the other kids who were all staring at me.

Glancing down as I felt my face warm from the memory, I looked at the back of my hand and wished it was a little bit paler so I wouldn't look so tan—that I could look more like the other kids. I was still staring at my hand when a woman walked up to me, her dress swaying around her knees.

"Hi there, honey—you must be Katherine. I'm Diedre's mom, Mrs. Neal." She wrapped an arm around my shoulder and started walking, gently pulling me along with her. "All the kids are playing outside since it's so warm today, but we'll have pizza and cake in a little while, and then…"

Her voice faded as I followed, her softly-spoken words no match for the rushing of the electricity in my ears. Once we were inside and she showed me where to put Diedre's present, I asked her where the bathroom was. She walked me down a short hall and pushed a door open.

"Right in here, honey."

"Thank you," I said quietly, walking in and closing the door behind me.

I sat down and started to pee when my stomach cramped up and all my food from earlier in the day came rushing out as diarrhea. Feeling my eyes burn with tears, I gritted my teeth refused to let them fall—I was getting better at that. I couldn't stop them from reaching my eyes yet, but

I could usually keep them from falling now. Then I tried to take a deep breath like my foster mom told me to do when I was angry, but that just made me dizzy; my chest wouldn't expand to let more air in. Instead, it felt like it was getting smaller and smaller and I was breathing really fast.

After I thought nothing else would come out of my body, I wiped, flushed, and washed my hands, but I didn't want to leave the bathroom and walk into the group of kids outside the door. I also knew I had to, that I couldn't stay in the bathroom the whole time, even though I wanted to do exactly that. Turning the handle, I walked out and down the hall. Pausing, I looked at all the kids crowded around a table with fresh pizza on it, Mrs. Neal helping everyone grab plates and napkins and pizza slices.

I couldn't make myself join them.

Instead, I walked out the door I'd come in with Mrs. Neal and found a swing on the side of their porch where there weren't any windows and sat down. It was so much easier to breathe, in the fresh air, by myself. I don't know how long it was before everyone came rushing out the doors to run around again, no one having noticed that I wasn't inside, but I hoped enough time had passed that I'd be able to leave soon. I knew my foster mom wanted me to make friends, but how was I supposed to do that? I didn't know anything about birthday parties. And I was invisible to them, anyway.

early april 1993

My eyes scoured the embankment behind the barn, breaking every few moments to glare at my foster mom who was standing a few feet away, hunched over to look at the ground. My sister wasn't far from her, squatted down as she scoured the earth, too. I was mad at both of them.

My foster mom had told us we were going outside to look for some quartz behind the barn. But I hadn't wanted to go outside right then—I'd wanted to read longer, so I'd said no. It was *my* decision, not *hers* what I did with myself. But she told me I had to go whether I wanted to or not. I told her that no, I wasn't going because I didn't want to, then I told my sister not to put on her shoes or jacket, either—that she was staying inside with me until *I* decided we were going outside.

However, Laurel didn't listen to me! She'd put on her shoes and jacket anyway. She used to listen to me all the time, no matter what. It made my foster mom mad every time I told my sister to do something different from what *she'd* told her to do, but I didn't understand why; she wasn't our mom. And *I* was the one who took care of my sister—not *her*.

But after we'd argued for a while, my foster mom had gotten so angry that she'd threatened to call our social worker again if I didn't do what she told me. I screamed at her to call her, that I didn't care, though I'd gotten my shoes and jacket on anyway. I didn't care that my foster mom was mad at me for misbehaving; it was just that she was threatening to make me go live in another foster home *without* my sister. After previous arguments and talks with my foster mom and social worker, I'd written down my plans for improving my behavior so they wouldn't do that—it didn't matter to me if I went to another house, but I didn't want to leave my sister behind.

My foster mom was talking to Laurel about something she'd found in the dirt, but I wasn't listening; I was just staring at her, getting angrier and angrier. I wanted to scream and cry and stomp my feet and pick up handfuls of gravel from the driveway and throw it all at them. I hated them for getting along, and I hated that my foster mom was acting like nothing was wrong; why wasn't she angry, too? She'd yelled about calling my social worker, but now she was acting like nothing happened.

"Katherine," she said, looking over her shoulder, smiling even though I was mad. "Look what your sister found."

I glared at her and didn't move. I was going to show her that I did what I wanted, when I wanted. But my sister was grinning, and my curiosity won out over my determination to stay right where I was. I flung my hands down to my sides and trudged over a few feet closer to see what was sitting in my foster mom's palm.

"It looks like a dirty rock," I muttered.

"Well, it's a dirty mineral," my foster mom said. She shifted the object around in her hand, using her thumb to wipe off some of the bright orange dirt. As she did, I could see the clear-ish white of the object in her hands and walked a few steps closer.

"It looks like a crystal," I said, my eyes rounding in awe. A crystal! She had *crystals* in her yard?

"Here, take a look," she said, placing the item in my hand.

I turned it all around, looking at it from different angles, trying to wipe it clean, which reminded me of a question I'd never asked. "Why is this dirt orange?"

"It's called red clay. There's a lot of it in this part of Virginia. It's very hard, too, so once things start to dry out, it'll be much harder to find things out here. But I have gardening tools you girls can use if you take care of them and put them back when you're done. Come on, I'll show you."

After retrieving some trowels from the tool shed that my foster mom said used to be an outhouse, we all headed back to where we'd been by the embankment behind the barn. On the way, we passed a smattering of little yellow flowers.

"Oh, buttercups!" my foster mom exclaimed.

I stopped next to her, the excitement in her voice piquing my curiosity, and watched as she bent and picked a single flower.

"Now, buttercups are smart little flowers. You hold them up under your chin—like this," she lifted her chin up an inch or so and held the flower underneath, "and if your chin turns yellow in response, it means you like butter. Let's see if it's right, shall we?"

I stared at her, already knowing the answer; the color was reflecting off the flower petals. Everyone's chin would turn yellow.

"Is it yellow?" she asked.

"Yes!" my sister cried out in earnest.

"Well, that settles it, then, it's right! I definitely like butter."

"Try me, try me!" my sister shouted.

"It's just a stupid reflection," I muttered.

My foster mom's eyes darted in my direction, then back to my sister. "Okay, chin up," she said to Laurel, ignoring me.

I rolled my eyes and headed back to the embankment without them as my sister's giggles filled the cool spring air. By the time they made it over a few minutes later, I already had a small pile of the rocks my foster mom had called quartz.

"Did you find anything else yet?" she asked.

"There's other stuff in here?" I asked in response as I looked up at her.

"Of course. All these rocks you see are *something*."

I thought about what she'd said and it made sense to me—everything had to be something. And I had a lot of the quartz—there seemed to be a ton of those little rocks in the clay. But was there anything even cooler in there?

"What's the coolest rock here?"

She laughed. "*That* I don't know."

"Do you have a book about it?" I asked, thinking back to the hundreds of books she had.

"I don't think I do," she replied, her brow furrowed. "We can check together, but I don't think I have a book about rocks yet." She paused, studying me. "Maybe we should start a list for when we go to the Green Valley Book Fair next weekend. What else should go on that list, I wonder?"

I shrugged.

"What else would you like? I told you that you girls can each pick out a few books of your own while we're there."

I thought about it for a moment. I would love to have my very own dictionary that I could keep with me to look up words instead of using my foster mom's since I always had to put it back after I used it. "A dictionary?"

"That's a great idea! Okay, so a dictionary and a book about rocks. Anything else?"

I shook my head from side to side and then turned back to using the trowel to dig in the clay embankment.

late april 1993

Just follow the fence line. Just follow the fence line. Just follow the fence line. I'd wanted to explore the woods behind the barn where the sheep were, but my foster mom had told me to go by myself.

"You're perfectly capable," she'd said. "And there's a fence to keep the sheep in, so just follow the fence line and you'll end up back where you started."

"But what if I lose the fence? If I look at something and get lost?"

"Then just pick a direction and walk only in that direction until you find the fence again. Then follow the fence. You'll be fine. You're smart—you can do this."

I hadn't believed her, but I hadn't wanted her to know that—or how scared I was to go out there alone. So, off I'd gone on foot by myself. About an hour had passed, and when I saw a dead sheep carcass, I started to panic; I hadn't thought it would take me that long. Had I gotten lost? Would I end up rotting in the middle of the woods like that poor sheep because no one could find me?

No, I thought. *She's right, there has to be a fence or the sheep would get out. So, this fence has to take me back. Maybe that was just a really old sheep.* Just then, I saw another sheep on the other side of a small clump of trees, munching on the tall grass, and its presence helped my heart slow and the electricity in my body started to subside.

My eyes drifted from the sheep to the tree trunk in the center of the nearby clump of trees—the biggest one there. Slowly, I followed the trunk up, craning my head back as far as it would go in order to make out the branches at the top. *Wow, it's huge! I think that's the tallest tree I've ever seen.*

As I began walking again, I moved more slowly, my head often tipping upwards to see the tops of the trees I was passing, their branches outlined all the more clearly against the backdrop of neon blue sky and cottony white clouds. After a while, once I'd gotten far from the dead sheep, I could smell the woods around me. It was musty, the odor of rotting wood and leaves and damp earth and crisp breeze. The smell became familiar as I explored, and I found myself purposefully taking deep breaths through my nose so I could keep the scent in my nostrils. My muscles felt relaxed and soft in a way they never had before—the closest was the day I'd rolled cigarettes with Linda and my brothers in West Virginia. I felt like I belonged, not like I did at Diedre's party. Being in the woods was so much better than being around people, I realized. I liked the trees; they were predictable and quiet and strong.

*****

The water streaming into the sink basin was a thick, murky orange from the clay I was cleaning off my rock finds that day. Lots more quartz, but a few I hadn't identified yet. I usually took my new *Rocks & Minerals* pocket guide with me, but it was drizzling outside, and I didn't want to ruin the pages by getting them wet, so I'd left it in my room. Once all the clay was rinsed off my little treasures, I used soap to wash them and my hands, wincing a bit.

I'd had so many I'd been afraid they would tumble from my fingers when I headed back down to the house, so I'd squeezed to hold them tight. When a few really sharp edges cut into my hands, I'd immediately released them, and all the rocks and minerals had fallen to the ground. I'd picked them back up and slowly, deliberately, closed my hand over them as the razorlike edges caused slight discomfort that progressed into pain. With my fingers white, I squeezed as hard as I could as my eyes filled with tears, blurring my view of my fist. This time, I didn't hold back the tears and they streamed down my cheeks. My hand had hurt, but I'd liked it, and now as I cleaned the clay out of my cuts, I felt a little better.

Once I'd identified everything I'd found, marked them in my book, and added them to my growing rock collection, I sat down on my bed and pulled out my diary from under my pillow. I'd gotten it new at the book fair when I got my book on rocks; it wasn't big, but it still had a lot of pages, and the best part was that it came with a lock on it. After grabbing a pencil from the cup on the table and retrieving my key from one of my drawers, I wrote about what I'd found and how I'd made myself cry. Then, I wrote about Michael, a boy I had a crush on. I wondered if Michael would kiss me. I'd been kissed before—once. I still missed the boy who'd done it. Closing my eyes, I thought back to when it had happened.

It was after my dad and I stopped living with my Aunt Sissy that we went to stay with some of his friends for a week or so. The house was in the woods somewhere, big with a large porch at the end of a long, secluded drive. Surrounding the house was a large yard with very short grass and a big gravel parking area. By evening the day we arrived, there were a lot more kids there. At seven, I was the youngest, and the oldest was about thirteen. The other kids didn't like me and were mean, calling me names like "cow" and Fat-ass, except for this one boy. His name was Josh, and he wasn't quite two years older than I was.

At first, he followed me when I ran off crying to find somewhere to hide after the others called me names. Moments after I'd tucked myself into a closet or scrambled under the front porch or even hidden inside a clump of wild shrubs, he'd be there. Silently, he'd join me, sitting down next to me and wrapping his arms around me while I hugged my knees and cried. After the first couple of days, he started sticking up for me, telling the other kids to leave me alone when they made fun of me. The kids responded by making fun of him, too, and I felt so guilty that he was being called names because of me, but he didn't seem to care about what they said about anyone—including himself—except me.

At night, the kids slept in a cavernous basement in sleeping bags on the floor, all the adults upstairs in bedrooms. Josh moved his sleeping bag next to mine and slept by my side every night, a barrier between the other kids and me.

On the last night, the teasing was worse than ever, and I cried in my sleeping bag so hard my sides hurt and snot was running out of my nose. Josh sat in his sleeping bag next to me, arguing with the kids who'd made me cry, but I pressed my hands over my ears to block out the sounds. After a while, Josh got up and walked out of the room and I cried harder. I hadn't understood all week why he'd stuck up for me or been so nice, and I'd been sure he'd get sick of me; it seemed I was right.

I was surprised when he returned a minute later with tissues.

"Here," he said, holding them out to me.

I took them from him and blew my nose over and over until all the tissues were filled with snot and piled up on the other side of my sleeping bag.

"Is the little piggy done crying now?" someone shouted out, kicking off a round of laughter.

My eyes immediately filled with tears that spilled over again, burning my skin as they fell. I wanted to curl up so small I would just disappear, but I couldn't.

"Come in here with me," Josh said quietly, his blue eyes watching me as he held up the unzipped side of his sleeping bag.

I shimmied out of my sleeping bag and slid in with him, burying my face in his chest while I sobbed. He wrapped his arms around me and hugged me until the tears subsided. I needed more tissues, but I didn't want to get up. The other kids seemed to have forgotten about me or fallen asleep, and I felt like I was in a safe bubble that would burst if I moved. Instead, I reached down and pulled up my shirt, using the hem to clean my nose out. Shifting around once I was done, I got comfortable with my head next to Josh's, our noses almost touching, and closed my eyes. I felt my body gradually get heavy and relaxed as my breathing slowed.

Something soft touched my lips unexpectedly and my eyes popped open just as Josh pulled back; he'd just given me a kiss. Setting his head back down, we stared into each other's eyes for a long time, and then he leaned forward and kissed me again, another peck. And then he pressed his lips against me slowly, holding them there for a moment, then sliding his tongue out and pushing it between my lips. I tried to remember what I was supposed to do from the movies I'd seen as I opened my mouth and began kissing him back. After a few minutes of kissing, he hugged me tight again and I fell asleep that way, wishing my dad and I didn't have to leave the next day.

I stared at the page in my diary, wondering where Josh was, what his life was like, if my dad still got to see him even though I couldn't. I liked Michael, but I liked Josh even more, and I really missed him. I was sure he wouldn't have let those kids in the trailer park beat me up or make fun of me if he'd been there. Looking back down at the page in my diary, I decided to write a letter to him in there, and if I ever found him one day, I'd give it to him.

before you have the chance

"Here's one of the more unusual and problem-creating symptoms that can develop from unresolved trauma: the compulsion to repeat the actions that caused the problem in the first place. We are inextricably drawn into situations that replicate the original trauma in both obvious and less obvious ways."

-Peter A. Levine

late may 1993

"Do you want to come over this weekend?"

I was talking to a girl in my grade—Ella—as we were about to get off the bus by my driveway. I'd been to her house before, but I wasn't sure if it was only because her mom and my foster mom decided I should be invited over or if Ella really wanted us to be friends. I shrugged.

"My mom will make us blueberry muffins and we can watch my favorite movie."

"Okay. I'll ask."

There was a flicker of excitement in my belly, but I pushed it away—I'd never kept a friend for very long. Though Ella was one of the first people who talked to me and she still did, so maybe she really wanted to be my friend after all?

That would mean I had three friends... if they stayed my friends: Ella, Brad, and Ruth. I'd met Ella on the bus, Brad at school, and Ruth at church, though we were all in the same grade. I didn't know why Brad talked to me at school, but he did. He smiled a lot, and when he did, he looked like Josh; his hair and eyes were the exact same color. I liked him instantly and felt safe around him, just like I did with Josh.

Ruth talked to me, too, though she had other friends already, and she'd invited me over to her house once. I liked Ruth and her mom a lot—they were so nice and always calm. But I still got really nervous around her; I was worried I'd say something wrong and she wouldn't want or be allowed to be my friend anymore.

"Can I go to Ella's house?" I asked my foster mom.

"Sure, but I can't drive you right now."

"Oh," I replied, feeling deflated. "Okay."

"You can walk, though."

Ella's house wasn't far from the road where the bus dropped us off. I could walk up the driveway, down the road a little ways, then cut through between two houses, a strip of woods, and then I should be in her backyard or only a house or two down. But what if I was too far over and I went through the wrong yard and that person got mad?

"I don't know if I remember which yard I go through," I said.

"Yard?"

"Yeah, where Ella cuts through when she gets off the bus."

"Oh! I wasn't talking about going up there. You shouldn't walk through other people's yards. You can walk through right here," she said, pointing in the direction of the pond. "The creek that runs out from the pond? It goes through the woods here and it ends at the road through the subdivision where they live. You just turn right and go up the hill when you reach the road."

My stomach clenched as I thought about going through the woods by myself. "What if I get lost?"

"You won't," she replied, turning back to what she was making in the kitchen. "Just follow the creek. You didn't get lost behind the barn, did you?"

I shook my head. "No." Maybe she was right, and maybe I could do it. "Okay."

Turning, I walked a few steps to the small table in the kitchen near a built-in shelf that housed cookbooks, a notepad and pen, and the old rotary phone we used to make calls. I loved using that old phone. For some reason, I felt so grown-up having to use my finger to turn the dial—though it could be really frustrating if you messed up a number because then you'd have to hang up and start all over. Picking up the receiver, I slowly said the numbers aloud as I turned the dial, grinning at the sound it made when I released it and it spun back to the starting position.

"May I talk to Ella, please?" I said when someone answered. I was sure it was Ella, but my foster mom said it was polite and good manners to always state who you'd like to talk to, even if you thought they were the one who'd answered the phone.

"It's me," she replied.

"You should say 'this is she,'" I said, repeating what my foster mom always said if we answered any other way. "I can come over. I'm going to walk through the woods by my house to get there."

We talked another minute and agreed she would meet me at the bottom of the hill where the creek ended, then I set off for my afternoon at her house.

*****

The sounds of Ella's mom in the kitchen reached us in the living room, and I knew the smell of blueberry muffins would soon fill the house.

"I wrote a new song on my keyboard," Ella said. "Do you want to listen?"

"Sure," I replied.

Ella wrote songs a lot. I would help her with the words sometimes, but never the music part; I was still learning how to read music and to play the flute my foster mom rented for me.

My foster mom had said everyone should know how to play an instrument and asked what I'd like to play. I didn't hesitate before I told her the flute. She'd promised I could try the flute then change to another instrument later, if I wanted; I'd shaken my head from side to side. The flute was the only instrument I wanted to play—it was a way for me to remember my mom.

To Ella, I said, "Maybe I can try to play my flute while you play the keyboard sometime?"

She nodded. "Okay."

I listened to her play on her keyboard and helped her change some of the words in her song until the muffins were ready for us. Her mom served us each a plate with a muffin, still warm from the oven.

"Are you interested in gymnastics, Katherine?" Ella's mom asked me after I took my first bite.

I shrugged. "I've never played any sports. But my foster mom said she wants me to try soccer this summer."

"Soccer is awesome," Ella said. "So is gymnastics. You should do it with me! There's a camp I go to for it in the summer."

"I'll tell your foster mom about it," Ella's mom promised.

"I'll show you what I can do when we finish eating," Ella said.

I nodded again and we finished our muffins as we answered her mom's questions about school, which only had a few more weeks left. She asked if I was looking forward to the summer and I told her I wasn't, that I wished we could go to school all year; I loved school and wanted to go every day. She laughed and said she'd never heard that; instantly, my face felt hot and my stomach turned. Once her mom had collected our plates, I followed Ella outside where she showed me she could do a cartwheel and could almost do a handspring as I watched, my eyes wide.

"That's gymnastics?" I asked.

"Yeah," she grinned, doing another cartwheel.

"I wanna learn!"

"I'll teach you," she said, turning to demonstrate a cartwheel.

By the time I went home, I couldn't wait to ask if I could do gymnastics camp with Ella over the summer.

*****

I looked up at the two people in my foster mom's kitchen and wished they'd never come. Jean had introduced them as her parents when they arrived a few weeks ago and we were told to simply call them Grandma and Grandpa to make things easier. I'd never had a grandpa— mine died when I was a baby—but this man looked grouchy, even when he smiled at us.

As they all talked, I was trying to wait to ask a question; Grandpa did not like it when my sister and I spoke. He was always telling us—mostly me, since I talked more than Laurel—that children were to be seen and not heard, that we needed to keep whatever we thought was important to say to ourselves. Grandma said it a lot, too, and they were always shushing me and interrupting me to tell me to talk more quietly when I *was* allowed to say something. It made me feel so angry and guilty at the same time. My foster mom often told me I was loud and that I talked too much, but after her parents came, she told me to stop talking a lot more.

I also hated that every time I asked for something, it seemed to make Grandma and Grandpa mad. If I didn't like something, they also got mad. They kept telling us we were ungrateful and telling our foster mom that we were just taking advantage of her. They said when you had nothing, you didn't have a right to not like something.

"You aren't family—Jean doesn't owe you anything. You keep that in mind because you can go back to where you came from any time," they said often.

I hated them every time they said that. Our social worker had told us we would never live with our parents again when they took us, so we would never have our family again. But Jean and her parents would never be our family, either.

june 1993

On the first day of soccer practice, my foster mom introduced me to the coach, a man who looked younger than my dad and had dark brown—almost black—hair and brown eyes. "This is Mr. Kerry. He's going to pick you up and drive you to Strasburg on the days you have practice." He smiled as she turned to me. "And this," she said to Mr. Kerry, "is Katherine."

"Hi there, Katherine."

"She's never played soccer," she added.

"Well, this is going to be *lots* of fun," he said warmly, smiling.

A couple of weeks later, I was sitting in his car with my seatbelt on while he filled his gas tank. Like every other time I was in his car, I felt so sick I thought I might not make it the twenty-five minute drive without throwing up; I was dizzy and sweating and having a hard time breathing. He always asked me questions about school, and I answered, although I preferred to be left in silence when we were in his car. I could count to one hundred and then start over again and see how many times I could do that between when I sat down in his car and when I could finally get out.

I watched him walk inside to pay for the gas, wishing I'd never have to sit in the car next to him alone ever again. Playing soccer was a lot of fun, but I didn't want to play because I had to keep riding alone with Mr. Kerry. His car door opened and he climbed in, smiling as he always did, and held out a candy bar in my direction, like he did every time he had to get gas when I was with him.

"Here you go," he said.

"Thank you," I said, staring down at my hands.

He pulled his seatbelt across his chest, pushed it into the holster, then turned the key in the ignition. I watched, wide-eyed, as his hand reached from the key to the gear shift. *Please don't touch me. Please don't touch me.*

Please don't touch me, I chanted silently. He never once had touched me—except for a pat on the back during practice like he did to everyone—but every time we got into his car, I was sure he was going to do it. I was sure he would put his hand on my knee and slide it up my thigh. I knew exactly what would happen because I had nightmares about it at night; he would touch me like Elmer had and I wouldn't be able to do anything about it. I'd be frozen like I was when Elmer did it. Except he would make it hurt even more—like the colored pencils did. And if I told anyone, they wouldn't believe me. Or they would think I liked it because I hurt myself with those colored pencils.

If I didn't stop him, like I didn't stop Elmer or Terrence, maybe I *did* like it and just didn't know it?

*****

My stomach was fluttering in excitement and I was bouncing in the back seat of the car. Glancing over, I could see my sister felt the same way I did.

We pulled into a driveway in a subdivision and my sister and I practically flew out of the car, racing ahead of our social worker. There was a glass storm door and the front door behind it was open, so we could see inside where there was a large crowd of kids, mostly a few years older than us. I scanned every face until I found the faces of my brothers—faces I hadn't seen since before our mom went into rehab.

"I see them! They're right there! Look, Laurel, look!"

My knees bounced as we waited at the front door after our social worker rang the doorbell. A tired-looking woman came to the door and glanced at us without smiling, though our social worker smiled at *her.* The woman opened the door and let us walk in without even saying hello to us. Our social worker started speaking, but I didn't stay to listen—I tore across the room and barreled into Al's arms.

"Hey, sis," he said, hugging me back.

I squeezed as hard as I could and never wanted to let go, though I did a few minutes later as Al laughed at me so I could turn, teary-eyed, to hug James.

"Everyone go downstairs until lunchtime!" the lady ordered.

When she spoke, the room quieted, and everyone immediately stood and started filing to the basement. I looked around with my eyes wide in surprise—everyone was so well-behaved.

"Go on," our social worker said kindly. "You go play with your brothers for a while."

When we got to the basement, James started playing a game of tickle with Laurel and I sat down next to Al; I couldn't wipe the grin off my face.

"We're in a home now, too. It's different, though. We live out in the country on a farm, and she has lots of animals and her own woods. Oh, she has sheep! And we watched a guy come and... shear—that's the word—all their hair off and then we use these things our foster mom calls paddles, like this"—I used my hands to demonstrate pulling something apart—"to make all the dirt fall out. She said she'll show us how it gets spun into yarn. Isn't that really cool? Oh, and she grows vegetables and fruit and we can go pick them every day and she said she'll teach us how to make jam and can sauces and jams and other foods this summer and we have chickens and two dogs—Princess and Sunny—and two cats—Molly and Juno. Molly is the fattest cat I've ever seen and she's my favorite color— she's orange—and Juno—"

"Whoa, whoa, whoa, sis." Al laughed, grabbing me so I couldn't move and giving me a noogie on my head. "Slow down. I don't think I've ever heard you talk this much!"

I looked down in embarrassment. *I should be quiet—seen and not heard.*

"I didn't mean to shut up," Al said a moment later when neither of us said anything. "I meant just *slow down.*"

I looked up at him. "Is this where you've been the whole time?"

Al laughed bitterly and looked away from me toward the other side of the room. "Hell, no. James and I didn't get some nice house like you have. The longest we've been in one house was three months."

"Why?"

He looked back at me and studied my eyes for a moment. "Doesn't matter, sis."

"Yeah, it does. Tell me why."

He took a deep breath and let it out slowly. "All our families have beat us."

My heart stopped. "What?"

He laughed again, the sound cold. "Yeah, they haven't done anything recently because you guys were coming to visit, but they rough us all up a lot."

I looked around and started counting. "There are six of you?"

He shook his head. "No, not everyone's home right now. There's ten of us here."

"Ten?" I asked, incredulous.

"Yeah. They do it for the money."

"But... but *how*? My foster mom said they don't give that much, that the clothing allowance isn't even half of what you really need."

"They get more for us."

"What do you mean?"

"We're 'problem kids' so they get more money for us. And there's a lot of us here. Then they just don't buy us clothes or anything like that, and they lock the food up so we can't eat except when they want to feed us. Today, they'll give us whatever we ask for because you guys are here—whenever there's a visit, they let us eat anything. But if we eat too much, they'll punish us later."

I started shaking my head from side-to-side—he had to be lying to me. But then I looked around and saw that all the kids were as knobby-skinny as my brothers; it couldn't be natural that they were all that skinny, right? I looked back to him and noticed the shadowing on his face. Could that be an old bruise?

"I'm going to tell my social worker," I said. "They have to fix it."

He laughed. "Sis, they don't give a shit about us. It's just a job to them. And all the families are like that."

I shook my head from side-to-side, refusing to believe it. "Well, I'll tell my foster mom, then. She's not like that. She'll make them fix it."

He laughed sadly and put his arm around me. "It's good you got a good home. But don't waste your breath."

Maybe I should tell them to switch me? My brothers could go to my foster mom and I could go somewhere else? They'd been in foster care much longer than I had. It wasn't fair if they were in all these bad homes and I got a good one the first time; they deserved it way more than I did. My chest tightened in guilt for having what my brothers should have had.

july 1993

My foster mom had told me a few minutes earlier that Ruth's mom had called and invited me to come over again, then asked me if I'd like to go. I'd said no. She was surprised and asked me if I was sure, and I'd said yes, then gone up to my room.

Now, I laid on my bed, staring at the ceiling. I'd gone over to Ruth's house and spent the night last week and we'd had so much fun. Her mom had played on their piano and we'd played with her dog outside and watched movies. All of a sudden, I'd gotten really sad when we were watching a movie and I didn't even know why. Because I wasn't expecting it, I couldn't keep my tears in, and I'd cried in front of Ruth and her mom. When her mom asked me what was wrong, I'd said that I missed my mom and dad.

They'd sat down, one on each side of me, and wrapped their arms around me, but it just made my heart hurt when they did that. I'd wanted to scream at them not to touch me, that I just wanted to curl into a ball and be left alone. But I'd liked it, too. When my tears had stopped, my nose was stuffy and my face was sticky, and Ruth's mom suggested I take a hot shower while she got out ingredients for us to bake cookies afterwards, so Ruth had walked me upstairs and showed me where the bathroom was.

"I'm sorry you don't have your parents," she'd said, her voice quiet. When I glanced at her, she looked like she was about to cry herself and I felt even worse.

"It's okay," I'd lied, forcing a smile. "Don't feel bad." I swallowed and looked down at my feet. "It's better anyway. I miss them, but it's better here." My voice cracked with my last word. I'd meant what I was saying—about it being better—though it didn't make it hurt less. But I hadn't wanted my friend to feel bad because of me.

Now I was so embarrassed about crying over there that I didn't want to see her again aside from Sunday School. She and her mom were the nicest people I'd ever met, and I'd made them upset and worried over me—they didn't deserve that. If I went over there, I might make them sad again.

Pain started in my chest like it always did when I got upset, and my eyes started burning with tears that I willed to remain where they were. But I felt like I couldn't keep them in anymore, and that made me really angry that I couldn't control it. In a huff, I got up and went downstairs, stomping the whole way.

"Why don't you go outside and play?" my foster mom suggested as I reached the first floor.

I shook my head. "I don't want to."

"Your sister is out picking flowers—why don't you go pick some with her?"

"I said I don't want to!" I shouted at her. "I just want to read!"

My foster mom started talking about my attitude again, and I tuned her out; I just wanted to be left alone. Turning, I saw my dictionary and grabbed it off the side table. I wasn't sure where I'd left my book, but I didn't care anymore. I headed back up the stairs to my room and threw myself on my bed, determined to learn every word in the English language; it would give me something to do other than think about how conflicted I was about being friends with Ruth until we went on vacation in a few weeks.

august 1993

My foster mom, Laurel, and I were in Canada on a summer road trip for our vacation. I hadn't been sure what to expect, and my foster mom had warned me that we wouldn't have as much fun if I had a bad attitude the whole time, but so far it had been pretty fun. My favorite part was that she'd asked me to sit in the front seat and be her navigator.

Prior to leaving, she'd taught me how to read a map and we'd planned out a general route to take and talked about how to make adjustments on the road if there was a road closure or we wanted to take a detour. And then we'd hopped in the car and she'd trusted me to tell her where to turn, what roads to take. It was a big responsibility, and I'd taken it seriously because I didn't want us to get lost. My foster mom had already told me several times that I was navigating wonderfully and I was really proud of myself. Even though Laurel and I were supposed to take turns, unlike when she usually got off the hook when she didn't want to do things, I didn't mind at all that Laurel didn't want to navigate because I liked doing such an important job.

We were at a point in the trip where we had to take a huge ferry, where we drove the car onto it below deck so it could carry us all to the other side, then we'd drive off toward our destination. As we rode the ferry into dusk, I didn't want to go below deck and leave the air whipping around us; it felt and tasted of freedom. I couldn't really even hear my own thoughts over the sound of wind, and I felt at peace standing near the railing on the deck with the forced silence.

But I couldn't stay—it was time to go down to our car and my foster mom called to me. I ignored her and stayed where I was as if she wasn't first calling—then shouting—for me to follow her. She walked over, irritated, and told me it was time to go inside. I glared at her, my eyes narrowing, and refused.

"NO! You can't tell me what to do. You can't make me do *anything*—you're not my mom and you never will be!"

She got angrier than I'd ever seen her as she tried over and over to get me to follow her and I kept refusing. I knew I could outlast her. And then she'd send me back, just like she always threatened when we got into arguments. Just like Grandma and Grandpa kept telling me would happen, just like I overheard them telling her she should have already done. None of them really wanted me, and my foster mom was going to get rid of me anyway—it might as well happen now.

"You'd better get your ass down those stairs right now," she said through gritted teeth.

I could tell her hold on her temper was tenuous. I'd never pushed her this far; she'd never cussed at me. I knew she was close to losing what hold she had. And I wanted to destroy it more than anything in the world right then. "No," I said, my voice steel.

My head snapped to the side and it took a moment before the familiar tingle started and I comprehended what had just happened; she'd slapped me in the face just as my Aunt Pauline used to do. I was simultaneously dumbfounded, furious, and had a sense of satisfaction that I'd been right that if I pushed hard enough, she'd snap. We stood there glaring at each other for a moment, both of us breathing hard as tears stung my eyes from the burning on the side of my face.

"We're going downstairs. *Now*," she said.

What would she do about it if I kept refusing? Would she slap me again? Something worse? I sat down right where I was standing.

She glared at me for a moment, clenched her jaw, then grabbed the sleeve of my sweatshirt and started walking. She dragged me across the deck, through the doors to the inside, which is when I started screaming at the top of my lungs. She dragged me down to the lower deck and dragged me around the maze of cars until we'd reached ours.

"Get inside the car," she bit out as she dropped my sleeve.

"No!" I shouted back, though my voice was wavering this time.

After a moment of glaring at me, her face hard, she opened the door on the other side of the car for my sister to climb in, and then she got into the driver's seat herself. I remained outside the car, my back leaning against the tire, as tears fell from my eyes, until the announcements blared that we were approaching the dock. I knew that meant that cars would be driving off the ferry and I didn't want to get run over, so I dried my face using my sleeves, clenched my jaw to hide that I'd been crying, and climbed into the back seat of the car.

hatred and gratitude

"When we are in pain and fear, anger and hate are our go-to emotions."
-Brené Brown

september 1993

"All the chores need to be done or no one gets an allowance," my foster mom said.

I glared at her. "But Laurel—"

"Katherine, I said it doesn't matter. It has to be done."

Though I wanted to scream, I settled instead for a cross between a growl and a screech. I hated my foster mom, and I hated my sister. And I hated my parents. My mom didn't even care enough to see us. Our social worker had taken us to see our dad once last month—at a McDonald's, that way he wouldn't know where we were living—but then he'd left again.

He said it was impossible to do everything Social Services was telling him he had to do so he could get us back, and he kept talking about our hair; he was angry my foster mom had cut it. I told him what she'd said— that it would be healthier this way, that we could grow it back out if we wanted. I hated my short hair because people always thought I was a boy, but it was getting longer. My foster mom kept reminding us that hair always grows, which I told my dad, but that just made him angrier. And we'd worn our nicest outfits to go see him, but he didn't like our clothes, either—he said we were dressed like white snobs, which made our new social worker get mad and tell him he couldn't say things like that. My dad said we didn't look like his kids anymore and told *me* that he couldn't even look at me with my hair short.

He wouldn't look at me, my mom wouldn't even try to see or talk to me, my foster grandparents wouldn't let me say anything, and my foster mom wouldn't listen to me. I hated all of them. Turning away from my foster mom, I stomped up the stairs to my room.

"You have to help me clean up!" I shouted at my sister.

She laughed. "No, I don't!"

"If we don't do it, we won't get our allowance."

"I don't care," she said.

"I hate you!" I screamed at her.

We got an allowance every week if our chores were done. We were always instructed to divide our money between short-term and long-term savings, immediate spending money, and tithing. Our foster mom would not buy the toys or candy or whatever else we wanted between holidays and birthdays, saying that was the point of our allowance—except that she always bought them for Laurel anyway. Laurel would cry until our foster mom gave in and got the stuff for her, but if I tried that, I was told I was old enough to know better. But we had chores that had to be done to get our allowance, regardless of who did it. And my sister didn't care if they got done, because she knew she'd get what she wanted anyway. I needed my allowance, though, so I could buy more books.

I lunged toward my sister, wanting to hold her down and shout at her until she said she'd do her half of our chores, but I missed, and she skirted around me and ran down the stairs. Chasing after her, I almost slipped on the stairs and caught myself at the last moment. When we got to the first floor, our foster mom shouted for us to stop fighting, but I ignored her; she didn't understand.

My sister ran behind her, hiding as she giggled like it was a game, and that made me even angrier.

"I hate you!" I screamed, lunging forward again.

"Girls! That's enough fighting!" my foster mom shouted as I chased my sister around the dining table. "You girls need to learn to get along—you're all you've got! That's it, no one else. You have to take care of each other, not fight."

I'd heard those words almost every day for months, but they just made me want to scream. Grandma and Grandpa already reminded us that we didn't belong and weren't part of their family, that we didn't have a family at all anymore. I didn't need to be told again—I hadn't forgotten.

october 1993

I didn't want to go to the Halloween festival they were having at the school; I just wanted to stay home and read or watch a movie. Or go to bed. Anything but go to the Halloween festival. But my foster mom had insisted that my sister and I go. That was bad enough, but my costume made it worse.

My foster mom believed in using what we had available whenever possible. Except that my sister was too small for any ideas she had from home, so she'd gotten a few things from the store and done her makeup so Laurel looked like a doll. The only thing she'd bought for me was a beard; I was chubby enough that with a pillow, she could cinch her jeans around me. I also wore one of her flannel shirts and a straw hat, suspenders, and had Grandpa's walking stick. She said I looked great as a farmer.

I knew I looked stupid, though. And I felt stupid. And I didn't like Halloween anyway because it was too scary. But she insisted that I go because I needed to make some friends. When we arrived, she ushered me into the auditorium, and I stopped walking as the first laughs reached my ears. I was the only kid in there *not* wearing a purchased costume, and I was the only kid there who was dressed like a short, fat farmer. For the next hour or so, I did what I was supposed to, pretending that the laughter and pointing didn't hurt my feelings, holding back my tears like I'd been teaching myself to do until I got home.

Once my sister was asleep, though, all those tears came out, soaking my pillow. I cried until I fell asleep. But I hadn't been asleep for long before I woke up, my chest seizing, certain there was something under my bed. The creature had been in my dream, had reached me when my dad deserted me as I tried to run from it, and I could hear it breathing, a heavy pant coming from the creature that was part man and part monster. I was paralyzed with fear and felt like I was going to die because I couldn't move any of my muscles, not even to breathe or blink. If I did, it would know I was there and would attack.

Sweat started pouring down my body and a small breath reached my lungs. My fingers twitched; I was getting control over my body back. But the creature would know, so I couldn't stay where I was. My eyes darted over toward my sister, but I knew she was safe; the creatures only ever wanted me. Squeezing my eyes shut tight for a moment, I sprang into action, standing and leaping off my bed as far away as I could in one continuous movement. My feet were already moving as I landed on the floor, and I slammed into the wall at the top of the stairs as I tried to make the turn to go down them without slowing.

A few stairs in, my feet slipped out from under me and I landed on my tailbone, bumping down the next few steps. Sharp pain shot through me, but it was quickly dulled by my fear and I was on my feet again, racing to get into my foster mom's room before the man-monster could catch me.

"Jean?" I asked, my voice breaking into a sob as I stood next to her bed. I could feel the heavy breath on my neck and knew if I turned, the creature would grab me.

She moaned a bit and blinked. "Katherine?"

"I'm scared."

She didn't reply, simply lifting her blankets up. I leapt into the bed, turning so my back was against her chest and I was facing out; I couldn't leave my back exposed. Jean tucked her arm around my middle and was back asleep in seconds. I laid there engaged in an internal tug-of-war. The monster I'd run from was lying in wait for me to get up. As soon as I left Jean's bed, it would grab me and then it would touch me before it killed me—all my nightmare creatures and men wanted to do the same thing. I couldn't leave where I was.

But I was also intensely uncomfortable with my foster mom's body touching my back—I didn't like to be touched. Even when my sister climbed into bed with me now, I'd scoot all the way to the edge of the bed, practically falling off if I had to, so there would be space between us. However, my foster mom had already been on the edge, so I had no space to scoot away. And when I tried to close my eyes and think the happy thoughts I recited to my sister when she was scared, I couldn't. I could see and feel the man-monster's hands and breath on me, my foster mom's body behind me became his, her arm tucked around me was his, holding me in place so I couldn't escape him.

I stared wide-eyed into the blackness in front of me, my falling tears keeping my eyes lubricated so I didn't have to blink very often. Once the first light from the rising sun started to brighten the room, I finally dozed off.

november 1993

The sting worsened and my tears fell harder as I used the washcloth to clean out the cut on my chest; I'd already used the tweezers to pull out the

122

splinters. I dried the skin around the new cut and tried to hold it closed to slow the bleeding, thinking back over what had happened, my heart skipping in fear and anger all over again.

Shaunte was our new foster sister and I hated her; she was *so mean* to us all the time and liked to beat us up. She had gone after my sister and I'd blocked her, having had enough of her torment, and said she could leave us alone and we'd leave her alone since we didn't like her anyway. She'd responded by calling me fat, and I'd shouted that at least I wasn't a thief like her—during her first week staying at a woman's in-home daycare after school, she'd been kicked out for stealing the lady's jewelry.

Instead of coming after me to hit me like she normally did, she reached over from where she was standing and grabbed a large, splintery section of wood from one of the logs comprising the wall and threw it at me like a knife. I'd just gotten out of the bathtub when I stopped her from beating up my sister, so I was naked and the wood sliced into the left side of my chest about an inch or two above my nipple.

She'd laughed when I screamed, and laughed harder when she saw little chunks of wood sticking out from my skin. I'd told her I was telling on her and ran to tell my foster mom, but she hadn't listened. She'd told me that she'd had enough of all our fighting, that she didn't want to hear it and that we needed to figure out how to get along ourselves. That's when I'd started crying in anger, though I was trying really hard not to.

After two ruined band-aids, I finally managed to get one to stick to my skin instead of my fingers as they pinched the cut together—as soon as I let go, it started bleeding really fast. I'd gone back to my foster mom after I cleaned out the big wood pieces and told her that I thought I might need stitches, but she told me I was being a hypochondriac and to just go put a band-aid on it.

*****

"Before we start, let's all go around and talk about what we're thankful for," my foster mom said as we all sat down for Thanksgiving dinner.

The table was overflowing with food and I was mesmerized by how much there was, how many different kinds. There was turkey and stuffing and mashed potatoes and green bean casserole and creamed spinach and sweet potato casserole and more. In addition to the four of us, my foster mom's kids—her son, Jack, and his wife, Kendra; her daughter, Sue, and her husband, Andy—had joined us for the holiday.

With my dad's family, whenever we had a family gathering for any reason, there was always loud arguing between at least a few people, kids fighting amongst each other after being banished from the company of the adults. This was so different—not one person had an argument or fight; they teased each other, but there was only laughter. They were all smiling and seemed genuinely happy to be there. My foster mom's kids had talked to my sister, Shaunte, and me, asking us questions about school, and we'd all played games together: *Gin, Sorry!,* and *Go to the Head of the Class,* which was my favorite. Shaunte had even been nice to me.

I looked around quickly, but carefully, and no one seemed to be irritated by my foster mom's suggestion. As my foster mom went first, my head started spinning thinking about all the things I was thankful for that year.

"I'm thankful for having a happy and healthy family," she started. "For having a home for all of us to be together. I'm thankful that we have plenty to eat and warm clothes to wear."

Yes, I'm thankful for those things, too. And I'm thankful for Jean and that we didn't go to a home like my brothers where they beat us, and for learning to play the flute and for horseback riding lessons and soccer and gymnastics and for camp and for having so many books to read and—

"And I'm thankful for these girls," she continued. "Thankful that you came into my life and that I'm able to provide a home for you. Thankful that you kids are so resilient."

I scooted my butt back and forth as I tried to sit up a little taller when she smiled at my sister and me after she spoke. I'd heard the word other times when she was talking to our social worker, our teachers, and her friends; I'd looked it up in my dictionary, so I knew it was a good thing to be resilient. Warmth and pride flooded through me that I'd made my foster mom proud of me.

When it was my turn to speak, my heart pounded hard in my chest. I wasn't sure what I should say, which things I should choose, and I didn't want to say something stupid and ruin my foster mom being proud of me.

"I'm thankful for being here," I started. "And that my sister is here with me. And for all the things we get to do that we've never done before."

It was all true, but I looked up at my foster mom's face, anxious for her reaction. She smiled and her eyes looked glassy; she was happy with what I'd said. My chest started to swell with pride again as everyone started filling their plates. The smile on my face was so big my cheeks hurt. *I've never smiled until my cheeks hurt.*

With that thought, my smile faded. I bet my brothers weren't smiling. They were in another new foster home—I'd told my foster mom what they said and she'd reported it—but would their new foster parents be nicer to them? Did they get enough food at their new home?

And wherever they were, were my parents smiling? My mom and Linda were probably cold and hungry while I was warm and had as much food as I wanted. My dad must be lonely with none of us there with him.

Guilt suddenly drowned me; I had so much the rest of my family didn't have. How could I deserve something they didn't? And I'd just proven that I didn't deserve it at all—what kind of person was thankful for not being with their parents? I missed my mom and my dad, but I knew I wouldn't have any of the things I was thankful for if I was with them, and a part of me was glad I wasn't with them. I realized then that I'd deserved everything that had happened to me, and that I didn't deserve for them or anyone else to love me.

How could a person who was grateful they weren't with their parents be lovable?

like i wasn't even there

"Most days, I wander around feeling invisible, like I'm a speck of dust floating in the air that can only be seen when a shaft of light hits it."

-Sonya Sones

january 1994

My whole body was filled with electricity as we drove. It was the start of the second half of fourth grade, but I was going to a new school. My foster mom had pulled me out from my class at the school I went to with my sister and Shaunte. I'd heard her and my social worker talking about it, and I'd learned I was being moved because of something that had happened with Shaunte.

My foster mom had taken us all shopping for clothes at a small department store in town. Shaunte and I went into a dressing room together to try on some clothes and she also had a handful of training bras to try. She tried them on, but instead of taking them all off, she left two of them on when she put her shirt back on.

"That's stealing!" I hissed.

"Shut up!" she hissed back at me. "Of course it is! This is how you do it."

"You shouldn't steal," I whispered. "It's bad. If you just ask, Jean will probably buy it for you."

"I don't care," she responded.

I stared at her for a moment as she readied herself to leave the dressing room. "I'm going to tell on you."

"No, you won't, or I'll punch you in the face. And I have two—I'll just tell her you asked me to steal the other one for you."

I glared at her and wanted to say that our foster mom wouldn't believe her, but I realized that I didn't know if she would or not. Probably so—no one ever believed me. "Don't steal in front of me anymore," I huffed, following her out of the dressing room. I wanted to tell on her, but I didn't want to get in trouble for it, so I didn't.

But my foster mom found the bras anyway and asked Shaunte about them. In spite of me not telling, she still said they were for both of us. I denied it, but my foster mom didn't believe me since I'd been in the dressing room with Shaunte. She said if I hadn't been involved, I would have told her, and that not telling her meant I was just as guilty as Shaunte. We had to go back into the store and tell the owner what we did, but I was angry and refused to say anything because I hadn't taken anything. The owner told my foster mom that she was only allowed to come back in if she went by herself; Shaunte and I were never allowed to step inside again or they'd call the police.

And now my foster mom was about to drop me off for my first day of Seventh-Day Adventist private school because of it. I was introduced to the class when I entered, which had about twenty students already, from third grade to fifth grade. Everyone stared at me, their heads turning to follow me as I found my seat, and I thought I was going to be sick.

When we stopped for lunch, I couldn't remember a single word the teacher had said from the morning; I'd barely managed to not cry or throw up. I followed everyone to the lunchroom, though I had to pee. Looking around, I didn't see any signs for a bathroom and the teachers hadn't told me where one was when I arrived.

"Excuse me," I said to the girl standing in front of me, after a deep breath to gather my courage, but there was no response. I tried again, louder, but she ignored me, continuing to talk to her friend.

I started to panic because I had to go so badly that I couldn't hold it, but I was too afraid to get out of line to look for one. My chest contracted as I tried to hold in a sob, and when that happened, my bladder released and pee started running down my leg. My eyes widened and my breath stopped; I couldn't remember ever having peed my pants in public. The warmth kept flowing, though I tried to will it to stop, and my head darted from side to side as I searched for some sign that someone noticed. By the time I was done, it seemed no one had even looked in my direction. Glancing down, I realized you couldn't tell that my pants were wet, the thick corduroy hiding the tell-tale moisture, and my boots were holding what hadn't been absorbed by my pants. My socks and feet were soaked, but at least no one knew.

february 1994

I usually played alone during recess. The rest of the kids would be playing four-square or were engaged in a soccer scrimmage I was never allowed to participate in, while I played alone on a set of parallel bars that were about three feet off the ground. I would jump and straighten my arms, holding myself up on one of the bars and then with a grand swing of my feet, flip forward, my belly as the fulcrum for me to spin.

I couldn't quite make the full circle, though, and after a while hopped back down to my feet, breathing hard. Thinking back to watching the more advanced gymnastics classes from the camp I went to over the summer with Ella, I hopped up and tried again.

After several more attempts, each one closer to completing the circle, though not quite making it, I hopped back down and stood with my hands on my hips, warming in my jacket pockets, as I caught my breath. It was cold outside, though aside from my nose and hands, I was warm—my cheeks were hot, even. As my exhales created white puffs in front of my face, I surveyed the rest of the playground and playing fields, watching the other kids. Almost all of them were friends already and had known each other since they were in kindergarten. There was one girl they didn't talk to very much—Rochelle—but they were still friendlier to her than to me. Most of the time, they just pretended I wasn't even there.

My shoulders raised up with my next breath, a deep one, and fell as I sighed it out. *Oh well.*

Ducking under the first bar, I popped up between the two bars and jumped to rest my weight on my straightened arms again. This time, I wanted to do a fancy backward dismount I'd seen the other older gymnasts do. I'd rock backward, swing my feet up and over my head into a back flip, except that I would let go part way through and land on my feet, standing.

I started swinging my dangling feet back and forth together to build some momentum and felt I was getting close. *One...two...three!*

Disoriented, I started coughing and sputtering—it felt like there was no air in my lungs. Blinking back the tears that were freezing my face, I realized I was on my back under the parallel bars. *I guess I fell.* I sat up and looked around as I continued trying to drag air into my lungs, but I couldn't see any of my classmates. Or my two teachers. In fact, there wasn't anyone outside—I was completely alone. *How much time has passed?*

My legs wobbled as I pushed my way unsteadily to my feet and made my way to the back doors into the building. When I stumbled into the classroom a moment later, I was still wheezing a bit, my chest not yet recovered from having the wind knocked out of me. My teacher startled when I entered, asking me where I'd gone, her eyes narrowed in irritation.

I was confused by her question—I hadn't gone anywhere. I'd never come inside. I realized as she stared at me, waiting for me to respond, that no one—not my teacher or her assistant or any of the twenty-something other kids in my class had noticed my absence.

Mumbling an apology, I walked to my desk, removing my jacket and hanging it over the back of my chair as quickly as I could. My teacher's voice started in the background as she turned to the blackboard, but I wasn't listening to her. Instead, I stared at the woodgrain on my desk. Why was I even there? No one wanted me in that class; the kids and teachers didn't even notice me most of the time and weren't friendly when they did. My sister hated me, and my parents didn't want me. My foster mom threatened to send me away whenever we fought. I didn't have any friends. I was an orphan who—at best—was an inconvenience to everyone around me.

What's the point in being alive? No one would even notice if I wasn't. Maybe I should just kill myself.

april 1994

It was a beautiful, sunny day; blue sky, few clouds, the warmth from the sun chasing away the early spring chill that lingered in the air. The ground was soft under my feet as I followed my classmates toward the track for our physical fitness testing.

Rochelle bumped her shoulder into mine, wearing her characteristically large and goofy grin around her thick-rimmed glasses. "I'm going to be the slowest person out there, don't worry."

I'd confessed to her that I wasn't very fast and knew everyone would laugh at me. Looking sideways at her, I grinned back. "No, *we* will. I'll run with you."

I didn't understand why they even made her do the tests. Rochelle— my only friend at the private school—had an inoperable brain tumor. She said the doctors told her it messed up her hormones, so it stunted her growth, meaning she was the shortest person in our class and the only person shorter than me, and also made her develop breasts before anyone else. She'd always gone to the private school, so the other students knew her but only sometimes included her.

We'd become friends not long after the day I fell off the parallel bars; she'd just started coming over to talk to me during recess, always with the same huge smile. At first, I'd answer her if she asked me a question, but that was it; I didn't understand why she was talking to me. But one day she'd started whispering into my ear about how one of our classmates, Marc, thought he was going to win the World Cup one day after he tripped over the soccer ball and fell when he was showing off and I'd laughed so hard I snorted. After that, I was always by her side.

I didn't understand why she always seemed so happy when the rest of our classmates had ceased including her in games when we became friends, but when I asked her, she just shrugged and said she didn't care. Every time she did that, I was fascinated and stared at her, trying to figure out her secret to not being bothered by everyone else.

A few weeks before the fitness test, I'd been really worried about her after she was gone for a few days, not to mention missing my only friend there, but I didn't have her phone number. The teachers didn't seem to be surprised that she was gone and said she'd be back when she was feeling better, but that didn't make me any less worried.

When she had returned—smiling like she always did—she'd looked different. Tired. She had circles under her eyes and she wasn't quite as chipper as normal. When I'd asked her if she had the flu or something, she'd laughed.

"No," she'd said. "I have a brain tumor."

My heart had stopped. "You're kidding, right? Was that a joke?" It must have been—she was so cavalier.

She shook her head from side-to-side. "Really."

"So... what, then? You'll have surgery or something to take it out?"

"No, they can't operate on it."

"Oh. So, it's like... just there, but not hurting anything."

She smiled. "No, it's getting bigger. They can't do anything about it. It's just going to get bigger. In a few years, I'll die from it. If I'm lucky, my doctor says I'll live to be twenty."

I stared at her in disbelief. But I could tell she wasn't lying to me.

"It's okay, though. Sometimes I don't feel well, which is why I missed school. But most of the time, I'm fine. My doctor said that will change, but for now I should just be a kid and do kid things while I can."

Okay? No, it's not okay! I screamed in my head. She kept smiling at me, waiting for me to accept what she'd just told me, but I was speechless.

Suddenly, I'd understood her secret: she wasn't bothered by what other people thought because she was too busy trying to enjoy life while her tumor allowed her to live and play. I admired her, though at the same time, I was heartbroken. My friend was dying.

rhoda's favorite game

"As a survivor of abuse, I would do anything, would endure anything, if only I could protect another from being subjected to those same experiences."

-Katherine Turner

june 1994

"Another little girl is coming to stay with us for a while," my foster mom said. "Her name is Rhoda. I knew her before I met you girls. She's a couple of years older than you, Katherine."

My sister and I nodded. I hoped she wasn't like Shaunte, who'd thankfully gone somewhere else. My stomach turned as I remembered what my sister had told us the day Shaunte left: the entire time she lived with us, she peed on mine and my foster mom's toothbrushes every morning. My sister had caught her doing it the first time and Shaunte promised never to pee on my sister's toothbrush if she didn't tell us, so my sister had kept the secret until Shaunte left. I hated her for doing that—I felt so betrayed that she kept that kind of secret, knowing I was brushing my teeth with Shaunte's pee every day.

"Do you have any questions before she comes?"

We were sitting on the sofa and I looked around the room, thinking. "Why is she coming here?"

"She has a very tough home life with her mom."

"She doesn't have a dad?" I asked, feeling an immediate kinship with the girl I'd never met.

"Her dad isn't really in the picture," my foster mom replied. "And her mom is... abusive. She beats Rhoda. So does her mom's boyfriend. Her mom's boyfriend has also... touched her kind of like how you were touched, Katherine."

132

I nodded, a wave of nausea passing over me at the reminder, my entire body suddenly enflamed and my heart racing. In my mind, I pictured Elmer touching someone else the way he'd touched me, and I wanted to punch him in my vision, save the other little girl by telling him to do it to me instead.

"When is she coming?" my sister asked.

"I think this weekend. I have to talk to her mom again. This isn't through Social Services like it is for you girls. Her mom refuses to do that, and she'll only let her come here if we have our own agreement." My foster mom paused and took a deep breath. "Rhoda has been in situations and seen things you girls haven't. She can have a bit of a temper, but some stability should help—you kids are resilient."

I nodded again. "I hope she never goes back after she comes."

july 1994

"Hi, Daddy!" I shouted into the phone receiver with excitement. We hadn't heard from our dad in months, and it had been even longer since we'd seen him. He'd only visited once more after that first time we saw him at McDonald's, almost a year ago.

"Your grandma died," my dad's sad voice came over the receiver in response to my greeting. "A few days ago."

"Grandma Virginia?" I asked.

"Yeah. She got sick and never got better."

"I'm sorry, Daddy," I said quietly. I was sad that my grandmother had died, but I was even more sad that I could tell how upset my dad was.

"I can't talk right now, but I wanted to call and tell you that your grandmother is dead. I'll call another time, okay?"

"But... but..."

"I can't talk. I love you girls."

I wanted to respond, but already heard the click indicating he'd ended the call. I glanced up from where I'd been staring at the floor into my sister's expectant face—she'd been waiting to talk to our dad, and I had to tell her that he'd hung up first.

august 1994

"Let's play house," Rhoda suggested.

My heart started racing as I looked up at her from my book. "No, I don't want to."

"Me, either," my sister chimed in.

"Come on, let's play," Rhoda said with a grin.

She may have been smiling, but I wasn't fooled. She didn't really mean house, not like my sister and I used to play. We *hated* Rhoda's version of it. I shook my head from side to side.

"Yes," she said, the air suddenly charging with anger.

I knew I had two choices, though they both arrived at the same destination: I could agree and play her game, or I could refuse, and she'd beat me up until I played her game.

"Why don't we do gymnastics—you can help me do walkovers?" I tried.

"No, we're playing house."

Our roles were the same every time we played her version of the game. Rhoda was always the dad or boyfriend, and sometimes she would even dress up, putting together more masculine clothing combinations, and she always spoke with a deeper voice once the game began. I was always cast as the mom or girlfriend, and I was sometimes directed to wear a dress. And if I couldn't talk Rhoda out of it, my sister played my daughter.

The game almost always started the same way: I was doing something like cleaning or cooking while Rhoda waited in another room so she could achieve a realistic element of surprise when she suddenly came barreling in, yelling obscenities and detailing how worthless I was. But I never knew precisely how the next phase of the game would unfold.

Sometimes she would grab me by the arm or hair and shove me toward wherever the closest bed was located. Once I was on the bed, Rhoda would give me specific instructions on what I was to do next. Most often, she would throw me around on the bed as she resumed her constant stream of abusive language and began tearing at my clothes. She would demand I do something and then begin to force me immediately after the words left her lips—she'd made it clear the first few times we played this game that I was always supposed to resist and fight back against her, rather than do what she was demanding. The penalty if I didn't was her hurting me more.

She would call me names like "slut" and "whore," say things like, "You like that, don't you?" and rub at my crotch with her fingers or lick and bite my nipples. At some point, she almost always pinned me down by my arms and humped me, sometimes with clothes, sometimes without, reminding me that I needed to try to fight her off. Other times, I was forced to do those same things to her, and I was instructed to moan—loudly and frequently. There were other days when the acting wasn't quite real enough, though, so the violence had to be ratcheted up a notch until I had tears spilling from my eyes and real cries of pain escaping my lips.

My foster mom didn't know anything about Rhoda's game—I wasn't sure if she'd believe me even if I told her. She was always telling us to figure out how to get along and that she wasn't going to solve our disputes. No matter how many times I tried to tell on Rhoda for hitting us when she didn't get her way, Jean refused to listen.

I hated the game, and I *hated* Rhoda when she made us play it, but I couldn't help wondering if she was only forcing us to do the same things she'd been forced to endure, and the thought filled me with sadness. I worried that, if I told my foster mom and she believed me, Rhoda might have to go home, and I knew horrible things happened to her there. I decided I'd much rather play her game than make her get sent away. But that didn't mean I wanted to play if I had a choice.

"Come on, Rhoda," I started, my eyes darting around as I scrambled for ideas. "We don't like that game. We can play a board game, or ask Jean if we can watch a movie? Or... or... we could—"

"No! I want to play house!"

Rhoda lunged onto my bed as my sister scurried around her and ran down the steps.

"Stop it!" I shouted, trying to push her off, deciding I'd rather fight than play her game again.

"Shut up!" she yelled, her fist darting forward.

I'd known the hit was coming and turned my face, leaning away as far as I could with her on top of me, so her knuckles hadn't hit my cheekbone full on; it still hurt, but it could have been worse. I tried to snake my arms to the same side, thinking I might be able to use them to push her sideways and then jump off the other side of the bed. Just as I started to push, her fingers closed around my escaping wrist and pulled, pinning it down against the mattress. Her other hand wrapped around my other wrist and I knew there was no hope of escaping; she was much bigger and much stronger than I was. I kept struggling anyway as she pinned my hands down to the mattress and started roughly humping me.

"Oh yeah," she said, her voice now altered to the deep voice she used for her game. "That's it, I like it when you fight me, you know it makes me hard."

"GET OFF OF ME!" I screamed at the top of my lungs.

"Keep screaming. I know you really like it," she replied.

"I HATE YOU!"

"Shut the fuck up, ungrateful bitch," she replied.

One of my hands was suddenly free and I moved to shove at her shoulder, but I hadn't been quick enough. Before I could push her away, I screamed out in pain; she was squeezing and twisting my nipple through my shirt with her fingers.

"That's what you get," she said, her hips still humping me roughly as she pulled harder on my nipple. "Shut the fuck up and take it."

In a fit of frustration, I growled and tried to push her off anyway, though I knew it was useless and it only made her pull harder on my nipple until I dropped my arm, tears streaming down my temples as my body bounced under hers.

"Take your clothes off."

I wanted to argue, but didn't see the point, letting her grab my shirt and yank it off so hard it jerked my head when it got caught under my chin.

"Fight me!" she demanded as she grabbed the waistband of my pants.

I bucked half-heartedly as she pulled down my shorts and panties, her fingernails leaving long red scratches on the outsides of my legs. Once she had my pants off, she climbed over me and pinned my wrists down again, then rammed her knee between my legs.

"OW!" I shouted, more tears squeezing out as I closed my eyes.

"Oh yeah," she said, her knee ramming into me again and again.

*****

That night, I gritted my teeth and clenched my jaw tight, seeing Rhoda over me as I rammed the colored pencils inside me, though her face shifted into Elmer's, then Terrence's, and then back again as I cried into my pillow. I'd told myself I wouldn't use those colored pencils anymore, but I always had nightmares after Rhoda's game, and sometimes if I hurt myself enough, it helped.

What's wrong with me?

136

words and more words

"Every secret of a writer's soul, every experience of his life, every quality of his mind is written large in his works.

-Virginia Woolf

december 1994

We'd been above the clouds for at least twenty minutes. My nose had been glued to the cold glass of the tiny window since we'd taken off, barreling down the runway as I fought to keep my head from resting back against my seat in order to watch the ground blur by while we picked up speed—I'd never been in an airplane. My sister, my foster mom, and I were flying to Florida to spend Christmas with Grandma and Grandpa; we'd agreed that I would have the window seat on the way out and Laurel would have it on the way back.

"Can you still see anything?" my foster mom asked from her aisle seat.

I looked from the window toward her and shook my head. "Not anymore. It's like an ocean made of clouds."

"Ah," she said, her fingers moving her knitting needles rapidly.

I watched her needles move for a moment as she looked down and counted under her breath. She'd taught me to knit like her months earlier, but I'd given up on it—it was so tricky. I tried as hard as I could to do a good job, but I ruined it just like everything else. My scarf had varying widths and big holes from where I dropped stitches without realizing it. Jean had said it was a great first scarf, that learning to knit isn't easy and just takes practice, but when I'd looked at it, I'd just wanted to cry and throw it away. Her eyes lifted as she stopped counting, flitting over me, pausing on my sweatshirt. Her lips pursed slightly and her brow creased.

137

"What a trip that was," she sighed with a shake of her head, nodding at my shoulder. "You were simply impossible! I almost sent you back, you know."

Glancing down, I gazed for a moment at the big black grease stain that wrapped up over the shoulder of my sweatshirt—the same one I'd been wearing when she'd slapped me and dragged me to the car on the ferry in Canada. I nodded, wanting to erase that memory and wishing she wouldn't bring it up every time I wore the sweatshirt, one she wouldn't let me get rid of as long as it still fit. "I know," I said, looking down at my lap.

I could hear her sigh again as she looked down at her knitting and started counting the stitches she'd finished while we spoke. "Oh, damn," she muttered, undoing the last few stitches.

Turning, I looked back out the window, but nothing had changed. A quick reach forward and the tray popped down from the back of the seat in front of me. From the little bag I'd put in the seat next to me, I dug out my pencil and a little green steno notebook, which had a beat-up cover and was missing several pages. Jean had given it to me prior to our departure when I'd asked for a notebook to write a story. She'd told me to choose from her collection of leftover notebooks; she didn't toss them once they were used until there were no longer any clean pages.

Flipping past the first few pages that I'd filled while we were waiting to board the airplane, I read the last few paragraphs I'd written. The words washed through my mind, erasing my surroundings and replacing them with the scene in my story. Tipping my head back, I closed my eyes and thought about what should happen next to get me closer to how I knew I wanted it to end. Once I saw it all in my mind, all my characters interacting and talking like I was watching part of a movie, I opened my eyes and began to write.

*****

"I want to go to the poooooooooooooool," my sister whined next to me.

"Shhhh—be quiet!" I hissed at her, my pencil moving feverishly across the page.

Laurel wanted to go swimming, but she wasn't allowed to go alone. I was prone on my belly, the sliding glass doors to Grandma and Grandpa's small backyard and the canal that flanked it directly ahead of me. I wouldn't have minded the fresh air while I was writing, but the previous day, there had been a huge alligator in the yard and I wasn't going to take any chances that another one was out there hiding where I couldn't see it.

"Katherine, come on! I'm bored!"

I looked up, glaring at her. "I don't care. Go ask if you can watch T.V. or something. Or you can read one of the books I brought—they're all in my bag."

"Jean said I can't watch T.V. until I read something."

"Then go read something!"

"I don't want to," she whined.

I rolled my eyes. I didn't understand why she was so resistant to reading. Jean's rule was that we couldn't watch anything on television until we'd spent at least thirty minutes reading—then we could have thirty minutes of T.V. I didn't care about T.V. and preferred to read, so the rule didn't bother me at all; Laurel, however, was just the opposite.

"Then ask Grandma or Grandpa for some paper and markers or crayons and go draw or color. But leave me alone—I'm busy right now."

"All you want to do is write in your stupid notebook!"

"It's not stupid!" I screamed at her.

"Yes, it is! You just don't want to wear a bathing suit because you're too fat!" she shouted back at me.

"At least I'm not too skinny!"

"I'd rather be skinny than fat!"

"Girls!" Jean said, walking into the room. "That's enough!"

I glared at my sister, but bit my tongue. *I hate you*, I thought, hoping she could read my mind.

"You guys have been cooped up in here for too long—it's a beautiful day. Go outside."

"I want to go swimming," my sister pouted.

"I think that's a great idea," Jean said.

"Fine, but I want to finish this first," I piped up.

"You've been writing in that thing non-stop since we got to the airport," Jean said. "You can write in it later. But we're here for only a few more days before we go back to winter in Virginia. I want you to get outside, get some fresh air."

"But I'm in the middle of—"

"And it'll be there waiting when you get back," my foster mom interrupted. "Put it away and go outside with your sister for a few hours. Go to the pool and go swimming. Play shuffleboard. Pick oranges from the front yard. I don't care what you do, just do it outside and be back by dinnertime."

"Fine, I'll sit outside to write," I muttered.

"And leave your notebook here," she added.

My sister grinned and skipped away toward the spare room where our bags were as I glared at her back. Why couldn't they understand that I needed to finish my story?

*****

"My, you really are into writing that story," my foster mom said from her seat to my left.

We were on the plane, returning to Virginia after a little over a week in Florida. My sister had the window seat for the trip back, and my foster mom had said that she would only sit in the aisle, so I was sandwiched between them. Not that it mattered—I was focused on my story, finally close to the ending. My steno pad was full, and I'd gotten a handful of old, yellowed, three-hole-punch loose-leaf paper from Grandma that I'd used nearly all of. But I had enough space to finish—I was sure of it. I was nearly there.

"Uh-huh," I said, distracted by the scene in my mind that I was trying to translate into words.

"What's it for again?"

I ignored her question for a moment, finishing my sentence, and then proudly writing "THE END."

"It's not for anything—it's just a story I had in my head." I lifted up the page I'd just finished. "It's done, see?" I said with a grin. Seeing the final words filled me with so much pride.

"Oh, I do," she replied. "What are you going to do with it now?"

"Well," I said, thinking about it as I straightened the loose pages so they were not only in order, but also lined up. "I want to read it and fix anything I messed up, maybe change some of the words to better ones."

"Okay, you're going to edit it."

"Yeah, edit. And then I'm going to give it to Mrs. Jackson." Mrs. Jackson had been my teacher since the start of the school year, for which my foster mom had moved me back to the local public school.

"You're going to give it away?"

"No, I mean, I want her to read it." She'd encouraged me to write when I told her I liked writing things and that sometimes I had stories in my mind that weren't like the ones I read; she was the whole reason I decided to write this one down.

"What's it about?" Jean asked.

I ran through the story in my mind. Casey—the main character—was a few years older than me, fifteen or sixteen. Her dad had disappeared less than a year earlier, but before he left, he used to come into her room almost every night and touch her chest and between her legs and made her promise to keep it a secret. Now it was just her and her mom, but her mom was so upset that Casey's dad had left (and she had no idea what he did to Casey) that she barely talked to Casey; most of the time, she was lying in bed and drinking. Casey didn't have any friends because she spent all her time at home taking care of her mom and everyone thought she was weird. A couple of boys from her grade followed her home from school one day, first talking about wanting to touch her chest and her butt, then chasing her so they could catch her and touch her against her will. They were stopped by another boy from her grade, Mark, who was passing by and started yelling at the other boys, standing between them and Casey and offering to walk Casey home. Casey was too scared of Mark because he was a boy and too embarrassed by her mom to invite him inside when he asked if she wanted to do homework together, and was surprised when he showed up the next morning to walk to school with her. He started walking to and from school with her every day and they became really good friends. He told her he loved her, and she stopped talking to him because she didn't believe him and thought he just wanted to touch her, and she knew she wouldn't be allowed to say no if he was her boyfriend. But he wouldn't let her shut him out and proved that he didn't want to touch her and convinced her that she was always allowed to tell people not to touch her because it was *her* body; that no one should ever touch her if she didn't want them to. She blurted out what her dad used to do to her, sure Mark would leave her and want nothing to do with her because she was so dirty, but instead he refused to leave her alone and stayed with her the whole time she cried. He asked her to marry him and promised to always protect her and she said yes, knowing she'd always be safe with him.

I shrugged. "A girl who... she..." *How do I say I want to be like her?* "I don't know how to explain it."

"That's okay, you don't have to," my foster mom said.

I nodded and then turned back to my story; it was time to start editing.

late january 1994

My heart was pounding with each step—pounding so hard I thought it might knock me over when I was only halfway to her desk.

"Mrs. Jackson?" I asked, my voice sounding feeble and weak.

"Hi, Katherine, good morning!" she said, looking up from what she was writing on her desk, her eyes brightening. Mrs. Jackson always seemed so happy to talk to me; she was my favorite teacher I'd ever had, and it made me sad every time I thought about how close the end of the year was. I'd already asked her if she could move up each year so she could keep teaching me, but she said it didn't work that way, though she was flattered that I wanted her to do that.

"Good morning." I swallowed, squeezing the papers between my hands so hard the paper edges were cutting into my skin. I'd spent the last weeks reading and editing and reading and editing my story—my short novel, complete with chapters—and it was as good as I could make it. I'd thought it was perfect, but now I wasn't so sure. *What if she hates my story? What if my writing sucks?* "Do you remember when I told you I had another story in my head and you told me to write it down?"

"Yes! Did you do that—did you write any of it down?"

I nodded, trying to breathe normally because I felt really dizzy. "I did." Raising my hands, I held the steno pad and now-stapled loose-leaf pages up for her to see. "I wrote all of it down over Christmas break and I just finished editing last night. I was wondering if... hoping... Do you wanna read it?" I finally blurted out.

Her face broke into a broad grin. "I would love to—I'd be honored."

I beamed back in relief, passing her the stack from my hands. "Thank you so much!"

"Thank *you* for sharing with me." She flipped quickly through the steno pad and the stapled pages, then set them down in front of her and looked back up at me. "It looks like you put a lot of work into this."

"I did!" I said excitedly, immediately cringing because I knew I'd said it loudly and could hear my foster mom's voice in my ear telling me not to talk so loudly. My mouth opened to tell her more about all the rounds of editing I did because I was just so excited, but then I closed it because I didn't want to talk too much like my foster mom and Grandma and Grandpa always told me I did.

"Well, I'm very excited to read this and am honored that you want to share something so special with me. I'll start on it this week and will let you know once I've finished."

"Okay," I said quickly, my face feeling like it would split in half from my grin. I wasn't sure how I was going to wait for her to read it, but I knew I had to—excited or not, my foster mom was always telling us that patience is a virtue. And I already knew I couldn't bug her by asking her every day if she was done because then she might not want to read it anymore. I would just have to wait.

mid-february 1994

My foster mom was picking us up from school instead of us riding the bus because she had to be at the school in the afternoon anyway. She would get my sister from the elementary school next door first, then pick me up from the middle school after. That meant I got to hang out in Mrs. Jackson's room for a few minutes after the other kids all got on their buses. When that happened, I usually helped her clean up until my foster mom got there and was planning to do the same thing until Mrs. Jackson called me over to her desk.

"Yes, Mrs. Jackson? I was just going to clean up some," I said as I walked across the room.

"So, honey, I want to apologize that it took me so long to read your story. There have been some unexpected... illnesses at home and I wasn't able to read it right away."

"That's okay," I breathed out, my heart racing in anticipation of what was coming next. "I'm sorry you guys weren't feeling well. Is everyone okay now?"

She smiled at me, but her eyes looked glassy instead of her face lighting up like it normally did; something wasn't right. "Thank you. We'll be okay." She took a slow breath in and let it out just as slowly as she stared into my eyes and I almost turned away under her scrutiny. "Anyway," she started, her eyes sliding away and looking down toward the floor next to her desk. "I finished your story and I wanted to return it to you." She held out my stack of papers and notepad, but her eyes were on the story and not looking at me.

My heart plummeted—felt like it was smushed under an elephant's foot. She hated it, I just knew it. How could I have been so proud of it? "I'm sorry," I said quietly, reaching out and taking the stack from her.

"Why are you sorry, honey?"

"That you wasted time reading my awful story."

"It wasn't awful!" she said, her brows drawing together like she was confused.

"It wasn't?" I asked, unsure if I believed her.

"No, not at all. I could tell you worked very hard on it and I think you did a wonderful job. And I want to thank you again for sharing it with me." She looked up at me briefly and smiled again, but her eyes still looked like they were filling with tears.

"Did you like it, then?" I asked.

She opened her mouth, but then closed it without saying anything, looking down at the floor near her desk again. I'd never seen her act like that, and it was because of my story; it must have been really bad, and she was just trying not to hurt my feelings. Turning, I walked back to my desk to put the story into my backpack.

*****

"Thank you for coming," Mrs. Jackson said to my foster mom. It was a week after I got my story back and Mrs. Jackson had been acting differently toward me ever since. When she smiled, her whole face didn't light up anymore. I was sure my story made her hate me because it was so bad.

They'd told me to go sit and read for a few minutes while they talked, but I couldn't help straining to listen to them as they spoke in low voices. I heard my foster mom say something about my sister and me coming from a difficult situation, something about us being resilient.

Then I heard Mrs. Jackson. "Katherine gave me a story she wrote and I read it... It wasn't... normal..."

She kept speaking, but I heard nothing else, the blood rushing through my ears loudly and drowning out all other sounds. *Not normal.* I'd forgotten that I wasn't normal, that I wasn't like everyone else. *Of course* I couldn't write a good story like a normal person! If my story wasn't normal, what she meant was that it was really, really bad. My eyes burned and my chest hurt, but I willed back the tears.

I resolved that, as soon as I got home, I was going to throw away my no-good story. I shouldn't even write anything else, but I wasn't sure I could help myself—I loved to write. But I definitely wasn't going to share it with anyone anymore if I did.

firsts

"If you have a traumatic experience when you're young, it does fuck you up."

-Ozzy Osbourne

september 1995

"Katherine! It's for you!" my foster mom shouted.

"Coming!" I called back as I looked for a bookmark to mark my place in *Wuthering Heights*.

Must be Ella, I thought. She was the only friend I regularly talked to outside of school. There were a few other girls I was friends with, but we only hung out sometimes, and they didn't really ever call me. The only other person who used to call was Ruth, but I'd drifted away from her— she was too good a person—and she'd stopped calling and inviting me over weeks ago. I missed her, but it was so hard to be friends with her because she was so nice and perfect, and I was always afraid I would screw up or that she'd decide she didn't like me after all. As soon as we would get really close, I'd need to take a break from our friendship.

I picked up the receiver to the rotary phone from the kitchen table where Jean had left it. "Hello?"

"Hi, Katherine."

My eyes widened as my heart started racing. "Dirk?" I was sure it was his voice, but it couldn't be him—he'd never called me. I'd had a crush on Dirk since right after the last Christmas break, but he'd said he didn't like me back.

"So, I want to go out with you."

146

My heart stuttered and my chest strained. "Okay," I breathed out, my face suddenly hot. *I can't believe it—he likes me! He actually likes me!* It was the first time I'd ever been asked out.

"I want you to be my girlfriend."

My mouth flopped open for a moment before I remembered I needed to respond. "Um, yes, okay, I want to be your—"

"But there's one thing you have to do first."

"Okay," I responded quickly, my mind racing to guess what he might be about to ask for. A kiss? A promise not to be anyone else's girlfriend? "Anything."

"You have to give me a blow job at the movies this weekend."

Blow job... blow job... isn't that...? "A blow job?" I asked. I was pretty sure that was oral sex, but maybe I was confused.

"Yeah, I want you to suck my dick in the movie theater."

I laughed, shifting my weight as my body started to feel hot. "*Right.*" I shook my head—he'd gotten me with that joke.

"I'm serious. If you don't promise to give me a blow job, we're not going to the movies. And you're not my girlfriend until you do it. If you really like me, you'll do it."

"Dirk..." I started breathlessly. "You want me to-to-to do *that*, and do it somewhere public?"

"That's the deal if you want to be my girlfriend."

Time slowed as I thought about it, trying to imagine myself bending over his crotch in the movie theater and putting his penis into my mouth. My stomach churned and my throat burned with stomach acid. *That's disgusting.* And in the movies? My foster mom knew *everyone* in the town— literally, like *everyone*. Someone would see and they would tell her, even if I could make myself do it. She'd send me away, I knew it. And we'd finally gotten past what happened on the ferry and almost never fought anymore. I always listened and did my chores and didn't argue—at least not very often. I couldn't jeopardize that. I didn't even *want* to—guys pee out of their penises! Why would I want to put that in my mouth?

"No," I said. "I won't do that. I want to be your girlfriend, but I don't want to do that." I felt guilty for telling him no, like there was something wrong with me, and felt I needed to justify myself. "You know my mom is the county truant officer and school social worker—she knows everyone— someone could see—I can't get caught."

"If you want to be my girlfriend, you'll do it anyway."

My chest ached as my heart beat painfully and my eyes were near to spilling over with tears. "I guess I can't be your girlfriend, then," I said quietly.

The words were barely out of my mouth when he'd hung up. I put the receiver onto the phone carefully, not wanting to draw attention to myself so I could make it up to my room unnoticed and cry alone. Once I reached my bed without incident, I sat on the edge and clutched my sides, trying to squeeze away the pain as I sobbed. I was sure Dirk wouldn't have asked me that if it wasn't for my body. Looking down at my chest—at my already-developed breasts—I hated them. I wondered if I could wrap something around my chest to make it flat again. But what would it matter? The real problem was *me*—breasts and blow jobs were what guys liked from girls, and I was a girl, so I should do what they wanted. What was wrong with me that I didn't want to do that? It wasn't his fault for asking—it was mine for saying no.

october 1995

My face burned as I looked up nervously to make sure the lock on the door was secure so no one could walk in on me. Open in front of me was the period starter kit my foster mom had bought for me with an information booklet and a few of every kind of pad or tampon imaginable. I hadn't understood what you did with the tampons, and had almost blacked out from not being able to breathe when my foster mom had said, "You place it into your vagina." Just the mention of that body part from someone else was too much—even from a woman. I'd thrown my hands over my ears and told her I couldn't talk to her about those things as she shook her head and rolled her eyes at my "dramatics."

It had been bad enough when I'd told her I'd gotten my first period. Luckily, there hadn't been much blood. In fact, the spotting almost escaped my notice since it wasn't an unusual occurrence, thanks to the colored pencils. It wasn't until I remembered that it had been weeks—maybe even months—since I'd used them that I realized the blood spots must be from my first period. I thought girls didn't get them until they were older, but then reasoned it wasn't that strange for me—I also already had breasts, unlike most of my peers.

My foster mom hadn't believed me when I told her I'd gotten my period and asked her to tell me what to buy; not until I'd pulled down my panties and shown her the bright red little dots in the crotch. I'd thought I was going to die of embarrassment when she leaned closer, her face not far enough away for my comfort.

"What?" I'd asked rudely, fine with getting in trouble for having an attitude if it meant she stopped looking at my panties.

She shook her head slightly and sat back, looking up at me. "Nothing—it just looks like there's some old blood spots on there, too, that have stained. I don't think this is your first time spotting."

I'd felt like I was going to die of mortification when she'd said that, my brain scrambling around for some way to explain away the old blood spots without telling her what really caused them. When I came up short, I decided on attitude.

"Whatever," I said, rolling my eyes. "Like I wouldn't know the first time I got my period."

She looked at me sharply with her eyebrow raised; I knew it was the precursor warning for my behavior and my body slumped a bit in relief—I'd successfully distracted her.

But that embarrassment would be *nothing* compared to what I'd feel if someone walked in the bathroom door at that moment; I was naked from the waist down, squatting over a hand mirror, a tampon in hand as I tried to make sure everything was aligned the way it was in the picture in the little booklet. When I thought I had everything lined up correctly, I tried to insert the tampon, but it was resistant.

Of course, I thought. *Why would my body work normally?* I shifted and reset and pushed until I got the thing inside me and yanked back the applicator triumphantly. *I didn't need anyone's help!* But when I stood up, it was painfully uncomfortable. Grabbing the booklet, I read through the tampon section again and realized I might not have it in far enough. Following the instructions, I used a finger to push it in a bit further until the discomfort was more manageable.

But then I was stuck staring at my finger. There wasn't really anything on it, but I knew where it had just been. *In there—down in there.* The only other things that had ever been *in there* were my broken colored pencils and... *Elmer.* That meant I'd just done to myself what he had done to me. Did that mean I'd secretly liked what he'd done? I stared at my finger, disgusted by it and wishing I could just cut it off and throw it away—it was a kind of dirty that couldn't be undone because it had been *in there. In my...* I couldn't even think the word my foster mom had used so casually.

Careful not to touch anything with that hand, my heart beating slowly and painfully as my skin began to feel really tight and hot, my breathing labored, I took the two steps to the sink. Turning on the faucet with my other hand, I held my tainted finger under the stream of water and grabbed the bar of soap from the soap dish. I scrubbed a thick lather over my finger and rinsed, but I could still remember where it was. When it was soaped up the second time, I grabbed my foster mom's nailbrush and scrubbed until my finger was red and raw. I could still remember, could still feel Elmer, but it was the best I could do without severing my finger entirely.

Sighing and avoiding looking at my hand, I got my lower half dressed; I wasn't sure I'd ever be able to use a tampon again.

*****

Walking into the lunchroom, my eyes scanned for a place to sit and stopped when they found Ruth. She was sitting with some other girls in our grade—girls she'd been friends with since before I'd moved there. There wasn't space for me to sit, but I decided to walk over anyway. I'd missed her a lot over the last weeks, and I realized right then that I desperately needed her friendship. Maybe this time I could keep myself from pulling away from her?

"Hi, Ruth," I said as I approached.

"Hi, Katherine," she replied.

"I was wondering what you're doing this weekend," I started. "I'd like—"

"You can't just be a friend when it's convenient," one of the other girls interrupted me loudly. Her eyes were narrowed and her jaw clenched like she was going into battle, and everything inside me froze, unsure what was happening. "It's not fair that you think you can come and go from a friendship with her. You're either her friend or you aren't."

The silence over the table was thick as I stared at the girl, paralyzed aside from the tears filling my eyes. I was trying to will them back, but I was struggling to control them over the sickening pain in my chest and nausea in my stomach. I realized she wouldn't have said that unless Ruth had been hurt by my coming and going in her life. It had never occurred to me that she'd really *want* me around or like me enough to miss me when I took a break from our friendship. I never wanted to hurt anyone—least of all Ruth. I'd always been afraid of screwing something up and it seemed

I'd done it. I wanted to believe I'd never back away from her again, but I knew it was something I couldn't be sure of. She deserved so much better than that from a friend...and I deserved so much less than her.

I nodded at the girl and said, "You're right." I turned toward Ruth, but I couldn't look her in the eye; instead, I stared at the floor in shame. "I... I'm sorry," I said. And then I turned around and walked away. For the first time since I'd met her, I was going to do the right thing.

love and friendship

"When I first met you, I honestly didn't know you were gonna be this important to me."

-Anonymous

october 1995

"I can't stand her! She's so stuck up!" I shouted at the dinner table to my foster mom.

"You don't have to yell, Katherine," she said. "I'm sitting right next to you."

"I know, I'm just... ugh! All the girls just think they're better than everyone else. Their dad is nice, but they're stuck up."

"They are," my sister chimed in. "Lynn is the worst."

"No worse than Janey and Mae," I said.

"Okay, okay, that's enough complaining, girls," Jean said. "You've been complaining about them after every practice and every game."

"They think just because they came from Northern Virginia that they're better than everyone else."

Jean studied us for a moment. "You know, maybe you guys are jumping to conclusions about—"

"Not possible!" I interrupted.

"—those girls. Maybe they're just nervous. They just moved here, they don't have any friends, they don't really know anyone. Maybe they're really nice and just *seem* stuck up because they don't know how to fit in?"

"Mm-mm," I said, my head shaking from side-to-side. Glancing over, I saw my sister was doing the same thing. "Not possible."

"Really? Not possible? Are you sure?"

I rolled my eyes. "Okay, anything's possible, but it sure isn't likely."

"I have an idea," Jean started, looking at us both in turn, then continuing. "How about you invite the girls—the ones your ages—to go to Baltimore with us this weekend?"

"No!" my sister and I shouted together.

Jean held up her hand. "Just hear me out. I understand you don't like them. But it seems to me that it's ruining soccer for you guys. If you invite them to spend the weekend with us, maybe you can all figure out how to get along well enough to enjoy playing soccer on the same team again. I'm sure Sue and Andy won't mind—they have plenty of space—and I'm sure we can get a couple of extra tickets to the ball game. What do you think?"

"Fine," I said, realizing the idea had merit; I didn't want to keep being mad after soccer all the time.

"No!" Laurel shouted. "I hate her—I don't want her to come with us!"

"But Laurel," I said. "Jean's right. We don't have to like them, but if we can just get along, won't soccer be more fun?"

She crossed her arms over her chest. "Fine."

january 1996

"Enough giggling! You are disrupting the class, Katherine!" Mrs. Posey said sharply.

Though my face was already warm, I would guess it was now lobster red—it felt like an inferno as I bit the insides of my cheeks to stop smiling. I'd never been called out in a class for being disruptive before, but it had just happened in my first day of band class. As soon as Mrs. Posey looked back toward the front, I released the giggle I was holding in, though I tried desperately to do so more quietly.

I was in the front row with the other woodwind instruments, the other flutes to my left, the clarinets to my right. But there was a boy in the clarinet section I'd never seen, wavy bleach-blond hair down to his shoulders, though the bottom of his head was shaved, and the bluest eyes I'd ever seen in real life. I'd noticed him as soon as I walked in the classroom and he'd noticed me, too. My whole body had felt really hot and the skin on my face was tight like when I got really nervous or scared, though this time I couldn't stop grinning at him.

My eyes kept darting in his direction as I set up my flute and adjusted my music stand, and every time that happened, I found him already looking back, watching me. He started making faces when I looked up:

puffing out his cheeks like a chipmunk as he pretended to play his clarinet once, pretending he also had a flute by moving his fingers as if on a dainty piccolo and wobbling his head back and forth with his lips pursed. He was acting ridiculous, and I knew that, but I couldn't stop looking, and I couldn't keep from laughing at his antics, which continued throughout the entire class period.

"You're gonna get in trouble," Janey laughed as we walked out of class together. We'd become best friends—as did Laurel and Lynn—during that trip to Baltimore my foster mom had suggested. It turned out she'd been right about the girls actually being nice and just being nervous because they didn't know anyone.

"Did you see him? I couldn't help it!" I hissed as I craned my head around to see the boy walking out behind us. "He was acting insane. I couldn't *not* laugh."

"Your cheeks are red," Janey teased. "I think someone's got a crush." She bumped my shoulder with hers.

"No, I don't," I muttered, though I could tell I was blushing again.

"Well, I do," she said, looking over at me. "Do you know Bobby Thomas?"

"Yes," I replied. Until I saw that boy in band class, Bobby had the bluest eyes I'd ever seen, though he had black hair. "He flirts with everyone."

"He's soooooo cute," she said, a dreamy expression on her face.

I rolled my eyes. "Not as cute as that boy in band class."

"His eyes are so blue, though."

"Didn't you see the boy who was making me laugh? His eyes are definitely bluer."

"I don't care," she said quietly, obviously daydreaming as we walked. "Besides, I thought you liked Allen?"

I laughed and rolled my eyes. We'd met Allen, who was a year older, at a three-day band competition right before winter break—he played the trumpet. He also had blue eyes, though not a bright blue, and dirty blonde hair down to his shoulders. He flirted with every girl there, but he was also funny, kind of like the boy in band class. He'd given me his skateboard necklace and we talked on the phone sometimes. I kind of had a crush on him, but I mostly just liked talking to him. "We're just friends, I swear!"

"Suuuuuuuure," she laughed, bumping my hip with hers. "Oh, I forgot," she started suddenly, looking over at me. "I have something to tell you."

"But we're almost late to class."

"I'll write you a note and give it to you between classes."

"Okay," I smiled. "See ya."

february 1996

"Ooooh, let's go sit over there," I said to Janey, pointing across the lunch room. It turned out that Allen and the boy from band class, whose name I'd learned was Joe, were best friends. I was friends with Allen and madly in love with Joe, so that was exactly where I wanted to be.

"But Ella's over there waiting for us," Janey responded.

I glanced in the direction she pointed and waved to Ella—the three of us had become really close and usually sat together. "Okay, but I want to say hi to them first."

As I approached the table where Allen and Joe were sitting with a couple of other boys from our class, my heart started beating rapidly. When Joe looked up and stared at me, I couldn't breathe. I hated the way my body reacted to him, but I felt like I was being pulled toward him like a magnet.

Allen greeted me and we talked for a few minutes in the flirty style that Allen used to talk to everyone, and Joe stayed quiet, just staring at me. I wanted him to say something—anything. Scrambling for something to talk about, I realized he didn't have a lunch tray in front of him.

"Aren't you hungry?" I asked.

"Not for this shit," he responded, his face pinched in disgust.

"Well, you should eat *something*," I said. "How about some fruit? You can have my banana—I had one for breakfast this morning." I nodded my head toward the banana on my lunch tray.

"No!" he shouted angrily.

My heart skipped in my chest and my body flooded with electricity as my vision tunneled. I wasn't sure why he looked so angry that I offered him a banana. My mouth hung open for a moment as I tried to find something to say, but the only thought in my mind was to give him my piece of fruit. Shifting to hold my lunch tray with one hand, I grabbed the banana.

"Come on," I smiled, though my heart was racing uncomfortably, unsure what would happen next. "I don't mind—just take the banana." I extended my arm to hold it in front of him.

Joe's hand darted out and smacked the banana out of my hands. "Are you trying to fucking kill me?"

"I... kill... what? No... I..." I couldn't form a sentence and my eyes suddenly flooded with tears, the skin on my face pulling uncomfortably.

"I'm fucking *allergic* to bananas," Joe spit out, glaring at me.

My stomach contracted and I felt sick. "I didn't know that," I breathed. My mouth hung open for a moment, but I couldn't think of anything else to say. Anger at being accused of trying to kill him when I'd had no idea he was allergic to bananas, guilt that I'd tried to make him take a piece of fruit he was allergic to, and embarrassment at being yelled at in front of so many people—let alone by my crush—warred for prominence as I tried to breathe. Spinning on my heel, I walked over to Janey and Ella, setting down my tray. Without looking at them, I muttered that I had to go to pee and disappeared into a bathroom before the tears fell down my cheeks.

june 1996

An elbow jabbed me in the side and I glanced over to my left. Bobby looked from my eyes down toward his lap, then back up at me. Looking down, I saw that he was holding a folded piece of paper. I knew if we got caught passing notes, we'd get into even more trouble, but I was curious—he was my best friend's boyfriend, after all. Glancing over at the teacher in the small, silent room with us and confirming she wasn't watching, I reached over and grabbed the note from him.

While it wasn't the first time for Bobby, it was the first time in *my* life that I was in In-School Suspension, or ISS, for the day. Even though I'd begged him to stop, Joe continued to do stupid things that made me laugh during band class and I'd gotten into trouble one too many times with Mrs. Posey. So now I was stuck in ISS for the day *and* grounded for two weeks. At least it hadn't happened a few weeks ago; then I would have missed our big field trip to Washington D.C.

I didn't really like going into the city, though we went sometimes to see my foster mom's sister and her family and sometimes to museums. I always got really bad stomach cramps and diarrhea the entire time we were there—but it had been the best field trip I'd ever had. Janey was with me the whole time, and it was the first time I'd been on a field trip and had a friend with me. We'd walked around the reflecting pool between the Lincoln Memorial and the Washington Monument, talking about everything. When we'd gotten back to the Memorial side, we'd sat down and watched couples taking photos together in front of the reflecting pool with the Washington Monument behind them. We'd talked about which couples were the cutest and how long we thought they'd last. We'd agreed that, no matter what, none of their relationships would last as long as our friendship would—we would be best friends until the day we died, no matter what. And then we'd decided to cement it with our own reflecting pool photograph, posing like the couples we'd been watching and laughing like hyenas afterwards.

Careful not to make noise, I unfolded the note from Bobby; he wanted to know what I'd done to get into trouble. I scribbled a response and passed the note back to him. When he responded that he was glad to have someone pretty in ISS with him, I formulated a plan. Bobby was a big-time flirt, but Janey couldn't see it because she was head over heels for him. But I was going to get him to do something unforgiveable on paper so I could prove it to her; I was going to get him to ask me out and say he was going to hide it from her on that note and then give the note to her.

early july 1996

Don't cry. Don't cry. Don't cry. I chanted over and over to myself as I sat at the table in our new backyard patio set. We'd just moved into town from the farm a few weeks ago, and our new house was less than a mile's walk from the park and Janey's house. The last time I'd seen Janey was a few days prior when we'd fought at the park. We'd been fighting ever since that day of ISS.

I'd gotten Bobby to ask me out on the note and make promises about not telling Janey. But then I'd stupidly passed the note back to Bobby when he motioned for it. I figured he wanted to write something else, but instead he just wanted to keep the note; he wouldn't give it back to me. When I'd told Janey, she hadn't believed me, and I no longer had the proof. Then Bobby gave her the note and told her he was exposing *me* when she asked him about it. And Janey had chosen to believe him.

I was devastated. She was my best friend. We'd promised guys would never get between us, and then it was happening. I'd been crying every night for weeks and hadn't even wanted to talk to Joe, even though he called me almost every day. Janey and I had finally agreed that our friendship was over and that we would do an exchange to return each other's belongings at my house, so I was sitting there, waiting for her to arrive. As soon as I realized she was there, I clenched my jaw and summoned my anger to beat back the stubborn tears that wouldn't leave my eyes.

She glared at me and then started flipping through the clothes and jewelry I had stacked, pausing when she landed on her Celine Dion CD in the middle of the pile.

"Do you want to listen to it one last time?" she asked, suddenly looking more sad than angry.

"Sure," I replied with a shrug. I wanted to seem like I couldn't care one way or the other, but my heart was actually racing. "Let me get my CD player."

I hurried inside and returned with my trusty portable CD and cassette player and some batteries. I plopped in the batteries and skipped the tracks until I landed on "Because You Loved Me." By the time the song was over, we were both crying.

"I'm sorry," she said.

I nodded in acceptance of her apology. "Don't do it again?"

She shook her head solemnly from side to side. "No. Never. A guy will never come between us again. I promise."

We hugged and listened to our song a few more times. Then we plotted the most embarrassing way for her to break up with the guy who nearly broke *us* up.

becoming permanent

"Shame is the intensely painful feeling or experience of believing that we are flawed and therefore unworthy of love and belonging."

-Brené Brown

mid july 1996

My mind and heart were both racing as I tried to figure out why my foster mom had sat my sister and me down in the living room, saying we needed to have a family discussion. She smiled—did that mean it was something good? We sat expectantly as she looked at us in turn and my body started to feel heavy, small bolts of that old electricity firing at random.

"You know, I keep thinking back to when you girls first came to me, and it's amazing how much we've all changed since then. You're so incredibly resilient, both of you."

My eyes slid away as she grinned at us proudly, and I cringed before I could stop myself. Why did everyone always call us "resilient"? Our foster family, our social worker, our teachers, our foster mom's friends... they saw me smile and heard me talk about school and watched me make the honor roll and play soccer and flute and piano. They didn't know I cried myself to sleep every couple of nights or about my nightmares or the colored pencils. If they found out, they probably wouldn't call me resilient—my foster mom probably wouldn't look at me with pride anymore, either.

"So, we have a decision to make. As a *family*. It's important that we make this decision together—that it's not just mine."

I perked up and looked up from the floor with curiosity—what kind of decision could this be that we all had to make it together?

159

"I spoke with your social worker. You guys already know they haven't been able to find your mom since Katherine went to court right after you guys came."

I still can't believe I didn't recognize my own mother that day! And I knew she was sick, but why couldn't she just love us enough to try harder? She never once checked in with social services, then she disappeared. Social services had thought for a while that she and Linda might have been in Florida, but they weren't sure. No way she would have done that if she loved us.

Of course, I wasn't sure my dad was any better. The last time I'd spoken to him was the day he called to tell us Grandma Virginia had died. He'd never called again or met the requirements to have a visit with us again. Our social worker told us he showed up for his checkpoints a few times, but he failed his drug test. Heroin in his urine, she'd said. She'd seemed undecided about telling us that, but Jean had said if we wanted to know, we deserved to have the truth. We knew that he'd then been arrested and gone to prison for using and dealing heroin and cocaine. I could only assume those things meant more to him than my sister and I did.

"Your father, as you know, is incarcerated for drug dealing," my foster mom continued. "Neither of them have met any of the requirements in the plan created for you guys to return to them."

Nope, not even once for my mom, although they told us Linda showed up a few times in her place. I guess Linda loved us more than our own parents did.

"They're starting the process to terminate your parents' rights."

"What does that mean?" I asked.

"It means that you will never be allowed to go back and live with them. If they decided to get clean in a couple of years, you still wouldn't be allowed to go back, or even see them. Their rights to you guys as your parents legally won't exist anymore."

My eyes darted around the walls and ceiling, not seeing anything as I processed this information. "So, it's like they're not even our parents anymore? Like... this is it, we'll never see or talk to them ever again?"

My foster mom's eyes were serious as she nodded. "Yes, that's right."

The heaviness that had settled onto me when I sat down was suddenly lighter and I almost smiled. All I felt for a moment was intense relief; we would never be sent back. *What kind of horrible, worthless person feels relief to get news like this?* I thought with my next breath. *No wonder they didn't love me—I obviously don't deserve it.* As quickly as it had arrived, the relief disappeared, and I just felt sick with embarrassment and shame. *Wait… if there's no plan for us to go back, then where will we go? This home was always supposed to be temporary, just until we went back to our parents.*

"What happens to us, then?" I asked, now staring down at my feet.

"Well, this process will take a while—a year or more for your parents' rights to be legally terminated. In the meantime, social services will make you girls available in the system for long-term placement. Since you already live here and have been here for a while, I can request that your permanent home be with me, and that's what I'd like to do if you girls agree."

"Yes," I said quickly, looking up. "Absolutely. I don't want to go somewhere else."

"Same," my sister chimed in, speaking for the first time.

"Okay, great." Jean paused and smiled at us. "There's one more thing we need to decide and we have some time to make the decision, so you guys can think about it. I can request to keep you girls in permanent foster care, or I can ask to adopt you. But I want the decision to be yours."

"What's the difference?" I asked, my eyes now darting around again.

She explained that with permanent foster care, we would technically still be wards of the state, that we would continue to have regular visits from a social worker—though less frequently—and they would continue to provide her with a stipend. Once we turned eighteen, we would officially be out of the system. Our parents would technically still be our parents, even though they had no rights. When it came time for college, we would be eligible for financial aid as orphans, there would be no expectation of a family financial contribution.

However, with adoption, once the court date was over, social services would no longer be involved in any way. Jean would be our new mom—it would be changed on our birth certificates—and we would have no one designated as our father. For college, we would need to provide family income information and there would be an expectation of financial contribution from Jean.

After she finished talking, she sat quietly, allowing us time to absorb everything she'd said. My eyes continued to flit around as I started a mental list of pros and cons for each option, much the way I had for deciding which parent to live with when I'd been forced to choose. Removing all emotional involvement—what my foster mom, social worker, and teachers called "a remarkable ability to compartmentalize"—it was easy for me to come to a decision about what I thought we should do.

I dreamed of nothing but going to college one day—a good one. My parents hadn't finished high school and I was sure that was why they struggled as much as they did. On the contrary, my foster mom, while not wealthy, lived comfortably after getting a master's degree. Everyone we knew either struggled financially and had no secondary education, or did not struggle and had a college degree. I knew what group I had to be a part of, and that was one reason I worked so hard in school to keep my grades up. My sister complained all the time that I was so much smarter than her and that's why my grades were better, but it was because I did all my work and I never gave up, not that I was all that smart. No, going to college wasn't a question for me—the only question was which one.

Our foster mom worked for the public school system that didn't pay very much, and although she had lived a frugal life, saving for her retirement one day, she was still a single mom who didn't make enough to put us through college. It wasn't even fair to ask her to—she already had her kids who were almost old enough to be my parents. And we weren't *really* her kids—no one should expect her to use her retirement to pay for our college. Even if she did, I'd be limited in where I could afford to go, and I wanted to go to the best school I could. She knew that as well—we talked about colleges a lot already.

"Permanent foster care," I said.

"We don't have to decide today," she replied. "You can take some time to think about it."

"I did. Permanent foster care. If it really doesn't matter to you—"

"It doesn't—you're my kids now, no matter what your birth certificate says."

"Then permanent foster care," I persisted.

"Why do you choose that?" she asked.

"You said we would be eligible for financial aid with permanent foster care that we wouldn't get if you adopted us. I don't want money to stop me from going to the best college I can."

Jean nodded. "Okay." She turned to face my sister. "Laurel? What do you think? You've been quiet through all of this. Do you have any questions?"

"If you adopted us, would we have to change our last name?"

Really? That's what you want to know? I thought, shaking my head. *Who cares!*

162

"Yes. If I adopted you, I'd like you to take my last name. Does that mean you'd like me to adopt you girls?"

Laurel shook her head from side to side. "I just wanted to know. We can do whatever Katherine thinks we should."

"But what do *you* want?" Jean asked her.

Laurel shrugged. "I don't care. Whatever Katherine wants is fine."

"Okay," Jean responded. "If you guys have any other questions, just ask. I won't tell your social worker for a while so you have plenty of time to think about it and make sure this is what you want."

"I won't change my mind," I said quickly. I knew I wouldn't—my foster mom always told me I was obstinate, like a dog with a bone, once I made up my mind about something. But I thought that was better than waffling about everything like my sister did. "I do have a question, though."

"Sure."

"What about our brothers?"

"What do you mean?"

"Like... is this happening for them, too, or just for us?"

"Oh! Your mom's rights will be terminated for all of you. Your dad wasn't actually the legal guardian for your brothers, so there's nothing to terminate there. Your brothers will be available for a permanent placement as well. Though, it will be harder," she added more gently. "It's harder for them to find homes for older kids. Especially kids with behavioral problems."

I looked away, staring through the wall. *Behavioral problems.* That was one way to put it, I supposed. My brothers had been separated a long time ago for fighting constantly with each other to the point of broken bones and needing stitches. That didn't really help, though, even when they ended up in nice families that were nothing like the first families of theirs that we met. Now, James was in a group home because they couldn't find a family willing to take him, and Al was in another home after leaving a psychiatric hospital.

Shivering, I thought back to visiting him there; we'd only gone once and my foster mom had complained about what we saw. Al had been like a ghost. He didn't smile—not even once—even though he'd always had what my foster mom called a "charming grin" at the ready. He was usually happy to see us and gave us big hugs or spun us around, but not that day. He'd sat there, his face blank, responding only occasionally with one-word answers to our questions. We'd asked him if he even knew who we were, and he'd shaken his head "no." In the car on the way home, Jean had explained that he was like that from the medications they put him on, and that he never should have been medicated to that extreme—to the point that he didn't recognize his own siblings. She was furious and said she would see what could be done about it. I'd had nightmares for days about that visit, about my family not recognizing me, about me being drugged up and not recognizing other people.

How was it fair that after everything they'd been through, my brothers still didn't have a home, but my sister and I had lucked out from the start? That we'd only had one home, and now it was going to be our permanent home, while they had lived in more places than I could count on two hands? Why did I deserve it and they didn't? They'd had it harder than me—*they* should be the ones getting a permanent home—not *me*.

the "cool mom"

"A child that's being abused by its parents doesn't stop loving its parents. It just stops loving itself."

-Shahida Arabi

late july 1996

"Stop touching me," I hissed out with a giggle. I was equally flattered by and uncomfortable with Joe's insistent attempts to touch my bare stomach and my bikini-clad butt under the water. We were at a huge man-made lake with surprisingly cold water that had ziplines, slides, and more. It had taken a week to talk Jean into letting me invite Joe to come along with us.

"I can tell you like it," he said, bouncing his eyebrows at me as he reached out again.

"I said *stop*," I repeated, starting to get annoyed. If he didn't quit, I'd never be allowed to invite him again. My foster mom was watching us like a hawk from the picnic table on the shore.

"But why?" he laughed as he lunged after me.

I darted away, simultaneously amused and irritated. "Knock it off, I'm serious," I hissed at him again.

"Hey!" my foster mom shouted from the shore. "Hands above the water only, Joe!"

I glared at Joe. "I told you to stop—now you might not be allowed to come with us again."

"But you like it," he persisted.

"What makes you think that?" I asked, exasperated.

"Because your nipples are hard," he replied, staring at my chest.

I glanced down at myself, then crossed my arms, my face on fire. Unable to look him in the face anymore, I instead looked out over the lake. "Stop staring at my chest! They're hard because I'm cold, dummy."

"What?" he asked, his brow scrunched in confusion.

"They get hard when you're cold, too—not just when you're..." I trailed off, searching for words while being monumentally uncomfortable with our conversation.

"Turned on?" he asked.

"Yeah, that. It's usually because you're cold. You didn't know that?"

"No," he said, suddenly sounding angry. "My mom only told me your nipples are hard when you're turned on." Neither of us spoke for a moment, the silence growing more uncomfortable with every heartbeat. "I need a cigarette," he muttered.

"You smoke?" I asked, incredulous, as I turned to face him again.

"Yeah."

"That's so gross!" Just the thought of cigarette smoke turned my stomach and I envisioned my dad's face in front of me, his half-smoked cigarette hanging out of his mouth and bouncing around as he talked, the end held in place by his teeth. I smelled the stale cigarette smoke in his mustache and on his breath when he kissed me goodnight. Shaking my head slightly to clear the memory, I refocused on Joe, hoping he hadn't said something I'd missed because I wasn't paying attention. "How do you get cigarettes anyway?"

He shrugged. "My mom buys them for me."

"*What*? Your mom?" I balked.

"Yeah. My mom's not like other moms—she's cool."

early august 1996

It turned out Allen, Joe, and I all had birthdays within a week of each other; Joe's was the first of August, Allen's the second, and mine was the seventh. And even though I'd just turned twelve a few days earlier, I was antsy to be thirteen like Allen and my friend, Sarah, who was waiting at my house with me for Joe's mom to pick us up. Sarah, Allen, and I were all going to spend the day at Joe's house up in the mountains, and I was going to be the youngest person there.

An enormous, old black car pulled into the driveway and Sarah and I looked at each other excitedly—Joe was my boyfriend, and she had a crush on Allen. A woman with red hair was behind the wheel and I knew that must be Joe's mom. Joe was in the front seat and Allen was already in the back.

"That's the biggest car I've ever seen," I said to Sarah as we walked toward the car.

"I know," she replied, laughing. "It's huge!"

"Well, you must be Katherine," the woman with red hair said. "I'm Joe's mom, Jan Ludwig. My other kids call me Mrs. Ludwig, but that makes me feel old. You can call me Jan."

"Hi, Jan," I said. "Nice to meet you." I looked over at Joe. "Hi," I said, blushing and quickly looking away under his intense gaze. "I didn't know you had any siblings."

"I don't," he laughed. "Mom's a teacher. She's talking about her kids from school."

"Oh," I said, feeling stupid as my face leapt into flames.

Sarah and I climbed into the back seat as Jan backed out of the driveway. I sat quietly, listening to everyone else talk as well as I could over the sound of the wind rushing in through the open car windows. As we approached town limits, Jan turned off the small highway onto the main road that led over the mountain toward where they lived.

The voices around me faded out as I looked out the window; I'd never been on that road before and it was beautiful. To the right were large fields and the main river in our valley, to the left were small homes with large plots of land, and up ahead were mountains. Behind the mountains was a bright blue sky with soft white clouds. The inside of the car was hot from the humid August day, but the wind coming through the window was relaxing and freeing.

"Fuck you, you little shit!" Jan's voice rang out, bringing me back to the happenings in the car. She'd been exchanging flirty banter with Allen since we'd pulled out of my driveway, and this line had been directed to him as well, accompanied by her giving him the middle finger.

Allen laughed and so did Jan, and the conversation continued, though I couldn't hear most of it. The last words I caught before they all started laughing was Jan saying something about a pearl necklace. I smiled, desperately not wanting to look stupid, while my brain raced and scrambled in an effort to figure out why everyone else was laughing. No matter how hard I tried, though, I couldn't figure out what was so funny, and decided to swallow my fear of looking stupid and ask.

Jan's laughter was mocking, her giddy tone asking, "Are you kidding me with that question? How big of a dumbass can you be?" My face heated with embarrassment as her raucous sounds filled the car and floated out the windows on the breeze. After a long minute, her laughter tapered off and she spoke.

"You use your tits to jack off a guy—you know, squeezing them tight around his dick, like this"—she took her hands off the wheel for a moment to grab her breasts and squeeze them together—"until he—pfffftt—comes all over your neck. It looks like a pearl necklace made of jizz."

The skin on my face was tight and hot, and I felt nauseous. I tried to smile in the few breaths of silence that followed, but it felt like more of a grimace as the words digested and the image she painted flashed through my mind.

"You'd better to learn to like it," she said, looking at me in the rearview mirror, her expression grave. "That's how you get a guy, and you won't ever keep one if you don't do it. If you're going to date my son, you better get used to it now."

I stared at her, paralyzed as my body filled with electricity and my chest tightened, squeezing the air from my lungs.

"Every guy out there wants to come all over your face and your neck—all of them. You didn't know that? You might as well figure out how to like it."

All I could do in response was nod and look back out the window, suddenly feeling cramped in the car that only moments prior had felt so large and comfortable.

I couldn't get out fast enough once we arrived at Joe's house. As everyone stretched and Jan unlocked the front door, I looked around. We'd come up a steep gravel driveway after winding along a gravel road and I couldn't see any neighbors from where I was standing—only trees and a large pond down the hill from the house. I remembered Joe telling me on the phone that they had three acres, and I tried to figure out how far back their property went. After following everyone inside, Jan, Allen, and Sarah started talking about what movie we'd watch and Joe grabbed my hand, lacing his fingers with mine. I didn't really want to be around people—let alone be touched—right then, still uncomfortable from what I'd learned from Jan, but I didn't pull away; it wasn't *his* fault. Tugging on my arm, he pulled me into a room near the front of the small house.

"This is my room," he said, grabbing my other hand and leaning forward to kiss me.

I leaned back. "What are you doing?"

"Kissing you," he replied, leaning forward again.

"But—" I gave him a quick peck in return when he cut me off. "Your mom is right in there."

"I told you, she's cool. She won't care."

My eyes slid away from him and I stepped back; I felt like I couldn't breathe. As I scanned the closet-sized room that barely fit a small bed, I saw some damage on the wall.

"What's that?" I asked.

"What?" he asked, stepping up against me.

I stepped back again. "Stop. What happened to the wall?"

He sighed heavily and looked over. "Oh, that. I punched it."

"You punched the wall? Why?"

He shrugged and looked away. "I was pissed off. I did it when we were arguing on the phone the other day."

"You hit the wall because we were arguing?"

He shrugged again. "I have some anger issues."

No shit, I thought. Though it made sense. We'd stayed up all night on the phone a few times already and he'd told me all about his biological dad, who used to beat him and his mom up until she left him, and now he had nothing to do with Joe. He'd told me about how his step-dad, Dennis, beat him up sometimes, too.

"Joe!" his mom called out, interrupting my thoughts.

"Yeah, mom?" he responded, staring hard at me for a beat, then walking out of his room.

I trailed behind him back to the living room where Allen and Sarah were sitting and sat down with them.

"I want you to clean the litter boxes now," Jan said.

"But mom, I just did them last night, and everyone's here."

"And everyone can leave if you don't go do it right now."

"Why? I'll do it tonight anyway."

"Because I told you to do it now, whether you want to or not."

"What the hell—"

"Don't back-talk me."

"Fine, whatever," Joe muttered, walking out of the room.

Allen and Sarah started whispering to each other as Jan moved around in the kitchen. *Should I go help him? I should probably go help.* Joe returned a few minutes later just as I'd decided to get up and offer to assist.

"It's done," he said, glaring at her.

"Thank you, sweetheart," she said sweetly. "Give me a hug?"

I watched him walk over and they hugged for a moment.

"Can we watch the movie now?" he asked, pulling away from her.

"Sure," she replied, smiling.

I watched as Joe turned around and started toward the living room, but his mom started talking again when he was only a few steps closer.

"Look at those tight buns!" she said.

"Mom!" Joe shouted as Allen and Sarah started laughing.

My face felt hot again, and I wasn't sure what to do. They thought it was funny, Joe seemed angry, and I thought it was weird. *Do moms really look at their kids' butts like that?*

"What?" she said, laughing. "I can't help but notice how nice your ass is. And why don't you show them your abs?"

"Mom!"

"What?" she said again, still laughing. "You've got a nice, tight body—you should be proud. And the cutest little—"

"Mom—stop it!"

"Oh, come on, Joe, I'm your mom! I gave birth to you—I used to clean your little penis and ass, I can talk about them until the day I die."

"I said *stop!*" he shouted louder. I could sense the violence brewing under the surface as he stood there, his face and neck turning bright red and the veins in his arms popping out as he clenched his fists.

"Okay, okay," she laughed. "I'll stop."

Joe turned, sitting down next to me, and Allen leaned over.

"But your buns are just so nice," he whispered.

"Fuck you, Allen," Joe replied, but then they both started laughing. I watched, feeling as if I was in a foreign land as Allen made a few more jokes and Jan set up *Empire Records* for us to watch.

*****

"Can you get the phone, Katherine?" my foster mom called from the front of the house.

I put my book down and got up. "Yes!" I shouted back. Two rings later, I picked up the receiver. "Hello?"

"I need to speak with Katherine," the angry voice on the other end of the line said.

My stomach seized and I tried to place the voice. It sounded familiar, but I couldn't remember doing anything that would make someone angry with me. "This is she," I said quietly.

"What the fuck do you think you're doing dating my son when you're a little bastard child?" the voice shouted at me.

Son... dating her son... it must be Jan.

"I'm sorry," I whispered. "I don't understand."

"Joe told me your parents weren't married when you were born, which means you're nothing more than a bastard. And any children you have will be bastards, too, and you'll all rot in hell because bastards are eternally damned. How dare you date my son when you're a bastard? He's a good, Christian boy, and you? You were born out of wedlock! How *dare* you? You should have enough decency to stay away from everyone—especially my son—and keep from populating the world with more cursed children like you. The devil must be behind you talking to him..."

She continued speaking, but I couldn't hear anything else over the pounding of my heart, the rush of my blood in my ears. My hand was cramping from how tightly I clutched the phone receiver as she continued to berate me for long minutes as I said nothing.

"Stay the fuck away from my son, do you understand?" she yelled so loudly I jumped. And then I heard the tell-tale click of her hanging up.

Even so, I was still paralyzed, unable to move. Tears were running down my cheeks and I felt like I didn't deserve to be alive. I couldn't help that my parents had me when they weren't married; if that meant I was cursed, though, I didn't want to curse anyone else. But it wasn't my fault— how was that fair that I was going to rot in hell for something I had no control over? That was just one more reason—

I jumped when the phone began the tone to indicate there was no one on the other end of the line and hadn't been for some time. Hanging the phone up, I ran to my room and curled into a ball as I started sobbing.

*****

Joe tried to call a lot over the next week, but I was too scared to talk to him after his mom called me. I told him what she'd said and that we couldn't talk anymore. He'd said to forget about what she said, that she'd get over it, that she was just like that sometimes, but I'd refused to talk to him.

Then his mom called me out of the blue about a week later and apologized. She said she was sorry she'd gotten so emotional and yelled at me, but she'd been so worried about her unborn grandchildren that she simply couldn't help herself. That she'd talked to Joe and understood that just because we were dating at twelve didn't mean we'd get married and have children, so I could keep talking to him as long as I went to church and studied the bible and had a good relationship with the Lord.

"It's okay," I said quietly after her bizarre apology. I wasn't sure what else to say. I believed in apologizing when you've done something wrong, but I also felt like I was the one in the wrong for being a bastard and that she shouldn't apologize to me. I understood overreacting when you're worried—I'd done that and seen that happen in my own family enough times—so it made me feel worse that she was apologizing to me for that.

"Well, here's Joe," she said.

"See, I told you mom was sorry," Joe's voice came through the receiver.

I didn't really want to talk; I was dizzy and had a headache. "Yeah... can we talk later, though?"

"Why?" he asked, sounding panicked. "Mom apologized. You can't—"

"I know, I just—"

"—break up with me!"

"I'm not!" I shouted, frustrated with the whole situation and rolling my eyes. He was always so scared I was going to break up with him, so jealous of every breath I took that wasn't spent with him. "I just have a headache, that's all."

"I'm going to my grandparents' house today for a few days—they live in town by the park."

"Really?" I asked.

"Yeah. Well, Dennis's parents—Nanny and the Colonel."

"Okay."

"So, I'll come over later."

"Wait—you can't. I'm going over to Janey's house."

"Cancel with her."

"No," I laughed, though I knew he was serious. "I'm not canceling with her."

"Then I'll come over after."

"You can't," I said, exasperated. "I'll ask Jean if we can go to the park or something tomorrow."

"I can't wait that long. I'll come tonight."

"Tonight? Are you crazy?"

"Crazy about you," he replied.

I laughed and shook my head. "That was beyond cheesy."

"Yeah, but it made you laugh."

"I laughed because it was so bad, not because it was funny."

"But you laughed." There was a heartbeat of silence, and then he spoke again. "So, I'll see you tonight after ten."

"What are you talking about?" I asked, my heart racing. "You know I'm not allowed—"

"After Nanny and the Colonel are asleep, I'll sneak out. They'll never know."

"I am NOT sneaking out of my house, Joe," I said, having trouble breathing and my body on fire. "I don't do stuff like that." *Or smoking cigarettes and pot or skipping class or hitting things like you do...*

"You don't have to. I'll come in."

"What?"

"Your bedroom is on the outside on the other side of the house. I'll use the window."

"No, absolutely—"

"Yes."

"—not!"

"I'll see you tonight."

"No, you—"

"I love you."

"I love you, too," I said quickly, knowing if I didn't reply right away, he would doubt my feelings. "But you can't—"

"I'll see you tonight," he said, and then I heard the click from him hanging up the phone.

alternative use for a common object

"I mastered an alter ego, which I appropriately named 'Face.' Face was amazing. Everything was back to normal in my face world. Face became second nature, almost easy for me to conceal my truths. […] I was hiding behind Face. Regardless of how good Face was, and it was superb, it was completely external. Face became an ironclad barrier to my inside world."

-Rachael Brooks

september 1996

I took a deep breath prior to dialing, trying to separate my emotions from what I had to do, and I felt like my body was coming apart at the seams. I thought back to a painting I'd seen during our family vacation earlier in the summer.

In the painting, there was a young woman surrounded by trees and flowers, but otherwise alone. She was gazing around her with her lips raised in a soft smile, her eyes breathing contentment and peace. I was struck by the stillness in the image—I didn't know what it was like to sit still. I was always on the go—as my foster mom put it—always had something to do or had to find something to do to keep myself busy. I didn't like to let my thoughts wander too much. Even when I was sitting "still," like we did during church, my leg was always bouncing; my hips were shifting; my toes or fingers were tapping; I was chewing the insides of my cheeks, or pushing my lip into my mouth to use my teeth to scrape off skin, or picking at any tiny bump on my skin with my fingernails. I didn't understand stillness in the way that woman in the painting exuded it. It was almost uncomfortable to look at her, my own breathing and motion slowing as I gazed at the painting until I suddenly felt panicked and looked to the side, walking away.

I wondered what it must have felt like to be that woman. As the other end of the line rang, I tried to imagine myself as her, content with stillness, surrounded by nature breathing and growing and dying and cleansing the air all around me, but I couldn't grasp the sense of ease and peace and contentedness I saw on her face. I wanted to walk into the painting with her, ask her how she did it, beg her to teach me.

"Hello?" Joe's voice answered the phone.

"Hi," I said, my voice like steel. *Good.* "We need to talk."

I could hear his intake of breath. "What's wrong?"

"I heard a rumor—"

"It's not true," he interrupted.

"I didn't even tell you what it was, how can you say it's not true?"

"I didn't do it."

I took a deep breath. "I don't believe you." My words felt like a knife splitting my heart in half; I could no longer pretend I *did* believe him now that I'd said I didn't.

He started talking, telling me about how he had been hanging out with Dana—a girl in our grade—and that she was so interested in him, that he couldn't help it. That I hadn't been around and he'd thought I didn't love him anymore.

"How could you think I don't love you anymore? Why?" I demanded.

"You push me away sometimes," he replied. "You don't want me like I want you."

Time froze for a moment, my mind running back in time to when he'd spent those days at his grandparents' house, when he'd first snuck in my window. That night we'd made out, heavily, on my bed, but I'd refused to take my clothes off. The next day, we'd gone to the park, and he'd immediately started making out with me again on a picnic table there. I'd tried to tell him no, that I didn't want to do that in public, but he said if he didn't care, neither should I. He was so insistent that I hadn't known what else to do, and I could see in his face that telling him no destroyed him, so I'd let him put his hand inside my jeans, his fingers inside me. And then he'd shown up again that night in my room, insistent on peeling my clothes off. I loved him, and it hurt him when I told him no, so I'd let him. By the time I was naked, I felt nothing, my whole body numb. I didn't feel his hands on my skin, or anything between my legs when he'd taken both our virginities. He'd said it was an ecstasy he'd never imagined, like being in heaven and I'd smiled so he wouldn't see that I'd felt none of that—he'd think it meant I didn't love him.

I'd never guessed that saying no to sex after that would mean he felt unloved, but it had. But I couldn't go through with it as often as he wanted to—I felt sick to my stomach about it, hated myself after every time he touched me like that. My nightmares of being chased by men who would rip off my clothes once they caught me, putting their hands all over my body while I was pinned down, were back almost every night.

And being away from him to spend time with Janey and Ella meant he felt unloved because I didn't spend every second with him. But I had my friends, I'd known them longer than him, and I wasn't going to give them up for a guy. Besides, he was so intense, I sometimes just needed a break so I could breathe again.

I'd never thought he would betray my trust after the ways in which he'd been betrayed by his father, but he had. Guilt and anger both flowed through me, my body feeling impossibly heavy, and a new sadness squeezed my heart; I felt pain for him.

"But you cheated on me," I whispered. "I told you that I loved you. I told you why I wasn't with you, exactly what I was doing. I told you everything. I told you how important trust is to me, I even told you why. I even told you about my parents! And you had sex with Dana behind my back anyway."

"Please, Katherine, don't break up with me. I'm sorry. I'm so sorry. I didn't mean to, and it didn't mean anything. She didn't mean anything to me—it was just sex. It wasn't like it is with you. I don't love her like I love you. You can't leave me, you—"

"Just stop!" I shouted, my emotional separation finally failing and tears spilling over. I needed silence to think. "You broke my trust," I said a minute later. "I don't think I could ever trust you again."

"You can't do this, Katherine. I love you. I love you."

"Stop saying that! If you loved me, you wouldn't have cheated on me."

"I won't stop because it's true. I love you. I—"

"I can't do this right now. I need to think."

"Wait, don't—"

"Bye," I interrupted and hung up to the sound of his voice shouting from the other end.

The phone rang immediately and I lifted the receiver and hung it back up. After a few more calls, I took the phone off the hook so he would get a busy signal, and then I curled up into my bed and cried.

After a few hours, I knew I couldn't stay with him. It was pouring down rain, but I didn't care—I decided to walk over to his grandparents' house to do the final break up in person. I told my foster mom I was going to walk our relatively new, rambunctious young spaniel, Cookie, and then asked my sister to come with me. We didn't talk to each other very much—it was guaranteed to turn into a fight if we did, so we just avoided each other—but I needed someone there to make sure I didn't cave. I told Laurel I was walking over to break up with Joe and needed her to make sure I followed through. Like our foster mom, she didn't like Joe, so she was happy to come along.

We shared an umbrella on the way over, but I left it with her and walked in the pouring rain by myself up to the front door. When he came to the door, I knew he couldn't make too much of a scene because I could see his grandparents behind him and I felt my body sag with relief.

"I love you, but I can't be with someone who cheats on me," I said.

"Katherine, please—" he started.

"It's over," I said, cutting him off. As soon as the words were out of my mouth, I turned and walked away. I could hear him calling after me for a moment, but it wasn't long until the sound of the rain drowned out his voice.

"You're soaked, sis," my sister said, trying to hold the umbrella over me.

"I don't want it," I said. "I don't care." *Besides, the rain hides the fact that I'm crying.*

*****

I wanted to die. I had broken up with Joe only a few hours ago and didn't want to stay alive, to feel the way I did. Joe was intense and pushy and made me deeply uncomfortable sometimes, but he understood me in ways no one else ever had. I'd never believed in that kind of thing, but I'd felt like our souls had been destined to find one another, like our shitty pasts were there to bring us together. I didn't feel as alone when I was with him. But all those things made this pain in my chest so much worse; I felt like the essence of who I was had been shattered.

I'd called Janey, but she had said she didn't really like him anyway, and we ended up in an argument when I started defending him. She didn't understand why I was defending someone who cheated on me, and I was angry that he was being judged by other things that weren't his fault. My foster mom had seen me crying when Laurel and I got back and I'd told her that I'd broken up with Joe.

"Oh, honey, it's not that big a deal! There're so many other fish in the sea. Better fish, if you ask me," she added. "And you're resilient anyway, you'll bounce back. You'll forget what you ever saw in him by next week, I'm sure."

As I always did when I started thinking about maybe killing myself, something I'd done a handful of times in the past, I closed my eyes and imagined what would happen in the world as a result of my death, who might be impacted. I knew that life always marches on and the world keeps turning, and I realized how insignificant my life really was. Aside from the initial shock, would anyone really care long-term?

No. Probably not.

Except maybe my foster mom. Definitely my sister. "You've only got each other," my foster mom's voice rang in my ears. Even if my sister wouldn't care, I'd be leaving her alone if I killed myself. But instead of deciding against suicide at this point, this time, I wondered if she'd be better off. We fought all the time, anyway—she told me almost every day that she hated me, that I made everything harder for her because I did so well in school that our foster mom expected her to, as well. She'd be happier if I was gone, I realized.

I started sobbing harder to the point it felt like I was going to turn inside out. *No one really loves me. No one understands me, not really.* Everyone smiled at me as long as I was doing what they wanted me to, but that all changed as soon as I didn't, and it didn't matter how I felt either way. I felt completely worthless, but everything was "fine" because I was doing well in school and played an instrument and a sport. I was *resilient* and had overcome my past as if it had never happened.

But it *had* happened. And no matter how far down I shoved my memories, they kept coming back to haunt me in the middle of the night. They were behind every smile, taunting me, spreading blackness. I *wanted* to be as outgoing and happy as others wanted me to be—as I projected for their sakes, but I couldn't figure out how to do it. People didn't understand that and I couldn't explain it. But I hadn't needed to with Joe—he had that same blackness inside. But now he was gone.

I rolled onto my back—my body still wracked with sobs—and tried to stare at the light fixture on the ceiling, but I couldn't make my eyes focus. Instead, I heard the voices of people who knew me on some level talking about my death.

"I had no idea—she was such a great student, a joy to have in class. And she got along with everyone."

"She was a real team player on the soccer team. Who could have guessed something like this would happen?"

"Katherine was so nice, always willing to help. Dependable. I can't imagine what would have driven her to this."

The pain in my chest worsened because I knew it was true, and that it was because no one really knew me; no one really *wanted* to know me. What I had inside was too much: too dark, too uncomfortable, too unusual, too difficult to think about.

Too much.

My thoughts drifted to different ways in which you could die by unnatural causes as I stared through the ceiling into nothingness. I'd read a decent number of Agatha Christie mysteries from my foster mom's book collection, so I first started recalling various deaths from her novels, even though they centered more around murder. There was poisoning, which wasn't really an option since I didn't have access to anything like arsenic. What else?

Oh, maybe I can overdose on something.

I got up and rushed to the bathroom I shared with my sister down the hall, hoping I could avoid seeing my sister and foster mom on the way and the inevitable embarrassment from them seeing me crying. Once in the bathroom, I struggled to see through my tears, so I turned on the faucet and splashed handfuls of icy water on my face until they slowed. Satisfied I could see as well as I was going to, I dried my face and turned to the medicine cabinet.

Can I overdose on Midol? I pulled the bottle out and read the label; it was unlikely even if I had a full bottle, and I only had two doses left. I went through the few remaining bottles in our medicine cabinet, but there wasn't anything in there in sufficient quantity to be dangerous—only a few ibuprofen and Tylenol doses in total. I thought about just dumping all the bottles into my palm and taking everything there, but I hesitated. *Would it kill me or just make me sick?* I didn't want to be alive, have my stomach pumped, and then have to look at everyone's confused and disappointed faces because I'd failed. I needed to be sure it would work. There couldn't be any doubt.

Slamming the door to the medicine cabinet and crossing my arms over my chest, I started sifting through my Agatha Christie memories again. There was death by gunshot—as close to a guarantee as you could get in my mind. Put a small gun in your mouth, point it upwards, and pull the trigger. But my foster mom abhorred firearms and didn't own one, so that wasn't a possibility. There was suffocation, but how could I suffocate myself?

Back in my bedroom, I decided to try smothering myself with a pillow, but all that accomplished was making me black out temporarily and then waking with a pillow over my head. I decided to try plastic, but the only plastic I could find right then that would cover my entire head was used grocery bags, all of which had holes of various sizes in them, so that wouldn't work.

I was running out of ideas and started crying again in frustration. I needed a respite, a reprieve. There had to be a way to escape from the pain inside me. With the heels of my hands pressing into my temples like a vice, a memory burst free from the leaky vault where I had locked away everything in my past that I didn't know how to process.

Years ago, I'd walked into a tiny bathroom to find my mom unconscious in a tub full of bloody water after having slit her wrists. She'd survived, but that had only been because I'd found her not long after she'd done it and she wasn't bleeding out fast enough to die before the paramedics whisked her away to the hospital. I just had to wait a few hours until my sister and foster mom were in bed, then no one would find me until it was too late.

It would likely be traumatizing for my sister to find me that way, so I figured I should write a letter and leave it on the kitchen counter for my foster mom to find. It would be horrible for her to see, too, but it was better her than my little sister. And she was always awake and in the kitchen before us, so she would see the note and then could keep my sister from going into the bathroom and seeing me.

I wrote the letter and tucked it under my pillow for safekeeping until the right time to leave it on the counter. Over an hour passed as I walked around my room, looking at and touching objects that I'd saved over the years because they had some special significance to me and allowed the memories associated with them to wash over me one last time. I cried, but I also smiled; I felt at peace, like I was saying goodbye to the good parts of my life.

Next, I opened my photo album and flipped the pages starting from the back, thinking about when and where each photo had been taken. When I reached the very first page at the beginning of the book, I studied a picture taken a day or two after we arrived in foster care, the youngest picture I had of myself. My fingers trailed gently over my image and I had a bizarre urge to hug the little girl in the picture, but I dismissed the urge immediately, feeling stupid. *It's me—how can I hug myself, let alone my younger self?* The thought crossed my mind that it was fitting that when I looked at my photo album, it was as if I hadn't existed until I was eight-and-a-half years old, as if my life to that point had never even happened. But I knew it had, because the memories and the nightmares and the pain remained, despite my best efforts to eradicate them.

Finally, the time had come. I snuck quietly from my room to the bathroom and sat on the toilet lid for several minutes as I listened, straining my ears to make sure I hadn't woken anyone. And then I remembered that I had planned to sit in a tub full of water, but running the water in the tub would be loud and would undoubtedly bring my foster mom to investigate. *Well, shit.* I looked around, tears burning my eyes again. *I'm such a failure that I can't even manage to kill myself! Fuck! No, I can do this. So… I can't use the tub. But I can fill the sink with water— quietly. And then just rest my wrists in there to help the blood keep flowing.*

The sink was full of water when I realized I didn't have anything to use to cut myself. I could use a knife from the kitchen, but I would have to turn on the kitchen light, which would also wake up my foster mom and bring her to investigate. So, no knife. I had a new manicure set, though— I could use the manicure scissors. Surely the wicked-looking point on those would be sufficient to pierce a vein?

I grabbed the scissors in my fist, held my wrist in front of me, closed my eyes for a moment, saying a silent good-bye to my sister and foster mom. Opening my eyes, I dug the point into my skin at the base of my palm and yanked the scissors toward me with a quick jerk of my hand. A line of blood started slowly seeping through the damaged skin as I realized I would have to risk a knife from the kitchen if I was going to make it happen—I couldn't push hard enough with those scissors to rip open my vein. But instead of moving, I stared, transfixed, at the blood slowly beading and pooling on the underside of my wrist. The longer I stared, the more aware I became of the pain that pulsed with each heartbeat.

It was blissful. Everything else I'd been feeling up to that moment faded; it wasn't gone, but it was now in the background, no longer the most prominent draw on my attention. It was suddenly manageable. I continued to stare at my wrist until the blood slowed, then I rubbed at it under the water for a moment to watch the blood flow anew. Grabbing the scissors with my cut hand, I repeated what I'd done on the other wrist, quickly setting down the scissors on the side of the sink and watching both of my wrists in fascination as the pain inside retreated even further, taking a back seat to the pain from my damaged skin. I half-smiled as I watched the blood bead and tears of relief fell from my eyes to drip onto my lap and forearms.

There was a soft thud from somewhere behind me and I jumped, my heart instantly racing. If my foster mom walked in, I was positive I'd be sent to a psychiatric hospital. I shuddered, thinking back to that visit when my brother was there. If that happened, I might be so out of it that I'd tell them about what I used to do with the colored pencils... I shook my head in a failed attempt to banish those memories once and for all. I wanted to forget so it would be like I'd never done it. I couldn't breathe through the shame when those memories rose to the surface.

Fuck. Okay, I need more.

I grabbed the scissors and started them across the underside of my right forearm, line after line after line, until the memories of the colored pencils faded back to where I'd banished them. *Much better,* I thought, taking my first full inhale and exhaling slowly in relief.

As I studied what I'd done to myself, taking full, measured breaths, I realized I didn't have to die after all. I could live the way I was feeling right in that moment. I could just make myself bleed whenever I felt like I needed to die. The water drained slowly and I rinsed all remnants of blood carefully from the sink basin, already thinking about the next time.

keeping the family together

"Setting an example is not the main means of influencing another, it is the only means."

-Albert Einstein

november 1996

"Katherine, will you walk the dog?" my foster mom asked on a yawn.

"Sure," I responded.

I reached over and grabbed my bookmark, placing it between the pages of my worn copy of *Wuthering Heights*. I'd been reading it from cover-to-cover on repeat for the last few weeks; feeling all the pain Healthcliff experienced as an orphan who was rejected and felt worthless, all his pent-up anger and resentment, all his self-hatred, over and over and over. Glancing up at the shelves as I stretched out the stiffness from sitting in the same position for the last few hours, my eyes landed on *Do They Hear You When You Cry* by Fauziya Kassindja. We'd read that over the beginning of the summer as a family; it was about a young woman in Africa who ran away to escape female genital cutting and then was trapped in American prisons like a criminal instead of the asylum seeker she was. The book was gut-wrenching and infuriating, and my heart raced just seeing the spine. Reading that book had sparked an intense wave of nightmares, but the deep, sickening pain in the pages made her final achievement of freedom *that* much more rewarding. I wasn't ready yet, but knew I'd read it again soon; it was one of a handful of books I would never tire of reading because of the range and depth of emotion I could experience while immersed in their pages.

"Where you goin', sis?" Al asked, walking into the room as I headed to the coat closet to grab a jacket. He had moved in with us that fall. Now that we were in a larger house with an extra bedroom, my foster mom decided to try to bring our sibling group together. Social services had said James could not live with us, that he would be too negative an influence, but that they thought Al had a chance to reform. Of course, they wouldn't tell Laurel and me that directly, but Jean didn't keep things from us, so she always told us what our social worker said.

"Walk Cookie—wanna come?" I asked. We knew almost every neighbor in a several block radius, but I still battled a fear of the dark. It was easier with Cookie; having a large dog helped me to feel safer, though she was more likely to lick someone to death than growl at them. But even friendly dogs were supposed to sense when someone harbored ill-intent and would defend their owner, or so I'd read in our dog ownership book.

"Sure, I'll come," Al said, following me to the coat closet.

We weren't quite two houses down the street when Al pulled a pack of cigarettes and a lighter from his pocket, despite being only fifteen. I shook my head a bit, not really surprised—he'd already gotten into trouble twice for smoking pot in his bedroom and cutting a piece of the window screen out to use for his bowl.

"You could get caught," I said.

He laughed and shrugged. "I don't give a shit." He took a pull off the cigarette and exhaled the smoke. "Wanna try?"

"God no!" I replied with a laugh to cover the fact that my heart started racing.

"Come on, just do it."

"No, I'm good," I said, my hands suddenly slick with sweat and my breathing shallow.

"Dude, I don't want my sister to be a pussy. You're already a suck-up. Just take a drag."

His words pierced through me like he'd stabbed me with a butcher knife. Even though I hated that word, hated that he said it around me all the time even though he knew it bothered me, I hated even more that he thought that and couldn't accept him thinking poorly of me. I needed to make him proud to have me as a sister.

"Okay," I said. "I'll try."

He grabbed the dog's leash and passed me his cigarette. "Inhale it, too—don't be a pussy and just suck it into your mouth."

Okay. Make sure to inhale all the way, I thought. My eyes watered from the smoke as I placed the cigarette between my lips and took a quick, deep inhale. Even over the harsh bark of my choking cough, I could hear Al's raucous laughter. *Oh god, he thinks I'm a pussy.* Feeling defeated, like a failure, but also a modicum of relief, I held the cigarette back out to him.

"I can't do it," I said.

"No, do it again," he replied, ignoring my hand. "It'll get easier, you just have to do it more. Go on, take another drag."

One thing I was already really good at was putting full effort into anything that would make someone proud of me—I had no shortage of determination when I was motivated by pleasing someone else. By the end of that cigarette, you'd have thought I'd been smoking for years.

december 1996

The pointy needles of the tree scraped my arm as it shifted around under my hand, but aside from my sharp intake of breath, I didn't say anything. I just wanted Al and his friend, Michael, to hurry up with getting the Christmas tree screwed into the stand in our living room. Michael had shimmied under the tree right below me and kept looking up at my chest. My foster mom had told me that my shirt was too tight, though it was only tight across my chest, but Al and Laurel laughed and told me I looked like a hobo if I wore anything looser. I used to dress like a skater and I loved the baggy jeans and long, oversized shirts, but Al had said he didn't want to be seen with me dressed that way, so I'd started wearing clothes that fit. Except that my chest was always too big for them.

"Oh, sis, you're barefoot!" Al shouted, laughing.

My immediate confusion melted into comprehension with my next breath. "Al, don't—"

"Look, dude," he interrupted, talking to Michael. "Check out—"

"Al—no!"

"—her toes."

"Al, stop it!" I shouted, fighting back tears of embarrassment already. My toes were a little different from most people's—genetic, our doctor had said—so my big toe was significantly larger than my other toes, which were all very short and stubby.

"Just call her T-Toe," he laughed, ignoring me entirely. "For Tower Toe."

"I hate you," I hissed out as Michael's eyes traveled from my chest to my toes and his laughter joined Al's just as my sister started laughing, too. I wasn't sure what was more embarrassing: what Al had just done or when my sister pointed out to everyone at the town pool that summer that I had two long hairs growing on my lower back.

My foster mom walked out of the room to use the bathroom and as soon as she turned the corner, I glared down at Al. "Fuck you," I hissed. "You're an asshole."

My anger only made them all laugh harder. To get back at them, I let go of the tree, which nearly toppled over onto Michael. He stopped its fall just in time as they kept laughing. Turning, I walked to my room and grabbed a pencil out of my backpack after closing my door, my tears dangerously close to spilling over. But I was determined not to cry—I refused to be that weak or to give them the satisfaction of knowing I wasn't just angry, but upset. Flipping the pencil upside down, I sat on the edge of my bed and started rubbing the eraser vigorously back and forth on the back of my left hand. A few weeks after I'd broken up with Joe, I'd discovered it only took a few moments for the rubbing sensation to shift to discomfort and then pain as the eraser burned my skin. As the pain set in, my tears disappeared. Shoving the pencil back into my backpack, I returned to the living room.

"Oh, there you are," my foster mom said. "Michael just invited your brother *and* you over to help his family with their, tree, too."

"No thanks," I said, still angry. I didn't want to go just to be the butt of all Al's jokes in front of another family. Besides, Michael was *Al's* friend—not mine.

"Come on, sis," Al said, "It'll be fun."

"We'll have cookies and hot cocoa," Michael said.

I thought I detected an undercurrent of amusement in his voice, but wasn't sure until Al started laughing.

"What's so funny?" I asked.

"Nothing, just thought about a joke," he said. He was a great liar and could fool just about anyone whenever he felt like it—I'd seen him do it countless times about big things and small—but he was obviously lying this time. "Just come, sis."

I finally agreed and my foster mom made us promise to be home by Al's curfew of 11:00 p.m., though that was much later than mine. We left as soon as the tree was stable; Jean said she was tired anyway and we could decorate it the next day. She drove us across town and dropped us off at Michael's house after he assured her his parents would drive us home.

Al and Michael led the way and I followed through the front door, suddenly understanding why Al had laughed earlier. There wasn't an adult in sight. The living area—the air thick with cigarette and marijuana smoke—was filled with kids. Most of the faces were unfamiliar to me because they were several years older, but there were a few I recognized from my grade or the one above mine, though I'd never talked to them. After Al introduced them all quickly, I recognized the names: every person there was someone my foster mom had labeled as "trouble" and we'd been forbidden to hang out with under any circumstances.

I'd already been nervous, but my heart rate went through the roof and I couldn't breathe very deeply as my armpits rapidly produced buckets of sweat.

"Chill out, sis," Al said. "You're too uptight. You need to unwind. Think about something other than brown-nosing." He paused, pulling a cigarette out of his pocket and offering me one, which I gladly took, along with his lighter. "Besides, Michael wants to fuck you. He likes your tits." And then he walked into the room, leaving me standing by myself.

I was trying to figure out what to do when Michael reappeared. He started talking, but I was too dizzy and the rush of blood in my ears was too loud for me to hear anything he said. I walked off while his mouth was still moving, following Al and asking him for his pack of cigarettes.

"Damn, sis," he laughed, digging in his pocket. "You're lucky I have another one."

I gave him a tight smile and turned, finding an empty corner to sit in. As soon as my butt was on the floor, I leaned back against the wall and lit the cigarette Al had given me right when we walked in. As I exhaled my first pull, I tapped the flame-end of the lighter against the fleshy area below my left thumb. The tip was still hot and burned my skin, but I didn't mind. Wondering if my fingertips were as sensitive as that part of my hand, I pressed one to the tip; it was uncomfortable, but wouldn't leave a mark or blister.

Collin, a boy from my grade, came over and sat next to me. "Want some?" he asked offering me his joint.

I shook my head, holding up my cigarette. "No, thanks. I'm good."

Collin shrugged and took a deep pull, holding the smoke in for a long time, then blowing it out. Without warning, he reached over and snatched the lighter from my hand. He used his thumb to light it and held it between our faces as the flame burned bright.

"What are you doing?" I asked.

He nodded his head toward the lighter, but didn't respond. I watched, but didn't understand what I was looking for. *He's high—he probably doesn't even remember what he was going to show me,* I thought. Then, just as abruptly as he'd snatched the lighter, he let the flame go out and handed it back to me.

"Now," he said, nodding his head toward me. "Now put your finger on it."

Is he serious? That would burn the shit out of me. I looked up at him and he was staring at me, waiting. I felt like he was testing me, taunting me almost, and my spine stiffened; I didn't like being told I couldn't do things. Clenching my jaw in advance so I could temper my reaction, I placed my fingertip to the hot metal and held it as long as I could.

"Ow, fuck," I said under my breath as I yanked my finger off.

Collin smiled and nodded his head. "That's how you do it. That burn will hurt like a motherfucker."

He wasn't kidding—my whole hand felt like it was throbbing, though the raised red skin that I knew would be a nasty blister was only on the one finger.

After a while, Collin got up and wandered off to talk to someone else and I was left in peace. I wasn't sure what time it was, but was hoping it was close to time to leave—we'd been there for a while and I felt like my body was trying to kill itself the longer we were there. I watched as everyone passed around bottles of liquor, rolled joints, and homemade bowls, smoking cigarette after cigarette for something to keep my hands busy, declining every time someone offered me something.

Michael came over when I was nearing my last cigarette, falling more than sitting down next to me, a mostly-empty bottle of liquor in his hand, laughing hysterically at his clumsiness. I forced my lips into a smile when he looked at me, but I just wanted him to go away again; I didn't want anyone near me. His hand on my upper thigh was unexpected and my legs snapped together, the insides of my knees slamming into each other painfully.

"Sorry," I mumbled, not wanting to hurt his feelings.

"That's okay, baby," he slurred, his hand sliding toward my hip, then over my stomach as he approached my chest.

I was screaming in my head for him to stop, but didn't feel like I had a right to tell him to quit touching me. Even so, I couldn't take another second of what was happening and jumped to my feet, my sudden movement knocking him off balance so he fell to his side.

"Oh," he laughed. "Straight to fucking, huh? I like it."

"I have to pee, actually," I said, feeling sick to my stomach and riddled with guilt for not wanting to sleep with him. Although, the more I thought about it, the more I wondered if I'd really have a choice.

"I'll show you where the bathroom is," he said, trying and failing to get to his feet, spilling the brown liquid from the glass bottle in the process.

"Dude, you're fucking wasted," my brother called out, laughing.

"Al—where's the bathroom?" I asked.

He pointed and I practically ran, shutting the door hard behind me and locking it. I sat on the toilet and peed, washed my hands, then splashed cold water on my face. I needed to find a clock.

"We're going to be late," I said to Al a few minutes later, having found a clock that showed the time was 10:30 p.m. I knew we'd have to speed-walk if we had a hope of getting home by curfew from that far away.

"So what? Live a little, sis," Al laughed.

"I don't want to get grounded," I said.

"Fuck her, man. She's not our mom—she can't tell us what to do."

"Al! I'm serious—we should go. I don't want to get in trouble, I don't want to get grounded. If I do, I won't be able to do *anything* anymore, let alone with you."

"Fine, we'll go, goody-two-shoes."

I usually couldn't stand when he called me things like that, but in that moment, I just wanted to leave. I didn't care *what* he thought or called me as long as we could get out of there and go home.

march 1997

The school bus slowed at a new a corner on the way to school and I looked toward the front of the bus, curious. Had someone moved? Three new faces—all boys—filed onto the bus. They were all wearing baggy, torn clothes, had long, somewhat greasy hair, and brought with them a strong odor of stale cigarette smoke, marijuana mustiness, and alcohol.

I figured the first boy who walked past was the oldest because he was taller than the other two. His hair was jet black and his eyes an icy-blue when they found mine. His lips tipped up in a sneer and I shrank back a few inches in my seat. The second boy was the shortest, and he also had dark hair, but he didn't creep me out the same way the first boy had. The third boy I guessed was between the other two in age because he was in height. His shoulder-length hair was dirty blond, his eyes a subtle grey-blue, and his face softened when he smiled at me.

His smile was different—not like the first boy's or how most boys smiled at me. It was almost sad, like an acknowledgement of something I hadn't realized I was communicating. As he passed, I turned my head and watched him walk to the back of the bus and sit down, snapping my head forward when he turned and caught me watching him.

I told my foster mom that evening some new kids had gotten on the bus earlier, hoping to get some information from her—she worked in the school system, so she would surely know who they were.

"They got on your bus?" she asked, seeming surprised. "I didn't realize they'd be on your bus."

"Who are they?"

"The Milsons. Charlie is the oldest—he's sixteen—then there's Will, who's fourteen, but he's in your grade because he was held back, and Frank is the youngest and he just turned twelve."

"Hm." I replied, the smile from the middle boy parading through my mind. Now I knew his name—Will.

"They're trouble, Katherine, do you understand? Stay away from them. Stay. Away."

"Okay, okay," I said, rolling my eyes.

"I'm serious, Katherine. You are not allowed to even talk to them. Those Milson boys are bad news, they're into drugs—just stay away from them."

"I will! Jeez," I muttered.

*****

"You going to a party?" I asked Al that weekend.

He looked at me, his eyebrow raised. "Why? You wanna come? I thought you didn't like being around people getting fucked up."

I rolled my eyes. He was right, but I was hoping he wouldn't call me out on it. I went with him sometimes just to be somewhere that people didn't really expect anything from me. Sometimes they got a little touchy, but they usually got bored with trying to talk me into having sex with them and moved on, and when I was sitting there alone, I felt more like I belonged there than I did anywhere else. Though I got uncomfortable when they got really messed up because the guys became more aggressive and started fighting. Al called me a prude because I only smoked cigarettes when I went with him and wouldn't sleep with his friends, but I'd stopped letting it get to me as much as it did at first.

This time, though, I was hoping the new boys—specifically Will—would be there. My foster mom said they were into drugs, and those were the people Al hung out with, so I reasoned there was a good possibility I'd see them there. I'd seen him every day that week on the bus. Since that first day, I could see him scanning the seats as soon as he got on, his eyes stopping once they found mine. That soft-but-sad smile would appear and his intense gaze didn't leave mine until he sat down with his brothers. My stomach was in knots and my heart racing in anticipation of seeing him as soon as I woke up in the mornings. I didn't want to go all weekend without seeing him.

"I wanna come, okay?" I said to Al.

He laughed. "Sure, come along, sis."

Later that night, we walked into a house I didn't recognize and I saw Will immediately. My stomach fluttered and I couldn't tear my eyes away from him, though I knew I should look somewhere else. That same smile from the bus softened his face as he watched me, his gaze unbroken even when he took a drag from his cigarette.

"Wanna beer, sis?" Al asked.

I turned to face him, shaking my head. "No." I never drank or smoked pot when I was out with him, so I wasn't sure why he kept offering.

"You sure?" he persisted.

"Yes, Al, I'm sure," I bit out, irritated.

"Your loss," he laughed, chugging the beer he already had in his hands.

I turned, intending to continue watching Will from Al's side, but instead found him standing right behind me. When I jumped, his eyes twinkled and his soft smile turned into a full-on grin, his cheeks revealing dimples.

"Hi," he said. "I'm Will."

tête-à-têtes

"We depend on nature not only for our physical survival, we also need nature to show us the way home, the way out of the prison of our own minds."

-Eckhart Tolle

may 1997

I had more work to do, but I couldn't focus while I was sitting at the dining room table. Every few seconds a warm breeze carrying the sweet scent of freshly-blooming flowers wafted in through the windows and I'd find myself gazing out the window instead. *I can't stay inside—it's too nice out.* I decided to take my homework outside so I could bask in the fresh air and warm sunshine. I put my pencil and notebook into my textbook, closed the book, and walked outside barefoot, carefully watching the ground prior to each footfall to make sure I didn't inadvertently step on a bee.

The sun chased the chill from the air, and I pulled off the sweatshirt I'd been wearing after I set my books down in the grass next to a row of peonies that bisected the area under the curve of our long horseshoe-shaped driveway. The peony plants were numerous, large, and in full bloom—deep magenta and a soft, almost pinkish white. Each bloom was enormous—easily the size of my face—and the stems along the outsides had given in to gravity with nothing there to support them and were now resting in the grass alongside the plants.

I sat and opened my book, but the glare from the sun was so bright off the shiny white textbook pages that, even as hard as I squinted, I still couldn't make out the letters. I figured I should run inside and get my sunglasses, but was reluctant to leave the sunshine warming my skin. The sun just felt *so good*. Closing my book back up with the notebook and pencil inside, I tossed it into the grass a few feet away and laid down on my back.

It took several moments before the feeling of adjusting and sinking as the plush grass accommodated my body trickled off, though the sound of the grass blades shifting around was still loud in my ears, as was the slight movement of the peony leaves in the breeze.

My face heated and it felt like the sun was embracing me, showering me with love, and my breathing naturally slowed as I brought my hands up to rest on my abdomen, just feeling my belly rise and then fall, a welcome heaviness invading my body. After several breaths, I opened my eyes, raising my right hand to create a visor over my forehead, but I was oriented in the wrong direction to block the sun. I shifted around so the peonies were near my head rather than near my feet, and then looked up again. This time, I could gaze at the sky without being blinded and found myself studying the clouds. There was one that looked like a heart, another that looked like a rabbit. Yet another reminded me of mountains. My eyes flitted around, but I no longer found the heart I'd been looking at a moment ago; it now resembled a jelly bean, the cloud having flattened out.

Not a jelly bean, I thought. *Maybe more like a lumpy pancake?* My head cocked to the side. *No, definitely jelly bean.* My thoughts debated one another as I looked back and forth between the clouds, trying to determine exactly what shape each cloud resembled as they were already shifting and morphing into something new. Once I tired of the debate over the clouds, I closed my eyes again briefly, the sweet, subtle scent of the flowers heavy in my nostrils, but it felt strange trying to keep them closed with the bright light on the other side of them, so I lifted my lids again as I shimmied around until my head was pushing into the stems of the peonies. I gazed around, turning my head from side to side, but unless I tucked my chin down toward my chest, all I could see was the green stems and leaves, and the colorful, delicate petals of the blooms.

I remembered the painting I'd seen on vacation of the woman in nature; indeed, I was lying there in the flowers, trees less than fifteen feet away in every direction. My vision blurred as I relaxed my eyes, no longer focusing on any single thing, and pictured in my mind the network of roots beneath me. I imagined the roots of the peonies, smaller and closer to the surface, those of the trees larger and more extensive, deeper into the ground, holding up not only their own trunks, but everything else supported by their sprawling roots. I thought about how they would share the water when it rained, how they shared the sunshine they needed to grow, how they were in so many ways interconnected even though they looked from the top like disparate plants. My eyes fell closed as I moved my hands to the ground, palms down, and dug my fingers into the soft earth, imagining I could feel the plants communicating with each other, with me.

I think you're beautiful, I thought to the plants, knowing I didn't have to speak aloud to be heard.

We know, I heard back through my fingertips. *You're beautiful, too.*

I asked them if they were tired after the spring, creating all those new leaves and blooms, the intense growth period of perennial plants and branch growth on the trees, and they whispered they were, but they would have a chance to rest in the fall and winter.

That's why I love fall, isn't it? Because it's not a season of death—it's one of rest!

You get it, they responded.

I knew my conversation was as imaginary as the one I had with myself about the clouds, and yet it felt so real. It felt more like a private conversation with a close friend—a cozy tête-à-tête. The kind of friend you aren't worried about impressing. The kind you don't have to explain yourself to because they just understand you. I realized that was the secret of the woman in the painting—she'd been having a lovely chat with the wildlife around her. And I *knew* I was right because I felt that sense of peace, the stillness that I'd seen in that painting as I lay there on my back in the grass with my fingertips in the dirt, having a silent conversation with the trees and plants in our yard.

*****

"How do you like my crown?" I asked with a grin.

"I want one—make one for me, too," Janey responded as she sat down in front of me.

We'd decided to meet at the park. I'd arrived first and found myself looking around at the trees with new eyes after the peace I'd found in my yard the previous day. The last trees I noticed were the weeping willows— I'd seen them before, always found them to be beautiful and been drawn to them, but I saw them differently this time. The flexible branches poured between my fingers like water when I held my hand to them as I walked around the trunk. Then I gathered the fallen branches and twisted them into a crown I placed on my head as I sat at the base of the tree and leaned my back against the trunk. The low-sweeping branches swayed in the breeze around me like a protective barrier between the rest of the world and me while the crown seemed to draw out some of the darkness I had inside until Janey arrived.

"Okay," I smiled.

She pulled up a blade of grass and held it between her thumbs as she blew across it, creating a high-pitched whistle. "You've like... disappeared," she said, searching for a new blade of grass as I collected more fallen willow branches for her crown.

"I know," I said, guilt twisting my stomach. "I'm sorry."

I felt like I should say something else, but I didn't know what *to* say. She was my best friend, no question. But she wasn't part of the side of me that spent time with Will and his brothers, that hung out with new friends I'd made because of my brother and the Milsons.

"I don't get it," she said, tossing the blade of grass she'd picked. "They're all druggies."

"Eh, I mean... not really. Will and Ashley aren't." Ashley was the older sister of one of mine and Janey's classmates and she and I had gotten close because she was dating Frank.

"Don't they smoke pot?"

"Well, yeah, but they don't do the harder stuff."

"Really?"

"Yeah," I said, though I knew that wasn't entirely true and omitting the rest of the story felt like lying to Janey, something I never did. "I mean, Will said he used to, but he doesn't really feel like it since he met me. It's not like he's promised me he won't—so he could if he wanted—he just said he doesn't really want to anymore."

"What about Shanna?"

Shanna was our age and had moved to our town about a year before. Janey, Ella, and I had all been friends with her, but I started hanging out with her a lot after the Milsons moved to town. "We don't really talk anymore, but she only drank and smoked cigarettes."

"Did you guys have a fight or something?"

I froze and turned to stare at Janey for a moment, trying to decide if I should tell her what had happened. "No," I said, my mouth suddenly dry. "I just... something happened, and I..."

I'd been at Shanna's house a few weeks ago when her parents were both home—which was unusual because they traveled for work a lot and left Shanna and her nine-year-old brother alone for days at a time. Both of her parents were drunk—the only way I'd ever seen them—when her dad came barreling down the hall, violently angry. Shanna had told me that her dad beat her—sometimes because she was in trouble and sometimes because she stepped in to take it instead of her brother—but she lied about a lot of things, so I never knew if I should believe her or not. She had bruises sometimes, but I'd been around her when she was drunk and she tripped and walked into things a lot, so I hadn't thought much of it.

But that was the day I learned she hadn't exaggerated a thing. He started screaming that he was going to beat her ass because she'd been around "that nigger kid"—our friend Jon—as he made it to where we were in the living room. She jumped up from the sofa and ran. I stood and watched as her father chased her into her bedroom, slamming the door behind him. My feet started down the hall when I heard her screams mixing with loud bangs and thunks and his booming voice nearly drowning out her cries. Deciding I should get help, I ran to the kitchen where her mother was cooking.

As soon as I started speaking, she interrupted, telling me I should just ignore it and might want to just go home and talk to Shanna later. That Shanna had known better than to associate with any colored folks and this was her punishment for disobeying. My jaw hung open as I gaped at Shanna's mother, but she turned back around to the stove, humming as she sipped her wine and stirred a pot of spaghetti sauce. I returned to the living room where I sat on the floor, hugging my knees and rocking as I waited. I knew I should go (who knew what might happen if he discovered I wasn't the purely-white kid he thought I was?) but I couldn't leave until I'd made sure she was okay. He eventually tired of beating her and left her room, walking calmly back down the hall, right past where I sat without even acknowledging me. Once he was out of the room, my body—which had frozen when I saw him enter the hall—was able to move again and I ran into her bedroom. She was bleeding, one eye almost swollen closed, red marks and the beginnings of bruises all over her body.

"I'm so sorry," she cried as I rushed in and ran over to her.

"Why the hell are you sorry?" I said. "Oh my god, Shanna, you didn't do anything! Are you okay? You look like you need to go to the hospital, and we need to call the police. We'll go to my house and call—my foster mom will keep you safe."

She shook her head frantically. "No, you can't do that, he'll kill me and my brother if you do, you can't call the police," she said. "Promise me you won't call, promise me!"

I argued and she tried to convince me that it wasn't that bad. She explained that sometimes he grabbed her breasts and squeezed as hard as he could, told her he'd rip them off her for being a slut, before he beat her. I wanted to protect her, but she made me promise I wouldn't tell anyone what had happened. She swore that was the most I could protect her. She said she was planning to get emancipated in a couple of years if she could, but she might be gone anyway, that social services was already investigating them for reports of neglect, that that was why they'd moved from their last town.

I stared at Janey as everything that had happened with Shanna flashed through my mind and had no idea how to even explain it. Not to mention that I'd promised Shanna I wouldn't tell anyone. Even though it felt wrong not to, I hadn't even told my foster mom about it. I *had* asked her about Shanna's family being investigated, though; I was sure if social services was involved, Shanna and her brother would be safe soon.

"Did you know her dad is racist?" I asked. "Well, her mom, too."

She shook her head no. "Are they really? Shanna isn't."

"Yeah—and I know."

"What happened?" Janey asked, looking up at me.

I shook my head. "It's not something I can talk about."

She looked at me and shrugged. I could tell she was annoyed with me for keeping something from her, but she wasn't going to push it. We sat in silence for a while as I made her crown and she found blades of grass to use for whistling. I couldn't remember a time since we'd become friends that we hadn't filled every second of silence with chatter, but I wasn't sure how to talk about what I'd witnessed without breaking my promise and I couldn't eradicate from my mind what I'd seen and heard now that I was thinking about it.

"Here," I said once I'd finished her crown, holding it out to her.

She placed it on her head and grinned at me. "I miss you."

I looked away. "I miss you, too," I said quietly, and I meant it.

"Maybe I could hang out with you and your new boyfriend who takes up all your time?"

My stomach dropped and I shook my head. "No," I said forcefully. "I promise I'll do better. It's just hard since Jean said I can't talk to him, but you definitely shouldn't hang out with any of those people."

What I really meant was that I didn't want her around Charlie, Will's older brother; he creeped me out. I knew she wouldn't want to be around all the drinking and smoking and other drugs I pretended not to notice were there, but I wouldn't be able to forgive myself if she came with me and Charlie did to her what he did to *me*.

197

He had this bizarre custom when he greeted me. I would come to a stop next to Will and raise my hand to wave as I said hi to Charlie and Frank. Sometimes I received a similar greeting in return, but when the mood struck him, Charlie would dart forward and wrap his arms around me in a bear hug. While my arms were pinned to my sides, rendering me both motionless and defenseless, he'd cram his face past my raised shoulder and bite the base of my neck. I could feel the tips of his teeth increasing in pressure until they'd breached the flesh as if time was slowed down, and there was nothing I could do except scream at him to get off me. On rare occasions, he did unclamp his jaw and arms; I'd immediately back up, my hand clamped over my tender skin. More often, though, he'd release my arms only, his teeth still clinging to my neck, and begin to move around. Left, right, forward, backward, dragging me around with him and mangling my neck in the process.

Eventually, Charlie would remove his teeth from my flesh, his hot, wet tongue dragging across my skin to lick off the dripping blood. He'd laugh maniacally and talk about how he was "just fucking with" me or make jokes about being a vampire. Sometimes Will thought it was funny and laughed, too. Sometimes he was pissed and they ended up in each other's faces until I jumped in, assuring Will I was fine in order to keep them from starting to throw punches. I didn't want to cause a rift in their close sibling relationship, something I envied. Frank always thought what Charlie did was funny; he looked up to Charlie and went along with whatever he was doing. I was embarrassed that I was bothered by it—especially on those occasions when Will also found it funny—and ashamed that it terrified me.

"Why not?" Janey asked.

I shuddered. "Charlie's a creep."

"Which one is Charlie?"

"The oldest."

"He looks scary."

"He is," I quickly agreed, looking down at the grass. "He bites me."

"He what?" Janey asked, laughing. "You said he *bites* you?"

Looking up, I locked eyes with her. "He does."

"Where?"

"My neck," I responded.

"Seriously?"

Instead of responding, I used my fingers to pull back the neck of my t-shirt, sweep my hair over my shoulder, and pull off the band-aid there. Turning so my neck was facing her, I waited for her to look.

"Oh my god," she said quickly. "What the hell?"

It was my turn to shrug. "I don't know why he does it. He knows I hate it, but he thinks it's funny. He bites Shanna sometimes, too, when she hangs out with us."

"Jeez, Katherine. That's scary."

"Yep," I replied, taking a deep breath to try to calm myself down. Just the thought of Charlie made my heart race and my chest squeeze so it was hard to breathe, my stomach knot up with nausea and my whole body sweat. Closing my eyes for a moment, I tried to imagine the crown on my head pulling all the feelings I didn't want out of my body and the pounding in my ears and temples softened a bit. *Thank you,* I thought to the willow.

"Why do you hang out with them, then?"

"Will's my boyfriend, Janey—I don't really have a choice."

"You don't have to hang out with his brothers."

"But I do, because they do just about everything together."

"I don't think anyone is worth being bitten like that," she said, looking at me.

"Will isn't the one biting me," I said, laughing uncomfortably as I felt myself becoming defensive. "I'm not going to judge him because of his family. That would be hypocritical since I don't want to be judged because of *my* family."

And I can't lose him, I thought.

the summer of '97

"Rape is a word and it's the truth. It wasn't just a thing. It was rape."

-Rachael Brooks

june 1997

I couldn't imagine a more perfect moment—it was like dreams I didn't even know I had were coming true. I'd told my foster mom that I was going to Janey's house after school. It was the start of summer, which I didn't normally look forward to, but this time I was hoping it would come with extra time with Will.

Of course, I'd no longer have the excuse of hanging out with my brother because he'd just been sent to another foster home. He wouldn't stop smoking pot in the house and my foster mom and social worker had decided that he'd been a bad influence on me after I'd been caught hanging out with Will a few times. I was sorry Al had to leave and worried about what home he might end up in, but I didn't feel as upset about it as I'd expected. I'd been sure I was a terrible sister for not being more upset, but not even that guilt could keep my thoughts from Will for very long.

I was addicted to feeling like I could just be myself, however it was that I felt. If I was in a funk, he wasn't bugging me to be more smiley or happy or tell him what was wrong, as if I even knew. But I wasn't in a funk right then; quite the opposite. I'd confessed so many things I'd sworn I'd never tell anyone who didn't already know over the last few weeks, feeling relaxed and safe in his arms after sex, the only time we were away from his brothers. Sometimes I even had feeling for a few moments while we were having sex before the numbness came back. He'd insisted gently that I open up and tell him what I'd been through since he often appeared at my window to climb in and hold me or walk me over to his house when I called after a really bad nightmare in the middle of the night. I was ecstatically happy and felt certain I'd found the person I could be that way with for the rest of my life.

Will and I were lying on the ground in some tall grass, his brothers off somewhere else for once, blue sky and fluffy white clouds overhead, warm sunshine on our faces, our heads touching, our fingers intertwined. The smoke Will exhaled from his cigarette blew overhead, twisting in the breeze before dissipating entirely. He passed the cigarette to me and as I took a pull, he spoke.

"I love you," he said.

It wasn't the first time he'd said it—he said it after every time we had sex—but it was the first time he'd said it out of the blue like that.

"I love you, too," I replied, my voice shaking as my stomach performed summersaults. He took his cigarette back and we sat in silence for a while as he smoked and I used my free hand to shade my eyes so I could study the clouds. "I see a turtle," I said a moment later.

He started laughing, his fingers squeezing mine briefly as he did. "I can't believe you're looking for cloud animals. I haven't done that since I was, like, five."

I shrugged. "It's fun—you should try it again."

I could feel him shimmy around, getting more comfortable and waited, content. Closing my eyes against the brightness overhead, I used my free hand to gently twist the tall grass around and between my fingers, careful not to slide them along the blades and cut myself on their surprisingly sharp edges.

"You're crazy," Will suddenly said, "that's definitely a camel."

"No, that hump is a turtle back."

"Camel," he said, laughing.

We argued for a moment until the cloud had changed shape and no longer formed something recognizable. Will rolled toward me, reaching his free hand around to grasp the side of my head and pull me onto my side to face him as he rested his forehead against mine. "I've never been happy before," he whispered in earnest. "I really do love you."

"Same here," I whispered back. "I feel happier than I ever have when I'm with you." I paused for a moment, then added, "You make me feel safe."

"You *are* safe with me. I won't let anyone hurt you again."

I nodded my head against his, afraid if I tried to speak that I'd cry instead as I struggled to control my emotional response to his words.

"As long as you're with me, I'll protect you. I'll keep you safe." He pulled back, untangling our fingers so both hands were cupping my face. His thumbs ran over my eyelids and I opened them, finding his eyes a few inches away—moist, like mine. "I promise." He smiled. "I love you."

july 1997

"Come on, live a little," Charlie cajoled.

My body was rigid as it always was when he was near, especially when Will wasn't there, and he was in the bathroom at that moment. I shook my head. "No, thanks."

"You're so boring. Why do you even come over if you're not going to have fun with us?"

I looked toward the stairwell wishing Will would hurry up. "To see my boyfriend," I replied, laughing. "Not to get fucked up."

"But getting fucked up is the fun part," he replied, scooting closer to me on the large stained mattress we all hung out on whenever I came over.

"No, nothing about it is fun," I replied with a shudder, thinking back to the two times I'd let them talk me into trying things with them.

The first time, they'd talked me into using a beer bong during a party they were having at their house that night. Charlie had poured four beers into the opening and was getting ready to pour a fifth when I'd caved and walked away, trying not to throw up the vast amount of carbonated liquid in my stomach. The next thing I remembered was waking up to their mom shouting for Will to come get me because I'd passed out on the house's only toilet and she had to go.

The second time they'd assured me would be nothing like drinking was and I'd shared a couple of joints with Will and his brothers. Suddenly, everything around me was black and I couldn't understand why until I made sense of the words around me to realize my eyes were closed, but I had no ability to open them. For a while, I felt such intense hunger that I was sure I'd somehow traveled back in time and was living in the trailer with my mom again and tried to understand how Will and his brothers were there when I was younger. They'd fed me a sandwich that consisted of a thick slice of tomato between two slices of American cheese and then the three of them had to carry me home because I couldn't walk. After those two experiences, I'd staunchly refused anything that wasn't a cigarette, but that didn't stop Charlie from pushing whatever they had that day at me.

"You just haven't taken the right thing yet," he said, leaning toward me. My body filled with electricity and I froze, staring at his mouth as he talked, afraid he would lean forward and grab my neck between his teeth. "But this stuff—it'll make you feel so goooooood. Come on, just give it a try." He shoved a fisted hand toward me. "Hold your hand out."

"No," I said, shaking my head again.

"Just do it, come—"

"Knock it off," Will interrupted him from the bottom of the stairs. "She doesn't have to do ecstasy if she doesn't want to."

I could feel my face lift as I looked over at Will in relief and smiled. *I love you,* I thought.

september 1997

I arrived through the small, ground-level window into the dank, smoke-filled basement at the Milson house around 11:00 p.m., and the three brothers immediately began talking over each other to tell me about the "legit teepee" they'd erected in the back yard earlier that day. They'd worked hard and were proud of the result, eager to share with someone else. By the time we were finally making our way outside, however, Will had passed out. I shook him, but it made no difference—he didn't wake. Charlie and Frank laughed as Charlie called him a lightweight and said fuck it, they'd show me without him. While I was uncomfortable being away from Will with his brothers, I agreed in order to avoid any unnecessary confrontation.

The three of us made our way into the back yard and I was appropriately impressed with what they'd done. We walked around the outside while they told me about where the logs and cloth had come from, how they'd gotten the logs set into the ground, and how they'd affixed the cloth around them. They insisted I check out the teepee large enough for a few people from the inside. I walked in, Charlie and Frank following behind me as they talked.

My heart raced faster and faster the longer we were inside and I had an intense urge to get back out into the open. I spun around to face where we'd entered, intending to leave. However, Charlie was blocking the only way out of the teepee.

"So, you gonna fuck us or what?" he asked.

I laughed uneasily as my eyes slid to the side. *Surely he's kidding.*

"Who do you wanna fuck first?" he persisted.

"Neither of you. I'm your brother's girlfriend," I reminded him with a laugh that I hoped didn't betray my mounting panic.

"And if you don't fuck us, we're going to tell him you did. And you know he'll believe us. But if you do fuck us, we won't say a word."

I told him it would never happen and begged them not to tell Will that I had, sure it must be some sort of joke—a sick one, but a joke nonetheless. When he hadn't moved, I gathered my courage and told him I needed to get back home.

"You're not leaving until you fuck us," Charlie said, his arms crossed over his chest.

Time slowed as realization dawned that it was—in fact—not a joke. Behind me, Frank was chuckling as he removed his pants and boxers, which made a dull thud as they landed on the packed earth. All of my senses heightened momentarily, and I knew an instant before it happened that Charlie was about to touch me. He reached out, using his palm to shove me in the sternum, and my legs buckled under me. I could feel a shell of numbness spreading to encapsulate me as I fell, my body and brain and heart becoming suddenly sluggish.

"Take off your pants," Charlie ordered as he twisted his foot to put out the cigarette butt he'd just dropped and reached into his pocket for a fresh one. An excruciatingly slow heartbeat passed as his words registered, but I didn't move. "Now," he said slowly, grinning. His teeth glinted in a tiny ray of moonlight coming through the top of the teepee. I knew they were more yellowed than anything, but they looked a pristine white right then. "You ready, Frank?" he asked his brother without looking away from me.

Frank laughed again—a giggle, really—as he dropped to his knees near my legs. "Oh, yeah."

"Come on," Charlie said, half of his mouth tipping up in a grotesque smile. "You're gonna like it. I promise." He took another drag off his cigarette, blowing the smoke out with impatience as he stared at me, an edge to his voice when he spoke that made it clear he was getting his way, one way or another. "Now take your fucking pants off."

I was barely aware of my hands as they unbuttoned and unzipped my jeans, removing them as if they belonged to someone else. I was flat on the ground, but my body was in a freefall and shrinking away once I was naked below the waist. I laid there, staring at the roof of that teepee, at the way the tops of the logs crossed one another as they exited the top of the cloth. Listening to Frank's grunts as my body jerked backward in the dirt in rhythm with his thrusts. Feeling the tears slide down my temples, chasing one another in a race to the ground until they disappeared into my hairline as I laid there, unblinking. Smelling the cigarette smoke wafting lazily around the inside of the teepee, mixing with the humid late-summer air as Charlie smoked and watched intently.

I had no idea how much time had passed when Frank was done, shoving up and pulling on his pants as I felt his semen begin dripping out of me. I laid there, not moving, still staring at the top of the teepee and trying to imagine myself into a different reality as I listened to the sounds of Frank's pants going on, the zipper as he zipped his pants closed sounding so loud in the small space.

Maybe if I'm still enough and silent enough for long enough, they'll just go away. Or better, maybe I'll wake up to discover this is just another horrible nightmare.

"My turn," Charlie said cheerfully, already working at the waistband of his own jeans.

"No," I whispered. "Please, no."

"How is that fair? You've fucked both of my brothers but not me. I won't be the only one left out—you gotta fuck me, too."

*****

Once I was home that night, I tip-toed into the bathroom as quietly as I could and pulled out a fresh washcloth. I couldn't shower and risk waking my foster mom, but I had to do *something* to clean off the filth from the night. I dampened the rough, scratchy cotton and draped it over the sink as I stripped off my jeans. I didn't want to, but I touched my wet underwear and flung them across the bathroom. I couldn't throw away my pants without my foster mom asking questions about why I was getting rid of perfectly good clothing, but I would toss the offensive panties that bore the proof of what had happened.

I sat on the closed toilet lid with my legs spread apart, tears burning my face as they slid down my cheeks and dripped loudly onto the porcelain peeking between my naked thighs. My hands shook wildly as I neared my defiled skin with the washcloth and my frustration was barely containable when I couldn't will them to be steady as I approached the whitish crust on my inner thighs.

The washcloth swept across my flesh hard and fast; I wanted to remove as much evidence as I could as quickly as I could. Again, I swiped, harder this time, then dragged it back. Back and forth, back and forth, for long minutes as I held my breath. If I just scrubbed hard enough, I could eradicate what had happened as if it never had. I stared, lost, at my inner thighs when I was done. The top layer of skin was missing and they were raw and bloody. I would need ointment and bandages, which I pulled mechanically from the medicine cabinet, feeling calm. Emotionless. Detached. I knew I should be bothered by the sight of my mangled skin, but I wasn't. It was okay with me. In fact, it was *more* than okay—it was a wonderful distraction from my memory.

Eventually, my body started to get used to the pain as I lay in bed staring at the ceiling, and then my mind began to replay what had happened. I couldn't allow that to continue, so I reached down and used my fingertips to squeeze my assaulted and bandaged skin, setting off a new wave of searing pain that gave me a bit of a reprieve.

*****

My heart pounded and my body was screaming at me to stay in my bed, but I couldn't do that. I knew if I got caught sneaking out again, I might get sent away—my foster mom had threatened to send me to a group home if it happened again after she'd figured out I'd snuck out of my window again the previous week. That was the last time I'd snuck out—the night of the teepee.

I hadn't spoken to anyone, really, since that night.

I'd finally come to the decision that being sent away was something I wasn't willing to risk, but I had to sneak out one more time. I'd decided to tell Will and Ashley what happened, and now that I'd made the decision, I couldn't wait any longer to do it. I also needed to explain to Will that I couldn't continue to sneak out to see him at night because I couldn't risk being sent away. I wasn't sure what it would mean for our relationship, but I knew we'd find a way to make it work. We had to... I couldn't imagine a different scenario.

I climbed out of my window the minute I thought I could do so undetected and ran the entire way from my house to the Milson's house. I avoided even looking at Charlie and Frank, imagining to myself instead that they weren't even there, and headed straight for Will. But something was off. Charlie sat off to Will's side, smirking, but was being uncharacteristically quiet, and Frank was just watching intently. Will, meanwhile, didn't even raise his head. For a moment, I was terrified Will had done some sort of hard drug and wasn't okay.

Fear tore at my gut as I climbed onto the familiar stained mattress where everyone sat and crawled over to Will, calling his name, but he still wasn't looking up. However, he continued to smoke his cigarette. I was perplexed. *What's wrong with him?* I grasped his free hand, but it was limp between my palms. Tears filled my eyes and spilled over as I implored him to look at me, explaining that we needed to talk, that I had to tell him something. He showed not a single sign of even hearing me and I started to panic.

"He already knows," Charlie's voice startled me.

My head snapped toward him as my insides turned to bilious liquid. "What?"

Charlie took a long pull on his cigarette and directed the smoke into my face as he exhaled it. "You think we wouldn't tell our brother that his girlfriend cheated on him?"

The ground felt like it was swallowing me as his words slowly sank in. And then I was frantically, hysterically begging Will to talk to me, begging him to believe me that it wasn't like that, that I hadn't wanted what had happened. I was desperate for a chance to explain, but he wasn't allowing it. After a while, he raised his head and made eye contact with me, though only for an instant. The expression in his eyes—clouded with moisture on the verge of spilling over—was one of pain and betrayal. He shoved me backward away from him, then turned to slide off the bed. When I tried to follow him, Charlie flung his arms around me from behind, trapping me in place.

"He needs some space," Charlie said with his lips touching my ear.

My stomach jerked as it tried to eject its contents up through my esophagus, but I managed to swallow the acidic liquid back down. Before I could speak, however, there was a loud banging on the front door upstairs. I listened to the voices of the police officers explaining that my foster mom had called them after discovering I was no longer in my room, that they'd have to search the house for me.

As their footsteps started heavily down the stairs, pausing to talk to Will as he made his way up, I sprang into action. Charlie and Frank helped me escape via the window through which I'd entered, and my fingers crossed in hope there wasn't an officer standing outside to see. The yard was clear, but I wasn't sure how long that would last, and I shoved my way through the dense branches of some bushes in the back yard, grateful they kept me hidden when the officers searched the area with their flashlights a few moments later. My heart was in my throat and my body was happy to start running the moment I heard their car start down the street.

I ran until I reached Ashley's house on the other side of town. She was having a party that night, so her house and yard were filled with people. I spied Will in her living room when I walked in the front door and begged him again to talk to me as he pretended I wasn't there, greeting other people as if I wasn't in front of him, hysterical once more.

"What the fuck is that slut doing in my house?" Ashley's voice pierced the air, quieting everyone's chatter.

I turned away from Will to face her. She knew about some of the things in my past and understood me. She would know I wouldn't have willingly done something like that. She would believe me. "Ashley—"

"Fuck you, bitch!" she cut me off.

Where Will had been still and silent, Ashley was the opposite. Just as I had with Will, I begged her to just let me explain. As I sobbed, I repeated over and over that I hadn't had sex willingly, but she didn't believe me. Frank appeared next to her and she wasn't mad at him, only me. She lunged at me, beginning a violent attack, and I threw my hands up to defend myself. I told her I wouldn't fight her, that I just wanted her to listen. At one point, I used the backs of my hands to clear the tears off my cheeks, but I didn't get my hands back up in time, and Ashley's fist plowed into my face.

While the blow was hard enough that I stumbled backward, the pain I felt was in my chest.

I was seven years old again, begging my dad to believe me about my cousin molesting me as he accused me of lying. While I was processing my flashback, I had backstepped away from Ashley and was now standing at the top of the stairs down to the basement. Ashley took the opportunity my location presented and shoved me in the chest with both hands. Through the shock, I felt the sensation of freefall as I clawed for something I could hold on to, grasping nothing but handfuls of air.

*****

I stumbled across town once I left Ashley's house, struggling to see through my tears in the dark and tripping with nearly every step on unseen obstacles. I didn't consider turning myself in to the police as a viable option, but I did try to go home. In my emotionally devastated state, it made perfect sense to go home, climb back in my window, and pretend none of it had ever happened. It was unfathomable that things could get any worse.

When I reached my house, my window was closed and locked. I briefly considered ringing the doorbell so my foster mom would let me in, but quickly discarded the notion. I knew I would face a long stream of questions and lectures, bearing the full brunt of my foster mom's disappointment and anger as soon as she opened the door—if she was even willing to do that. I could just as easily see her refusing to let me in until I'd turned myself in to the police. Either way, in that moment, the alternative of running away seemed more palatable; at least I'd likely be able to keep to myself and cry in peace.

Turning on my heel, I headed back toward the Milson's house, hoping that Will would have returned from Ashley's by then and would be willing to listen to me. When I arrived, I found that Will *had* returned, but he still wasn't willing to talk to me. I sat in an adjacent area of the basement, again hoping that with me in the same general vicinity, he might decide to come talk to me at some point. Instead, I sat in an old, oversized reclining chair littered with cigarette burns, wrapped in a filthy, musty blanket as I cried so hard I thought my body might actually split in half. After some indeterminate amount of time passed, Charlie returned to the house and appeared behind me despite my silent prayers that he would stay away from me. On the contrary, he climbed onto the chair behind me. Between my emotional anguish and my intense fear of him, I was paralyzed; I couldn't make myself get up. I curled myself more tightly into a ball, my entire body rigid, and hoped with everything I had that he'd decide to just leave me alone.

Instead, he wrapped an arm around me, smashing the front of his body into the back of mine. He whispered into my ear, telling me everything would be okay, assuring me that I simply needed to give Will some time to get over his girlfriend cheating on him. Promising me that even though Will was mad at me, *he* wasn't. With each word he uttered, every hot and moist and disgusting breath into my ear and across my cheek, I became more physically ill until I was sure the next exhale would carry vomit out of my mouth with it. I tried to shove up to at least get my head over the side of the chair to keep from vomiting on myself, but Charlie's arm tightened like a vice and prevented me from moving. Everything in my body froze, even my roiling innards as he captured my neck between his teeth in a vicious bite. I couldn't even breathe as I felt his teeth piercing my skin. Just as I thought I'd pass out from the lack of oxygen, he slowly released my neck from his jaws and dragged his tongue across my skin to lap up my blood, much like a dog licks at a bloody wound on its paw. After a last long lick, he resumed his whispered reassurances into my ear. Eventually, my body exhausted itself and I cried myself to sleep.

A soft moan woke me sometime later while the basement was still dark. It took only the span of a breath for the sleepiness to fade and to be fully awake and cognizant of what was happening. Charlie had shifted me in my sleep so that I was on my back next to him in the wide chair. His left arm was wrapped around my back, his hand under my shirt and bra, latched onto my left breast. His right hand was wrapped around mine as he held it around his erection, moving it up and down as he moaned in time with the strokes. Time slowed as I tried to process the situation I found myself in and figure out how I might be able to extricate myself; Charlie was moving my hand faster and faster, his moans turning into grunts, and I knew what would happen soon. I decided to try to move as if I was shifting in my sleep, but the second I tried to pull my hand away, he squeezed my breast painfully and crushed my hand around him. Long seconds passed with nothing happening as I tried to force my panicked breathing to slow; I had to convince him I was asleep. *God, I wish I was actually asleep*, I thought. Slowly, he loosened his grip on my breast and started moving my hand again. Up. Down. Now a little faster, his hand squeezing harder, his grunts coming closer together.

*****

Once it was light outside, I left the Milson's house and headed back to try again to talk to Ashley. She was still sleeping, and her sister, Jessica, implored me to leave before she woke. I'd tearfully nodded in understanding, but explained that I didn't know where to go. She sighed and glanced over her shoulder, and then told me to follow her. She led me to a clearing in the middle of the woods across the street from their house, explaining they'd partied there before and that the police wouldn't find me there.

As she'd promised, she'd returned with a pillow and blanket, a flashlight to keep me company in the dark, books to read to pass the time, scraps of food she could fit into her pockets, partially-smoked cigarettes she collected from the street curb, and a handful of tampons since I was on my period. I'd bled through my pad that morning, my underwear and most of my black jeans were already saturated with blood, but I'd reasoned they could mostly dry if I had something to help staunch the heavy flow.

By Sunday afternoon, though, I knew I couldn't keep living in the woods, that it was time to go home and face whatever consequences were handed to me. I walked slowly across town, wishing I could skip the confrontation and just go straight to my consequences.

When I walked in, my foster mom's eyes widened in shock for a moment, and then she started railing at me for having snuck out again. For having broken her trust. *Again.* She was beyond disappointed in me and couldn't deal with me anymore. I was going to a group home indefinitely and she wasn't sure she would even allow me to come back again. That it would require trust from her to do so and she wasn't sure she'd ever be able to forgive me and trust me again.

I sat there, the bright cheeriness of the front room we'd dubbed the sunroom for just that reason mocking me, the belongings I was allowed to take in a black trash bag as I waited for my social worker to arrive. Though I was aware I deserved every angry word, every hurt and disappointed look, every disgusted grunt and facial expression, I was screaming inside, begging for her to stop yelling at me, to stop saying words like "disappointed" and "appalling." Wishing I knew how to tell her that I was already destroyed inside; everything I thought I was, everything I thought I knew, in catastrophic ruin. I was desperate to tell someone everything that had happened and wished she would just ask me "why" without all the yelling and judgment; ask me why and then wait and really listen to everything I couldn't find the words to say out loud, to hear it in the silence between the words I did manage to utter, to see it in my eyes. But none of those things happened, and as the minutes ticked by with her unhappy voice filling the air, everything inside me was consumed with the blackness, tainted with guilt and self-disgust and awareness of my own unworthiness to even be in my foster mom's home.

She was angry that I wasn't reacting outwardly, that I was staring into space, silent and expressionless. She thought I didn't care—she said as much. But what she couldn't see, and what I didn't know how to explain, was that I'd realized I hated myself more than anyone else on Earth ever could. I was filthy and disgusting inside and I didn't know how to fix it. Ashley's words about me lying, about how I must have wanted to have sex because I didn't physically try to fight them off me—that if I hadn't wanted to fuck Will's brothers, I would have fought to get away—were rolling around in my head, echoing in my ears. She was right that I hadn't fought them, so she must have been right about the other part; deep down, I must have secretly wanted what happened to me.

Why else wouldn't I have tried to stop them with something more than words? I had said no, but I didn't back it up with a struggle, so I must not have meant it; I must have been lying to myself that it wasn't consensual. What kind of fucked up person would do something like that? I deserved everything that was happening to me—I deserved *worse*. I definitely didn't deserve to be alive.

Why couldn't I have just died when Ashley pushed me down the stairs?

new housemates

"Don't try to win over the haters. You are not a jackass whisperer."

-Brené Brown

september 1997

The group home was a couple hours' drive from my foster mom's house, not far from several of the numerous neighborhoods I'd lived in with my biological parents. As the miles passed, my social worker tried several times to talk to me, but I ignored her. I knew anything she had to say didn't really matter and I'd gotten enough disgust and disappointment and anger from my foster mom. Instead, I spent the drive folding everything I felt into that little hole I'd found that day in court until I was mostly numb by the time we arrived; not angry, not upset, not anything.

As soon as my social worker left, one of the counselors gave me a tour of the house with bland indifference, introducing me to my housemates who scowled and glared at me as we encountered them. The complicated chore chart was explained to me and then I was left in my new bedroom at the far end of the second-floor hallway to unpack my handful of clothing, my portable CD player, and a handful of my favorite CDs—the only personal items I'd brought with me. The room—like every other room in the house—was small, with four beds each situated against a different wall. Three of the beds were already occupied, so I took the vacant bed immediately to the right, with the door to our tiny shared bathroom at the head of my bed.

Once I was unpacked, I laid back on my bed listening to the familiar songs by Usher and Linkin Park coming from my CD player and staring at the ceiling as I thought back to the day I'd chosen permanent foster care over adoption. I wondered if I'd have been sent away if we'd been adopted instead, or if I'd still be at home with the only family I had. I'd thought permanent foster care meant that Jean's home was mine, too, but realized it wasn't if I could just be sent to a group home like I had been and there was a chance I'd never be going back. Why hadn't I realized there were limits to being loved and accepted, and that I always had to earn those things? That being part of a family would always be conditional, predicated on not ever misbehaving? I couldn't help but wonder if it might have been different if I'd chosen adoption instead.

My stomach sank with regret at the choice I'd made, the first tendrils of doubt about an education being the most important thing in life wriggling their way in, but it was too late; the decision had already been made. There wasn't anything I could do now. And even if changing that decision were possible—I could never ask and risk the rejection I was sure I'd receive at this point. My new goal would be to return to everyone's good graces by being the perfect child. I would do everything I was asked to do, I wouldn't back-talk, I wouldn't hide anything or sneak out anymore, I would get even better grades in school, get better at soccer, practice the piano as much as I was told—anything. Everything. I would do it all so my foster mom and my social worker would only be proud of me, and maybe they would even forget any of this had ever happened.

*****

"Bullshit, cracker," one of my roommates, Teresa, said to me later the evening I arrived. "Ain't no fuckin' way you black in any way. Shayla over here—" she pointed to the only white kid in the home, who also roomed with us "—is blacker than you and she's fuckin' white."

"White chocolate," Shayla chimed in.

"I'm not lying," I said, my voice much smaller than I would have liked. My heart was racing and my body was filled with that long-familiar electricity, but I didn't want them to know. I'd learned at the community dinner that I was the youngest kid there and that I had the most innocuous offense: two of my housemates were serial shoplifters, almost everyone else had multiple assault charges—some even with weapons—as well as drug charges, and about half had destruction of property and attempted robbery charges. I was the only kid who'd never spent time in Juvenile Detention, and—as they'd pointed out at dinner—I didn't talk like them, but instead like "a stuck-up white bitch."

"Girl, I'm tellin' you, if you think your daddy was black, he was fuckin' lyin' to ya. Your mama fucked some white guy and ain't tell nobody." She barely got the words out before she was doubled over with laughter, my other roommates joining her.

"Lights out!" one of the counselors yelled from the doorway.

Thank God, I thought. Sliding my headphones out from under my pillow, I laid down on my back and stared up at the darkened ceiling as the tears slid from the corners of my eyes and down my temples, my pain escaping from the hole I'd shoved it all into only a few hours ago.

*****

I'd searched the few drawers I'd been allotted for my clothes, under my pillow, inside my pillowcase, and pulled every blanket off my bed—twice. My CD player was gone. I'd only turned it off to go down for breakfast and now it was gone. I knew I hadn't put it somewhere, but I checked again. After a long weekend in the woods where I hadn't really slept, then a sleepless night in a new bed, I was groggy; maybe I did something without realizing it?

On a whim, I walked across the room and grabbed a pillow from one of my roommates' beds just as she walked in the room.

"What the fuck you doin' in my shit, cracker?" she shouted.

Lifting up my CD player from where her pillow had been, I turned and glared at her. "Don't take my stuff."

"I don't know how that got there," she said, crossing her arms across her chest with a smirk. "But I'll tell you this—you go lookin' over here and touch any of my shit again, I'll beat your puny white ass into a fuckin' pulp your mama wouldn't recognize."

Not that hard, I thought. *She didn't recognize me already.*

Ignoring her, I returned to my bed and laid back after putting my earphones on, immersing myself in the music until the shout that it was time for school. I waited until I thought no one was watching and slipped my CD player into a sweatshirt in my drawer instead of putting it under my pillow, and then followed the rest of my housemates for my first day of school in the group home.

School was held in the basement, in a small, windowless room that was crammed with desks sporting attached chairs. A counselor at dinner the night before had told me that a single teacher, Miss Everly, was responsible for all of us, which spanned grades eight through twelve. When we were all seated, the teacher said for everyone to pick up where they'd left off during the previous class, then walked over to my desk.

"Hi, there. I'm Miss Everly. You must be Katherine."

"I am," I replied. "Hi."

"I haven't seen your transcripts yet, but I was told you're in the eighth grade. Was that right?"

I nodded.

"Okay, great. Here are your books," she said, handing me a small stack of books, followed by a notebook and some loose papers in folders. She explained that my textbooks would stay in the classroom, that we would be given the time we needed to complete homework assignments there, and gave me my assignments for that day. "Let me know if you have any questions—just raise your hand and be patient," she concluded with a smile as she stood.

I watched her move to the other side of the small room to help one of the oldest students who'd been cussing loudly about how stupid his assignment was. Looking back down at my papers, I picked up the pencil Miss Everly had given me and inhaled deeply as I held it in front of my face, the smell of the wood and lead comforting. I gazed for a moment at the eraser on the back, but I didn't dare try to burn myself with it; we were packed so closely in the room that no one could do something without being seen.

Once I'd finished my assignments for the day, I looked up at the clock and saw that an hour had elapsed. *It's going to be a long day*, I thought with a sigh. All the work I'd just completed was stuff I'd done in the last few years, in earlier grades. *Maybe she gave me the wrong work.* I raised my hand and waited.

"Yes?" Miss Everly asked when she walked over a while later. "You need some help?"

I shook my head. "No. I was wondering if you might have given me the wrong work to do."

"Was it too hard for you?" she asked.

"No, it was too easy. I already finished everything for today."

"Oh," she said, her eyebrows shooting up on her forehead. "Let me take a look."

I handed her my completed assignments and she scanned through them, shuffling from one page to the next as she stood next to my desk.

"Hmm." She looked from the pages in her hand back at me, studying me thoughtfully.

"Was it the wrong grade work?" I asked again.

"No," she said softly. "This is what I have to give you for eighth grade." She paused as she continued to study me. "Why don't you go ahead and work on your assignments for the rest of the week?"

I shrugged. "Okay." I would have preferred something challenging to occupy my mind—time would pass more quickly—but at least I'd have something to do.

*****

"Katherine, hang back for a moment, please?" Miss Everly asked at the end of that first day.

"Sure," I replied, sitting back down in my desk. I didn't mind staying behind to talk to my teacher, but I was worried my roommates would find my CD player before I got up there. *Please let this be quick.*

"Do you mind telling me a little about yourself?" she asked, as she moved around, collecting work and straightening desks.

"No. What do you want to know?" I replied, feeling a little suspicious about what she might be asking if that was her first question.

"What subjects are you taking in school?"

My body sagged a bit with her innocuous question, and I replied, telling her about the classes I had, what I was learning in them. She asked me a few questions here and there to clarify, particularly around math; she was surprised by my grasp of algebra already.

"It's normally taught in high school," I explained, "but they have a class for it at the middle school—there are a handful of us who are taking it early. Mostly it's just those of us in GATE, though there are a few other people, too."

"What's GATE?"

"It stands for Gifted and Talented Education. I've been in the program for a few years."

"So, it's an extracurricular program for really smart kids like you?"

I laughed. "I'm not really smart. My IQ testing was at the cutoff, but they decided to let me in anyway. The other kids in there are *really* smart. And it's during the school day. A few days per week, we go to a special room with two teachers for a couple of hours instead of our normal classes and we do logic puzzles and that kind of stuff. I'm always the slowest, but it's fun anyway," I shrugged.

Miss Everly sat down behind her desk, finished moving around the small room, and folded her hands in front of her as she studied me with the same thoughtful expression she had earlier in the day. Finally, she spoke. "Why are you here, Katherine?"

My face instantly leapt into flames and I looked down at the floor. I could tell she liked me and her opinion of me would change once I told her. "They don't tell you that?"

"They do—some of it, anyway. I haven't had a chance to read through what they gave me for you, yet. But I want to know from you. Why are you here?"

"Why do you wanna know?" I asked, feeling defensive. I didn't want or need another lecture.

"Honestly? I'm just trying to figure it out. You're smart, you're polite, you've obviously come from a better school district than most around here. I want to understand."

"I smoke cigarettes and I ran away from home when I got caught sneaking out of my house at night."

"Your parents sent you here for sneaking out once?"

I shook my head, still staring at my feet as the nausea in my stomach made its presence known. "I've been in foster care since I was eight—my foster mom sent me here. And I got caught sneaking out more than once."

"And you smoke? Why?"

I shrugged.

"What are your grades like?"

"Mostly As, sometimes Bs," I replied in relief that we were moving back to topics I could be proud of.

"Wow. Hmm." She was quiet for a moment. "So, I want to give you harder work, but I can't—I'm not allowed to. Regardless of how you perform, I'm under a strict mandate for what I can give to you for each grade level. But at this rate, you'll finish your work for the year in a matter of weeks. I think I'm going to have you help me out. You may have noticed today the other students here have not received the same kind of education you have and most of them are struggling to keep up—some are already a grade or two behind where they should be. But I'm only one person and I can't help everyone at once. After you finish your assignments for the day each morning, I'm going to have you help me answer everyone's algebra questions. How does that sound?"

Fucking horrible—they already don't like me. But Miss Everly was smiling hopefully at me and I didn't want to disappoint her. Besides, I *did* like the idea of not sitting there at my desk with nothing to do for hours on end. "Sure."

"Great! Well, I won't keep you any longer—I know it's chore time upstairs right now. I'll see you in the morning, Katherine."

"See you in the morning," I replied, heading to the doorway that led upstairs.

Once I stepped out of the basement stairwell, I walked directly upstairs and verified that my CD player was still where I'd left it. Filled with relief, I headed back down to review the chore chart; it was my turn to sweep the kitchen and vacuum the rest of the main floor. By the time I reached the closet under the stairs where the cleaning supplies were kept, my body was filled with electricity all over again; something didn't seem right. After the last twenty-four hours, it felt unnatural that everyone would be so quiet. But ultimately it didn't really matter—I just wanted to do what was expected so I could go back home.

I opened the door to the deep closet and stepped in to grab the broom and vacuum from their resting spots on the back wall and sensed someone's presence behind me. Before I could turn, my right arm was yanked backward and twisted up behind my back so I couldn't move.

"Ah!" I shouted, pain shooting through my entire arm.

"Shut the fuck up, cracker, or I'll break your arm," a voice said. I wasn't positive, but I thought it was the oldest guy there, though I couldn't remember his name. "You're going to do my chores. And anyone else's who wants you to do theirs. And if you don't, I'll beat the shit out of your snooty ass, got it?"

I could barely breathe, let alone respond, and my body was completely frozen in place. Squeezing my eyes shut as tightly as I could manage, I prayed with everything I had that the person behind me would release my arm and leave me alone. And a moment later, with a shove that had me ramming into the wall, I got my wish.

Don't cry, don't cry, don't cry, I said to myself as I grabbed what I needed to clean the floors. There was a part of me that felt angry and defiant—I wanted to walk up to the guy who'd threatened me, flip him the middle finger and tell him to go fuck himself and do his own chores. But the other part of me was too terrified of what he would do to me in retaliation.

Reading the chore chart, I started placing names to faces and figured out the guy who'd threatened me was Jack. His chore was washing the dishes after dinner, which the previous night had happened while the counselors remained seated at the table in the kitchen where we all ate; if that happened again, he wouldn't be able to make me do anything.

Turning, I headed back to the hallway, intending to go upstairs and listen to my CD player until dinner, but stopped short when I turned the corner. It looked like someone had dumped a bucket of dirt all along the hallway and I knew if I walked down a bit further and looked into the living area, it would be the same. I'd need to clean the floors again. Biting the insides of my cheeks to keep any tears from spilling over, I focused on stuffing my emotions back into the black hole where they belonged.

december 1997

It would be a miracle if I could stay awake long enough to have my assessment meeting the next day to determine if I could go home yet. My nightmares, which had been nightly when I arrived but tapered off to be only two or three per week, had returned to nightly over the last week; I felt like I was living in a constant state of dreaming.

But it would all be over soon. I'd been busting my ass to keep everyone as happy as I could—my housemates, my teacher, the counselors—so they would let me go back. I just had to make it to the meeting the next day. Then I could go home, go back to my school, do everything I could to stay out of trouble. I could stop dreaming about being chased and beaten and raped, I could stop imagining different ways I could kill myself whenever I was in silence for a few minutes.

My roommates and I were all in our shared room, passing the time. I was reading on my bed while the other girls talked and laughed with each other. Shayla got up and went into the bathroom, quietly shutting the door behind her. As the door clicked closed, the whir of the exhaust fan inside filled the air. People only used the fan in the bathroom for one reason—to smoke. Sometimes cigarettes, sometimes marijuana. No one should have been able to obtain either of those things since we were in a constant state of lockdown, but I had a hunch who the supplier was. One of the counselors, Paul, smoked cigarettes, sometimes showed up to work high, and was friends with some of the kids there. Paul had also been a counselor there when my oldest brother, James, had lived in the exact same group home a few years earlier and often reminisced fondly about how good my brother had been at basketball, telling me stories about how persuasive James had been. He often said he couldn't believe he got James' little sister, too; how it seemed I was going to be just like my big brother, except that I sucked at basketball.

A few minutes after she'd entered the bathroom, Shayla appeared and another one of my roommates went in. After my third roommate, Teresa, returned, she told me it was my turn. I hesitated for a moment as I gazed longingly at the bathroom door, the cigarette smoke that had by now snaked its way into our room enticing in my nostrils as I inhaled deeply through my nose. But I knew if I did it and I was caught, I didn't have a chance in hell they'd recommend I be allowed to leave.

"No, thanks," I said, looking back down at my book.

"Come on, cracker, don't be a pussy."

I shook my head.

"See ya'll, I told you this bitch lied about smoking, just like she lied about her daddy bein' black."

"I didn't lie about anything," I said, my jaw clenched as I set my book down next to me.

"Prove it," Teresa said, crossing her arms over her chest.

"I don't have to prove shit to you guys," I said, shocking myself.

"That's just cuz you're lying. We won't believe you unless you can take a drag off that cigarette without coughin'."

I shouldn't do this—I know they're baiting me.

"Pussy," Shayla muttered.

Shutting down the part of me that was begging me to ignore them, I stood. "I'm not a pussy. I'm not lying. And I'll prove it to you."

With a final glare in their direction, I walked into the bathroom. Pulling the door shut behind me, I leaned out the tiny open window as far as I could once I'd carefully lifted the burning cigarette from the window ledge and took a long, deep pull. There was an immediate, familiar head rush from the nicotine while I held the smoke in and a welcome softening of the hard edges inside my body as I took my time to exhale, watching the smoke slowly dissipate into the air. I closed my eyes after the next inhale to focus on the way the nicotine made me feel and forgot for a moment where I was. Instead of in a bathroom in the group home, I was lying in the grass with the sun warm on my face, sharing a cigarette with Will the day he swore he'd always keep me safe.

I was inhaling my third and last drag on the cigarette, still lost in that memory of feeling loved, when I was startled by banging on the door. Randy, the counselor on duty that afternoon, called through the closed door for me to open it, that he knew I was smoking, that one of my roommates had come to tell him. I was busted and there was nothing I could do to get out of it. I'd fallen right into the trap I'd known my roommates had set for me and had no one to blame except myself.

I sat in the counselor's office, explaining what had happened as I cried. For the first time since my arrival there, I talked about how the other kids there treated me, how they stole my CD player often and hurt me, how they sabotaged my chores and made me do theirs. He nodded as I talked and sat quietly until my cries tapered off. As the last of my tears were drying on my cheeks, he explained that I wasn't going home. In fact, I'd just added two to three more weeks—at a minimum—to how long I would remain in the group home if I didn't screw up anything else. He shrugged and said, "I'm sorry, but rules are rules."

I broke down, sobbing into my hands, repeating that I didn't belong there. He asked me why I felt that way, but I just shook my head. While I felt in my bones that I shouldn't be there, I couldn't articulate why to him.

He shrugged again. "If you didn't belong here, then you wouldn't be here. Getting caught smoking today only proves that you *do* belong here and aren't ready to return to a normal life. In society, you have to follow rules, and you're not following rules. I understand you're upset about it right now, but one day you'll be grateful this is happening."

I don't believe you, I thought, but I nodded anyway.

I was dismissed a few minutes later to go back to my room to a chorus of snickering. One at a time, they said they were so sorry I'd been caught and was stuck there with them now, laughing as they spoke. While I knew my eyes were already puffy and bloodshot from crying while I was talking to Randy, I fought to keep from breaking down again, not wanting my roommates to see me in the act.

And I resolved to do whatever it took to get that recommendation to return home when I was up for review again in a few weeks—no matter how my roommates decided to bait me.

friends and guys

"Life is not about who's real to your face, it's about who's real behind your back."
-Anonymous

january 1998

The phone rang for the third time just as I grabbed the cordless receiver from the wall and answered. "Hello?"

"Katherine? It's Cassie, hi."

Cassie? I couldn't believe she was calling me; she came from one of the most pious families in town and her father had been a pastor when he was alive. We'd been friends since I'd moved into town, but I was surprised her mom would let her even call me after I'd been in a group home for running away. We chatted for a moment and then Cassie jumped into why she was calling me. While I'd been away, Joe had started talking to her. He'd asked her out and she really liked him, but she didn't want to risk upsetting me; she'd only date him if I was okay with it.

I absolutely *wasn't* okay with it, but not for the reasons she was asking. I'd written him off—after he slept with Dana and broke my heart, I didn't really care what he did with his life. Except that I didn't want him around Cassie. I knew he'd be bad for her. I wanted to lie to her and tell her I would be upset if she dated him so that she'd tell him no, but I couldn't lie.

"He doesn't know how to be faithful," I said. "Seriously—you have no idea how many places he's stuck his dick at this point. I'm not even kidding, Cassie."

She acknowledged that she heard me, but I could tell she was smitten. She said she knew he'd done that before but that she didn't think he was like that anymore, that he wouldn't do it to her.

"Oh my God, Katherine, I don't mean it like that—I mean—if he did it to you, of course he'd do it to me because I'm nothing compared to you—I didn't mean I'm better than you—"

"Cassie! You're fine, I know you didn't mean it like that." I sighed. She didn't understand that she *was* better than me and that's why she should stay far away from Joe. "Just be careful, okay? I don't want him to hurt you."

"I promise I will," she said, excitement spilling from her voice as uneasiness filled my chest.

After we hung up, I paced around my room for a while, antsy. I wanted to *do* something, but I didn't know what. When I thought about Joe, I wanted to punch him in the face. The thought of talking to him ever again made me see red and my heart race erratically. But I knew I needed to do it, so I picked up the phone and dialed.

"Hi," I breathed into the phone after he answered, his voice making my heart flip over in my chest and all my feelings for him come rushing back. It seemed I didn't hate him as much as I thought I did. But I *was* still furious with him, so I just needed to focus on that.

"Hey," he said, sounding a bit baffled.

"So, I heard you're into Cassie now."

He said something in response, but I wasn't really listening; I was trying to find my courage. I closed my eyes and saw Cassie's face the way I knew it looked when she was excited, the way it must have looked when I was on the phone with her.

"You shouldn't go out with her," I blurted out over whatever he was saying. "You should leave her alone. She's *good*. You're going to fuck her up and destroy her, I know it."

"No, I won't!"

"Yes, you will—I know you will. Just... don't ruin her. And don't have sex with her. Please? Just don't."

He agreed that he wouldn't, but I knew that would change. As long as he thought sex was love, he would never be able to keep his word.

february 1998

"Let's do JV track this year," Janey said from where she sat on the end of my bed.

"Why?" I asked, scrunching up my face. "We hate running."

"Because we'll be seen if we do and it'll get us into better shape which could help for soccer tryouts."

"They're in, like, a year, Janey."

"I know, but it'll help! We can keep up running over the summer while we play soccer and then we can do cheerleading in the fall for—"

"Ew! No! I'm never doing cheerleading."

"Come on, Katherine," Janey whined. "I don't want to do it alone."

"Ella will do it with you."

"I know, but we should all do it together."

"Read my lips: Hell. No."

"It's great exercise and—"

"And short-ass skirts—which I'm too fat for anyway—and—"

"No, you're not and you did gym—"

"—bouncing around in tight shirts—"

"—nastics with Ella and—"

"—that my boobs won't even fit in anyway!"

"—you'd be great."

"I don't give a shit if I'd be great," I said, staring at her. "I'm not doing cheerleading. Period. I'll do marching band instead. Which you should do with me."

"I don't know if I'm going to keep playing my clarinet. And I want to do cheerleading."

"Go for it. But I'm not doing it with you."

"You're no fun!" she exclaimed.

"Whatever—you're the one who's no fun. Cheerleading? Oh my god, no. I can't believe you thought I'd do that!"

"You're the nerd who's going to do marching band."

I shrugged. "So? I like playing the flute. Besides, Allen does marching band."

"Have you asked him out yet?" she asked, wriggling her eyebrows at me.

"No, of course not. I'm not going to ask him out. We're friends. And Joe is his best friend anyway—that would be really weird for him."

"So? Joe was an asshole."

"Yeah, I know."

"And he's dating Cassie anyway."

I sighed. "I know."

"So ask Allen out."

"No."

"Fine," she said, grinning as she reached over to my nightstand.

"Janey," I said, a warning in my voice. "Don't."

"Don't what?" she asked, wriggling her eyebrows again as she started dialing.

"Janey! Don't! Don't you dare! If you even think about it, we're not friends any—"

"Hi," she said into the phone. "Is Allen there?"

"Oh my god," I whispered as I instantly became dizzy, my heart beating through my chest. "You can't do this," I hissed at her.

All my attempts to reason and dissuade her failed, however. And by the time she handed the phone to me a few minutes later, I had a boyfriend.

april 1998

"Look," Janey hissed into my ear, bumping her hip against mine. "Those two guys coming toward us—they're so hot."

I looked at the guys she was talking about and laughed. "No, they're not."

"Your opinion doesn't count—you don't even think Brad Pitt is hot and you like a bald guy over him."

"He's not *always* bald," I replied in my defense. I knew it was strange that I thought Bruce Willis was more attractive than Brad Pitt, but to each his own, as my foster mom often said.

Janey slipped her hand under my elbow and reached around, locking me into her side, giggling as we started to pass the two boys. They were both on the varsity track team, so we saw them practicing every day, but since we were on different teams, we didn't have practice together. I rolled my eyes in false annoyance; but I was more amused than anything by her silliness.

Both guys looked over in our direction as they passed by us, smiling with the cocky expression most of the male athletes I'd seen had perfected, and I shook my head—I was not interested in guys like that. I was perfectly content with Allen. As I turned to Janey to say something about how cocky they seemed, something landed hard on my left butt cheek and squeezed it. I flipped my head around, stunned, and the guy who'd been closest to me as they passed winked at me, then continued along with his friend.

"That guy just grabbed my ass!" I said through clenched teeth at Janey.

"Which one?" Janey asked.

"The one on the inside—closest to me."

"Oh, he's the hottest one—he must like you."

"What? He doesn't *know* me! And I didn't give him permission to grab my ass. That's seriously so fucking gross. Ugh. I don't care who he is or how hot he is or isn't, he thought he could just grab my ass?"

Janey tilted her head. "I mean, he's really cute, but I guess you're right."

"I *am* right. That pisses me off."

"Screw that guy."

"Yeah, screw that guy," I agreed. *If I see him again, I'm going to flip him off.*

But did I really have a right to be that mad? I mean... he didn't *hurt* me. And Janey's reaction made me think I should have been flattered. But I didn't want some random guy grabbing me. I wished my boobs and my butt were smaller so they wouldn't draw so much attention. I looked down at my legs and how much skin was exposed and tugged at the hem of my shorts to pull them lower on my hips and cover more of my leg. My track shorts were comfortable, they weren't snug, but they really were much shorter than anything I normally wore. *Maybe I should get bigger shorts.*

*****

"Can I talk to you about something?" I asked my foster mom, my stomach in knots.

She didn't look up for a moment, her eyes moving back and forth across the page until she reached the end of her paragraph. Then she laid her book down open across her lap. "Of course."

"Promise me you won't say anything to anyone?"

She studied me for a moment in silence. "Probably."

Okay, fair, I thought.

My eyes filled with tears and I had a flare of anger in response; I hated getting emotional in front of people. "Um..." I looked away out the window to the right of the fireplace at the maple tree there and studied the trunk as I tried to steady my breathing. "I'm worried about something and I don't know what to do." I turned and looked at her.

She looked back at me, her face blank and waiting for me to continue. "Okay," she said after a moment.

I started crying when I opened my mouth to speak, the tears spilling over and down my cheeks, dripping off my chin. "I think Cassie's anorexic," I said. I *didn't* say that it was all my fault, that it was because I was a bad influence on her. That I had broken up with Joe, so he was free to date anyone he wanted, and he chose her. That if I hadn't broken up with him, I could have protected her from him. That she never would have started down the path of self-destruction she was on if I hadn't been responsible for someone showing her the way.

"Why do you think that?" my foster mom asked.

I explained that Cassie talked often about being fat, that she was getting skinnier and skinnier, that if she had even a few drops of extra dressing on a salad that she would get upset, but that often she didn't even eat. Everything I knew came spilling out as I demonstrated how all of the evidence together pointed only at anorexia and she was inclined to agree with me. She asked me if I had talked to Cassie about it.

"I tried," I said. "But it didn't make any difference. And I'm worried about her—*really* worried. I don't know what to do."

"Well," she said, swallowing and shifting around a bit in her chair and folding her hands over her middle. "What are your options?"

My foot bounced violently as I put off responding. I knew I only had one option, really, but I didn't want to say it out loud. "I have to tell her mom," I answered through my tears. "But Cassie will hate me for doing that. She'll never forgive me for telling her mom."

I stared out the window and cried for long minutes, trying desperately to figure out some option I hadn't considered, that I hadn't thought of. Wishing I wasn't so certain about what was happening. Wishing there was some other way to help her. As the minutes ticked by, my chest caved in more, making it harder to breathe.

"Okay," my foster mom said, breaking the silence. "So, your options are to do nothing while Cassie is starving herself, but you'll still have your friendship, or to tell her mom so she can do something about Cassie's anorexia and possibly lose your friend. Is that right?"

I nodded. "Or I could ask someone else, like you, to talk to her mom," I added weakly.

"Is that what you want to do?"

I felt that option would be the same as lying to Cassie. "No."

"So, which of those is the worse scenario?"

How could she even ask that question? "Cassie staying anorexic!" I shouted.

"Okay," my foster mom responded, her voice still calm and measured.

I took a deep breath. "But I don't want to lose our friendship. And I don't want her to hate me, to feel like I betrayed her. I don't want to betray her, I just don't want her to keep hurting herself."

"It's a difficult decision to make."

I nodded in agreement, but I knew there never really was a decision to make. Even if she hated me for the rest of our lives, I would do what I thought was right. That afternoon, when I knew Cassie wouldn't be home, I walked over to her house and knocked on the door, wringing my hands as I waited for the door to open. When her mom answered, I looked down immediately; I couldn't make eye contact. I was too ashamed. *God, I shouldn't even be here doing this. It's all my fault. I'm such a bad influence.* I opened my mouth and started crying. *Damn it!* I swiped the tears away with my hands, took a deep breath, and then betrayed my friend's trust.

may 1998

"You have a package," my foster mom said one day after Janey's parents dropped me off at home after track practice.

I had no idea who might have mailed me something and felt some excitement over the surprise. I took the small package from her and tore it open. Inside, I found a cassette tape and a letter in a handwriting I recognized—it was from Cassie! She'd disappeared not long after I talked to her mom and no one knew where she was. Her mother had only said that she was in another state in a center that could help her and that she couldn't give me a phone number to talk to her or even address to write her because she wasn't allowed to have contact with anyone outside her immediate family while she was there.

My face broke into a painfully large grin as I shouted who it was from, and I smoothed out the creases in the folded paper. Leaning back against the kitchen counter, I held the paper between two hands and started reading. By the time I finished the first sentence, my stomach was unsettled, and my grin was now an unsure smile. By the end of the second sentence, I was no longer smiling at all and felt positively nauseous. And by the end of the letter, I was angry and flung the papers on the counter. I had an urge to take the cassette tape and fling it at the wall.

"What's it say? How's she doing?" my foster mom asked.

"Who knows?" I shouted. "This is bull! *That*—" I pointed at the letter "—isn't her! It's like someone dictated to her what to write and it's all crap Cassie would never say."

"What does it say?"

"Some junk about how she's writing to me to save my soul, that I need to turn to God, and he would heal me like he healed her, that she was praying for my soul and in the meantime, she sent me some Christian gospel music to listen to that she enjoyed and thought I might, too." I paused and huffed. "Cassie doesn't even like Christian gospel music!"

"Are you sure?"

"Yes. It's like someone told her what to say. Where the heck is she, anyway? And what are they doing to her? She needed help, but this isn't help—this... this is like brainwashing! *None* of this is Cassie."

My anger faded after I shouted everything at my foster mom, and in its place, I felt a deep sadness and a heavy wave of guilt. If I hadn't said something to her mom, she wouldn't be in some super-secret compound place being brainwashed until she wasn't really Cassie anymore.

This is all my fault.

november 1998

I unfolded the note Janey had pressed into my hand as we passed in the hall. We often exchanged notes between classes to talk throughout the day since we didn't have a lot of classes together, and I'd handed her one as well.

My eyes scanned over the sheet of paper I held in my lap as my biology teacher started writing on the blackboard at the front of the class, my stomach clenching in frustration at the words on the paper. *You've got to be kidding me—how could she?* I'd just learned that the same guy who'd grabbed my ass at the end of track practice, Trevor, had not only asked her out, but that she'd said yes and was going on a date with him that weekend. Fuming, I pulled out a fresh piece of paper from the binder in my backpack and a pencil and started writing furiously. She'd apparently had some lapse in her memory and forgotten that he'd grabbed my ass in the spring or that we'd agreed he was gross for doing that and I was going to make sure she remembered. No way in hell she could date that guy—she wouldn't.

I found her after class and didn't even bother giving her the note as we headed to the lunch room.

"You can't date him, Janey," I said immediately.

"Why not?" she laughed. "He's so hot."

"Why not? Because that's the guy who grabbed my ass, remember?"

"That was a long time ago."

"It was a few months ago."

"Come on, Katherine, I'm sure he's sorry. And people can change."

"No."

"Well, if I can't date him, you can't date Allen."

"What the hell does Allen have to do with Trevor?"

"Katherine," she said as we stopped at the back of the line to buy our lunches, turning to face me. "How many times has he cheated on you? How many times have you guys broken up already?"

I looked away, my face heating up. "He only kissed them. It's not like he slept with them or something. He'd be gone if he did that."

"*Only*? He kissed them! And you're still with him."

"I broke up with him!" I shouted, aware of how defensive I sounded, wondering why I was defending him.

"And then you took him back. Every. Time."

"He promised it won't happen again," I said weakly. Even *I* didn't really believe that. But I couldn't seem to turn my back on him, either. And other than that, he wasn't a bad boyfriend. My foster mom even liked him—who wouldn't? His dad was a preacher. He was cute, did well in school and was well-liked by everyone, played soccer and trumpet, was the lead guitarist, singer, and songwriter in his own band; every box was checked for the perfect boyfriend. "Besides," I added quietly as I leaned in to make sure no one heard me, "we had sex last weekend for the first time. He won't cheat on me again." At least I wanted to believe that—it would hurt so much worse if he did after that.

"What?" she shouted. "You didn't tell me?"

I shrugged. "I wasn't sure what you would think."

"I'm your best friend, you can't keep things like that from me!"

"Even though your best friend is a slut?"

She laughed. "You're not a slut because you had sex with your boyfriend, Katherine. You'd be a slut if you had sex with everyone."

I wanted to believe her, but I could hear Ashley's voice in my head calling me a slut the night she pushed me down the stairs—after I hadn't fought off Charlie and Frank. I could hear my foster mom's voice telling me the clothes I wore sometimes made me look like a hussy, that I was asking for a "certain kind of attention." I thought about my conflicted feelings when guys checked me out, how as much as I hated it, I sometimes liked it, too. And while Allen *was* my boyfriend, he wasn't the first person I'd had sex with. Or even the second.

I *must* be a slut.

a man is a man is a man

"It's easier to build strong children than to repair broken [adults]."
-Frederick Douglas

june 1999

"Can you come over?" Janey asked tearfully over the phone.

"Let me ask," I replied quickly. "Hold on, I don't have the cordless."

My mind raced as I searched the house to find my foster mom and ask if I could go over to Janey's house. I'd thought our friendship was going to be completely over soon; she was pulling away, spending more and more time with Trevor and less time with me. She'd told him when they started officially dating that I didn't like him because of what he'd done that day at track, and after that, she stopped calling me and stopped sitting with me at lunch. I'd started to give up on her.

I found my foster mom and she gave me permission. Within minutes, I was on foot headed to Janey's house, where I found her in her room, crying on her bed.

"Trevor and I broke up," she wailed.

Inside, I was relieved because I knew he was at the heart of me losing my best friend, but I knew better than to say anything right then. Instead, I sat next to her on the bed—holding her when she wanted it—and let her sob as much as she needed. She told me that he was controlling and forced her to do things she didn't want to do.

"Did he rape you?" I asked, my gut filling with dread and rage.

"No," she whispered. "But he forced me to give him a blow job. His... was in my mouth... after I told him no."

"Are you fucking serious?" I shouted, my hands fisted so tightly I could feel my fingernails cutting into my palm. I could feel vomit tracking up my throat, but the burn of stomach acid faded in the company of my rage. *I'll fucking kill him. I swear to God, I'll fucking kill that bastard.*

She nodded. "In his car..." she whispered, her voice trailing off at the end.

I jumped up to my feet. "Jesus Christ, Janey! How the fuck... And you stayed with him? Agh!" My whole body tense, I looked up toward the ceiling, willing myself to calm down. I wasn't mad at Janey—I needed to stop yelling at her. "You should call the police," I said—calmer—and started searching around her perpetually messy room for her cordless phone receiver.

"No!" she cried out. "I... no."

"You at least need to tell your parents."

"No, I can't do that."

"But Janey—"

"Katherine, please," she breathed out.

Her red and swollen eyes were pleading for me to let it drop, and while I didn't think I should, I did. "Okay," I finally agreed through gritted teeth.

As her tears began to subside and give way to anger, she rummaged in her closet and reappeared a moment later with something in her hands. She held it up as she sniffled, and I saw that it was the same photograph of us taken with the reflecting pool and Washington Monument behind us that she'd printed and framed for both of us years before. The frame's glass had a large crack running through it. She walked in front of me and placed it on her dresser where it had always been.

"H-he decided I couldn't be friends with you because you didn't like him," she started, using her shirt to wipe her nose. "He's the reason I stopped talking to you. When he came into my room the first time, he told me I needed to put away any picture that he wasn't in, starting with this one since it had you in it and he flipped it down like this." She placed the frame face down on her dresser for a moment, then placed it upright again. "I flipped it back up when he left and didn't think about it until he came over again. He saw it and walked over, grabbed it, and threw it into my closet. That's how the glass broke. There's a chunk missing from the wall where it hit, too."

"Jesus, Janey," I breathed out.

I didn't know what else to say. I wanted to find Trevor and do something—anything—to hurt him because he'd hurt my best friend. I wanted to be a shield to protect her from him from then on, and I wanted to find a way to take away the pain I heard in her voice and saw in her face. *I should have protected her from that asshole. I don't know how, but somehow.*

"I'm sorry, Katherine," she said. "I let him come between us and I never should have done that."

"It's okay," I said. It wasn't, but I didn't want her to feel any worse than she did. "It's no different than me doing stupid shit that got me sent away," I added, smiling at her.

"Oh, God," she responded with a small laugh. "You can't get sent away again, ever. That was awful. I was so scared."

"I know," I said softly, looking away. She'd given me the letters she'd written to me—one every few hours—the days I was missing while the police were searching for me. I'd read them over and over, shocked by how much she must have cared about me. Even though we were best friends, it had taken me by surprise that she cared *that* much.

After using her shirt to clean her nose again, she changed the subject. "Speaking of boyfriends... how's Allen?"

I sighed. "He's Allen. You know how he is. But he wrote me a song for Valentine's Day and he sang it for me while he played it on his guitar."

She nodded, looking away.

"But he also held hands with Autumn walking down the hall when we weren't even broken up. And he still flirts with everyone." I shrugged. "I did break up with him for the Autumn thing—that was a real dickhead thing to do. I don't even understand how we ended up back together. We always end up talking after we break up because we're friends and then suddenly we're dating again. I dunno. And I met his parents."

"That's big—how did that go?"

I wasn't sure how to answer that for a moment. I'd almost said they were racist, but Allen had sworn they weren't. Though I still couldn't figure out how that was possible. I'd walked up to their front door with Allen, my heart in my throat, afraid they wouldn't like me, and just before he opened the door, he'd turned to me and said, "Don't mention to my parents that you're biracial."

I'd looked at him in shock. "Your parents are racist?"

"No, no," he'd assured me. "Not at all. They don't have a problem with people of color. They just don't want me dating one."

"It was okay. They like me," I said to Janey. *Though they also don't know I'm half-black.*

She sighed and looked over at me. "Why do guys suck?"

I gave her a half-smile. "Who knows. But they do, don't they? All of them."

"Girls are so much better."

"Eh... *some* are," I laughed.

"*We* are."

"Agreed. Let's not let an asshole guy come between us again?"

"Never again. I swear."

july 1999

I was at Janey's house for a sleepover and we'd already eaten dinner. Laurel usually slept over with Lynn, Janey's younger sister, when I was there with Janey, but she'd already had plans with someone else; Janey's older sister, Mae, was at a friend's house for the weekend, so it was just the three of us. We decided to watch a movie they liked that I hadn't seen and headed to the living room. Just as we were settling in, their dad decided to join us and plopped down between his daughters. Janey and Lynn snuggled up with him to get comfortable, and I sat down rigidly a few feet away at the edge of the sofa. The movie started, but I couldn't make myself focus on it; I was too distracted by watching *them*.

I wanted what they had *so* badly.

My foster mom had been more of a parent than both of my biological parents had ever been, so I never really felt like I was missing out on anything, but right then, I desperately longed for a dad I could snuggle with, a dad who was there for me and cared about me. A dad who wanted to spend time with me enough that he coached my soccer team and would choose to watch a stupid movie with me.

A dad like my friend had.

After a while, he stretched out an arm that had been around Janey and used his hand to motion me over to join them. I hesitated, wanting to scoot over immediately, but uncomfortable with the idea of being so close to him. I didn't know what it was like to be close to a man—*any* man—with even a modicum of the comfort my friend and her sister obviously had.

My intense desire for even a taste of what I saw overrode my hesitation in the end, though, and I scooted closer. I mashed myself up against Janey and her dad wrapped his arm around my back, grasping my shoulder with his hand the way he had been doing with Janey. His attention returned to the television and I turned to face the screen, but I couldn't focus my eyes on any of the images that seemed to be appearing at the end of a long black tunnel. Instead, I was hyperaware of the pressure against my shoulder, the fact that it was a man's hand that was touching me. Breathing was difficult, but I was afraid Janey or her dad would notice rapid respiration and desperately tried to make my chest and shoulders move in a fashion that was more natural for sitting still. I wanted to enjoy the time I had, being included as another member of their family, but I couldn't; I just wanted it to end. I was too scared of hurting his feelings if I scooted away, though everything in my body was screaming for me to do just that and I was nauseous and dizzy. I hated that I couldn't just enjoy an evening and a movie with my friend's family, couldn't simply relax the way they were.

I hated that—as hard as I tried, as much as I projected I was—I couldn't just be normal.

*****

"Come on, Katherine, out of bed. It's a beautiful day, you need to go do something outside, not sleep it away."

I groaned and rolled onto my side painfully. I'd been fine when I came home from Janey's the day before, but sometime in the middle of the night something happened. I felt awful. My whole body hurt, every muscle was sore from my neck to my calves; my head was foggy and I had a pounding headache. I usually woke up around six every morning without needing an alarm, but it was now ten and I couldn't make myself get out of bed.

"I think I have mono or something," I said. "I don't feel well."

"Oh, Katherine, you don't have mono. That's ridiculous. Don't be so dramatic."

"I'm serious," I protested. "I really don't feel well. My whole body hurts. If not mono, maybe the flu."

"Is your stomach upset?"

"Not really, but I don't want food, either."

"I think you're fine. You just need to get up and move—you probably just didn't get enough sleep last night."

Well, that's certainly accurate, I thought. I'd woken up several times with nightmares that just wouldn't go away. But that didn't explain what was wrong with me; I had nightmares often and I never felt like this afterward.

"Come on, out of bed," my foster mom said, heading toward the kitchen from my doorway.

A groan escaped as I struggled to push myself up to sit on the edge of my bed. *I feel like I'm dying.*

*****

I'd been going to therapy off and on since I'd entered foster care, courtesy of a requirement from social services. While I didn't want to talk to a therapist at all, Jim was my favorite therapist I'd ever had. He was kind and soft-spoken, and never tried to force me to talk about things I didn't want to talk about, which meant we generally only chatted about what was going on at school or in soccer, sometimes about my relationship with my sister if we'd been fighting even more than normal. At first, I had stared tensely at the wall during every session, but I'd become more comfortable with being alone with him for an hour with the door closed, no longer had flashes of my nightmares or elaborate visions of being assaulted by him the entire time I was there.

I told him about the last day of school the previous week and that I'd spent the night with Janey. And then I shared that I'd thought I was sick with mono or the flu but that it had mostly dissipated already, so it couldn't have been. As I bent my head to take a sip of the hot tea I always made at the beginning of our sessions, watching the movie at Janey's house flashed through my mind. I remembered the tension in my body as her dad's fingers clasped the outside of my shoulder, how tired my neck was by the time the movie was over. *Holy shit,* I thought. *It was all from that.*

"Is everything okay?" Jim asked, pulling me from my thoughts.

"Yeah, why?"

"You stopped talking in the middle of a sentence and your eyes got big and your breathing changed."

"Oh," I muttered, embarrassed. *How is he so observant?*

"Would you like to share what you're thinking about?"

I glanced up at Jim. He was watching me, his face open and inviting, but not expectant, a crease in his forehead that wasn't normally there the only sign betraying he was concerned. *He has kids—I bet he's a really good dad,* I thought. *But I can't talk to him about this stuff—I can't talk to anyone about this stuff. He'd think I'm crazy. And he's a man.* I thought about denying that I was thinking about anything at all, but opted for honesty instead; I knew he was the one person who would accept my response no matter what it was.

"No, not really."

"Okay," he replied with a smile. "Anything else you want to talk about?"

I shook my head. "Nope. Game of pickup sticks?" We played in nearly every session once I was ready to stop talking unless I was so preoccupied that I couldn't even focus on that. It was my favorite part of our hour together and usually flew by. And while I didn't want to be in therapy, there was a part of me that looked forward to coming, knowing I could or could not talk about whatever I wanted and then play a game of pickup sticks without any pressure to do or say anything else.

He closed the notebook he was holding and reached over to place it on his desk along with his pen. "Sure. Set it up."

unwanted change

"The saddest thing about betrayal is that it never comes from your enemies."

-Anonymous

august 1999

I stared at Janey, my mouth agape as I struggled to find words. She'd just told me that she was officially dating Trevor again. I'd known that he'd been calling her often ever since their breakup at the end of the school year, talking to her mom when Janey wouldn't talk to him, but she'd sworn it didn't matter, that she was never going to take him back.

"What the hell?" I finally shouted. "He's an asshole—he's-he's controlling, he forced you to—"

"I know, but—"

"You promised no more—"

"—he's sorry."

"—guys would come between us, Janey!"

"He won't."

"Right. Because he didn't last time, either," I bit out as I clenched my jaw. I couldn't believe she was doing this.

"This time is going to be different. I already told him that he couldn't have any say in who my friends are, and he agreed."

"Bullshit."

"He did!"

"I don't care what he said, it won't last."

"I believe him."

"Then you're fucking stupid," I muttered.

"So are you!" she shouted. "How many times have you broken up with Allen because—"

"That's not the same!"

"Yes, it is!"

"No, it's not! Allen doesn't control me or force me to do things or tell me who I'm allowed to be friends with, Janey." Though I felt guilty for my words, because I was making it sound like Allen was perfect, when he wasn't. Ever since we'd had sex the first time, he'd been changing, so slowly I almost didn't notice. He was now jealous of any guys I talked to or looked at, and he backed me into corners when we argued so I couldn't easily walk away anymore.

Janey glared at me and I crossed my arms as I raised my eyebrow at her, daring her to argue with me.

"We're *both* stupid, okay?" she finally said with a half-smile.

I laughed, her response unexpected. "Okay, fine."

"You don't have to be such a bitch about it, though," she added.

My stomach clenched at her words as I heard myself in the last few moments. "I'm sorry," I said, looking down at my hands. *I'm worried about losing her friendship, so I call her "fucking stupid"?* It was like half of my break-ups with Allen, which were because I was sure he was about to break up with me and I instigated a fight until it happened. I always believed I was in the right when it was happening, but afterwards realized I'd started it.

What the hell is wrong with me? Why do I always push away the people I want to stay?

december 1999

My knee was bouncing up and down violently where I sat on the cold cinderblock bleachers in Atlanta. Our marching band had traveled to play in the halftime show in the Georgia Peach Bowl. We were in competitions for another two days after that, then we were heading home. We'd already competed for the day where we were and were now just watching the other bands take their turns to compete. I could feel the tension rolling off Allen where he sat next to me and was waiting for him to start yelling at me for something again.

He'd been a complete asshole since his grandmother had died a few weeks earlier, but it had gotten even worse on the trip. Everything seemed to set him off and he took all of his anger out on me. I'd tried everything I could think of to placate him, but nothing I said made any difference. Our mutual friends had been asking me repeatedly if I was okay and it was getting harder to plaster on my smile and assure them that I was as I made excuses for Allen. I knew he'd been close to his grandmother and was really upset that she'd died, but I was also getting sick of him taking that pain out on me.

"What are you looking at?" he asked, leaning in toward me.

"Just watching the show."

"You sure you aren't looking at that guy in front of us?"

I glanced away from the field to scan the bleachers in front of us; I'd barely even noticed the band that sat a few rows down. "No, I'm watching the band on the field," I replied, looking back up.

"I saw you look at him. How fucked up is that, you checking out another guy right in front of me?" he started, his voice quickly escalating in volume. "You want *that* fucking guy?"

"What? No, Allen, I—"

"I saw you fucking looking at him!"

"No, I wasn't," I hissed, hoping he would lower his voice; people were starting to look away from the field to stare at us.

"You're lying, I saw you. You're probably cheating on me."

"What?"

"I don't know why I'm with you when you're checking out other guys and you're always starting fights—you're such a shitty girlfriend."

"Allen," I said urgently. "Please. Not here."

He started to argue, and I could tell that he wasn't going to calm down, so I stood and begged him to take the argument somewhere else, relieved when he followed me as I led the way from the bleachers. I was mortified by what was happening and wanted to get as far away from other people as I could, so I led us past the bathrooms to a long wall under the bleachers that connected the two ends. The area was deserted—not a soul in sight.

Thank God—at least now no one else will see or hear us fighting.

I turned, my heart racing and tears burning my eyes, as he continued to bellow, backing me into the cinderblock wall behind me until my back was mashed flat against it and he was only inches in front of me. As I watched his face turn so deep a red it was almost eggplant in color, listening to his voice so loud my ears were ringing as the sound echoed off the concrete around us and my heart fluttering like a cornered rabbit's might, I got a small shock of anger.

How dare he treat me this way? *How dare he?* Maybe he was right and I couldn't give him what he needed, but that didn't mean he had a right to treat me the way he was.

"You're being so unfair to me!" I screamed over him. "I know you're upset about your grandmother," I continued, lowering my voice a bit, "but that doesn't make it okay for you to take it out on me. I'm doing everything I can to be here for you, and you're being an asshole to me. It's—"

"*I'm* the asshole?"

"—total bullshit!"

"This has nothing to do with my grandmother."

"Yes it—"

"No, it doesn't! This is about *you* being a shitty girlfriend!"

My back straightened and I squared my shoulders as my teeth clenched. I wasn't sure what was possessing me, but I said the next words loud, strong, and slow. "That's. Not. True."

"Yes, it is, goddammit!" he screamed. And then he plowed his fist into the wall next to my face, the side of his hand brushing my cheek just as my head had instinctively pulled a few inches to my left.

I was paralyzed, fear and shock freezing my entire body. *He almost punched me in the face. My God-loving, Christian-ska-band-leading, ultra-charismatic-friends-with-everyone, son-of-a-preacher, honor-roll boyfriend nearly punched me in the face.* The skin his hand had touched throbbed and tingled with awareness as I stared at him, unable to move or speak as everything around his head faded into black, and all I saw was his face.

Time had slowed, then suddenly went screeching back to a normal tempo. Allen shouted at me for being such a bitch and making him so angry as he cradled his hand, but I couldn't do anything more than stare at him as his voice melted into a low hum under the buzzing in my ears. I was used to him having mood swings; his temper could be explosive once something set him off, but I'd never been afraid of him the way I was in that moment. I knew if his hand had only been an inch to the side or if I hadn't moved my head at the last second, many of the bones in my face would have been smashed under his fist.

late april 2000

Janey, Ella and I were talking before soccer practice as we got on our shin guards and cleats at the edge of the field. Janey and I barely talked except during soccer because Trevor was controlling who she could be friends with again. She'd also started wearing sweatpants and baggy shirts, except on game days when we were required to dress up; something she confessed Trevor told her she had to do so that guys wouldn't look at her.

Ella glanced over to our new soccer coach, Mr. Andrews, who seemed to have a preference for our teammates. "I heard that Betsy went on a date with him and they had sex," she said. Betsy was a freshman.

"Ew, he's so gross!" Janey added.

"That's really sad," I said. "He *is* gross—he's a pedophile!"

They both nodded in agreement. Since the first day of tryouts, he'd made nearly everyone on our team uncomfortable, staring at our chests and our butts as we ran around on the field, making comments about how we bounced. Every day, he would flirt with some of us and ask girls out on dates—he'd been asking Betsy to dinner for a couple of weeks already.

"I can't believe the school didn't do anything," I bit out, angry. We'd written a petition to have him removed, explaining his sexual behavior toward us as well as his misogynistic tendencies that came out in comments about how we would never be as good as the boys because of naturally having shitty depth perception and things like that. Almost every single person on our team had signed the petition, and we'd given it to the principal, but nothing was ever done about it. "That's their job and they ignored us. I wish we could just have Mr. Myers back."

"Yeah. I heard he's sleeping on Mr. Aaron's sofa and that his divorce is really bad," Ella chimed in.

I'd heard the same thing about our former soccer coach, who'd informed us just prior to the start of the season that he couldn't coach us that year because of what was going on in his personal life. He'd been our coach previously, and while he was fairly new to soccer when he started coaching my freshman year, we'd done well under his style of leadership and we loved him.

I sighed. "I don't know, guys. I told Jean last night that I think I'm going to quit."

"You can't quit, Katherine!" Janey said. "You can't leave us to deal with him alone."

"You love soccer," Ella added.

"I know," I replied, "But I hate it right now. I hate going to practice every day. He's ruined everything I love about soccer. I can't stand being in practice with his eyes on me." My shoulders instinctively hunched up and my body shuddered. It was the most disgusting feeling, and if I couldn't get rid of it before bed every night, I was guaranteed to have nightmares, and I was exhausted from them.

"Don't give him the satisfaction of seeing you quit."

I looked up at Ella with a short laugh. "That's what Jean said." Turning, I saw Mr. Andrews getting out of his car and walking toward the field with the giant mesh bag of soccer balls and my stomach immediately dropped as my pulse skyrocketed. I'd been almost chilly sitting there in the early spring air, but now I felt like I was suffocating. My body wanted me to get up and leave, to stay as far away from him as I could. But if I did that, then he'd be winning—he'd have effectively driven me away from something I loved—and I'd be damned if I let him do that to me. "Okay—I'll stay. I won't quit."

early may 2000

My eyes slid down to glance at the face of my watch as Allen's voice continued shouting. We were arguing in the school parking lot near his car, but I was going to be late to soccer practice if I didn't jog to the field immediately. He'd been yelling since we'd walked out of the school, accusing me of cheating on him after I'd asked him about a rumor I heard that he'd gotten drunk and high the previous weekend. I wanted to yell back at him—and six months ago, I would have. I wouldn't have hesitated to tell him that he was being unreasonable and acting like an asshole. I wouldn't have hesitated to try to bring the argument back to my original question that he'd only briefly denied before the accusations started.

But every time I started to open my mouth, I clamped it shut, feeling his hand brushing against my cheek when he'd punched the wall next to my face in Atlanta. Instead of simply my boyfriend, I now saw him as a volatile being capable of causing me serious physical harm if I wasn't careful with my words and actions. I knew that after a while he would yell himself out and his anger would fade without me arguing with him, but I didn't have time for that right then. If I didn't head over to the field, I'd be late. And if I was late, I'd get more attention than normal from Mr. Andrews. Swallowing the fear that had my body trembling, I spoke up.

"Allen!" I shouted so he would hear me. "We can talk about it later."

"No—"

"I'm going to be late to practice!"

"This isn't over—"

245

"It doesn't have to be—we can talk, argue, fight—whatever you want, but we have to do it later."

"No, we're doing it right now."

"I can't, Allen!" I said, exasperated as I eyed the field. *Please let Mr. Andrews be late today.* "You know how Mr. Andrews is—you know what it'll be like if I'm late."

"I don't care! We're..."

He continued to shout, but I tuned him out as I stared at the soccer field. I needed to make a choice, and I decided I'd rather risk my relationship with Allen, risk pissing him off even more, than be Mr. Andrews's focus for the next couple of hours. I spun on my heel to head to the soccer field. With my first step, however, I was yanked back around by my right wrist. As I stumbled to gain my footing, Allen grabbed my left wrist, too, and started yelling again that I obviously didn't care about him at all—how could I if I was just going to walk away during an argument? I tried to reason with him, reminding him about Mr. Andrews, then tried to just pull my hands back and leave as I craned my head around and noticed that warm-up had started. My stomach dropped. *Fuck—I'm already late.*

"I have to go!" I shouted, my wrists still trapped in his fists.

"No! You're not going until we talk!" he bellowed back.

I tried to leave again, stepping back and attempting to jerk my wrists out of his hands. Without releasing his hold, Allen stepped backward and yanked, forcing me to stumble toward him.

"You're not leaving yet!"

"I have to!" I shouted back as I struggled to get away, twisting and pulling my arms. It was a useless endeavor; he was much bigger and stronger than I was, and until he decided to let me go, I couldn't do anything about it. I gave up and let him yell as I stared at my feet, silent, until he finally released my wrists and let me leave for practice.

*****

Reaching down, I picked up the loofah I'd dropped for the third time in a row, trying to force myself to focus on the task at hand: showering. But it was hard to shut off the mental replays of the afternoon, from Allen grabbing my wrists and jerking me around to Mr. Andrews's constant attention once I got to practice. With an involuntary shudder, I could feel my body covered in a thick slimy filth that had nothing to do with the sweat and dirt from soccer, but was a result of Mr. Andrews's eyes on my body. Every evening I had to shower that filth off, but it was thicker than normal this time, thanks to having been late to practice.

I twisted the loofah—now firmly in my grasp—around my legs in rough motions and felt a dull, achy type of pain in my wrists when I did. Lifting both of my hands into the stream of the shower water, I rinsed off the bubbles. My loofah dropped out of my suddenly limp fingers as I saw the cause of the pain I'd felt: bruises around both of my wrists like little cuff bracelet tattoos. *Allen did this to me... he left bruises on my body.* Using my fingertips, I probed every millimeter of the discolored and abused skin until I knew where the most tender spots were. *I'm sure he didn't mean to do this. It likely happened when I was trying to pull away; if I hadn't pulled, I probably wouldn't have bruised. He wasn't squeezing me that hard, was he?* I shook my head as I stared down at the bruises, feeling like I was somehow responsible. On one hand, he shouldn't have held on to me when I wanted to leave, but on the other, could I really blame him for the bruises if they were a result of me pulling away?

Regardless of fault, I need to wear long sleeves until these fade, I realized. If my foster mom saw those bruises, she'd lose all respect—all love—for me. She'd never see me the same way if she found out I had bruises from a boyfriend.

But what if it happened again? What if something else happened— what if the next time he punched *me* instead of the wall? I'd worked so hard to earn my foster mom's love back and it would disappear in an instant if something like that happened. I couldn't risk it. I would need to break up with Allen—for good.

duped

"Poisonous relationships can alter our perception. You can spend many years thinking you're worthless."

-Steve Maraboli

late may 2000

Sitting at a picnic table at the park down the road from my house, I took a deep breath and looked over at Allen. He was sitting on the tabletop next to me, telling a story about practicing with his band, but I hadn't been able to focus on what he was saying while I was looking for my willpower and tucking away my emotions into that black hole inside me.

"Allen," I interrupted, waiting for him to look at me. "We're over."

"No," he said immediately.

"Yes, we are."

"No way. I love you, Katherine."

"I love you, too, Allen. But this is the end for us."

"You say that now, but we'll be back together—"

"No, not this time. This is for good this time."

"Why are you doing this? What did I do to you?" he asked, his voice turning combative.

I took another deep breath and looked away; I couldn't keep eye contact when I said this next part. With my heart racing and the world beginning to spin, I answered his question. "I don't know anymore what you might do when we argue, so I'm afraid to argue, afraid to make you mad. I'm scared of you."

He scoffed. "Why would you be afraid of me? I'd never hurt you."

"You almost punched me in Atlanta," I said quietly, studying my fingernails. "And you bruised me when we argued in the parking lot that day when you grabbed my wrists."

"Those were only two incidents. And they don't count anyway. I *didn't* punch you in Atlanta, and you must bruise easily because I didn't grab you that hard in the parking lot. You're just looking for an excuse to break up with me, just like you always do."

I shook my head. "No, Allen, I'm not. I just can't date someone I think might hit me."

"You're overreacting, Katherine."

"I'm not. And it doesn't matter anyway—we're over, we're done. And I'm not changing my mind."

"I love you, damn it, Katherine!" he shouted, his face bright red and a few tears racing down his cheeks. "Please, Katherine, just give us one more chance. Just one."

When I saw that he was crying, my stomach clenched with guilt and the emotions I'd shoved into my black hole came rushing out. Suddenly I was crying, too, and nearly giving him the chance he wanted.

"I can't lose you—I won't let you do this, I won't let you break up with me," he said, his voice filled with emotion.

But something about him telling me he wouldn't *let* me do something dumped a bucket of cold water on that thought and ignited a surge of anger and defiance within me. Instead of giving in, I clenched my jaw and responded.

"You can't stop me from breaking up with you. We're over. You aren't my boyfriend anymore. And I'm not—never again will be—your girlfriend. Got it?"

I shoved up to my feet and started walking home. I heard him shouting after me, but I didn't respond; I didn't slow. I didn't give in.

For the first time, I was doing what was best for myself.

*****

My heart was racing as I laughed, trapped in the magnetic draw he'd always had. How had I let this happen? I'd sworn when I broke up with him for cheating on me three-and-a-half years ago that we were over for good. And then, somehow, Joe and I had started talking after Allen talked me into tutoring him in Latin. I'd stayed away from him when I wasn't tutoring him because I just couldn't control my feelings for him when he was near. But without thinking, I'd accepted his invitation to the movies the day after I'd broken up with Allen.

And now I was standing in the little gazebo across the street from the movie theater, dragging my feet about walking home, laughing at some stupid joke he made, and it was like we'd never been apart. He was getting closer to me, and my body was aware of the shifting of the air molecules as he moved and talked. I knew I should leave, that I had no business even being there right after breaking up with Allen, and yet I couldn't make my feet move. I'd told Joe we were going just as friends, but the look in his eyes was something far beyond friendship. As he got closer, my heart skipped and sputtered in my chest, I couldn't breathe, and the streetlights illuminating the dark of the night seemed to dim.

I can't kiss Joe. I can't—I can't do this. He's a cheater, remember? Just go—

My thoughts ceased as Joe pressed his lips to mine and then I was kissing him back. Excitement and guilt warred strongly within me and I felt sick. He pulled back, ending our kiss and I struggled to breathe.

"I have to go," I said, grinning despite my mixed emotions. And then I left like I should have minutes earlier.

*****

When I walked up to the picnic table at the park two days later, Allen was already there, sitting in the same spot on the tabletop that he'd been in when I broke up with him. I'd hesitated when he called me, tempted to just hang up the phone, but I'd listened instead and then agreed to meet him at the park to talk. I missed him, and the sound of pain and brokenness in his voice was more than I could say no to in that moment.

I settled onto the tabletop next to him, our feet on the bench, and he shifted a few inches so our knees touched. For a moment, I thought I would scoot away so we weren't touching, but I just couldn't find the willpower to do so. We sat in silence for a while as I waited for him to talk; I could tell he had something to say and I didn't mind waiting. It was actually nice to be near him again. After so many years of friendship and dating, it had been a long week without talking to him.

He started crying, trying to hide it by turning away and darting his other hand up quickly to swipe away his tears. "It can't really be over," he said, his voice thick and nasally and breaking at the end.

As gently as I could manage, battling the guilt that was crawling up my throat and threatening to make me cave and go back to him, I assured him it was. He reached over without looking at me and laced his fingers tightly with mine, his thumb smoothing rapidly back and forth across my hand, something he'd always done when he was upset. Long minutes passed in silence aside from the sounds of him crying and trying to clear his nose, and I used the index finger of my left hand to lightly draw patterns across the back of his hand that clasped mine. Prior to Atlanta, I'd seen his hands differently; I'd seen them play his trumpet and guitar, write me notes and create hand-made cards and write song lyrics, hold me when I was upset—his hands, his arms, all of him had been a safe place. But now I looked at them and wondered how much damage they could do, in how many ways. I knew they were strong enough that I couldn't break free of them if I wanted to, that they were capable of touching me in anger.

"I'm sorry," he said, breaking into my thoughts about his hands. His voice was still sad but had a note of resolution and acceptance.

"Was any of it true? The rumors?"

He pulled his hand from mine and turned his head away from me instead of answering. He started fidgeting, first picking at his cuticles, and then his fingers beating a rhythm against his knee. My stomach dropped and I felt sick, tears stinging my eyes. I'd expected him to say "no," I realized.

"You cheated on me!" I accused, my heart racing as I braced myself for an unpleasant revelation.

"You know I did," he replied, his voice tinged with impatience and frustration.

"Not the ones I know about. Were there more? Ones I *didn't* know about?"

After a tense moment, I began to get dizzy as I held my breath in anticipation of having my world flipped upside down again. He nodded his head slowly, still staring straight ahead. "Yeah."

"How many?" I demanded; the words had been ready on my tongue, only waiting for the reply I'd realized was coming.

He shook his head quickly from side to side.

"How many, Allen?" I demanded again, my voice as hard as my clenched jaw, anger and indignation having taken reign over the rest of my emotions.

"Why? You don't need to know that. You don't *really* want to know."

"Yes, I do. Tell me."

"It's just going to hurt you."

"That's *my* problem. I deserve to know what you were doing behind my back. That much you owe me after cheating on me."

He swallowed, glancing at me, then turning away again. "Thirteen."

I felt like I'd been punched or fallen on my back or in some other way had the wind knocked out of me as I struggled to catch my breath; I hadn't expected that. *Thirteen? He cheated on me with thirteen other girls, besides the ones I knew about? This can't be happening. That's... that's not possible!*

"Are you fucking serious?" I shouted, my eyes burning and stomach churning as the edges of my vision turned black and got fuzzy. I swallowed in an attempt to alleviate the sudden dryness in my mouth and when I continued, my voice was more subdued. "So..." I swallowed again. "What? You kissed all those girls? Made out with some of them?"

"Why the hell do you want to know this?"

"Because I deserve to know the truth, Allen!"

"Damn it, Katherine. It doesn't matter anymore. They didn't mean anything anyway. I loved *you*."

I loved you... *I loved* you.

I'd heard those words from him before... so many times before. Just as I'd heard them when I broke up with Joe for having sex with someone behind my back, and my gut told me this was the same as when that had happened. I desperately needed Allen to tell me I was wrong, though; it couldn't be happening again. Whatever he said next would determine my sanity, and I knew it right then, but I couldn't stop myself from pushing for the truth anyway. I *had* to know. Anything—*anything*—was better than uncertainty.

"Tell. Me."

"I had sex with them, okay? Those are the ones I slept with."

No way. No. Fucking. Way. He must be exaggerating. I can't...there's no...he must be lying. "Who?"

"No, I'm not telling you that."

"Who?" I insisted.

"It's none of your business."

"None of my business? You're telling me you had sex with other people, then with me, and it's none of my business? You made it my business when you did it while we were together! Tell me who!"

He rattled off the names, then I demanded he tell me when and where and who else was there until I had to admit that he was telling me the truth. In the process, I learned there were others he'd kissed or made out with in addition to the thirteen he'd had sex with, but I lost count of the others, all the faces swirling behind my eyes, each one bringing a fresh stab of betrayal. There wasn't a soul in school who didn't know Allen and I were dating; was there anyone who thought I was worth fidelity and loyalty? Worth *not* messing around with my boyfriend behind my back and then smiling at me as if nothing had happened?

"So, I'm inclined to think now that all the other shit I heard about you was true, too," I said, feeling deflated and beat up and not sure why I couldn't just keep my mouth shut and remain in blissful ignorance. "Do you drink and do drugs?"

He sighed, still tapping a rhythm against his knee. "Yes."

"What the hell, Allen? How are you doing all this shit and I don't know about it? I mean, there were rumors, but... How are you hiding all this from me?"

His face and neck turned bright red and I knew he was embarrassed about whatever he was about to say. "I paid people not to tell you," he said softly.

"You *WHAT?*"

I was sure I'd misheard him—there was just no way. I'd read books and seen movies where that kind of thing happened, the ultimate duplicity and manipulation. But that stuff didn't happen in real life, right? Let alone in our tiny rural town that would have to be ten times its size to qualify as a city. And it definitely couldn't happen to me, of all people; I wasn't that blind or stupid. It simply couldn't be true. Whatever else had happened, he certainly hadn't *paid* people to lie to me, to hide the truth from me. That... that was just *crazy*. No, I hadn't heard him correctly, that's all.

"Can you say that again?" I whispered.

He cleared his throat. "I paid my friends not to tell you, to lie to you if you asked, because I knew you'd be mad."

I *had*, in fact, heard him correctly. The world tilted sideways, spinning out of control. How could I possibly have allowed myself to be manipulated like that? To be that *stupid*? How could he have done that to me? Anger burned through my veins as I glanced over at his profile while he stared straight ahead, his red face betraying his lingering embarrassment; he was embarrassed by what he'd done, but it had worked... *I* was *mortified*. But it wasn't just him; it was all those other people who were complicit—who made out with him or had sex with him behind my back, who were willing to lie to me in exchange for some money... Could I really even blame any of them, though? I mean... how could I have been so fucking stupid that they could get away with it?

"I'm sorry," he said again, his voice stronger than it had been. "But I promise I won't do it again. I promise. This time will be different."

"*This* time?" I asked, bewildered, my mind still racing to process what he'd revealed to me.

"We're giving us another try, one more chance. You have to, Katherine. We aren't over—we're too good together."

"No, Allen, we—"

"I won't accept no, Katherine, not—"

"Allen!" I shouted, feeling a desperation to put an end to this back and forth. "We're over. For good. I..." I hesitated, though I'd already started. I wasn't sure I wanted to do what I was about to do, but felt I had no choice—he would finally accept that we were over if I did. "I went to the movies with Joe," I said quickly.

"What?" he asked, the air around us suddenly very still.

"The other night." I swallowed. "We kissed."

"You cheated on me with my best friend?" he screamed.

"No!" I shouted back. "We broke up a week ago, Allen! I told you we were over, and I meant it."

"That doesn't matter," he roared back. "Let's go." He grabbed my wrist, and while I didn't want to follow him, I did anyway—I didn't even try to get away as he stormed to his car. "Get in," he said through clenched teeth.

Dread filled the pit of my stomach and I knew I shouldn't, but I opened the door and got in anyway. I was afraid of not doing what he said. As he peeled out of the parking spot, his tires kicking up and spewing gravel in all directions, I closed my eyes briefly and prayed we wouldn't get into a wreck. As he flew down the road, far exceeding the speed limit and blowing through a stop sign, I asked him where he was taking us, but he wouldn't respond.

I figured it out when we started down the road I knew Joe lived on, his mom and stepdad now living temporarily in another house the next town over from Allen and me. Allen skidded to a stop at the top of their gravel driveway and launched himself out of the car as he was still shifting into park, his door left wide open. Frozen, I watched from my car seat as he barreled toward Joe, who was in his yard, and—without a word of warning—punched him in the back of the head.

Shouting ensued as Dennis, Joe's stepdad, flew out the back door of the house toward Allen, but the blood rushing through my ears was so loud

I couldn't make out any of the words. I was terrified, but I couldn't move. Allen jumped back into the car and I knew I shouldn't be in there with him. My body was frozen, however, and a split-second later, Allen was fishtailing down the gravel road away from Joe's house.

By the time we reached the paved main road, he'd calmed to some extent, and pulled over at the first gas station as he started shouting.

"Dennis called the fucking cops. They're coming, so you need to get rid of your cigarettes before they get here."

"What?" I asked, trying to process what he was saying through the elevating panic inside.

"Your cigarettes! Give them to me!" he shouted.

I fumbled around in my purse, pulling out the pack of cigarettes there; I'd forgotten I had them, the first pack I'd gotten since I'd returned from the group home. Allen grabbed them and spun around to the back of the gas station as blue lights came into view down the road. Reaching through his open window, he chucked them into the woods and pulled back around to the front, parking just as the two police cars pulled in.

One car parked and the officer walked up to us while the other pulled around behind the building. Allen got out of the car and talked to the first officer while I sat in the front, replaying everything that had just happened and locking up my emotions, one by one. The second officer appeared a few minutes later, holding the pack of cigarettes Allen had thrown into the woods, holding them up and tilting his head.

"I believe you threw these out your window," he said, shaking the pack between his fingers.

"They're not mine," Allen said, pointing inside the car toward me. "They're my girlfriend's—I was getting rid of them for her."

My heart stopped—I couldn't believe he'd just done that. He was already in trouble—what would he gain by telling them the cigarettes came from me? I did the only thing I could think of right then and leaned toward the open window, glaring up at him.

"I'm not your girlfriend," I said loudly.

june 2000

I stood at the end of my driveway, watching Allen pull away again, wondering how I'd become this person, how I kept thinking there was something there that wasn't. Every time he'd called since I'd learned about the extent of his lies, I'd answered. And since the police had decided not to tell my foster mom about the cigarettes, every time Allen asked to see me, I said yes.

He'd pick me up and drive me to the expansive orchard behind his family's property, parking under the trees off the main road. As the sun tracked low and the horizon bathed everything in an orange glow, he'd talk about trouble he was having in class or soccer, an argument he'd had with his parents, or about the new song he'd written or sermon he was planning to give that coming Sunday in his father's church. He'd tell me how much he missed me and how sorry he was for everything, how he was struggling without me to talk to every day. Despite my resolve, tears would escape, and I'd tell him I missed him, too. He'd wrap his arms around me and hold me as I cried, telling me how much he still loved me, occasionally cradling my face and using his thumbs to clear the moisture from my cheeks.

As my shoulders shook against his chest, his hands would slide down my back, smoothing back up under my shirt against my bare skin. He'd grab my hips and lift me onto the hood of his car, if I wasn't already sitting there, all the time whispering into my ear about his regrets and his love for me. He'd kiss my lips as he used his fingers to undo my shorts or jeans and tug them down with my panties to puddle at my ankles, leaving my bare ass on the dirty metal of his old car's hood as he reached into his pocket and pulled out a condom. And then he'd screw me on the hood of his car.

When he was finished, as soon as I reached for my clothes around my ankles, I would feel the weight of regret over my head, trying to suffocate me, as my mind exploded with questions.

Why did I do that? Why can't I tell him no? Why does he always have a condom in his pocket? Does this mean he really loved me after all, that he regrets what he did? Or was he just horny and knew he'd be able to get into my pants because I still love him? Why do I feel so desperate for him to love me back?

He'd laugh sheepishly, blushing, as he waited for me to finish redressing my lower half and say we probably shouldn't do that anymore since we weren't dating. That he'd love to spend more time with me, but he had to be somewhere. Every time he spoke those words, my heart would sink because I'd realize he'd just wanted to have sex and I'd allowed myself to be used. Again. Then he'd drive me home, smiling as he navigated the streets, occasionally reaching over to squeeze my knee. My skin would burn where he touched me, shouting for him to return the warmth of his hand and take anything he wanted as long as I could have his love, while at the same time my stomach turned, and I wanted to snap my knees together and glue them that way so he could never again consider venturing there.

His foot would remain on the brake as he pulled up in front of my driveway, telling me it was great to see me. I'd gaze at him for a moment, wondering if he would kiss me or tell me again that he loved me the way he had when he'd picked me up—we'd just had sex, after all—but he'd just slide his hands around on his steering wheel, still grinning, waiting for me to get out. I'd open the door and climb out of his car with my heart struggling to pump. He'd smile and—with a final wave—drive off.

I always watched him go, like I was right then, my body heavy and slimy with self-loathing I knew I couldn't scrub away, a feeling that would return once the pain from rubbing my skin with my pencil eraser faded. Every time, I thought it would be the time things were different, and I held my breath as I waited for him to honk or tap his brakes or turn his head—some sign that thoughts of me lingered with him as he went.

But he never did any of those things. Not even once.

hija gringa

"Seeking validation will keep you trapped."

-Unknown

june 2000

I was standing outside the Reagan National airport with a cross-body purse and a suitcase, smiling as I waved good-bye to my foster mom and my sister. Turning, I took a deep breath and walked through the doors, looking around for the check-in counter for my airline and a bathroom; my digestive tract was *not* happy with me. It was a sensation I was intimately familiar with, something that happened anytime I traveled into an urban area or crowds of people, and I knew I had only moments to find a toilet.

With luggage checked in and after several trips to the bathroom, I bought a bottle of water and sat down in a chair by my gate, glancing up at the board to make sure my flight was still on time, and then pulled out my worn and weathered copy of *Wuthering Heights*. Also in my purse was an English-Spanish dictionary, a stack of flashcards I'd made by cutting index cards in half that was held together with a rubber band, my passport, and a folder burgeoning with papers: two printed copies of my itinerary and AFS exchange paperwork, printed copies of every email containing information about my upcoming summer abroad, and all the information I could find online about the small Chilean town I'd be living in a few hours south of the capital of Santiago.

When my foster mom had introduced the idea of me doing a summer exchange program with American Field Service, or AFS, after my interest in the Spanish language and Latin-American culture bloomed, I'd jumped on the offer. After a year of saving my wages from working on the weekends, my allowance, and raising money with the AFS-recommended fundraisers until we could afford the trip, I was en route to Miami for three days with all the other students in the US who were traveling to South America.

As I sat there in the airport, however, I didn't have the same confidence I'd had when I decided to do the program; if I was so stupid and blind that I hadn't seen everything Allen was doing—how could I possibly handle an exchange program? But even with the intense doubt and fear I now harbored about this solo trip to another part of the world, I was relieved I would have a forced distance from Allen since I couldn't figure out how to tell him "no." I was hoping that I'd be able to find myself while I was gone.

*****

The next several days of stateside and overseas orientations, broken up by the thirteen-hour flight from Miami to Santiago, had flown by in a blur of feeling so nauseous I couldn't eat—and if I did, it passed immediately through me—and pasting on a smile to hide my discomfort and fear. Most of this had fallen away, however, when those of us headed to the sleepy little town of Cúrico were loaded onto the bus that would take us there, along with the woman who lived in the town and would be our Spanish language teacher a few days a week as well as local AFS coordinator, Mari.

We hit the road on the first day in over a week that it wasn't raining, though our drive began with the skies dark and threatening. Less than thirty minutes into what was supposed to be a two-and-a-half hour bus ride, however, the clouds began to scatter, a neon blue peeking between them. Mari told us then that we would be taking several detours along the way and our trip would be significantly longer than anticipated. There was severe flood damage from the rain along the sole major road to our destination; there were sections of road missing and closed, necessitating that we—and everyone else traveling—detour along bumpy dirt side roads, many only a single lane wide, and none intended for the volume of traffic they saw.

As we got further from the city, the landscape changed dramatically, showcasing the poverty-stricken countryside that was newly devastated from the rainfall. Long lines of people walked alongside our bus heading toward the city. They carried packs and young children stacked several feet out from their backs, their arms filled with as much as they could carry. Their clothes, their skin, their hair, their belongings—everything was covered in a yellowish-tan mud. Their faces were all vacant, barely even registering us passing them. I couldn't keep myself from staring at them, my gut clenching at the somehow familiar expressions on their faces, and my body started to feel tight and hot.

"Many of the poor make houses from scraps of metal and woods along the riverbank," Mari explained. "When the river floods, they lose their homes and everything they do not carry in their arms."

"Where will they go?" I called out through the silence that followed.

"Most will go to the city to try to sell something on the street for food."

"Are there any shelters? Anything?" I asked.

"No, I'm afraid there are not," she replied sadly. "Our country still needs to do work on the infrastructure."

The tears that had been building as I watched the people passing us spilled over. I wanted the bus to stop. I wanted to open my suitcase and pass out the clean, warm clothes I had packed inside, give them the bottle of water I had in my hands for them to drink. I wanted to usher them onto the bus and have the driver take them wherever they needed to go, wherever they would have shelter and food. It didn't seem fair to me that we were so well-equipped to take care of ourselves and we were the ones on the bus while those who truly needed it were fighting to put one foot in front of another through the mud with miles to go in order to reach an uncertain future after having what little they had in life destroyed.

My chest ached, and I leaned my forehead against the cold glass of the bus window as tears burned tracks in my cheeks from my eyes to my chin. As it became harder to breathe, I wanted to rage and destroy something because I couldn't help those people. If I lowered the window and leaned out from the bus, I could probably touch them as we passed each other, and yet there wasn't a damn thing I could do to help them, and that knowledge was as infuriating as it was crushing. After a while, the other students on the bus started chatting excitedly with each other again, asking Mari questions, and I couldn't blame them; what we were doing *was* really exciting. But I couldn't even summon up more than minimal excitement for the months ahead when I knew there were men and women and children newly homeless, without food or clean water or even a makeshift shelter.

My excitement finally made a comeback when we arrived in Cúrico to meet our host families. Mine was a mom, dad, and two girls (one about eight months younger than me, the other about two years younger). They also had an older son in the Naval Academy in Santiago, but he lived on campus. Despite the unexpected and long delay in picking us up from the bus station, most of the families there were smiling, excited to meet the students they were welcoming to their homes for the next couple of months. As soon as I laid eyes on my host family, they welcomed me with literal open arms, enormous grins, and twinkling eyes. I fell in love with them immediately.

Once bundled cozily into their small car, my host father asked me in broken English how the bus ride had been. I wanted to smile and make a good impression—I certainly didn't want to come across as whiny or unappreciative—but I couldn't mask my sadness when my eyes filled with fresh tears.

"It was okay," I said quietly as my voice broke. "There were a lot of people who'd lost their homes in the flooding."

My host father's face clouded as he glanced at me in the rearview mirror and his eyes softened. He translated what I'd said to my host mother, who didn't speak any English, and her face fell, too, as she nodded her head quietly.

My host father explained they owned a small farm with some vegetables and pigs that was the main source of income for their family, that several of their workers' homes had flooded, that they were staying in a building on his farm intended to house equipment and had no electricity, but it was better than the alternative. He told me he'd take me out to the farm once the land had dried out some, that he couldn't drive out there right now or his little pickup truck would get stuck in the mud since the road onto the property was just a path that had been cleared through the fields. He asked if I'd ever been to a farm and I explained that it was different from what he did, but that I'd lived on a farm for a few years and he beamed once again. My host sisters, one on each side of where I sat in the middle of the back seat, each had their arms wrapped around one of mine and were grinning from ear to ear in their excitement to have me there. I couldn't remember ever seeing anyone in my life so excited to have me around. I couldn't understand why they were so excited about *me,* but felt I could bask in that glow indefinitely. Despite the sadness I'd seen on my way there, I felt warmth take root inside me; sitting in that car full of strangers, trying to communicate despite our language barriers, I felt like I belonged... I felt loved.

*****

I settled pretty quickly into life with my host family. My host father was interested in everything about life in the United States, with an endless stream of questions about my life and the culture there. He wanted to practice his English, so he had a rule that he could only talk in English to me, but because my Spanish was woefully inadequate, I was only allowed to talk to him in Spanish. If I couldn't, he would tell me how to say what I needed after we managed to communicate and then I had to repeat my English in Spanish. The family, like all there, was patriarchal, but my host father was respectful and kind; his family obviously adored him, and I grew to as well.

The whole family was very affectionate and they all welcomed me as one of their own. My host father introduced me to everyone we met as his "hija gringa" or, roughly translated into English, his foreign daughter. My host mother adopted the term as well, and my host sisters called me their "hermana gringa." My entire body warmed at the endearments—especially coming from my host father—and I felt more a part of their family than I'd ever felt a part of any family, including my own biological family.

Because they were on the other side of the equator, what was my summer in the states was their winter, though it was milder than winters were in Virginia. Even so, it was cold. Inside the small houses, upper-middle-class families like the one I was living with had a single heating unit installed in the wall that would run for an hour a day to keep the temperature indoors manageable. You wore sweaters and socks during the day and at night added on a beanie for sleep under a pile of blankets. You planned your laundry several days in advance; the clothes going from the washer to the clothes line for sometimes a couple of days until they freeze-dried and were brought in for ironing. Meals were slow and relaxed and loaded with food and lunches were followed by a siesta.

Especially that first week, my family doted on me. They asked me constantly if I was warm enough, and when I kept laughing and assuring them I was fine, they explained they had been told they had to buy a heater for my room but they hadn't done so yet. I was baffled; why would they buy a heater for my room? They explained that other students in the past had complained about being cold in the houses and all the host families had been advised to keep their homes warmer while the students stayed there. They were already running their existing heater for two hours a day instead of the normal one, but couldn't run it more without polluting the air with toxic fumes. My stomach sank when they told me they were changing what they were doing to accommodate how my life had been in the United States—I felt guilty and mortified on behalf of my country. The purpose of the trip was to experience another culture, not demand it adjust to be more like ours.

I explained that to my host family, assured them that I didn't want anything to be done differently simply because I was there, and they were surprised. They explained they had also been instructed to serve more food at meal times because of complaints from students and their families in the States that they hadn't had enough food to eat, and again I was baffled and ashamed of my country. It suddenly made sense why my host mom was always serving me seconds and thirds against my assurances that I was full, even though everyone else had stopped eating already. I vehemently promised them I didn't want them to do that anymore, that I wanted to experience life with them, not force mine on them. I couldn't keep from apologizing for my own culture of excess and expectation that the world adjust to accommodate us.

Soon enough, we fell into a comfortable routine. Three days per week, I walked about a mile to the small building where I attended language classes and cultural field trips with my fellow exchange students, led by Mari. We visited beaches with black sand, expansive vineyards, tiny villages, museums. We practiced vocabulary and verb conjugations, discussed local idioms and turns of phrase, talked about how that part of the country had a dialect where they tended to leave off the final "s" in words when they were speaking. We took frequent breaks to have a smoke next to the fire with a cup of coffee or hot chocolate to warm our fingers.

Two days per week, I squeezed into a uniform better suited to my host sister's taller and slimmer frame and layered on sweaters and finally a coat, thick socks, and two pairs of pants and traveled to school with my host sisters. I sat through classes bouncing my legs rapidly in an attempt to warm up; the rooms were all fresh air, glassless windows and open doorways to the outdoors. I didn't know enough Spanish to follow the lectures at first, but I did my best to keep up and complete the work anyway, enjoying the challenge.

The boys and men opened doors and let the women and girls go first. Couples who were dating would stand together chatting to their friends, and the boys had an arm draped comfortably over their girlfriends' shoulders. The pace of life was slower, more relaxed. There seemed to be more mutual respect between peers and between children and adults. I was fascinated by how different it was from the US and fell deeper into love with not only my host family, but the entire culture with each passing day.

Within the first few weeks, I was practically the only exchange student from my group who didn't have a boyfriend or girlfriend there and I felt left out, like there was something wrong with me. If I could just be like them, find a boy from there who liked me, I just *knew* I'd be treated well. It would mean that I was worth something after all, that maybe I hadn't deserved everything Allen had done and everything else that had happened to me. Maybe I could stop staring at the computer screen at night, crying when I didn't have an email from Allen; crying harder when I did and he was sure to include some reference to making out or having sex with someone else. My host family was confused about why I was so upset every night and I felt guilty; I didn't want them to think I was ungrateful.

I needed something to happen to prove to me I was worth more than that so I could maybe start to believe it myself.

mid-july 2000

As we often did, several of the other exchange students and I were taking a walk through the small town, their local significant others joining up with us. When one of them arrived, he had an unfamiliar face with him and introduced the new guy as Rodrigo. Everyone else waved and said "hola," then Rodrigo started walking next to me.

Rodrigo was possibly the tallest person I'd ever seen in real life—easily a foot taller than me, if not more—and I wondered immediately if he played basketball. I discovered when I tried to ask him that he spoke no English and struggled to understand my limited Spanish that came with a heavy American accent. We continued to try to communicate, however, both of us more amused than frustrated by our entertaining train wreck of an attempt at carrying on a conversation. Every time I struggled with a word, he smiled at me, a broad, easy grin that brought crinkles to the corners of his eyes. I was filled with a fluttering sensation in my chest when he smiled at me like that and it was getting harder to think clearly.

We'd been walking for a while and I was starting to get hungry. Looking up, Rodrigo was grinning down at me and the fluttering was so strong it took my breath away, leaving me struggling to find the words I needed.

"I'm... I mean... Tengo hombre," I said.

Rodrigo's face split as his smile grew wider and he bent over slightly as he started laughing, and I heard laughter coming from everyone else as they glanced at me. My heart skipped as I tried to figure out why; *I said tengo—I have or I am—hom—oh shit, I said I have a man.* I burst out laughing with everyone else.

"No, no," I said through my giggles. "Tengo *hambre.*"

"Suuuuuure," one of my fellow exchange students said with a wink.

We all continued to laugh, and I could feel my face redden with embarrassment that I'd made such a silly mistake. I could read and write Spanish with relative ease, but when it came to listening and speaking, I struggled to recognize and recall words and conjugations. I wanted to say that I was embarrassed by my error but didn't know the word. Applying a rule of thumb that was often helpful, I adjusted the English version of the word.

"Estoy embarazada."

Everyone's laughter deepened, and when I asked why, they were laughing too hard to respond, so I dug my pocket dictionary out of my bag. Flipping the pages to find the word I'd said in Spanish, I read the entry and realized I'd said I was pregnant. Snorting with laughter, I flipped to the English section of the book and found the correct word. We all laughed together as we continued meandering along the main avenue looking for a place to grab a basket of fries together. While I'd made mistakes that had everyone clutching their sides in laughter, it was something everyone did at some point—it was part of learning a new language—and I didn't feel like I was being laughed *at.* It was a subtle difference in how people behaved that I hadn't been aware of until right then, thinking back to the shame that accompanied making mistakes of any sort in front of my peers at home.

I looked up often as we walked, unable to stop grinning at my own mistakes, and I always found Rodrigo looking down at me, a friendly answering smile on his face, his eyes twinkling as he walked along, his hands in his pockets.

late july 2000

Cyndi, my host sister closest in age to me, and I were at a discotheque with Ciri, an older exchange student with whom we were spending the night.

We'd already been there for a few hours, alternating dancing with sipping on Piscolas—a Chilean drink comprised of Pisco and Coke that Cyndi insisted I try. I knew Ciri was there somewhere, but I hadn't seen her in a while.

"I'm going to smoke a cigarette!" I shouted so Cyndi could hear me over the din.

"I go too," a guy standing nearby said. He was one of many guys and girls who'd danced with us since we'd arrived, chatting with us when we took breaks, interested in who I—"la gringa"—was.

"Okay," I nodded, heading for the door.

We stepped out the front door together. He lit my cigarette for me as I started shaking from the cold—I was not dressed for hanging out outside in the middle of the night in a Chilean winter.

"You want truck? No cold," he said in broken English.

I nodded vigorously. "Yes, please," I said, my breath choppy from my body shaking.

He started his truck after opening the passenger door for me to climb in and closing it behind me, blasting the heat and cracking the windows so the smoke would have an escape route. We smoked in silence aside from my chattering teeth and the sounds of our exhales, the interior dimly lit by the nearly full moon above filtering through the smoke that wafted around inside the truck cab. When we finished our cigarettes, I tossed the butt out the crack in the window and rubbed my still-cold hands together in front of the vent that was finally blowing warmish air. He raised the windows when he finished his cigarette, but instead of turning off the ignition, he turned and said he wanted to kiss me.

I laughed, flattered and taken aback, but quickly agreed; a kiss in a foreign country sounded like the kind of romance I was hoping to find. Our lips met and his hands instantly went up the back of my shirt as he shoved his tongue into my mouth. I pulled back, laughing again, though this time it was to cover my sudden discomfort. I shook my head back and forth, repeating the word "no."

"Si, si, amor," he replied, scooting closer to me on the bench seat.

I grabbed the door handle as my body flooded with electricity, realizing he wasn't getting the picture that I was saying no, but nothing happened. *When did he lock the doors?* I turned my head, trying to find the lock in the dark as he tugged up the back of my shirt and went for my bra clasp, my stomach clenching with dread. Flipping back around, I said "no" again, but he kept repeating "si" in response, snagging one of my hands and shoving it onto his bare penis. *How the hell did he get himself out of his jeans that fucking fast?*

"No! No quiero! Por favor, no quiero!" I shouted, hoping I was saying I didn't want to do it; in my panic, my knowledge of Spanish became elusive, and I could only think of what to say in English.

He continued to repeat one word—the Spanish word for yes—using a hand to grab my hair and holding my head still as his tongue touched my face, my neck, and his other hand attacked my long skirt. He stopped abruptly when his hand made contact with the pad I was wearing; I was on my period. He asked something I didn't understand but I went out on a limb assuming he was asking me if I was bleeding and shouted, "Si! Si!"

There was nothing for a long moment aside from the loudness of my shallow, panicked breathing as I waited to see if he would let me go or not. He shifted suddenly so his back was against his seat again. Using the hand that still had my hair fisted in it, he shoved my head down, stuffing his erection into my mouth as I fought against my gag reflex so I wouldn't choke. As he forced my head up and down until he'd filled my mouth with his semen, tears fueled by fear and relief fell from my eyes onto his body; he was letting me off with a blow job. I'd never been so happy in my life to have my period.

As soon as he was done, he went around and opened the door for me to climb out and I realized the door simply didn't open from the inside. He draped an arm over my shoulders as we walked back inside as if we were a couple, and I was too scared and confused to do anything but allow it. My eyes scanned the crowd frantically when we walked inside, looking for Cyndi; I suddenly realized how unsafe we really were and would never forgive myself if something like what I'd just experienced had happened to her because of my absence. When I found her, my whole body sagged in relief and I ducked out from under the strange guy's arm as I beelined over to her.

*****

For the rest of the night, I hadn't left my host sister's side, an expert fake smile on my face. When we'd gotten to Ciri's house for the night, I'd listened to the sounds of them sleeping as I chain-smoked the rest of my cigarettes and watched the moon travel across the sky and fade as the sun began to rise for the new day. I'd hoped that the smoke would cleanse the taste of a stranger's semen from the inside of my mouth that lingered beyond having brushed my teeth so many times I'd lost count. It didn't.

Now, everyone was awake and it was time to return home. But I wasn't ready to go; I felt sick thinking about seeing my host father after the previous night's encounter. I was afraid he would look at me and know what had happened. That he would be disgusted, regret that I'd come there and would want me to leave early. I called another host student and asked her if I could come to her place for the day. She said she had tons of homework but was fine with me hanging out in her room while she did it.

The day passed quickly, a blur of smoking cigarettes and playing Tetris on her computer. I found the intense focus required for the simple game to be soothing and couldn't seem to stop. My head throbbed from staring at the screen, and my fingers were cramped from holding the same tense position for hours on end, but I was unable to turn it off until I could no longer put off returning to my host family's home.

*****

It had been a week and I was finally able to stop thinking about the discotheque every waking moment and had hope that the nightmares that had started would start to taper off soon. Everything on the outside had continued as normal, despite my fear that every time someone looked at me, they would know what had happened and be disgusted with me and never talk to me again.

"Hola," a familiar voice called.

I looked up from where I'd been staring at the ground as I walked with the other exchange students through town to see Rodrigo jogging over to our group. I smiled, but that same fear of being discovered gripped me. He fell into step next to me and soon my fear dissolved.

We decided as a group to stop in at a café in town for soda, fries, and a little warmth, and ended up there for hours as we played games and chatted and sheltered from the wind that made the damp air feel bitterly cold against our skin. I spent most of my time listening and observing, not feeling up to the chattiness I normally engaged in, my mind scattered and continuously going blank as it had for the past week. But I was keenly aware of Rodrigo's eyes on my face anyway. When it was time for everyone to head to their respective homes for dinner, he looked down at me, obviously nervous, and then his eyes darted away.

"I like you. Walk... tomorrow. Please?" he asked in broken English.

I stared at him, dumbfounded that he'd just spoken to me in English—he hadn't spoken a single word of the language when I'd met him. I decided to respond in Spanish. "Si, me gustaría mucho," I said, crossing my fingers that I'd correctly conjugated the verb so I was saying, "Yes, I would really like to."

*****

My host father invited Rodrigo in when he knocked on the door; he'd told me he wanted to talk to him before we would be allowed to leave. I followed and stood near where they sat in the living room, listening to my host father ask Rodrigo questions about his family, where he went to school, what he did for fun, and more. I felt so loved as I listened that I had to fight the tears that wanted to surface. *If only you knew what I did the other night, how stupid I really am, you wouldn't care so much,* I thought.

After forty-five minutes, I figured they must be nearly done talking and decided to use the bathroom while they finished up. As I peed, my heart started racing and my stomach flipping over, everything beginning to dim and turn fuzzy. I stared down between my knees toward the floor, trying to will my heartrate to slow and my breathing to normalize, not sure why they were suddenly so out of whack. My eyes slowly focused from the blind stare they were in and I noticed the crotch of my bare panties between my knees.

What if Rodrigo is like that guy in the truck? I thought, beginning to wonder if I shouldn't take a walk with him. But it was too late; he was already there. Backing out wasn't an option—it would be rude and might hurt his feelings. I reached over to open the under-sink cabinet, pulling out a thick overnight menstrual pad, unwrapping it, and sticking it onto my panties.

Just in case.

We walked around town until well past sunset, working hard to communicate with one another. Rodrigo showed off the handful of English words he'd learned, explaining he'd started studying the day he met me. We sat next to each other at a picnic table in the main square and he asked me if it would be okay for him to hold my hand and my heart swelled. When he walked me back to my host family's home, asking if he could kiss me before placing a soft kiss on my cheek, I nearly cried with relief that he was proving not everyone was like the guy in the truck, and with shame that I'd been so afraid of this kind boy.

*****

"Hola," I said, smiling up as Rodrigo joined our group's walk about a week and a half later.

I'd been seeing him nearly every day since he'd first come to the house to take me on a walk. As I'd come to expect, his face lit up when his eyes found me, as if I was the sun and he'd been living in darkness. The confusing mix of emotions that had become familiar engulfed me as I knew it would; I felt so whole and lovable as I watched him fall in love with me. I was excited to spend time with him because I enjoyed just being around him and his perpetual grin when he was with me made me see everything in a more positive light. But I also felt almost sick with guilt; as much as I liked him, and as much as I wanted to, I simply couldn't seem to feel as deeply for him as he felt for me.

"Hola," he replied, his cheeks turning pink as he blushed and held out his hand.

I grinned, butterflies fluttering in my stomach as I took the papers he held out to me. He wrote me letters daily—sometimes more than one per day—in a mixture of English and Spanish and gave them all to me each time I saw him. Sometimes he wanted me to read them with him, and other times, I saved them for after I'd gotten home. I treasured each one, collecting them carefully in the drawer of my nightstand.

Once I got back home that evening, I knew my host father would ask if I'd seen Rodrigo, as he always did. He didn't like that I spent so much time with Rodrigo, sure Rodrigo was bad for me because he came from a public school in a country where public education was only for the extremely impoverished families. Every time he told me Rodrigo would never amount to much because of his background, I felt ashamed for disappointing him and guilty that he had no idea that I came from something much, much poorer than Rodrigo. I felt like an imposter in his home, and I was so afraid of how he might see me if I told him about my past that I couldn't force myself to do it.

august 2000

I woke the morning of my birthday and dressed in my uniform for school with my host sisters the same way I did every other day. I walked down the short hall and turned, freezing in place, unsure how to process what I saw. The dining table had a few wrapped gifts sitting on it, but the biggest surprise was the wall. Behind the small table were two walls of mirrored glass that joined into a corner. The glass was covered with messages and notes from everyone in my host family, in both English and Spanish, little drawings and designs, all done with my host mother's lipstick. My host sisters, squealing in excitement behind me, told me about how they'd all snuck out of bed after I was asleep to do it, that it had been my host father's idea because he had to leave early and wouldn't be there to wish me a happy birthday when I woke up. When they asked if I liked it, I couldn't do anything more than nod my head up and down, my throat closed with emotion. My host mother walked in and the three of them engulfed me in a giant hug and I broke down and cried. I could feel their love for me, some strange girl from another country who they'd accepted and welcomed as one of their own. I cried because the feelings were so intensely foreign and wonderful, and I cried because I didn't know how I was going to walk away from it in less than two weeks.

When my host father picked all three of us up from school that day for the lunch hour, my host mother was also in the car, and I wondered briefly why since she was always home serving up lunch so it was on the table when we walked in. Instead of driving us home, my host father drove around the corner from the school to the home of some friends of the family. Their home was decorated and a feast was laid out, a thousand-layer cake prepared just in honor of my sixteenth birthday, more of their friends and extended family members present for the celebration as well.

I couldn't believe how many people were there, how much trouble everyone had gone to for my sake. I was intensely grateful and uncomfortable with how much effort had been expended on my behalf—it was wonderful and too much at the same time. I wouldn't have been upset if they hadn't even remembered my birthday; I would have been excited for them to simply wish me a happy birthday before I'd left for school. But all they'd done? I didn't know how to accept that.

*****

My heart pounded as I scanned the bus station for about the millionth time. I wasn't looking for anything, but I couldn't focus. My host father was talking about some of the silly language mix-ups we'd had over the summer, and everyone was adding on as he did, laughing, but our eyes were all glassy, our eyelashes damp. As my eyes began another scan, Rodrigo appeared around the corner of the bus station, running toward us.

What's he doing here? School was in session, so he should have been in class. He jogged over, barreling into me, wrapping his arms around me in a tight hug that lifted me off my feet. He said he skipped school because he had to see me one more time before I left, that he hadn't been able to even sleep because of my impending departure.

"Te amo," he whispered as something wet touched my cheek and he set me down.

He loves me... he said he loves me. I gazed into his tear-stained face and couldn't comprehend how someone so sweet could care about me that much. My jaw trembled violently moments later as I looked from his face to those of my host family from my seat on the bus, my hand pressed against the glass, until we pulled from the curb and I could no longer see them. Though the tears on my cheeks were hot, burning my skin, the rest of my body felt cold and empty, as if there were parts of me I was leaving behind.

surprises

"Betrayal is the only truth that sticks."

-Arthur Miller

late august 2000

A deep sadness had taken hold of me as soon as I left the bus station in Cúrico and only deepened once I arrived in the US, though I covered it with the same broad smile I used to cover everything else. Within that first week, I received an envelope with multiple letters from Rodrigo talking about his dream of coming to the US when he turned eighteen to make a life with me. He spent pages describing his love for me, describing how I had hijacked all his thoughts, how he'd never felt so happy in his soul. I hated myself more with every word I read, knowing he was too good for me, knowing I could never feel about him the way he felt about me.

I'd spent a lot of time thinking about the night at the discotheque, how monumentally stupid I'd been to go outside alone with that boy, how lucky I'd been that I hadn't been forced to do more than I had. And I was thinking about that guy again a little over a week after my return as the asphalt passed under Allen's car tires. When he'd called and said he wanted to catch up, that he'd missed me over the summer and asked if he could pick me up, I'd agreed despite the tightening in the pit of my stomach. I was desperate for something to make me feel normal again, desperate to feel loved by someone about whom I cared deeply.

We arrived at the orchard and he parked in the same place he always did, but I ignored the voice in my head that told me he'd only called me to get laid. He asked me about the summer and I told him about the landscape, from the black sand beaches to the Andes Mountains with tops so high they disappeared into the clouds. I told him about the differences in culture, from the patriarchal society to the midday lunch and siesta. I described my host family and how they'd worked so hard to ensure my comfort and about everything they'd done for my birthday. I talked and talked, my eyes glassy, about all the wonderful things I'd fallen in love with and desperately missed now that I'd returned, but I carefully avoided any mention of Rodrigo or the guy in the truck. I was unsure how Allen would react to my stupidity the night of the discotheque or if mention of Rodrigo would trigger his violent jealousy the way the mention of Joe had at the beginning of the summer.

Allen smiled as he listened to me, and suddenly I realized that instead of sitting next to me on the hood of his car, he was standing in front of me, his hands on the bare skin of my thighs below the hem of my shorts. His thumb started rhythmically circling a flat mole on my left thigh as he looked down and his focus shifted to my legs.

What is it with that damn mole? Joe and Will had also been drawn to it; it seemed to be a magnet for sexual attention. I looked down where Allen's thumb continued to circle it and felt a deep loathing begin to take root.

"Hey, A-allen," I stammered, my heart racing as I reached down to stop his hands from moving any further up my thighs. "I thought we could just talk." Despite my intent to come across as confident and authoritative, my voice was soft and hesitant.

Instead of responding, he raised his head and looked at me for a moment. Then, pulling his hands out from under mine and wrapping them around me, he pulled me closer to the end of the hood and up against the erection between his legs as he began kissing me.

"I missed you so much," he whispered a moment later as he worked to unbutton my shorts.

Stop! Just Stop! I screamed in my mind, but I said nothing; I did nothing; I simply allowed him to continue, though I felt nauseous at the thought of having sex. Within a few rapid breaths, Allen was inside me, though his face in front of me kept morphing into the face of the guy in the truck and I was barely even aware of what Allen was doing as I fought to banish the unwanted imagery.

Allen suddenly paused between thrusts. "You're loose," he said, his voice loud and hard. "Who'd you fuck in Chile?"

Tears stung my eyes, and I clenched my jaw, ready to risk his temper, ready to fly in the face of my undercurrent of fear of him becoming violent toward me, and shove him out of me, screaming at him to go fuck himself when shame washed over me, dragging my shoulders down instead. How I could be so indignant when I was stupid enough that I'd almost gotten myself raped? So idiotic that I'd had been forced to give a stranger a blow job and swallow when he was done?

"No one," I replied, though my voice was weak. "Not since you."

"I don't believe you," he replied quickly. After a short pause, he rammed his hips into me so hard it hurt, and I had to bite the insides of my cheeks to keep from making any noise. He'd never been rough with me during sex, and I had the fleeting thought that it had been accidental. My body jerked backward, the skin on my bare ass catching painfully on the hood as he did it over and over, and I knew it was intentional. I bit the insides of my cheeks harder, trying not to make a sound or cry, realizing I was going to be bruised by the time he was done. A slight metallic taste invaded my tongue as he continued to thrust into me violently; I'd bitten so hard the insides of my cheeks were bleeding.

"You feel that?" he asked, panting as he paused. "You feel how loose you are? I know you're lying. I know you've been having sex with someone else."

Could a tampon make me seem loose? I usually avoided them, but I had used one earlier in the summer during my first period on the trip—could that be why I was loose to him? I wanted to suggest that to him, wanted to keep arguing, to tell him he was wrong, tell him what had actually happened the one time it had been a close call, but I couldn't. He already didn't believe me; he'd never believe what had actually transpired. And what did it matter, anyway? I might as well have—the guy's dick was already in my body in some way.

My tears finally broke free, spilling over silently as Allen kept commenting on how loose I felt between ever more painful thrusts. He continued commenting all the way through his orgasm, while I was redressing myself, as he drove me home. I listened wordlessly to him telling me I'd been having sex with someone else, and when I got out of his car, I didn't stand and watch him drive away this time.

Instead, I walked straight inside the house and directly to my room. Grabbing a needle from the travel sewing kit I'd unpacked from my trip and left on my dresser, I sat down on my bed and scratched away at the mole on my thigh until the skin was bloody and unrecognizable. Staring at it, I felt nothing but hatred toward it and saw it as a failing in my body, a way my body was betraying me by teasing guys into wanting me only for sex; I wanted it gone or so damaged with scar tissue it was repugnant. Once I had slapped a band-aid over it to keep from bleeding on my sheets, I squeezed handfuls of my inner thighs in my fists, wishing I could remove any skin that had ever been touched by a guy and cried myself to sleep.

october 2000

"Hey, Laurel," I said after opening the door to her room. "Do you wanna go to a concert with me?"

She looked up at me from where she was painting her nails over a paper towel on her bed. "Why?"

I almost told her to forget it because she was so rude, but I bit my tongue; even though we practically hated each other, I really didn't want to go alone. I would have invited Janey or Ella, but Janey was still with Trevor and he wouldn't let her do something like go to a concert with me, and Ella was ultra-social and I wasn't up for talking to every soul who'd be there.

"Allen asked me to come see his band play tonight out near Orkney," I responded, knowing she liked the music his band played. "And I really don't want to go alone. I could use a little moral support since we're broken up," I added, nervous about being so honest with her.

She studied me for a moment. "Okay, sure, I'll come."

We hopped into my mom's old Volvo and headed out just as dusk fell. We arrived and positioned ourselves so we could see the entire band, but we weren't front and center. I didn't really even want to be noticed by anyone aside from Allen. A few songs in, Allen strummed a familiar chord; I knew what song he was getting ready to play. My heart soared. The song was going to be his apology—for cheating on me, for getting violent, for using me for sex, for accusing me of having sex when I hadn't and then hurting me during sex, all of it.

"This song is special to me," he started, strumming another chord mindlessly. "I wrote this song about the girl who stole my heart, the girl who made my whole world suddenly make sense. She's the love of my life— I can't live without her."

I recognized his words—it was the same dedication he gave every time he performed the song, a version of what he'd said to me right before he sang it to me the first time. My whole body hummed and trembled, my stomached filled with butterflies, and I couldn't stop grinning. *Whatever else has happened, he really loved me after all. And he still loves me. That's why he wanted me to come—to tell me that with this song.*

"This song is for you, Clara," he concluded.

Everything in my body seized, everything around me except his face went black for a moment. *Clara?* Clara was the last girl he'd told me he had sex with behind my back before I broke up with him. Suddenly, I remembered him mentioning her in his sporadic emails to me while I was in Chile and realized he must have been dating her. *I wonder if that happened before or after he had sex with me?* Finally, I turned and saw familiar faces who'd heard the song during other performances looking at me with pity. I noticed Clara by the stage, beaming as she screamed out that she loved him back. And there was Allen, grinning down at her as he started to play.

"I have to leave," I muttered to my sister. Turning without waiting to see if she'd heard me, I ran outside as his voice started singing the first verse of the song he'd written for me to another girl. My first exhale of the crisp fresh air outside brought stomach acid with it and I bent over, emptying my mouth of the burning liquid that splashed onto the gravel under my feet. Laurel arrived next to me as I dug into my purse for the cigarettes I'd started buying again the day after Allen had accused me of being loose. My fingers shook as I pulled one out and lit it, my tears dripping off my chin onto my neck. I smoked it hard, barely exhaling between drags, and pulled out another as soon as I finished the first. I ranted off and on to my sister who stood by, her pity and sympathy palpable.

How was I still so fucking stupid?

*****

The harsh ring of the phone startled me, and I jumped. Sighing, I glanced over at the phone, then looked back at the bloody letter A I had just burned into the back of my hand. *Shit, I shouldn't have done that.* I'd meant to burn myself with the pencil eraser and I was thinking about the other night when Allen had dedicated my song to Clara, but I didn't want anything to do with his name on me. Hopefully, I could keep it from scarring into a noticeable letter; I'd have to be more cognizant of what I was doing next time.

As the phone rang a second time, I set my pencil on my nightstand and lifted the receiver to my ear.

"Hello?" I answered.

"Katherine, I'm so sor—" Allen's rushed voice started.

"Fuck you!" I screamed over him, slamming the phone back down.

I panted as if I'd been sprinting and my eyes were burning with tears that wanted to break free. Why was he still trying to call me? That was the sixth time since the concert, and they all ended the same way. I was never going to waste a breath talking to him again. Didn't he get that? He wasn't worth it—wasn't worth my tears, either. Clenching my jaw, I willed my tears back, refusing to cry over him any more than I already had.

november 2000

I had finally started answering Joe's calls after the concert fiasco with Allen, and it had only taken a few conversations before we were dating again. There was no such thing as just friendship with him, though I'd tried it. A magnetic force pulled us violently together if we weren't far apart; there was simply no in-between. That same force had my heart pumping harshly in my chest, my breathing slightly labored, my skin tingling right then as I walked next to him; it's how it always was when he was near.

"Um," Joe said as he stopped and scratched the back of his head, then reached his hand back down so both of his hands held both of mine. "Allen told me—"

"You and Allen are talking?" I interrupted, incredulous as I remembered what Allen had done to him before I went to South America.

"Kinda," he replied, looking away for a moment. "Anyway, Allen told me that... that you..."

"That I what?" I asked, my vision black and fuzzy as my heart pounded. *What the fuck did that asshole say?* I still hadn't spoken to Allen since his concert, and just the thought of him filled me with a rage that scared me.

Joe took a deep breath and exhaled. "He said you fucked someone in Chile," he said quickly.

"What? He told you that?" I said, the air rushing from my lungs as if they'd been punctured.

Joe nodded, looking down toward our feet where we stood at the cross-country course. "He said you guys fucked when you got back and that you were loose."

I could tell by the way his veins were raised that Joe was trying to contain his anger and I knew why; he'd called and called—and I hadn't answered—for weeks after I'd returned. He was so intense, and I just hadn't felt like I could handle being near him or even talking to him when I'd gotten back. I'd known he wanted to get back together, and I hadn't been prepared to make a decision.

"What are you trying to ask me? If I fucked Allen or if I fucked someone in Chile?" I said, my voice hard as I flung his hands back at him and crossed mine tightly over my chest. "If it's such a big deal to you what I did or didn't do when we weren't even talking to each other, maybe you should have asked *before* we got back together." I wanted to piss him off; I wanted to make him angry and tell me I wasn't worth the trouble, push him past his limits to see if he would hurt me, though I couldn't for the life of me figure out why I wanted any of that to happen. I loved Joe—I'd always loved him—why would I *want* him to walk away from me, *want* him to snap and hurt me? It didn't make any sense. And yet, I did, especially after what he was asking me.

"Both, I guess," he said, clenching his jaw.

Bingo—I'd pissed him off even more. It wasn't hard; he was the most jealous person I'd ever met. "Yes, Allen and I had sex when I got back," I said, intentionally using the word sex to make it sound more emotional and consensual than it had been; for some reason, I wanted to hurt Joe. "And yes, he said I was loose." *Though I can't fucking believe he said that to anyone else.*

"So, you *did* fuck someone in Chile."

"Does it matter?"

"No."

"Then why are you asking?"

"Because I want to know if it's true."

"Well, Allen said it was, and he'd know, right? Since we've been fucking for years?" I said, feeling a stab of pain in my own chest for being so intentionally cruel. I knew it was wrong, yet I couldn't seem to stop myself.

"Just tell me if you did or not."

"It doesn't matter what I say—no one ever fucking believes me anyway," I bit out, my whole body on fire with rage.

"Katherine," Joe started, his voice unexpectedly even though I could still hear the anger underneath. "I believe you if you say it's the truth. Period."

I stared at him for a moment and tears stung my eyes; my chest felt like it was caving in on itself and my rage was suddenly gone. "I didn't sleep with anyone while I was gone," I said quietly, staring off at the mountains in the distance. "I don't know why Allen thinks I'm loose, but it's not from having sex, because I didn't. I was almost raped," I added, my voice cracking as my tears spilled over, "but I wasn't. I didn't have sex at all. I swear." My jaw trembled as the mountains disappeared in the blur created by the moisture spilling from my eyes and I turned back to glance at Joe.

"I believe you," he said as soon as my eyes found his. His face was drawn, his jaw clenched. "Do you want to talk about it?"

I shook my head. "No."

"I'm here if you do," he replied. "And I'm so glad you're okay."

february 2001

The day's assignment in the creative writing class I was taking for the spring semester was to write a poem about anything I wanted. It could be happy or sad or neither; the only requirements were that it be a non-rhyming poem and that it be organized around an obvious central theme. *Well, I've got that covered.*

I'd just broken up with Joe—again—because of him cheating on me. Again. He'd made out with someone he worked with at a fast-food restaurant. I'd only figured it out because he started accusing me of cheating on him out of the blue; I was beginning to realize his paranoia about me cheating on him seemed to ratchet up when he was cheating on me. It always started with us fighting because he didn't think we spent enough time together, then moved to him accusing me of not loving him anymore because I didn't have the same interest in sex that he did. Then came the accusations of me cheating on him.

Of course, I'd nearly caved and gotten back together with him in the next breath when I made the mistake of looking into his eyes. There was something about his eyes, the depth of pain I always saw there, everything they told me about who he was underneath all the shitty things he did, that made it nearly impossible to say no to him when he asked for anything.

Picking up my pen, I began to write.

Your Eyes
I think it was your eyes
That doomed me for life.
They stopped my heartbeat
And captured my soul.
Those baby blue stars looking at me
Caused me to forget all your wrongs.
I believed every one of your lies
And had faith in your love for me.
When I looked into your eyes,
I found myself floating... lost.
Every time I looked away
A piece of me was left behind.
Now I have looked for the last time
Only to find you possess all of me.
If I had never seen your eyes
I might be happy now
But I lost my soul looking into yours
And now I am left in torment...
Broken, helpless, and longing for you.

march 2001

"My dad's been having an affair," Janey told me from where she sat on my bed. She'd broken up with Trevor—for good this time, she swore—and we could now spend time together again.

"Oh my God, Janey," I replied, shocked. "Are you sure?"

"Yeah. With a woman he works with. She's not even that much older than Mae."

"Oh, Jesus. I'm so sorry."

She nodded, staring blankly at my bedroom wall.

"How's your mom?"

"Not good," she said quietly. "They're either fighting or she's crying."

"Are they going to try to work things out or... or... not? I mean..."

Janey shrugged. "I don't know right now," she replied, her voice cracking.

I leaned over and wrapped my arms around her. "I'm so sorry, Janey. I'm here, whatever you need, okay?"

She nodded against my shoulder as she cried. "I know. Thank you."

"Love you."

"Love you, too."

*****

"I'm going to the grocery store—you girls need anything?" Jean asked as she grabbed her purse and her keys.

"I need some tampons," my sister said.

Tampons... when was the last time I had my period? I couldn't remember and I'd never bothered to try to keep track—normal for me was irregular and meant anywhere between three and six weeks between periods. But I was fairly certain it had been closer to two months since I'd had one. *No way I can be pregnant.* Joe and I had been dating off and on for months, and there was no relationship with him without sex, but it just wasn't possible; I was just paranoid. If I didn't have my period in the next couple of days, I'd take a test to prove I wasn't pregnant and then ask to go to a doctor.

*****

My heart was alternately not beating and trying to burst out of my chest a few days later after I'd driven a few towns down to buy a pregnancy test where I was less likely to be recognized under the guise of running out to get ice cream at the local Dunkin' Donuts. *No. No way. This can't be happening.* I grabbed the box and read the instructions again; again, I read that two lines meant pregnant. Looking back at the stick, I confirmed again that there were two bold pink lines. *Maybe I waited too long to look— it's a two-pack, I'll just pee on the other one, too.*

I ripped off the wrapper from the second pregnancy test, grateful for the first time in my life that I had a small bladder that meant I was already able to pee again, and held the stick under my urine stream. As soon as I'd emptied my bladder a second time, I lifted the stick and watched the moisture travel across the window. Two lines appeared simultaneously; there was no doubt what it was telling me.

I'm pregnant. I'm sixteen and I'm fucking pregnant. Jean will never forgive me; she'll never love me again. I fucked up everything.

Again.

unlovable

"I still think the greatest suffering is being lonely, feeling unloved... That is the worst disease that any human being can experience."

-Mother Teresa

march 2001

My hands shook as I wrapped the positive pregnancy tests in toilet paper and dropped them into the trash can. Turning, I walked straight to my foster mom's bedroom. She was already in bed for the night, reading in her nightgown, and I started to cry hysterically as I knelt on the floor next to her.

"What's wrong, Katherine?" she asked, setting her book down on the bed next to her.

I blubbered, spraying tears and spit and snot. "I'm afraid to tell you."

"Afraid?" she asked, drawing her face back in confusion.

"Y-you w-w-won't love m-me anymore," I stuttered out, my chest so tight I couldn't breathe.

She laughed a little and pursed her lips at me like "oh, come on, grow up, of course I'll still love you," but I knew it was only because she had no idea what I'd done. Slow, painful minutes passed with me sobbing, opening my mouth to tell her and then closing it, my chest contracting to keep the words from escaping and destroying every vestige of love and affection I had.

"Oh, come on, just spit it out already," she said after a while, having grown impatient with my emotional display.

And so I did—two little words. "I'm pregnant."

There was a beat of silence as I watched my words sink in, her eyes widening in realization.

"Oh, jeez. How could you be that *stupid?*" She muttered a bit to herself as I cried harder; I'd known she wouldn't love me anymore. "You could ruin everything you want in your life! Everything!" she shouted, shaking her head at me, disappointment oozing from her in every way, her eyes hard. "I hope that few minutes was worth it," she bit out, her face scrunched as if she'd just eaten something unsavory. "What are you going to do?"

I looked at her, confused for a moment. "Do?"

"Yes, Katherine—what are you going to do? Are you going to have the baby and keep it? Have an abortion? Have the baby and give it up for adoption? You need to decide, and you need to do it quickly."

"What do you think I should do?" I asked through my tears. I hadn't even thought about that—the only thing that had been on my mind was how she would react.

"It's not my body—it's yours. And your decision. I'll support whatever you decide, but it's not up to me."

"You will?" I asked, surprised.

"Of course I will—it's not my decision to make."

"You'd let me have the baby if I wanted to?"

"It's not my place to stop you. But if you have a baby, you'll need to live somewhere else where you'd have the right kind of support to be raising a baby while you're in school."

I nodded, looking down. "I understand. Of course," I said quietly. After a moment, I added. "I'm sorry."

"I bet you are," she said. "Go to bed. I'm too disgusted to look at you right now."

I nodded again, understanding—it was what I'd expected—and shuffled back to my room to figure out what I was going to do.

The next morning, I went to the kitchen as soon as I heard Jean moving around in there, even though I didn't need to get up for school yet. My body was heavier than it had ever seemed, as if the weight of the world rested on my shoulders. My eyes were puffy and red and burned from crying all night. But I'd made a decision and wanted to tell her while my sister was still asleep; I didn't want her to know.

"I made a decision," I said quietly, my arms wrapped tightly around my waist as I looked past her shoulder at the dark window; I was too ashamed to make eye contact.

"Okay," she said, not looking up at me from where she was preparing her breakfast and coffee.

"I'm going to get an abortion."

"Okay. Why'd you decide on that?"

I took a deep breath. "I'm sixteen. I'll be lucky to graduate high school if I have a baby, and there isn't a chance I'd ever be able to go to college. And then I'd be no better than my parents and any baby deserves better than that."

"Well, I'd imagine you'd split the responsibility with the father," she said.

Oh, God, no—I hadn't even thought about that. And with Joe's mom? Hell. No. I shivered at the thought of her being involved in the life of a baby of mine.

"Do you even know who the father is?" Jean asked casually as she walked to the dining room.

"What?" I asked, following her as my stomach dropped. Surely, I'd misheard.

She sat down and picked up the newspaper and started reading, speaking without looking up. "You're pretty promiscuous, Katherine— seems to me you spread your legs for anyone. I wouldn't be surprised if you didn't know who the father was."

I stared at her, speechless. My mouth hung open as I tried to find words, but I clamped it shut as a wave of nausea passed over me. Gritting my teeth, I refused to succumb to it and worked to lock up every shred of pain her words had just created, shoving it all down into that black hole deep inside.

"I don't do that. And yes, I know who the father is. It's Joe."

"Oh, jeez," she muttered. "You can't tell him—he'd tell his mother and that woman is crazy."

"I have to tell him," I replied. "He has a right to know."

"Only if you were going to keep the baby."

"I can't keep this from him," I said. "But he'll respect my decision. And he won't tell his mom if I tell him not to—I trust him."

Jean cocked her head at me. "I wouldn't be so sure." She took a bite of her toast and read the paper as she chewed and swallowed. "And you're sure you want to get an abortion?"

"Yes. I can't raise a baby—it wouldn't be fair to the baby."

"There's adoption, too. If you wanted to carry the baby, you could put it up for adoption once it's born."

"I know, but I don't want to do that. I don't think I *could*. I can't imagine carrying a baby and then being able to give it up."

"Okay," she said. "Find a clinic out of state so you won't see anyone you know. If anyone finds out, it'll be worse than if you just carried the baby. Don't tell anyone—especially not Joe."

*****

"Just tell me who it is, Katherine—I know you're fucking cheating on me!" Joe shouted over the phone a few days later.

"I'm not cheating on you," I said through my tears. Ever since I'd seen those two pink lines, I hadn't been able to talk to him; all my energy went to trying to process what I was about to do, shove every tiny emotion into my black hole, and try to act completely normal for the rest of the world. But while it was convincing for everyone else, I couldn't fool Joe. He knew something wasn't right—he just wrongly assumed it was that I was cheating on him, like he always did.

"Stop lying to me!" he shouted again. "Tell me who it is!"

"I'm not lying," I cried softly. "I swear." I'd told Jean that I wouldn't tell anyone I was pregnant, but I couldn't keep it to myself anymore. "I'm pregnant, Joe."

There was silence for the span of several breaths, and then he spoke. "You're pregnant? Like, we're going to have a baby?" he finally said, sounding excited.

"No—I'm getting an abortion."

"No, you're not," he said immediately.

"Yes, I am," I responded.

"That's murder, Katherine."

I rolled my eyes. "No, it's not."

"Yes, it is, and you can't murder our child!"

"For fuck's sake, Joe!" I shouted back, "I'm not murdering anyone! And it's not your decision—it's *mine*. I shouldn't have even told you."

"Shouldn't have told me? I'm the father, of course you have to tell me. That's my baby, too."

"It's not a baby yet," I muttered.

"It is—and it's our baby. We'll raise it together and—"

"And how do you think that would look, Joe? What kind of life would that be? Neither of us would finish high school—"

"So, you're putting your wants above our baby's needs?"

"NO!" I screamed back at him. "You know my parents never finished high school and look how that turned out for my sister and my brothers and me! It's not fair to a baby to be raised like that."

"But we'll have help, Katherine—my mom loves kids—"

"I don't want your mom anywhere near a kid of mine."

"Why the hell would you say something like that about my mom?"

"Right... really? Your mom called the police on you and had them lock you up in Juvenile Detention because you tried to protect yourself when she attacked you."

"That wasn't her fault—she thought I called her a bitch—"

"It doesn't matter what she thought. She shouldn't have started kicking you in the balls, Joe!"

"I shouldn't have pushed her—she's a woman."

"She's a woman who's bigger than you who was attacking you—you had every fucking right to defend yourself and push her away from you. It's not your fault she tripped and twisted her ankle. The cops should have taken her instead of you."

"You don't understand my mom, Katherine, she's—"

"I don't care. I don't want her raising one of my kids, ever."

"Then fine, we'll do it on our own."

"No, we won't, because I'm getting an abortion."

We spent the next hour arguing over whether he had a say in what was done about my pregnancy and whether abortion was murder until I couldn't argue any longer and told him I couldn't talk to him for a while, promising I'd consider changing my mind in exchange for his promise that he wouldn't tell his mom.

*****

"I told you not to tell him," my foster mom said angrily. "That crazy woman was calling me in my office all day telling me she wouldn't let me force you to get an abortion. What did you say to Joe? Do you really think I'm forcing you to get an abortion? I told you this was your decision—if that's not what you want to do, you don't have to do it."

I wanted to shout and jump up and down and pull my hair until I had none left in my scalp, slam my forehead against a wall, then climb into a hole where no one could find me. I wanted to lay on the floor and kick and scream like I was a two-year-old throwing an epic temper tantrum. And I desperately wanted to hit something; I was filled with molten rage that Joe had broken his promise to me.

"I know it's my decision," I said through clenched teeth. "I told him that. I'm sorry she bothered you."

"She's probably going to tell the whole town, too. I told you to keep your mouth shut about it."

My head hung as I studied my feet, my rage fading into shame. "I know. I shouldn't have told him. I didn't think he would... it doesn't matter. I trusted him and I shouldn't have."

The phone rang as I finished speaking and my foster mom and I looked at each other.

"It's probably that crazy woman again," she said. "I wouldn't answer it if I were you."

I knew she was right but thought maybe I could make Jan stop if I talked to her, so I walked to my room and grabbed the receiver on the third ring.

"Hello?" I said, using my other hand to press into my temples; my head was suddenly throbbing.

"You have no fucking right to kill my baby!" Jan's angry voice poured over the line. "If you—"

"It's not your baby," I said quietly. "And *I'm* choosing to get an abortion, not my foster mom—"

"You are *not* getting an abortion and murdering my unborn grandchild—that's my baby! I won't let you. I'll have the police stop you."

"You can't stop anything, it's legal," I said, though it was getting harder to force my voice out over the pounding of my heart. *Besides—I'm a bastard—you should be happy I'm going to abstain from giving birth to a child cursed for eternal damnation.*

She started screaming again and I hung up the phone without saying anything else. When the phone started ringing again, I laid down and pulled my pillow over my head, trying to drown out the sound. When it started ringing a third time after the voicemail had picked up, I lifted the receiver an inch, dropped it back into the cradle to hang up, and then lifted it again, leaving it ajar to ensure any further calls would simply receive a busy signal.

A few hours later, however, there was a knock on the front door. I knew in the pit of my stomach it was Joe and his mother, but I walked to the door anyway. Joe stood on the porch, his mother still in the car in our driveway. In his hands was a pink stuffed bear that he held out toward me.

"This is for our baby. I know it's a little girl. Don't kill her, please," he said, tears spilling over and falling down his cheeks.

I stared at him for a moment, refusing to touch the bear. "You need to leave," I said flatly, my emotions finally cooperating and hiding away in my black hole.

"Katherine, I'm begging—"

"No, you lied to me. You promised you wouldn't tell her, and then you did."

"I had to! I needed—"

"Leave. I mean it. Just go."

"It's like you don't even care!" he shouted, still crying.

I shrugged and stepped back inside my house, shutting the door in his face. After he'd left, I wanted to sit on the porch and watch the rain that was rolling in, and when I opened the door, the pink bear was on the bench on the porch, a small note tucked between its arms: *For our baby girl.*

early april 2001

"Katherine!" Janey said breathlessly. "Why didn't you tell me sooner?"

I shrugged and wiped my eyes. "I was trying not to tell anyone, especially after what happened when I told Joe. And you have enough you're dealing with anyway."

She looked away and sighed. "I told you my parents are getting a divorce?"

I nodded. "I'm so sorry, Janey."

Turning back to me, she smiled, though her eyes were watery. "I'll be okay. And I'm still here for you, too. I wish you'd told me sooner so I could have been there for you."

"You don't hate me?" I asked with a small laugh to cover how worried I was. I knew her family was pro-life and wouldn't agree with the fact that I'd gotten an abortion.

"Of course I don't hate you, Katherine. And my parents wouldn't either if you let me tell them—you're like family."

I smiled softly. "Thank you. I feel like you guys are a second family, too. But even so, please don't tell them."

"Okay, I won't."

"Promise?"

"Promise. Have you told Ella yet?"

I shook my head. "No. Not sure if I will."

"You're not going to tell her?" she asked, surprised.

"I want to, but I know she'll tell people. I've never told her something important that I really wanted kept a secret and had her honor that—she always tells people. I can't risk the whole town finding out. I'm sure I'll tell her one day, but I can't right now."

She nodded. "How are you feeling?"

"I'm fine," I said, flipping on my cheerful voice. "It was uncomfortable—like really bad cramping—but it didn't hurt after or anything. I bled a lot, though. But I'm fine now."

She stared at me without saying anything for a moment and I started shifting around, uncomfortable. *I wonder if I have enough time to smoke a cigarette before one of her parents gets home.*

"I mean, are *you* okay?"

"I just told you—"

"No, Katherine, I mean… like… are you upset? Are you okay with what you did? You know… are you *okay*?"

It was my turn to stare at her. "Sure, I'm fine with what I did, really. I mean, it's done, I kind of have to be okay, right?" I laughed.

"No—you don't," she replied soberly.

I opened my mouth to reply, but stopped abruptly as my eyes filled with tears. *I don't?* I looked down at my hands as my jaw started trembling.

"I don't know if I'm okay," I said quietly.

just another angsty teenager

"All it takes is a beautiful fake smile to hide an injured soul and they will never notice how broken you really are."

-Robin Williams

late april 2001

Movement caught my attention and I looked up anxiously from where I was working on another poem at my desk. Every time the door started to open for the last week, I'd scrutinized the person walking in, looking for any sign of anger. After a recent sharing of work where we had to read and critique pieces—poetry as well as prose—written by our peers, I'd had some concerns about several of my classmates. I knew if they found out I said anything that my life would become hell, but I had no choice. If there was truth in what they were writing, I had at least one classmate who may be suicidal, another who was self-harming, and two who were being abused by their parents. I knew there wasn't a damn thing I could do about it, but my foster mom was the school social worker—it was her job to try to do something about these things—so I'd told her my suspicions. It turned out she was already aware of some of what I told her, that the families were already under investigation, and she promised to look into everything else. And while I'd known deep down that I was doing the right thing, I also knew that's not what others would think.

Instead of one of those classmates, however, it was Clara walking into class, and my stomach clenched as it always did. Having to see her in creative writing class all semester had been torture; every time I looked at her, I flashed back to the concert when Allen dedicated the song he wrote for me to her. I'd been nonplussed that first week of class when she'd come in and sat down near me, eagerly asking me if I had any advice for her

291

about dating him. In my mind, I envisioned myself punching her and knocking that smile off her face. She'd had sex with him when she knew he and I were dating; I couldn't believe she had the gall to talk to me the way she did, to treat me with so little respect, as if I was completely worthless.

But I did nothing about it either. I plastered on a smile that first day and wished her luck with someone who had so little concept of what it was like to be honest and faithful, as if her question to me had been the most natural thing in the world. I tried to tell myself I wasn't giving her the satisfaction of seeing me angry and upset and hurt, though I knew that was a lie and that I was just so anti-confrontational that I couldn't make myself tell her what I really thought of her.

My animosity toward her fled, however, as I took in her appearance—she looked like shit. She had big circles under eyes, her hair was unkempt, and she had light bruises on her forearms. Bruises in shapes that I recognized because they were just like the ones I'd had on my wrists. I'd heard that Allen had started knocking her around at parties they went to together when they got into arguments, heard that he'd even punched her in the face once but that she'd covered it with make-up.

I felt sick to my stomach as I watched her come in and take her seat. I didn't wish a violent relationship on *anyone*—not even her. It seemed that what Allen did with me had just been the beginning; if I'd stayed with him, I'd be the one with bruises I was trying to cover with make-up. I'd be the one he was jerking around, the one he was punching. My whole body shuddered at the thought, but when I looked at her face, all I could feel was a growing sense of guilt. I wanted to apologize to Clara, explain to her that it was my fault because I'd left him, leaving him able to abuse someone else. Explain that if I had just stayed with him, I could have protected her and any other future girlfriend, from his anger. Apologize that I hadn't done so.

It should be me under those bruises—not her.

*****

I pulled into Janey's driveway that Saturday, feeling heavy and in need of some time with her to keep me from reaching for some implement to make myself bleed. I'd decided after I'd mindlessly burned the A into the back of my hand that I needed to stop doing things like that to cope. That meant I was smoking more, but I'd figure out how to quit doing that later. For now,

I wanted to stop doing things that could possibly get me locked up in a mental hospital if someone found out.

She'd told me that things were really bad at her house—her dad had moved out and her mom had been in bed for over a week, barely getting up to use the bathroom, even less often to shower, and not really eating at all. I needed her to keep me sane, and likewise, Janey needed me for support. I took a deep breath as I closed my car door and started pushing everything toward my black hole, forcing a smile to my face when I neared her front door; she needed me first.

I knocked, even though they'd told me countless times I didn't need to—it just didn't sit well with how I'd been raised to *not* knock before entering a house that wasn't mine—and then walked in when no one answered. The house was quiet inside, though I could hear a soft murmur coming from somewhere near the back of the house and headed in that direction. I found Janey and her mom in her mom's bedroom, her mom crying in bed, and Janey sitting next to her.

Her mom's eyes looked over to me and she gave me a half smile. "Hi, Katherine."

"Hi, Mrs. Notsin," I replied with an answering smile, reaching over and giving a brief rub to her blanketed calf.

"How are you doing?" she asked.

"Me?" I responded, taken aback. *She's the one who's depressed and in the middle of a divorce.*

"Yeah," she said softly, her brow furrowing. "Janey told me about the baby."

My heart stopped for a moment and I turned to Janey who looked down and refused to make eye contact.

"I'm fine," I said, still staring hard at Janey. "I don't want to talk about it."

"I think of you as another daughter," she replied. "I'm here if you do."

The only person I wanted to talk to about it was your daughter, but apparently that was a mistake.

After a few minutes of small talk, Mrs. Notsin said she wanted to be left alone so she could take a nap and Janey and I walked to her living room.

"Where are Lynn and Mae?" I asked.

Janey shrugged. "They're gone a lot—who knows. Probably at a party." She looked up at me, finally. "I'm sorry, Katherine. I... it was a lot and I had to talk to someone about it."

I nodded, understanding what she meant, but it didn't help with the feeling of betrayal in my chest. I'd trusted her when she said she wouldn't tell anyone. "So, what are we doing today? Should we try to get your mom up to watch a movie with us or something?"

Janey looked away again. "Actually... you can't stay."

"What?" I asked, figuring I hadn't heard her properly.

"Trevor is coming over," she said quietly.

For the second time, my heart stuttered. "What? Why? You guys are broken up." Janey didn't reply and I had a bad feeling in the pit of my stomach as my heart started pounding. "Right? You guys *are* broken up still? You promised that wasn't going to change."

Tears began tracking down her cheeks. "I don't have a choice, Katherine. Mom has been talking to him every day since all this stuff happened with my dad. She says he's the son she never had."

"So what? That doesn't mean you have to date him!"

"I know, but Mom wants me to give him another chance. She said it's not fair of me to shut him out when he never would have treated me that way if I hadn't let him, and she's right."

"No, that's bullshit, Janey."

She shrugged and wiped her eyes before using her shirt to clean her drippy nose. "Mom begged me. She said it's the only way she can be happy again. I have to."

"No, Janey—"

"I already got back together with him."

"You can't do that," I said breathlessly. "Janey... you promised me! Your mom is wrong, it's his fault, not yours. Don't you remember why you broke up with him?"

"I do, it's just—"

"No," I interrupted, "you obviously don't remember. Let me remind you. He forced you to give him a blow job, remember? He controls everything you do—what clothes you wear, who you talk to. Don't you remember that you got into a fight with him when you went to a bookstore with your mom without his permission? A Christian fucking bookstore with you own mother, Janey! That's fucking crazy!"

"I know," she said quietly. "But I'm not going to let him control me this time. I just have to do this for Mom."

"Your mom is so fucking selfish," I muttered.

"She's destroyed right now," Janey retorted.

"I know, but that doesn't give her a right to coerce you into dating someone—let alone someone like Trevor. She's not thinking about what that relationship does to you. You have to say no, Janey. I'll be here, right behind you, for all of it, I promise. Just don't do this."

"I told you, I already did. And he's coming over today to cheer Mom up."

"So, you're telling me I'm not allowed to stay because he's coming."

"I mean... no," she said quietly. "But you know how he feels about you, so it would be better if you weren't here."

I stared, unblinking, at the wall to my left, trying to fight back the tears and the pain threatening to overwhelm me. Janey had been my safe place—I was closer to her than to anyone else in my life and I was her oldest friend. We'd forgiven each other for so many screw-ups and even had our own song.

But Janey was choosing to turn her back on our friendship, on our history together, on *everything*. She was breaking her promises and abandoning me. And not only that, but she was doing it *because of a fucking guy.*

may 2001

Mrs. Stratford was handing back our last few writing assignments and my heart was pounding in my chest as I waited for her to get to me. I'd used my words to bare the pain I normally hid, hoping that would help, much like a pressure valve. The last weeks I'd clung to new friends as Janey began to grow distant again, but it hadn't been enough to fill the void her friendship left. I had Joe in my life, but we were in a constant state of fighting about *something*. Either we weren't talking enough or seeing each other enough or having sex enough for him, or he thought I was cheating on him, or he was cheating on me, or I was fighting with him about him skipping class to get high with one of his friends, or arguing about whether he was smart enough for school if he just applied himself, or if he was too stupid and fighting a system that was secretly plotting to make sure he failed, as his mom had told him.

My foster mom had no idea I was smoking again and was happy enough that I was getting good grades, even though she was still cold toward me the way she had been since she'd found out I was pregnant. She trusted me enough that I occasionally went to parties with my new friends—all with permission from her—because I had no interest in drinking or getting high and was happy to be the designated driver in the group every time. My teachers all liked me because I did my homework and studied and performed well in all my classes. I was doing well and improving in soccer; my flute teacher was impressed with my vibrato. I was a reliable employee at the job I'd gotten as soon as I'd turned fourteen and obtained a worker's permit, and filled as much of my free time as I could with hours there.

And yet, no matter how many times I ran down the list of reasons I should be happy, why the smile I pasted on my face should be genuine, nothing changed. I was burning myself with erasers and cutting myself with safety pins again when I found time I couldn't fill with some sort of activity. Sitting with the peonies didn't even help anymore. I barely slept, and when I did, those minutes were spent running for my life while faceless men and demons were in hot pursuit, their fingers grabbing my clothes and clutching at my body, my screams heard by no one. I was filled to bursting with a sense of being an imposter no matter what I was doing, no matter who I was with, and I hated myself for not truly being what everyone wanted to see, for not being as resilient as everyone seemed to think I had once been.

But I hadn't been able to wear my mask for these writing assignments, and I was worried what was going to happen as a result. None of my peers who read them had batted an eye, just as they hadn't at anything else I'd written during the year. Ms. Stratford had only smiled when she'd handed back every other assignment. But these were more literal, and I was sure she'd be worried—I knew *I* would be if I read them from someone else. As I waited, I recited the pieces in my head to give me something to focus on other than the excruciating slowness of the passing seconds until Ms. Stratford got to me.

> *Not what I seem*
> *I smile, laugh, and play—a front*
> *Though I have everything I could possibly want*
> *There's nothing missing from this life of mine*
> *So why can't the light of happiness shine?*
> *I ask myself the reason for my tears*
> *Why my heart's being disemboweled with spears*
> *I don't understand what makes me cry*
> *And nothing I do gives me the answer why*

Today my life is light and gay
Yesterday all I could do was pray
I have friends, a family, smarts and a guy
But something is missing and that's why I cry
I can feel the void taunting my soul
And it turns the sun, even, blacker than coal
I sit and I think and I go insane
Sadness seems like my life's refrain
I pick up a book, but am unable to read
I cannot write, though I feel the need
I ponder what's happened years past in my life
Reliving the pain, the anguish, the strife
To have lived through it all is an amazing feat
But I can feel the weight of the mortuary sheet
"I know I look happy to you!" I shout
Happiness drains from the inside out

Bittersweet Chorus
Life is imbued
With pain and strife
And lies
And I experience all of it
Each time I choose to care about you

There are empty promises
Of wishes to be fulfilled
And unpleasantries to be avoided
That I realize every moment
I think of you

I see the brazen misleadings
And feel the pain
Of deceit
And silently I wonder
Why I cherish you
Then I understand:
I have to forgive

The troubles you cause me
Before I learn the more to love you,
Precious life

Ms. Stratford got to our row and I couldn't breathe, my entire chest locked as I waited, hoping I could quickly figure out how to respond to whatever she said or asked. I forced myself to look up at her when she got to me the way I always did, trying to act as normal as possible. *This is it,* I thought. *I finally let my mask slip and someone's going to say something.* Everything around her faded into a fuzzy blackness and I felt sick as she looked down, shuffling through the papers in her hand to pull out mine.

"Here you go," she said, smiling broadly. "Nice work." She held the papers out to me, already glancing down for the next student's writing as I slid mine from her fingers.

That's it?

I'd been expecting something—anything—more, even just a look. But nothing. It was business as usual. I'd been so terrified of being discovered, of someone finding out I wasn't the person I projected myself to be. And the worst that I could imagine hadn't come to pass. I should feel relieved—elated, even. I'd managed to skate by undetected, which was what I'd wanted.

But I didn't feel relief; instead, I was angry and upset. I wanted to take a sledgehammer to my desk and I wanted to curl into a ball and cry. Instead of feeling triumphant, I felt like I was falling apart. Flashes of my foster mom rolling her eyes and shaking her head when I got mad or distraught paraded through my mind, the dismissal of every display of emotion as excessive and simply attributable to hormones.

Apparently, I'm just another angsty teenager, I thought, bitter, as I started shoving everything into that black hole once more. Though, this time, some of the anger refused to cooperate, lingering instead.

becoming castration queen

"What I never say out loud is that rape makes you want to turn into wood, hard and impenetrable. The opposite of a body that is meant to be tender, porous, soft. Sometimes I'm too angry, seething after reading a rape story, *I need to slice a dick off.*"

-Chanel Miller

june 2001

"I have to go. And it's just for a few days," I said, failing to keep my exasperation from seeping into my voice. "Trust me, I'd be skipping the Naval Academy part if I could, but Jean's making me do this because it would be a free education."

Joe and I had been arguing ever since I'd told him I was going to be gone for the better part of a week to do some college visits. Starting the next day, I'd first be spending four nights at the Naval Academy, followed by two nights at St. John's College, both in Annapolis, Maryland. St. John's—dubbed "the book school"—was one I was intensely interested in, with their unique approach to education that began with the original texts in the original languages for every subject, something that didn't scare me off as a straight-A Latin student. On the other hand, however, I had the opposite of interest in the Naval Academy—I was averse to required intense physical activity outside of playing soccer and couldn't stomach the thought of learning to use weapons. However, Jean had told me there were two college visits I had to do whether I wanted to or not, or there would be no college visits at all, and the Naval Academy was one of them. I'd known a few months ago that I'd be going and that part of the three-day program would involve physical fitness testing, so I'd started running every day to avoid being a total laughingstock when I was there. The result was that I was the thinnest I'd ever been, which earned me compliments from my foster mom, extra attention from just about every guy since I had an accentuated hourglass shape now... and Joe's insistence that I would cheat on him while I was gone.

"I know you'll find someone else if you go," he said.

I growled in frustration. "I'm not going to look for guys—this is about figuring out what college I'm going to. That's it. There's going to be sample classes and lots of physical testing and training and God knows what else at the Naval Academy—we have this thing called 'plebe day' and I'm afraid to find out what that means. And then just sample classes at St. John's. And then I'll be home."

"Still..."

"No, not 'still'—just trust me. I've never cheated on you and I'm not about to. It's more likely that you'll cheat on *me*..." I laughed, though I meant it; I had very little faith in Joe's ability to be faithful, even though we'd talked and he seemed to understand that I couldn't keep going in this cycle of being destroyed by him and then trying to trust him again. A next time would be the last time because there would be no trust left to resurrect. But I also knew it always happened when he felt like I was pulling away because I wasn't physically there enough for him, and he saw my going to college visits alone as pulling away from him.

"No, I won't," he said, his voice full of conviction.

*****

I knew I should be hanging out with the other kids for lunch and then socializing until dinner—the first scheduled activities for the visit at St. John's—but I laid on my bed in my room there instead, wishing I had a cigarette... or five. I couldn't even think about eating or talking to people. I hadn't been looking forward to the Naval Academy, but it had been so much worse than I'd imagined. Tears stung my eyes as I thought back over the last few days.

I'd been the only prospective student there—out of hundreds—who hadn't been in JROTC; I didn't even know what that was. The only marching experience I had was from marching band and we weren't anything spectacular, so on the first day when we were told we'd be competing by platoon in a marching competition on the last day, I'd panicked. And then I made a fool of myself when I had to ask what an "about face" was, followed by tripping over my own feet and falling on my face when I tried to execute it. And things had just gone downhill from there. I was the least physically fit person, failing every single fitness test: distance run, sprints, crunches, pull-ups... everything. We ran everywhere throughout the day and the slowest person stayed in front; in my platoon, I was always that person and it made us late to almost everything.

And then there was plebe day. That was a kind of hell I never could have imagined, and my roommates told me they were going easy on us because, in the session the week before ours, two kids had been hospitalized as a result of what they were forced to do. I'd never in my life been called so many names and been screamed at in my face the way I was that day, someone else's spit all over my cheeks and nose and forehead as they cussed me out and told me I was completely worthless. I'd never been so dizzy from being unable to breathe—so close to passing out—as that day during which the feeling never faded. I'd even thrown up, something I almost never did; I hadn't been able *not* to since the first thing we were ordered to do after breakfast was chug water until we threw up. We were given physical tests of endurance—like holding a push-up position for five minutes—and if someone dropped before the time was up, more time would be added. Of course, my muscles had failed in every one of those tests and my peers suffered angrily as a result.

St. John's was my top college pick, but I couldn't make myself engage in the activities right then. All I wanted to do was disappear for a while—days or even weeks—and try to forget the last few days. Every time the events started to play through my mind, my body felt paralyzed and I sweat profusely, dizzy and unable to breathe. I couldn't keep tears from my eyes and I just wanted it all to stop. My fingers itched to grab my pencil, but I didn't want to accidentally have a burn show while I was in the activities the next day. Instead, I wrapped my fingers around my biceps to keep them from reaching into my bag.

When I got up to use the restroom after staring into nothingness and replaying the events on repeat, I had tiny bloody crescents where my fingernails had been. *I guess I'm wearing a cardigan for the next few days, even though it's hot as hell outside.*

*****

How is this happening? How could they do that to me? My breathing was getting choppier with each rapid heartbeat, an invisible vice keeping my lungs from moving, and the blackness on the outside of my vision had encroached so only a tiny point at the end was still lit. I felt like a cornered rabbit that knew it had no way to escape. *I give up. I just... I give up.*

I'd learned that Joe had been over at Janey's house while I was at the Naval Academy and St. John's. That he'd spent the night over there, invited by Lynn. I hadn't needed to ask to know why he'd been over there, though I had anyway, deliriously hoping I was wrong. He'd denied it, but when I'd confronted Lynn and asked her, she'd told me the truth. And hearing the girl who up until that moment I'd thought of as another sister admit that she'd invited my boyfriend over, had sex with him, and was intending to date him hurt in a way I'd never experienced. It had felt as if there was an actual blade being pushed slowly into my chest, through my heart, out my back, and then left there.

I'd flashed to all the times Lynn had joined Janey and me when I was over, distraught over the loss of a boyfriend, and I'd hugged and comforted her along with Janey. I'd made her tea and cooked for her and talked to her. I'd stuck up for her at school and with friends when someone had badmouthed her, calling her a bitch or a whore. I'd defended her and cut people out of my life for her. And then she'd intentionally pursued my boyfriend when I was out of town.

And he'd willingly engaged with her! The same guy I'd forgiven so many times already, the same guy I'd thought understood there would be no coming back from cheating on me again. The very same guy I'd spent countless hours talking to about our lives once we were married one day, the same guy I'd now given more of myself to than anyone, the same guy I'd bared more of my past to than any other person I knew.

And to top it all off, they'd done it while I was away, being screamed at and having every insecurity and fear triggered, being convinced by strangers that I was, in fact, as completely worthless as I'd thought for so long.

"I can't believe you cheated on me!" I screamed.

"Katherine... it's complicated."

"No, don't 'Katherine' me—it's actually pretty simple. You stuck your dick in her," I said through clenched teeth, trying to make it sound as crude and disrespectful as it felt to me.

"I don't love her the way I love you," he pleaded. "Please, Katherine, I'm sorry, I'm so sorry."

"Fuck you and your sorry!"

"You were gone, and you were pulling away from—"

"No, I wasn't!" I screamed at him. I was so sick of hearing that as an excuse for him cheating on me. "That's bullshit! And when you think you're losing someone, you fucking talk to them—you don't cheat on them!"

"Katherine—"

"NO! We're done—over. Period. For good. You can go fuck whoever you like, and it won't make any difference to me anymore. You're free to stick your dick anywhere you want, whenever you want."

"I'm begging you," he cried, tears on his face.

Seeing him so upset, so tormented, did something to me inside. I hated seeing him that way, and I understood he had a fucked-up way of equating sex with love, that he had no self-confidence or sense of self-worth and that it fed his insane jealousy and determination I would leave him. I knew that he was looking for feeling loved every time this happened. But just the fact that I realized that and felt bad for him infuriated me in a new way and I hated him from the depths of my soul for it.

"You can go fuck yourself!" I shouted. "Don't ever talk to me again."

I turned my back to where he stood in the parking lot outside the fast-food restaurant where I'd picked up a second job for the summer to supplement my income at the catering business—as bad as fast food pay was, it was way better than my catering pay—and headed inside for my shift, ignoring all the looks and low whistles and comments coming from my coworkers and others who'd witnessed the display.

*****

I'd almost decided not to go to the party I was pulling into, not feeling much up to socializing only a few days after I'd broken up with Joe, but I'd already promised I would go—it was a birthday party for one of my coworkers, Christy. All of us who worked together at the restaurant and were in high school or had just graduated were attending, along with a few other of her friends.

"Beer? Liquor?" Dirk asked for at least the tenth time. I'd eventually lost my crush on him after I'd gotten over being devastated when he wouldn't date me unless I gave him a blow job in the movie theater when we were eleven, and now we were friends. While we never hung out, we did occasionally talk on the phone, usually about work or when he needed help with a homework assignment from school, sometimes to give him advice about a girl he liked.

"No, thanks," I replied. "I'm serious—I'm not drinking tonight."

We'd been playing card games and listening to music mixed with the chorus of frogs and insects and I'd laughed as I watched everyone else who was drinking get sillier and sloppier.

"But we're playing *Asshole*," Christy chimed in. "You can't play if you don't drink—it wouldn't be fair to everyone else."

"Yeah, that's not allowed," someone else chimed in.

"Don't be such a goody-goody," Chase added, laughing. Chase was a year older and had just graduated. While he'd been nice enough at work— he had a "good ol' boy from next door" vibe and was always smiling—I'd never hung out with him outside of work.

Fuck it, I thought. *I don't want to spend another second thinking about Joe or Allen or Will or that guy in the truck or Frank and Charlie or fucking anyone else.*

"Fine! Fine, fine!" I said, holding up my hands in a gesture of surrender.

"What do you want?" Dirk asked.

"I don't care—whatever you wanna give me."

He passed me a can of beer and I lifted the tab, puncturing the aluminum. Lifting the cold beverage to my lips, I took a large gulp. It was cool and refreshing, some light beer that tasted almost like seltzer, though because I didn't drink, I could already feel the warmth from the alcohol when that swallow reached my belly and I wanted more of it. I tipped the can and emptied the remainder of the liquid in one go.

*****

My head turned sluggishly to the side and everything around me seemed to blur, reminding me of those time-lapse photographs of busy streets with streaks of light where the cars had passed during the exposure period. Everyone else was laughing and talking around me; someone laughed so hard they fell off their chair. I struggled to make sense of what everyone was saying, but the words were garbled in my mind. There was a dark haze over everything, and I felt like I was swaying even though I was sitting down. *I think I'm wasted. How much did I drink?* Even if I didn't touch another drop of alcohol, it was going to get worse once the rest of what I'd sucked down like water hit my blood stream, though I wasn't sure how much worse because I couldn't remember the time lag between ingestion and intoxication. Or how much I'd downed in that time.

I might actually black out. I shrugged to myself and decided I didn't care. *In for a penny, in for a pound, as Jean would say.* Besides, blacking out would mean a reprieve. I realized I might have had so much that I'd end up with alcohol poisoning and come to in an emergency room. I might even have had so much that I would never wake up at all.

That's okay with me.

*****

My diaphragm contracted to expel something in my throat that was blocking my airway, but then it moved again. I thought I heard grunting over the loud ringing in my ears, but I wasn't sure, and everything was pitch black. *Why can't I see?*

I realized my eyes were closed. Forcing them open took exceptional effort, especially considering the rhythmic blocking of my throat that had me fighting my gag reflex and the sensation of motion that made me feel off balance. I wasn't even sure what position I was in; was I standing? Sitting?

My eyelids slowly peeled back to reveal the answers to my questions, but it took me a few moments to process and understand what was going on. I was in a small, dimly-lit room that was vaguely familiar, though I wasn't sure why for a moment. Then I remembered Christy had given us a tour of her house and this room was in the basement. I was on a twin bed against the wall, on my hands and knees, and Dirk was lying on his back under me, his unzipped jeans and boxers pushed low on his hips, his pubic hair suddenly getting closer to me. As it did, my airway became blocked again just before I felt pressure on both sides of my head yanking me upwards. Finally, everything clicked: I was in Christy's basement with Dirk's penis in my mouth as he guided my head up and down over it.

When the realization hit me, I wanted to spit out what was in my mouth, but I couldn't even figure out how to make my body cooperate to sit back and pull out of the grasp he had on my head. *Well, I guess he's getting that blow job after all,* I thought. *Actually, maybe I'm dreaming. This can't really be happening. Maybe being that drunk—*

My thought was cut short when my stomach contents rose rapidly as I choked, my mouth slammed against Dirk's pubic bone, my effort to stave off my gag reflex failing when he shoved himself into my throat. Unexpectedly, I was pushed backward and the pressure on the sides of my head disappeared as Dirk removed his hands and used them to strip off my shorts and panties, pushing and moving me around like a rag doll. By the time I could process what he was doing, he was already done and pulling me down on top of him. I felt like one of those giant blow-up decorations in front of businesses or in people's front yards around holidays, clumsy and unstable, being pushed around by an external force with no power of my own. Through the haze and confusion, pain signals from the unexpected intrusion reached my brain. *I guess I'm not imagining this after all.*

*****

I was lying in a tent next to the house by myself, crying. Gut-wrenching sobs with snot running down my face, though I was trying to make as little noise as possible—people were passing out for the night and I didn't want them to hear me. Something rustled outside my tent and I tensed, afraid there might be a bear, and clueless what I should do if it was. Not that it would have mattered if I did know—I was so drunk I wasn't sure I could make my body cooperate. The sound of the zipper rising confused me because I was pretty sure a bear couldn't and wouldn't do that, but I had no idea what could be there instead.

"Can I sleep in here?" Chase asked quietly from the tent entrance. "There's nowhere else to crash."

"Sure," I responded in relief, trying to sound chipper rather than like I was crying, failing miserably when my voice broke. Then I sniffled loudly because I was having trouble breathing. *Great, this is so embarrassing. As if everything else in my life, everything else tonight, isn't already a clusterfuck, now I can't stop crying in front of someone I barely know.*

"You okay?" he whispered as he stepped in and zipped up the tent behind him.

"Yeah, I'm fine," I replied as brightly as I could, though I was fairly certain my words had been slurred—talking was unbelievably challenging.

"You know Joe's an asshole, right?" he whispered.

I snort-sobbed. "Yeah. I know." *Though that's only a small part of my fucked-up life. It's not like he's the only one who cheated on me; I wasn't good enough for Allen to be faithful either; they only wanted me for sex. Not just them, but everyone—all of them. And now Dirk...he...I...oh, God.*

Turning, I laid back down and curled into the fetal position, hugging my knees with my back to Chase. My body jerked unnaturally as I tried to hold in my cries, mortified that I couldn't locate my black hole so I could get control over my emotions. Chase shifted and scooted behind me, settling down, but after a few minutes, he rolled and rested a hand on my shoulder. My sobs broke free at the gentle touch—a comforting gesture— and I allowed myself to cry until exhaustion took over.

*****

Someone was gently caressing my arm in my dream, warm breath on my neck. I couldn't see his face because he was behind me, but I knew it was Joe and it was Allen and it was Will. It was none of them, but it was all of them, and it was a gesture of care, an offering of apology. I let out a ragged, teary breath and felt for a moment that I was less broken. That I hadn't deserved what they or anyone else had done to me. That maybe I was lovable. If they were apologizing, then maybe I wasn't at fault for everything that had transpired with them.

But then I was being moved around, and my warm feelings dissipated as I realized I had only been half-dreaming. Someone was indeed caressing my arm and their hot, moist breath was on the back of my neck, but that someone was Chase. Or was this still part of the dream? I shifted onto my belly and the breath left my neck, but now my shorts were sliding down my thighs. Was I hallucinating? I must be; I'd just be still and the hallucination would stop. Then the clothes covering my lower half were catching my knees as they continued down my legs. I squeezed my eyes shut and the sensation of spinning convinced me I must be imagining things, though this wasn't something I wanted to imagine right then—I just wanted to be left in peace. My shorts and panties were now around my ankles, hot hands touching my hips.

"What are you doing?" I asked, foggy and disoriented and still not entirely sure I wasn't hallucinating. Long fingers wrapped around my hipbones, and with a tug, my dead weight was lifted off the ground until I was wobbling a bit on my hands and knees. "I don't understand. What's—"

I was cut off abruptly when he shoved himself inside me, his hips slamming me forward. My arms gave out, so I was now on my elbows, and my head fell to the ground between my forearms. My whole body felt like a live electric wire and the skin on my face tightened, my eyes flooding with fresh tears. Everything between my legs felt raw and burned while Chase held me in place, a tight grasp on my hips as he moved quickly in and out of me. I wanted to flip around and kick him away from me, dart out the tent and drive away or scream at him to get out of me and to tell me how the fuck he thought he could do that to me.

But nothing happened—I couldn't make myself do any of those things. Just as I hadn't been able to with Dirk earlier that night. Just as I hadn't been able to stop Allen when he was hurting me during sex as he accused me of sleeping around while I was away for the summer or that guy in the truck in Chile or Charlie or Frank or Elmer or Terrence. I must have secretly wanted all those things to happen to me because I couldn't make myself fight to stop them, no matter how hard I was screaming at myself to do so.

Please let this be a dream—a bad dream that I'll wake up from soon. Chase's breath came in bursts as he increased his speed, and the thought of what was coming next made my stomach clench with nausea. *If this whole night isn't a bad dream, I'm going to have cum from two guys inside me.*

*****

The next morning, I dragged myself out of the tent and headed to work, realizing I wasn't hungover because I was still buzzed from the alcohol coursing through my veins. As the pavement passed slowly under my car, I tried to sort out what had happened the previous night versus what my mind might have been fabricating, thanks to being wasted. But there was no doubt I hadn't been dreaming; the soreness between my legs was proof of the reality. And no matter how I looked at it, I couldn't see things any other way—I'd chosen to get so drunk that I couldn't distinguish between dream and reality, let alone stop two guys from having sex with me without my permission. Though I'd let them—I hadn't fought against them—so I must have wanted to do it, right? And if I didn't say no and try to stop them, was that consent? How else would they know? I mean, I'd tried to ask Chase what he was doing, but he'd done it anyway. But I hadn't told Dirk no. Or had I? I couldn't remember. I couldn't remember how I even got down to that room or anything before I came to with his dick in my mouth. But that was my fault if I was too drunk to stop him. I must have been asking for it because I chose to get that drunk—I must have wanted to be used for sex. *By two different guys. In the same night.*

That thought was horribly nauseating, and I had to swallow down the stomach bile that made it into my mouth, the acid burning my throat. *You can't just have sex with someone without caring, right? Even if I hadn't wanted it, they must have cared. They must have cared so much they couldn't help themselves, right? Or something like that? Isn't that how that works? I mean, I'd heard from Joe and Allen so many times that they couldn't help themselves when they wanted sex because they just loved me so much. There must be something there. I can't just be a sex toy to them.*

With my buzz for support, I felt brave enough—and desperate enough—to confront them both at work. The stakes were too high not to—if they did that to me and *didn't* care? I couldn't even consider that alternative; just the thought made me feel violent toward myself in a new kind of way, like I wanted to beat myself in punishment.

The first of the two guys I saw was Dirk. With a deep breath, I started, staring at the ground.

"U-um... last night... I-I..." I took and released another breath. "I think... no, I mean, we... did it mean—"

His sharp bark of laughter as he bent over cut me off.

"That was just for fun—you think it meant something more?" He laughed like he was surprised. "I never would have fucked you, of all people, if I hadn't been so drunk and horny."

My heart stopped, and I felt like I'd shrunk down several inches, melting into the ground, but I tried to speak anyway. "But—"

"Just pretend it never happened because it never would have if I wasn't shit-faced. If you tell anyone, I'll deny it, so no one will ever know if you don't say anything."

Pretend it never happened? I came to with your dick in my mouth, not understanding how I'd gotten there. And I should pretend it never happened?

Chase let me finish my sentence when I approached him a few minutes later, but he assured me once I was done speaking that what he'd done had meant nothing, that he had no feelings for me. That he wouldn't have even considered fucking me if he wasn't wasted next to me in a tent and horny as hell. He stared wide-eyed into my face, as he implored me with panicked urgency that I couldn't tell anyone because his girlfriend couldn't find out, that he was going to ask her to marry him. I was dumbfounded—I'd had no idea he even had a girlfriend.

I realized that, to Chase and Dirk, I was just a drunk slut, there for them to use. And I knew if anyone else ever found out, they'd think the same thing. After all, even if I hadn't wanted to have sex with them, I'd been drunk—I deserved it. At least that's what everyone would say, so it must be true, right?

I had a tendency to avoid thinking about the past at all costs, but I thought back to all the people who had hurt me since I was a young child as I went through the motions at work. So many of them were males. Kids, teens, adults—but so many of them males. In my mind, they all—Terrence, Elmer, Charlie, Frank, Will, Joe, Allen, Dirk, Chase, that guy in Chile, even my dad and Trevor—were the same. As I thought about each of them, rage welled up within me, choking me with its thick viscosity, and got stuck as it began to seep out of every pore. I looked around and hated every single male I saw.

I hated Chase and Dirk. I hated the nice old man who came in every Sunday morning for breakfast before church and the dad who came in every Sunday afternoon for a bucket of chicken for his family after church. I hated the man driving the car next to me at the stoplight, even though I'd never seen him. If the person had a penis, I wanted him so far away I couldn't see him, and if I could, I snarled, my face contorting in rage and disgust, and if he looked at me for any reason, I flipped him my middle finger. If I even thought they glanced at my chest, I went on attack, saying every vile thing I could think of, spitting out every derogatory curse word I could remember in the moment. If they tried to speak to me, I told them to go fuck themselves.

Fuck guys. I don't need them. And if one ever thinks he'll touch me again? I'll rip off his dick. I won't even cut it—that would be too easy, it would heal neatly. I'll grab and twist and pull until it rips off. Maximum pain, maximum damage.

I talked about Lorena Bobbit being my hero, how I admired her for taking matters into her own hands to stop what was being done to her, for getting rid of the problem. I started drawing pictures of myself ripping off penises, holding the bloody appendages in my hands. I swore to myself that if a guy ever tried to stick his penis in my mouth again, I'd bite it off. My peers nicknamed me Castration Queen.

The whole problem with males came down to what was between their legs—get rid of that, and the problem would go away, I reasoned. I fantasized about meeting and falling in love with a guy who had been castrated, believing that was the only way I would ever actually be happy.

Loved.

Respected.

Safe.

over the edge

I felt worthless, stupid, and endlessly guilty. How could I have let that happen?
- Rachael Brooks

early october 2001

How did I end up in this situation? How did I let myself look past everything that had happened and find myself willingly walking around the cross-country course with Joe by my side? There wasn't a single reason I could logically recite to anyone to justify even being civil to him, let alone having this conversation. And yet, something inside me that I didn't understand struggled to hold anything against him. That same part of me understood in some way why he was the way he was and wanted to help him heal. And because of that, I was now walking beside him and trying to find words. I'd agreed to consider giving a relationship with him another try a week ago—only a few days after he'd called simply to apologize for everything he'd ever done to me—but he'd just told me that Lynn had called him the night before and I had a bad feeling about what was going to follow those words.

"And?" I asked as emotionless as I could. "I thought you guys broke up."

"We did—a while ago."

"Okay..."

"Her period is late, and she thinks she's pregnant. She's going to take a test tomorrow."

My chest felt like I'd been hit by a sledgehammer, but I started laughing. It was slow at first, more like a chuckle, but soon I was practically doubling over as I walked. "You've got to be fucking kidding

311

me," I muttered more to myself than him. To Joe, I said, "Is it even yours? I mean, you guys broke up because she was cheating on you, right?"

He nodded solemnly. "I don't know if it's mine. But it could be. She was sleeping with both of us when she would have gotten pregnant."

We walked in silence for a bit, but my laughter was fading, and in its place were tears that felt icy against my skin in the cold autumn air. "I'm guessing she'd keep it."

He nodded. "She won't get an abortion. And you know my dad walked out on me when I was little—I can't do that to my own kid. If it's mine, I'm going to be there for it." He inhaled and exhaled slowly. "Would you be willing to be a stepmom to mine and Lynn's kid?"

The tears kept falling, but my laughter returned at the craziness of the situation, the craziness of his question. "You know how ridiculous that question is, right?"

"I know, but it is what it is. I won't turn my back on my kid if it's mine. And I don't want to live without you in my life, Katherine. I understand if you wouldn't do it, but I'm begging you right now. I wish I didn't have to—"

"Well, that would have been easy enough to prevent—don't fuck someone else behind your girlfriend's back. Right? I mean, I would have thought that would be common sense, but apparently not," I continued, lashing out intentionally, wanting right then to see him suffering from even a fraction of the pain he'd caused me. "Just like I guess it's not common sense that even if you're going to cheat, you definitely shouldn't fuck your girlfriend's best friend's little sister because that's almost the same as fucking your girlfriend's sister. Maybe you just need a list of people not to fuck—how about we just say anyone who's not your girlfriend? Would that work?"

I looked sideways at him, my eyebrow raised, waiting for a response. I knew I was being an asshole—I even felt a pang of guilt for it deep in my chest—but I couldn't help it. That was so much easier than letting loose the pain that was trying to escape the hole I'd shoved it into. As I watched, Joe's face crumbled.

"I'm so sorry, Katherine. I told you that. I don't know what else to say."

I shrugged. "Maybe it'd be easier to believe if you hadn't done it so many times already. Or if you hadn't dated the person you cheated on me with." I cast my eyes upwards as if I was honestly trying to figure it out. "Probably both, actually." After the words were out, I could feel the anger subsiding again. I didn't want to show that I was getting upset, so I started walking faster.

"Katherine, wait," Joe called.

As he caught up to me, he reached out, grabbing my bicep. My arm shot forward, jerking out of his hand. "Don't touch me right now," I bit out, my teeth clenched so hard my jaw ached. "Just... don't."

late october 2001

"I told you that you have to stop coming over here," I hissed at Joe when he woke me up by tapping at my window in the middle of the night. "We're going to get caught if you keep it up."

"I had to see you," he whispered back as he climbed in.

Joe had officially been added to my foster mom's do-not-associate list, which made dating him difficult, though not as difficult as it would have been if Lynn had actually been pregnant. I'd tried to explain to my foster mom what I could see about him that she and other people seemed to miss, but I had obviously failed because it didn't make any difference. She reminded me that he'd had sex with Lynn—something I'd regretted telling her as soon as I'd uttered the words when she saw me sobbing the day I found out. Though she likely would have found out anyway because Laurel immediately ended her friendship with Lynn when *she* found out, and Jean would have noticed the sudden disappearance of Laurel's best friend in her life. Regardless, she told me I couldn't have any contact with him anymore.

Not only that, but Joe's mom had pulled him out of school for his senior year. She'd said that she was going to homeschool him, but Joe had confirmed what my foster mom predicted—Joe's mom was doing nothing to educate him. Instead, his mom had told him he needed to get a full-time job, which he'd done. But all this meant that I generally only saw him when he was able to join me on my walks at the cross-country course or when he snuck into my room in the middle of the night.

He pulled the screen down, then twisted around on his knees, falling into my arms, squeezing so tightly it was hard to breathe as his body shivered. It was always the same when he saw me, even if it had only been a day—it was as if he'd been gone for years. His whole body melted when I wrapped my arms around him, and I could feel the energy in the air shift as at least some of his ever-present tension dissolved. I was a balm for him, and I knew it.

We talked, whispering about our days, and then he began to kiss me urgently. I always had mixed feelings about his strong sexual desire; I knew he equated sex with love as he always had, but I felt less able to say no than ever. I loved him with everything inside me, but he was incapable of understanding how that was possible if I wasn't as sexually interested as he was, though I'd tried so many times to explain it to him. I knew that his lack of understanding, combined with his own baggage from his parents and his earlier childhood, was why he needed sex to feel loved and that *that* was ultimately behind every time he'd cheated on me. But I also couldn't go through that again. I knew he'd been faithful since we'd gotten back together—I'd always been able to sense a shift in his energy when he cheated on me long before it came to light—and I hadn't sensed that since Lynn. I'd made the decision to make an effort not to deny him sex again, driven by the fear of my own destruction if he cheated on me again.

After, we lay wrapped in each other's arms as he trembled for long minutes. As always, I was torn between wanting to remain close after and wanting to be completely alone, but I was working on locking away the latter urges along with my aversion to having sex since I didn't understand why I felt that way. My fingertips ran gently up and down Joe's spine as his breathing evened out and his body became heavy.

I want to want this—why can't I? It's not—

My thought was interrupted by sounds of movement in the house and I froze, my body flooding with electricity. I listened for a moment, unmoving, as my foster mom's footsteps neared, followed immediately by the sound of nails clacking on the linoleum in the kitchen—she was taking the dog out.

"Get dressed," I hissed quietly to Joe. "And hide somewhere just in case. I'm going to use the bathroom and stall her if I have to."

I tossed on my nightgown and stepped out of my room, walking heavily to the bathroom. After flushing and washing my hands, I walked out, colliding with Jean in the hallway.

"I can't believe you," she seethed, her face red.

"What are you talking about?" I asked, trying to feign sleepiness as my heart beat out of my chest.

"I know he's here," she replied, turning toward my room.

"What? No one's here," I said, panicking as I hoped Joe had gotten himself hidden.

I followed on my foster mom's heels as she flung open my door and flipped the switch to turn on the light. Joe was at the foot of my bed, still situating his pants. My vision instantly narrowed as everything on the edges turned black.

"Get out of my house," she gritted out. "You can leave the way you came—right out that window."

Joe grinned back at her and took his time as I screamed at him in my head. My foster mom was shouting at him, but I couldn't hear her over my own internal voice and the blood rushing through my ears. I knew what he was doing was a reaction to being scared and anxious—he'd done it enough times when his mom lost her temper, and even with me for me to know that—but my foster mom didn't care to understand that. Once he was out the window and walking away, Jean finally turned to me.

"Jean, I—" I started.

"You little slut," she interrupted. And then she spun on her heel and walked out of my room.

I was still sitting on my bed, her voice in my ear and tears wetting my cheeks, when the sun came up and it was time to get ready for school. I missed everything in class because the only voice I could hear was hers. *You little slut.* Instead of going to the lunchroom, I avoided everyone I could and headed to the classroom of my junior year English teacher. Somehow, I'd started going to her room that year when I needed quiet. I could sit and do nothing or eat or do homework or even chat and she was fine with any of it. She would listen if I wanted to talk but never pressured me to open up about what was on my mind.

"Can I sit in here during lunch today?" I asked quietly, staring at my feet.

"Of course. Are you okay?" she asked gently, her concern obvious.

I shook my head from side to side but couldn't find my voice.

"Do you want to talk about what happened?"

I shook my head again.

"Okay, but I'm here if you do."

I eventually did, crying as I told her that my foster mom and I had more or less had a fight, that I'd screwed up again, done something she would never forgive, and that she'd said something to me that was destroying me, but I couldn't make myself repeat the words aloud. I could have if I hadn't believed them, but the reality was that I did. All those guys who'd in some way been inside me—whether I'd wanted them to or not, I still hadn't stopped it from happening. It was my fault. Secretly, I must have wanted it, right? Or else it wouldn't have happened? Even though I had nightmares about it and thought I would pass out when I even thought about so many of those guys, I hadn't stopped it, so something deep, deep down must have wanted those things to happen—something so deep I couldn't seem to find it. My foster mom was right.

I am *a slut*.

november 2001

Oh no. Oh shit. Shit, shit, shit. Come on, Volvo, you can do it... come on... just make it to the gas station... Ah, shit.

My car had just died on the main overpass that crossed over the interstate and I was alone, unsure what to do. It was Saturday and I was supposed to be headed up to clean the Unitarian church my foster mom had started attending; as an extra side job, I'd picked up cleaning the church every Saturday. But now I was stuck on the overpass and I wasn't sure what to do about it. Up ahead, I knew Joe was parked in the Wal-Mart parking lot, waiting for me. To find time to see each other, even though I was forbidden from seeing him and his mother had threatened to kick him out if he ever stepped foot on the property of the Unitarian church because it would curse his soul, he'd started joining me on my cleaning excursions. We rode together, and then he'd help me complete the cleaning, usually leaving us with enough time for a roundabout way of returning that wound through beautiful back roads rather than flying down the interstate. But right then I was stuck and had no way to get to the church or to tell Joe why I wasn't showing up, and I knew Joe would immediately think the worst.

First things first, though—my car was blocking traffic, so I needed to get it out of the way. I squeezed both of my hands around the steering wheel. *I'll get you towed,* I thought, speaking silently to the car. *Please don't be something majorly wrong, okay?* The old used Volvo—a 1986—that my foster mom had bought the week my sister and I arrived on her doorstep had become mine not quite a year ago. My foster mom had picked me up from my college visit to St. John's in a new Honda Accord and said she intended to get rid of the Volvo by giving it to a junk yard. I'd begged her to give it to me instead, and eventually we'd agreed that I could keep the car as long as I paid to fix whatever mechanical problems there were in order for it run safely, I paid the insurance for it, and I replaced all the tires, which were nearly bald. We'd taken it to a mechanic's shop and I'd crossed my fingers—hard—that the mechanical issue would be minor. I nearly cleared out my savings to pay the $1,200 to have everything done, but I'd figured I had time to build it back up. And I had, but I would need it for college, so I was hoping it wasn't going to cost a fortune to fix whatever had just gone wrong.

I hopped out of the car when traffic came to a stop due to a red light and jogged the rest of the way across the overpass, past the exit ramp from the interstate, to reach the gas station and repair shop on the other side. I walked in and spoke with the man at the counter, asking if I could use his phone. I tried to call my foster mom, but she didn't pick up the phone, so I agreed with the man at the counter to have them tow my car.

*****

"What's that?" I asked, eyeing the used maroon Toyota Corolla in our driveway.

"My new car!" my sister shouted excitedly.

Confused, I looked over at her. "Your new car? Why did you get a new car?"

"Because I didn't have one."

"How much was it?" I asked her.

"Eight thousand."

"Whoa! You're making the car payments for that? How can you afford that on top of paying for insurance?" I asked, shocked. My sister never wanted to pay for anything, but Jean had told us she'd never buy us a car, that that was the kind of thing we had to do for ourselves. My sister also didn't work a lot—I was sure she didn't make enough every month to make both car and insurance payments.

She laughed. "No. Jean's paying for everything."

My stomach dropped and clenched as the skin on my face got hot. *That's not fucking fair! How is that fair? She never pays for anything for me—ever!* My fists were clenched and my jaw tight as I walked through the house looking for my foster mom.

"You bought Laurel a car?" I shouted.

She looked at me sharply. "No. I bought *a* car."

"So, it's for both of us?" I asked, my ire fading.

"No. You're not allowed to drive at all. It's for your sister to drive."

My stomach clenched. "What?" I asked breathlessly.

"You've lost your driving privileges."

"What?" I shouted. "Why?"

"First, you've been sneaking around to see Joe. Second, you wasted a lot of money because you didn't call AAA to tow your car."

As soon as she said the words, my heart dropped—I'd totally forgotten about AAA in the moment. "Why does that even matter? I'm paying for it—it's not coming out of *your* pocket."

"It was wasteful because you were too air-headed to—"

"I'm not air-headed because I forgot! And I tried to do the right thing by having it towed to the mechanic you prefer!"

"And that was so far away that it cost a fortune to tow the car there—if you weren't going to use AAA, you should have had it towed the few feet to the shop right there."

"I was trying to do the right thing!" I shouted back, feeling it wouldn't have mattered what I chose to do, that it would have been wrong regardless. She turned back to her book, but I wasn't done. "Do you know how much it's going to cost to fix the Volvo?" I asked. I was pissed she'd bought a car for my sister, but not because I wanted it for myself—I really liked my old Volvo and just wanted that back.

She glanced at me briefly before looking back down. "I told Skip to keep the car and do what he wanted with it—use it for parts or something. I figured it would be something major. He called this morning and it was actually only the spark plug that needed to be replaced, but I'd already given it away."

I couldn't breathe—my chest wouldn't move. "You... you got rid of my car?"

"That wasn't your car," she said sharply.

"Yes, it was!" I screamed back, tears starting to fall. "You were giving it away and said if I paid for everything it needed that it was *mine* and I did that! I spent over a thousand dollars and you gave it away when all it needed was a spark plug?"

"I'm sorry, Katherine," she said, still looking at her book, but her voice was that same cold tone it had been since my pregnancy—she didn't really care at all.

I turned and started out of the room. "I hate you," I said through clenched teeth.

318

june 2002

I opened the passenger door and slid inside Ella's car, pasting a smile on my face as I pulled the door closed. Not only was I without a car, but I now didn't even have a driver's license; I'd gotten a speeding ticket and because it had been my second one while I was under eighteen, I'd lost my driver's license.

Jean and I had been civil to each other for the last couple of months, but that was it. I wasn't expecting her—or my sister, for that matter—to attend my graduation ceremony. I knew Joe and his parents would be there and I had plans to go to dinner with them to celebrate, but I was going to ride over with Ella.

As we drove the few miles to school, she chatted excitedly as I smiled and nodded, but I was struggling to pay attention to what she was saying. I couldn't believe I was about to be the first person in my biological family to graduate from high school. Or that I'd fucked things up so badly that the only parent I'd had for the last nearly ten years—over half of my life—probably wasn't going. That we weren't really even on speaking terms. That it was the same for my sister, who I'd been reminded countless times was the only family I really had.

What the hell am I doing?

late july 2002

"That's enough of the deceit, Katherine. I won't tolerate any more lying, any more disrespect because you think you can do whatever you want while you're living under my roof. You're almost eighteen and you'll be able to make your own decisions then. But until then, you will follow my rules. If you can't do that, you can leave. Today."

We'd been fighting daily about me seeing Joe again. I'd stopped caring about even trying to hide it; I didn't have the energy. With college coming up in less than two months, I needed as much money as I could save, so I was working full shifts at the catering business and McDonald's. Because I didn't have a car, I woke at 3:45 a.m. so I could toss on my clothes and speed walk the nearly two miles to McDonald's to work the opening shift. Later in the day, once that shift was over, I'd walk the half-mile to my catering job. If I could, I'd see Joe between shifts. Otherwise, I tried to see him at night once my catering shift was over.

I knew what I was doing was dishonest—even though I wasn't trying to hide it anymore—and I knew it was blatantly disrespectful. I felt guilt and shame for doing things so contrary to my nature, and yet I continued to do them. I couldn't figure out why, where my reasoning kept breaking down in the moment, so I stopped even trying. This was just who I was now. Maybe it was who I'd always been—I didn't know. I never felt like I knew who I really was.

"Fine. I'll be gone this evening," I said, forcing my voice to sound like I was talking about the weather the next day even though I could feel the tightening in my body and the emotions surging toward my eyes. Turning so she wouldn't notice, I walked to my room and picked up the phone. It was a Sunday morning, and I knew Joe should be home before his family headed to church.

"Hello?" he answered.

"Jean kicked me out," I said right off the bat. "I have to be gone today."

"Okay," he said without missing a beat. "We'll pick you up after church. Have your stuff ready."

I was sitting on the front porch, my clothes, my flute, stuff I'd acquired for school, and a handful of my favorite books tossed into two fifty-five-gallon trash bags, empty enough for me to easily carry them around.

How fitting, I thought angrily. *How darkly poetic that I'm leaving exactly how I arrived—with everything I own in trash bags.*

welcome to college

"I hate the feeling when you really don't have any emotion. You feel so empty. You're not happy, you're not sad. You're nothing. When your mind is spinning but you can't feel anything."

-Anonymous

mid-august 2002

As soon as I'd turned eighteen, Joe and I had driven a little over an hour with his mom and bought a car together. I had a small investment account I'd contributed to as I grew up and I'd emptied it for the down payment. Joe and I had no credit, and his mom's credit was awful thanks to bankruptcy and a chronic inability to pay her bills on time. The only person who had good credit was Dennis, but he would never consider co-signing on a loan. In fact, Jan and Joe hadn't even told him they were doing it; we'd bought the car during the week while Dennis was away for work. The little used two-year-old Mazda Protégé was beautiful to us—a far cry from the unreliable and unexpectedly expensive ten-miles-per-gallon 1972 Oldsmobile Joe was driving. We'd agreed to 23.9% interest since they were the only dealership willing to give us a loan, and made an appointment to return a week later to have the windshield replaced since it had an enormous crack in it.

The windshield replacement would take all day, and it was pouring rain. I turned to Joe. "What do you wanna do?" I asked, knowing our options were limited. *Maybe we can walk through the bookstore—there's a Barnes & Noble down the road.*

"Let's get tattoos," he replied, wriggling his eyebrows at me.

I rolled my eyes in return—I *hated* tattoos and he knew it. They just looked so... *trashy.* Why would anyone do that? But I knew Joe loved them, everyone in his family having at least one, if not many. "Sure," I said, joking. "Let's get tattooed." I shook my head, following him into the loaner car we had for the day. He turned the key in the ignition and pulled out of the parking space at the dealership. "Do you know where we're going?"

"Yep—you'll see," he replied.

I looked out the window, mesmerized by the rain as he drove. I wasn't sure where we were going, but I didn't really care right then; Joe was in the best mood I'd seen him in in a long time. About twenty minutes later, we pulled into a parking area and I looked at the sign.

"Joe," I started slowly. "What are you doing?"

"We're getting tattoos," he said cheerfully.

"No, we're not," I replied forcefully. "At least *I'm* not."

*****

I bent and gently ran my fingers over the bandage on my ankle that covered the raw and sore skin underneath. They'd said it would be a few more days before my tattoo should really start to feel less sore and be less susceptible to infection. *I still can't believe I went through with it.*

At Joe's urging, I'd picked out a gothic-style butterfly outline and chosen the outside of my right ankle for it. He'd picked out a cat with its claws out to go on his chest, and was adding our first initials to the design—wouldn't it show my dedication to him if I did the same? And so, I had, adding a letter to each butterfly wing. *Not as bad as putting someone's full name on your body,* I'd reasoned.

*****

The atmosphere in the small, overflowing car was heavy—choking, really—as the miles continued to pass under the tires. Hundreds of miles were behind me, but I still had hundreds of miles to go to reach the college I'd decided to attend in a residential neighborhood in St. Paul, Minnesota. Visiting this school had been the other college visit my foster mom had told me I didn't have a choice about, and I'd grudgingly attended the weekend-long organized visit for multicultural prospective students in the early fall. By the end of the first day, I'd secretly thanked my foster mom for making me go—Macalester was definitely going to be on my short list for schools. By the time I was boarding the plane to return to Virginia, I was already filling out the application for early-decision admission. I'd hoped with everything I had that they would accept me, and they had. I'd immediately withdrawn any applications I'd submitted for regular admissions decisions to the other colleges on my list and completed my paperwork to accept the offer of admission to my top pick school.

Joe, however, wasn't thrilled. But there was no way in hell I was giving up my dream to go to my top pick for a school, especially when the school was as good as Macalester was. I'd never really felt like I fit in anywhere, but the closest I'd ever felt to fitting in had happened during that weekend I'd spent there, and nothing was going to make me change my mind about attending.

I was going to miss him, of course, but that wasn't going to sway my decision to go. While I had my doubts about *him*—whether he'd be okay emotionally, whether he'd remain faithful with so much distance between us—I knew *I'd* be fine. As I neared the school, I could feel a shield, almost, going up behind me, blocking out anything that had come prior to that moment, and all I could think about was the next few years at school. It infuriated people when that happened; my foster mom, my sister, my boyfriends—especially Joe—so often accused me of not having feelings when they expected me to be overcome by them. Accused me of being insensitive or uncaring. I knew it wasn't that; I just had this shield that kept me separated from my emotions sometimes. It was that thing that my foster mom and social workers had called my remarkable ability to compartmentalize, but what they didn't understand was that I'd never had any control over when it happened and when it didn't. Sometimes it just... *happened*.

early october 2002

My midsection caved in on itself as I tried to keep my sobs at bay; I needed to clean myself up and get to class. But I couldn't stop the tears from streaming down my face in the bathroom stall, and there was no way in hell I could go back to my room until I'd calmed down. *I won't give her the satisfaction.*

Despite honestly answering the questionnaire to be matched with someone compatible, my assigned roommate, Jess, was *not* a good fit. When we'd met on move-in day, she and her mother had openly laughed at me in front of all the other students and their families for having driven from Virginia instead of flying, carting my meager belongings for college with me instead of having them shipped, and not having two loving parents there with me. They had flown from Boston as a family and had Jess' belongings shipped out to arrive that day. They huffed and clicked their tongues in pity and superiority for hours, and by the time her parents left, I no longer felt like I belonged. Instead, I felt like an imposter who had no right to be in college—let alone a good one.

That had only been the beginning; the discord between us had escalated daily until she now intentionally kept me awake at night even though I had an 8:00 a.m. calculus class, which I'd just slept through because I was so tired. Calculus was the only class I couldn't afford to miss because it was the one that might get a grade low enough that I'd lose my scholarships. I'd signed up for multivariable calculus as the natural next step after taking AP calculus my senior year in high school, and it was a required class for my intended first major in math. But a week after the drop date, when we started working with equations beyond three dimensions, I started having problems. Nothing made sense anymore, and I was suddenly in a constant state of confusion. I started going to tutoring five days a week, which was hard enough since I was not only taking eighteen credits, but also played flute in the campus concert orchestra and worked twenty hours a week in the admissions office as part of my financial aid package. Every spare moment was devoted to calculus—I often even missed the hours the cafeteria was open and had dropped a lot of weight as a result of missing so many meals. I desperately needed that five hours of sleep I allowed myself each night.

november 2002

I glanced up at the clock on the wall in the tutoring center as I packed up my backpack—it was 8:45 p.m. Which I already knew if I thought about it because that's when my tutoring sessions ended. *Duh.* Sighing, I zipped my backpack closed and rubbed my eyes; I was so tired I could barely think straight. But I'd spent nearly the entire day working on calculus in preparation for tutoring and I had work to do for all my other classes as well. Running through what classes I had the next day, I decided to focus on my research paper, which meant I'd need to run to the library. As I buttoned my ankle-length coat, my stomach rumbled—I'd missed dinner. And lunch. And breakfast. Again. There was no hot food anymore, but if I hurried, I could swing by the café inside the cafeteria and get a coffee and a muffin before they closed in fifteen minutes.

With a deep breath to brace myself as I walked out the front door into the cold, I jogged the best I could with my heavy backpack to my dorm a few buildings down to exchange my calculus books for my research binder before rushing to the cafeteria. After tucking my muffin into my backpack, I headed toward the library, walking as I enjoyed the aroma of coffee wafting from my cup up to my nostrils in the cold, crisp air, the most relaxed moment I'd had since I'd woken before calculus class that morning.

Not much longer, I thought as I sat down and pulled out my notebook and muffin. *I just have to hang on for a little over a month, then this semester will be over. Calculus will finally be over. I'll be able to take a breath and figure out what the hell I'm going to do with myself while I'm on break in Virginia—oh, fuck...*

My stomach clenched as I realized I'd forgotten to call Joe. Again. He'd wanted me to call before tutoring, since the time zone difference made it later in Virginia, but I'd been doing work up until the minute my tutor was ready for me, desperately trying to get done what I needed to so tutoring would be most helpful. It was far from the first time it had happened. I'd tried to explain how much work I had, how I couldn't guarantee when I could call or how often, but he didn't understand. He was angry and upset because we didn't talk enough, hurt that I wasn't as affected by our separation as he was.

It wasn't that I didn't miss him, though that's what he thought. I just had so much to do that I couldn't focus on anything else. That shield that had gone up as I traveled across the country was still firmly intact, so while I missed him, I wasn't upset by our distance, either. I didn't know how to explain that, though, and no matter how hard I tried, he didn't understand; he didn't believe that I hadn't found someone else at school. I knew he would already be wrecked if I ran back to my room now to call him because I was late, just as I knew he wouldn't sleep until I *did* call, unable to turn off the images his mind conjured of me with someone else. I knew we'd spend so much time on the phone arguing about what I'd been doing, how I could have forgotten to call him; time that I desperately needed to get my work done so I could keep my grades up.

My eyes burned with tears as I felt a brief desire to just throw my hands up and surrender—just give up. Why was everything I did so difficult, like swimming against a current? I was just so tired, so sick of trying and barely not failing. Maybe I really didn't belong there, after all—

maybe I didn't belong in college. But I didn't even have time to ponder that thought right then; I needed to get back to my dorm and call Joe so I could then work on my research paper.

I looked down to re-pack my backpack and saw my muffin sitting next to my notebook, untouched, and a wave of nausea passed over me. *I'll just save it—maybe I'll be hungry tomorrow.*

early december 2002

"Oh my God... no, no, no... please... don't do this, don't do this!" I shouted at my computer as my heart skipped wildly in my chest.

"What's wrong, Katherine?" my new roommate, Ana, asked as she walked over. After I'd talked to my RA about the problems with Jess, she'd moved in with Ana's roommate and Ana had moved in with me. She and I had gotten along from the first day we'd roomed together.

"My computer... it won't... look—it won't boot up!"

"Let me see if I can help, okay?" she said with a soft voice, gently pulling my hands away from my laptop and sliding it closer to where she stood next to my under-bed desk.

I watched, my eyes filling with tears as she confirmed the charger was both connected to my computer and the wall, as she pushed and held the power button repeatedly, as she looked for a way to remove the battery... all to no avail.

"I'm fucked," I whispered.

"Call IT and tell them it's an emergency," she said, walking back to her side of the room.

"I don't even know the number and I can't look it up because—"

"I'm already getting it for you," she said calmly, looking over her shoulder to smile at me. She walked back over a moment later with a post-it. "Here's the number. Call them. Then use my computer to email your professor. I have some things I need it for, but you can use it otherwise."

"I just..." I started, my tears spilling over as I stared at my overflowing 4-inch binder that represented a semester's worth of research and organization and notes. But the purpose for it all—my thirty-five-page research paper that was half of my grade for the class and due in less than a week—was on the hard-drive of my computer that wouldn't boot up. I didn't have time to recreate anything near the caliber of what I'd spent so many weeks on, and I couldn't afford to even try because it would mean sacrificing the time I needed to be studying for finals in my other classes—especially calculus. I'd managed to keep a B in the class—the lowest grade I could get and keep my scholarships—but barely. I didn't have any cushion to do poorly on the final. "I don't know what I'm going to do," I finally said. "I can't do... I... where would I even start? I mean—"

"It'll be okay," she interrupted. "They might be able to fix it—it might even be something easy. And I'm sure your professor will work with you."

I nodded, hoping she was right.

late december 2002

I thought back on how eager I'd been as I sat in the airport waiting to board my plane a few days ago. I'd been excited to be back in a place where everything felt familiar and to be able to spend time with Joe—despite having to be around his parents—after the record levels of stress I'd experienced during the semester, like my computer faltering at the worst possible time. The machine had mysteriously started working on its own three days later and two days before the paper was due, though I had no assurance it wouldn't happen again.

I'd known that the friction I'd had with Joe during the semester would be compounded once I was back in town with him and I wasn't looking forward to that pressure, even though I was looking forward to seeing him. But, overall, I'd still been excited about the upcoming flight to Virginia. The time away would be a break from the intellectual pressure I'd been under and an opportunity to make a little extra money.

I never should have gotten on the damn plane, I thought.

Joe and I had been fighting almost every second since he'd picked me up from the airport, and being around his parents so much since they were home for the holiday was intense in a way I hadn't expected. I'd known Dennis was an alcoholic from living there for a few weeks over the summer, but I hadn't seen him much because I was working two jobs. And while I was going to be working in my hometown after Christmas until I went back to school, the last few days leading up to Christmas, during which we'd all been together all day, had been a nightmare.

Dennis was either angry, his eyes cold and hard even as he smiled, or making thinly-veiled sexual innuendos to the rest of us, and I often found him staring at my body. I wished I had more sweatpants and sweatshirts because I wanted to be drowning in my clothes when I had to be around him. As always, Jan had my head spinning, one minute laughing and joking and the next screaming and throwing things at us. They congratulated me on finishing my semester, but then Dennis kept telling me about classes that were "actually hard" and Jan would talk about how everything she'd ever done in school was much more challenging. We went out to dinner and Jan screamed at the waiter, accusing him of trying to kill her because there was lettuce on her burger, but I was sure I'd seen her eating a salad in the fall. I was mortified as she cussed at him and told him to take her plate before she went into anaphylactic shock and wished I could hide my face.

The last week of my trip home, Joe and I fought endlessly about me returning to college, about whether or not I was pulling away from him, about whether or not I'd found someone else while I was there. I laughed, but I wanted to scream at him for always thinking he was at the center of everything, explaining that even if I'd had that as a goal, it couldn't have happened because of how much time school itself took. He said he couldn't be apart from me again and I told him he had to because I was going back. And then again for another three years after this one was over. He'd shouted and told me I didn't love him the way he loved me, that he didn't understand why I was so uncaring, and my frustration gave way to sadness and I cried. Then, as I used my shirt to blow my nose, he held out his hand and asked me to marry him.

I looked down at the ring and froze—I'd know that ring anywhere. I'd seen it and the matching wedding band in an antique store in a nearby city about a year or so earlier. We'd gone to a coffee shop in the same area and were walking around after when we decided to enter the antique shop and browse around. There'd been many beautiful things in that shop, but something about that ring set had called to me. I'd chatted with the shop owner about it, discovering it had been made for a woman in England a few generations ago and was passed down for a while until there were no more heirs and it ended up in his little shop. I knew it was more typical to want a large, flashy engagement ring, but this small, delicate, understated set spoke to me. It was simple and elegant at the same time, small and tasteful and beautiful.

"H-how...how did you...?" I asked, shocked. It was a lot more money than I could fathom spending on jewelry.

"I worked a lot, and I sold my snowboard," he said, his eyes red and still moist from crying as we fought.

328

My eyes rounded; his snowboard had been his most prized possession. "Yes," I said.

He crushed me in his arms after sliding the ring onto my finger and we cried together. "I have to go back with you," he said.

I nodded. "Okay. We'll figure it out."

When his mom saw the ring and started calling me her daughter, and Dennis calling me his daughter-in-law, it made me feel sick. I didn't understand what my problem was—they'd been nothing but nice to me, allowing me to stay there, and yet I felt ill at the thought of being related to them.

And now, I was walking up to the front door of my former home, twisting the ring around to hide the stone, to see my foster mom and my sister for only the second time since I'd moved out the previous summer. I knew if Jean saw the ring, she'd be even more disappointed in me and I didn't want to get a lecture from her. I also felt like a hypocrite for knowing I was going to walk in and smile and pretend like all was hunky-dory when I was miserable. But worst of all was knowing that I hadn't defended her when Joe's parents made comments about her being uptight and bitchy as they dropped me off at the house. I hadn't agreed, but I hadn't said anything either; instead, I'd bitten the insides of my cheeks, which were now sore and swollen. I'd been too afraid of how they might react, but I'd hated them for saying those things. I didn't agree with my foster mom, and we didn't part ways on good terms, but that didn't mean I was okay with people saying things like that. I just didn't know how to speak up when I was reliant on the people making the comments.

minnesota

"I believe the effects of intergenerational trauma shape us much more than we might realize."

-Jason Large

january 2003

My foot was bouncing violently as I stared at the computer screen; it was the last opportunity to change my spring semester classes. Any changes after that day would mean missing the first class. *What should I do?* I couldn't just major in literature or Spanish—my intended second major— because there'd be no guarantee I'd get a job after college. How many times had my foster mom told me that I needed something practical? That's why I'd chosen math for the first major, but now that it wasn't option... what was I going to do?

I glanced over the classes again. If I switched something out for a third philosophy class this semester, since I'd already taken one the previous semester, I'd have a philosophy minor. The right side of my mouth tipped up and I shook my head—I wouldn't do that. I wasn't in love with philosophy. I was only taking two more classes because I'd loved the professor, and he was only there for a year while one of our tenured professors was on sabbatical.

I just needed to stick with what I'd already selected and try to figure out what to do prior to the end of the semester. Besides, I felt confident I could handle the workload for these classes, and that was vital since I was starting another part-time job bartending at Fuddruckers; it was the only way we could afford to have Joe living up there. Even though he was renting half of a bedroom in student housing, the cost of that, his food, the car, the shockingly high cost of car insurance in that state, and the money

Dennis was charging him for the car he'd torn the transmission out of when we were sixteen well exceeded what he could make working his job manning a brick oven for a restaurant in downtown Minneapolis.

You know this schedule will work and you know you can handle it. You already made a decision—just stick with it.

february 2003

"You should have called us first," one of the police officers said, his voice both bored and annoyed.

My stomach clenched even tighter as I tried not to throw up, fighting back tears as my whole body shivered in the cold. I was standing with Joe outside the house he was living in as we talked to the police. It was late—nearing midnight—and well below zero degrees Fahrenheit outside.

Only hours earlier, I'd parked the car a block down from my dorm while I ran inside to change from my shift at Fuddruckers before driving to pick Joe up from his job. I'd hesitated because there were clothes and CDs sitting out and St. Paul was a city, after all. But I'd reasoned that nothing would happen in the twenty to thirty minutes it would take for me to return. The car was parked in front of the middle school next door to campus, the sun was only starting to set, and there was an event at the school, meaning the area was flooded with kids and their parents entering and exiting the school in constant motion.

When I returned twenty-five minutes later, rushing into the driver's seat to shelter from the cold air outside, it took me a moment to process that something was seriously wrong. I sat frozen as I slowly looked around, then released a short scream. The entire front passenger window was shattered across the front seat and floorboards, and the car had been stripped bare. I hadn't been gone long and realized they could still be in the area. One could even still be in the back seat, I realized, too scared to look. I jumped out, running inside to find someone to come back and look with me, so I wouldn't be alone if there was someone still inside my car.

We inspected and verified there was no one there. She urged me to call the police, but I couldn't think clearly and insisted we pick Joe up first. She agreed to accompany me on the drive and sit in the car so it wouldn't be stolen while I went inside to get him, holding a blanket up in front of the missing window to block some of the wind. As we drove, I went to push in the car's lighter so I could smoke a cigarette without digging around to find my lighter in my purse, but the manufacturer's lighter end was missing.

My heart beat more furiously against my chest as I struggled to wrap my head around that detail. Take clothes and loose change? Yes. Take checkbooks tucked into the visor? Of course. Jumper cables from the trunk? Sure, okay. But the built-in lighter end from the car manufacturer? What the hell? It was that quality of being so utterly illogical and unpredictable that got to me the most—people who behaved that way, I knew, were a different kind of dangerous.

When I'd told Joe as we walked down to the car together, he'd also admonished me for not calling the police first and my stomach had dropped. *How can I be that stupid? Of course I should have called first!* But all I'd been able to think about was Joe sitting there and waiting for me, not knowing why I wasn't showing up, and I hadn't been able to do that to him. But I'd obviously made the wrong decision, which was only emphasized by this police officer, and I was filled with a sickening shame that, for someone who was supposed to be somewhat smart, I was actually really, really stupid.

"I'm sorry," I whispered to the officer in return. "I... I'm sorry."

"Yeah, me, too," he said in his half-bored, half-annoyed voice. "We might have been able to do something about it if you'd called us sooner. But now?" He shrugged. "It's not likely. Don't keep anything in your car anymore—it's not safe."

Thank you, Captain-fucking-Obvious, I thought angrily. But then I realized that I was the one who'd done something that indicated I was too dumb to realize that fact and nodded, thanking him.

april 2003

Seconds turned into minutes and minutes into hours, and yet I couldn't do anything but lay on my back and stare at the ceiling only inches in front of my face. I knew I had work to do, but I was unable to stop thinking back over the weekend, over what I'd learned earlier that morning... that seemingly benign Sunday morning.

Friday afternoon had kicked off one of Macalester's weekends during which it hosted multicultural high school students interested in attending the school. I'd looked forward to the weekend, proud to be part of the organization that hosted it, remembering it was during one of those weekends that I had fallen in love with the school myself. Not only that, but it was another attempt to eliminate barriers caused by wealth disparities; like their admissions, acceptance for the weekend program was on a need-blind basis. The weekend represented my favorite aspects of Macalester outside of its academics.

Unfortunately, the weekend happened to fall right before several exams and a milestone for an important paper. I was present at all the organized activities, but I didn't do much else with the high school girl who was assigned to me. I felt guilty because I knew I should spend more time with her, but I also couldn't risk my grades and my admission status. I arranged for her to spend the time between organized activities with other hosts and their prospective students, and everyone involved, thankfully, seemed content with the arrangement. She also lucked out, getting to sleep in my bed instead of using her sleeping bag on the floor in my dorm room, because I spent Friday and Saturday night in the library, allowing only a thirty-minute nap here and there.

Time flew by in a blur of research, documentation, and studying, and suddenly Sunday morning had arrived. Yawning and downing buckets of coffee, I made my way to the admissions office to assist with debriefing the high school students on their experience over the weekend and ensuring they were on time for their transportation to the airport. It wasn't long after I arrived that I heard the news, however.

Just after midnight, a man who wasn't a student somehow entered the dorm building next to mine. He found his way into a room where one of our host students and her high school senior were in bed, and held the host student at gunpoint while he raped the high school girl. Nothing like that had happened before—not on the campus itself or in the residential neighborhood surrounding it. While campus was in a city, it felt more bucolic and I'd generally assumed I was safe since I'd arrived.

What if feeling safe had meant I was careless? Even though campus was small, there were so many faces I didn't recognize every day. What if a number of them weren't really students, but rather imposters? How many times had I, like others, held doors open for the people behind me when I entered and exited my dorm and the academic buildings? Ten times a day? Twenty? More? What if it had been me? What if I had opened a door for someone who didn't belong and it had been myself, my host student, or others in nearby rooms who'd been assaulted? I hadn't been at the building where the rape had happened, but if I had, I probably wouldn't have thought twice, wouldn't have known I *should*.

What if I'd already done that and just didn't know?

What if someone else had been raped and kept silent because I'd held a door open for someone?

may 2003

Despite the passage of several weeks since the rape, I felt more like a zombie than anything else as I moved with the throngs of other people heading to class. I was barely sleeping, my nightmares of old having returned in force, filling my nights with scenes of chase and rape when I closed my eyes. But that was only the beginning. The second I decided to step foot outside my dorm every day, I entered a heightened state of awareness and felt like I was in a thriller movie where the camera gets close up on someone who's being pursued, their eyes impossibly wide as they dart around trying to figure out if the people around them are truly strangers or well-concealed antagonists.

For the first few days after what happened, I panicked when it was time to change classes, the students moving en masse to enter and exit the buildings, holding doors open sometimes for long minutes at a time. What if the person behind me wasn't actually a student? What if they followed me in, then hurt someone? I got tunnel vision and felt nauseous, staring wide-eyed at every face, trying to discern if I'd seen them before, if they looked capable of harming another human being. My knees barely held me up by the time I made it to my seat in my classes and I couldn't focus for at least ten minutes, the professor's words a blur of white noise in the background. Sometimes, I never heard a word the whole class.

Passing the exterior entry doors where dozens of students were headed, I beelined for the ashtray on the side of the building that housed my next class and pulled out a cigarette. Since arriving in Minnesota, I'd smoked infrequently during the day, preferring to arrive to class and get set up for taking notes with time to spare. But my new routine involved a cigarette at every class change, putting it out at the very last second to allow me to run from the ashtray to my classroom and walk in seconds before the professor started lecturing. I knew it made me appear irresponsible and lazy, but it meant I could enter the building with no one around me, eliminating the fear of accidentally providing building access to someone who didn't belong.

early june 2003

I still couldn't sleep, staring at the dark ceiling over my head, listening to Ana's deep breathing on the other side of the room—she'd fallen asleep hours earlier. Based on the frequency they'd been occurring, I figured I had about a fifty percent chance of a nightmare-free night, and those odds weren't bad after the nightly occurrence for weeks following the campus rape.

What am I going to do? I had a week left and no idea what classes I was going to take in the fall. No idea what subjects to even consider. When I thought about the options, my chest felt tight and I couldn't breathe—it was like drowning under a wave in the ocean. My plan—the plan I'd had for *years*, the plan that had taken me *years* to decide on—was no longer possible. And I hadn't had a backup; it had never occurred to me that I'd need one. I'd picked something I was good at—really good at—and the thought had never crossed my mind that I could suddenly *not* be good at it.

My foster mom had talked to me about being a lawyer on more than one occasion when I was growing up because of the way she said I would mince words during arguments. I couldn't stomach defending someone I knew was guilty or prosecuting someone I knew was innocent, though; I knew I'd end up fired and disbarred the first time I was expected to. The only other thing Jean had often talked about being a good course of study to provide financial stability was something in business and then one day getting an MBA.

However, Macalester didn't have a business program at all—it was a strictly liberal arts college. Macalester and the University of Minnesota a few miles away had an agreement whereby students from my school could take a certain number of courses there, provided they weren't courses offered by Macalester, but I would have to transfer if I wanted to major in business. And if I tried to transfer somewhere, I might not be able to afford to go; not many schools were need-blind in the way Macalester was and I wasn't sure I'd qualify for scholarships somewhere else. On the other hand, I couldn't just keep going to Macalester without having a plan. I only had scholarships for four years; I couldn't take five to get my undergraduate degree. And if I ended up deciding on a major that meant I had to attend a different school, I would have wasted money that Macalester could have given to another student in need.

I can't do that. I can't take something from someone else. But I also can't make a decision. It's too much pressure. I just need to take a break. Students in other countries take a gap year before attending college... I'll just take one after my freshman year. The leave policy said I could take up to a year off and keep my scholarships. I just have to return by the fall of 2004. I just need a year to try to figure out what to do. Joe and I can get a cheap apartment and just live up here, then I'll go back next year with a plan in hand. I can do that.

late june 2003

"You're a very hard worker," the man sitting at the bar said.

The part-time job I'd started after winter break as a bartender at Fuddrucker's was now my full-time job, though it wasn't enough; Joe and I were barely paying our bills and tearing through the money I'd saved for textbooks in the fall while living primarily off boxed macaroni and cheese.

I half-smiled in response, hoping the man—a regular—would tip me well. Working hard was never a guarantee that the tips would be reasonable. I knew if I could be flirty, it would help, but I just couldn't make myself flirt with strange men getting drunk every night. A week earlier, as we neared closing time, a customer who'd been at the bar for hours asked me for my phone number. I'd heard that I should offer a fake phone number when that happened, but that didn't sit well with me. Instead, I'd smiled and politely declined. He badgered me, trying to talk me into giving it to him as I continued to shake my head. I flashed him my ring, explaining that I was engaged to be married and was not going to hand out my phone number. Digging into his pockets, he then held up both of his hands.

"It's your choice, honey," he said. He shook a hundred-dollar bill that was in one hand. "Give me your phone number and this is yours." He raised the other hand, pinching a penny between his thumb and forefinger, and shook his head as if he was disappointed in something. "No phone number, and this is what you'll get for a night of hard work."

I smiled and said I understood, but that I wasn't going to give out my phone number. He flung the penny at my chest and walked out the door. He was muttering as he went, but my heart was pounding and blood rushing through my veins too loudly for me to hear his words. *I'm not cut out for this kind of shit.*

But the man who'd just spoken to me had never treated me in that way. He was always respectful, usually quiet. His wife had joined him once or twice, and they got a bit raucous together, but only telling stories and laughing.

"I could use an employee like you," the man continued. "How much do you make here?"

I laughed, a little uncomfortable with his question. *Isn't it bad form to talk about your pay?*

"I bet I would pay you more," he persisted when I didn't respond. "I need a supervisor and I see you working in here, working with other people, making sure everything is done. You have leadership ability. My wife and I own a Dairy Queen and we agree you would be a good fit for what we need. And the pay for a supervisor is pretty good—better than here, I'm sure."

I started to decline his offer, but paused instead. Joe and I were struggling financially—if I could make more money, that would be a significant help. "How much?" I asked.

july 2003

"So, it looks like I could make a shit-ton of money here. It says must be personable and willing to work directly with customers, which I already do—"

"What's the job?" Joe interrupted, reaching over to grab the cigarette we were sharing from my fingers.

"I don't understand exactly, but it's for a vacuum company. They have an open house kind of application and meet and greet this weekend. I think I should go."

"Sounds fishy to me that you could make that much money. And what happens if you don't do what they want? Is the whole thing commission-based?"

"It sounds like it's not. I can go to the info thing and find out," I shrugged. "What do we have to lose? I have to find something. We aren't making enough—"

"I know."

"—and I can't stay at Dairy Queen."

"I know," Joe said again with a sigh.

The job had been okay at Dairy Queen, but I hadn't moved to supervisor yet, so I still wasn't making any more money. Not only that, but on my first day there, Don and Rosie, the owners, had talked about how excited they were to have me and their vision that over the next year, I'd take on management of the store so they could open another one. It seemed that, while I'd told them I was going back to college the next year, they were convinced I was going to work for them indefinitely. I couldn't work there for the next year under that pretense, so I'd immediately started looking for a new job.

Guilt shot through my chest, making my heart skip. It felt like a betrayal that I was even looking; Don and Rosie had been kind to us. They'd had us over for dinner several times, followed by hours of playing card games and drinking, then sent us home with bags of groceries since they knew we were struggling to feed ourselves. As guilty as I may have felt about it, however, I couldn't even consider giving up my education, and in the meantime, I needed to be able to pay my bills.

*****

I tried to take a deep breath to calm my nerves, but my chest would not expand fully. *I hate first days.* Reaching over to the glove box, I pulled out a handful of napkins and soaked up as much of the sweat in the armpits of my shirt as I could. *I wish I didn't sweat so much when I was nervous.* With a final sigh, I climbed out of the car and headed toward the doors; even if it meant wet armpits, I didn't want to be late for my first day.

During my interview, the friendly and laid-back woman had explained that I would be part of a sales team, that I'd make a base hourly wage plus commissions, and that my commissions were based on our performance as a team. While I'd confessed that I wasn't entirely comfortable with the idea of trying to sell something, she'd assured me it was a completely different kind of sales.

It had been a week since I'd been in there and I recognized the hallway. When I reached the door I'd walked through previously, I plastered on a smile, twisted the knob, and pushed the door open. If I hadn't already quit my job at Dairy Queen, I would have turned around and left. The outer room that had been filled with desks and chairs and friendly faces and soft music was empty, save for a few boxed vacuums stacked near the wall to the left. *Where was everyone?*

My heart started beating faster than it already had been and I felt the tell-tale dripping of sweat from my armpits. Something didn't seem right— I knew I should leave. But if I left, then I wouldn't have a job at all. Whatever was happening, I *needed* to make it work. Gritting my teeth, I walked in and headed toward a door on the other side of the room.

mid-august 2003

I rolled my eyes as I powered my cell phone off; I couldn't handle Joe's anxiety and jealousy right then. We'd been on the road for work for two days and I knew I hadn't made even a dollar yet. I'd learned that first day that I only received a base pay after a certain number of demonstrations had been secured; demonstrations that I was responsible for securing by knocking on doors and trying to bribe the owners to let us in by shoving a gallon of Sunny D or laundry detergent into their hands. I'd had moderate success at first, but as I was coached to be more persuasive—what felt abusively persuasive to me—I found myself unable to talk my way into a single door. I spent hours every day, from sunrise to sunset, knocking on doors without making a dime.

I'd promised myself that I would do better on this trip; we desperately needed the money. And the stress from our financial situation was compounded by the fact that Joe and I fought daily about everything— *especially* my job. It infuriated me that he didn't trust me, and I lashed out at him, scared it was a cover for him cheating on me again, though I didn't have that feeling I'd always had when he was. On a tubing trip with several of my coworkers that Joe had also attended, I'd even kissed one of them goodbye in front of Joe just to piss him off. I'd only meant to kiss the guy's cheek, but he'd turned and pressed his lips into mine. I'd been furious, but had been too embarrassed to let anyone know that—especially Joe—so I'd pretended that had been my intent and Joe and I had fought for days over it.

Not that I could blame him. With a few exceptions, my team consisted of a group of the most unsavory people I'd ever spent that much time with, many of them felons with rap sheets a mile long, filled with violent offenses: robbery, assault, possession of illegal firearms. While I smiled and smoked my cigarettes, laughing at their off-color jokes and sexual innuendos, inside I was on constant alert, hyperaware of everything around me. I had digestive issues resulting in the longest-running case of diarrhea I'd ever experienced.

I'd smoked pot with my team a few times, succumbing to the pressure from them when I was the only one who didn't want to partake, even being interrogated by one of my team members about being a plant for the police if I didn't join them.

That night, however, they were drinking. Everyone. And heavily.

We were in a decent hotel for the night—definitely the nicest one we'd ever stayed in during our overnight trips—that had a pool and jacuzzi. After tossing my phone into my purse, I pulled out an extra set of clothing to wear since I didn't have a bathing suit and—unlike the other college girl I worked with, Nicole—I wasn't comfortable just wearing my underwear and bra.

I'd never liked being hot, never really understood the allure of a hot tub, but I followed Nicole into the big jacuzzi, wincing as I slid down into the steaming water. *I hope she wants to get into the pool soon.* The guys kept bringing beers over and I declined, watching Nicole accept each one. When she reached her fourth, I finally accepted—desperate for something cold to drink as I battled dizziness from the heat—and sucked down the can of light beer like water. It wasn't long until the dizziness worsened and I accepted another can of beer, thinking it would help.

When the second beer failed to help, I decided I had to get out and cool off. As I tried to stand, I stumbled a bit and struggled to get out of the jacuzzi.

Nicole laughed. "When you drink in a hot tub, you'll get trashed."

Fuck, I thought. I hadn't intended to get drunk, but I could tell I was as I stumbled sideways, fanning my face with my hand in a desperate search for some air flow.

*****

Am I dreaming? I wondered as I stared ahead of me. My body felt like it was floating and there was a throbbing originating from the top of my head. I knew that opening my eyes was going to hurt, so I kept them closed as I tried to piece together what had happened. I remembered getting out of the hot tub, though even that had a haze over it as if there'd been a thick fog. There was a flash of my head smashing against something, a flash of leaning over the pool, though I wasn't sure what happened first. And blood—I remembered a lot of blood. I remembered a towel that was soaked with it, someone joking about us being charged for the ruined linens.

I started to take a deep breath and nearly threw up. *Jesus, I feel like shit. Did I drink more last night? I can't remember...*

Gritting my teeth, I forced my eyelids to open. There were bodies all around me in various states of dress, everyone asleep in a pile. *Oh god.* Slowly tipping my chin down, I verified that I was wearing clothes and breathed a sigh of relief. Using every ounce of effort I could summon, I pushed myself to sitting, then to my feet, and shuffled slowly into the bathroom. There had been a body pressed against my back when I'd woken, but I'd refused to look when I got up; I didn't want to know.

I slowly pushed the bathroom door closed behind me and locked it as I flipped on the dimmest light available. With as deep a breath as I could muster without triggering the nausea again, I lifted my chin to look in the mirror. In the center of my head, right where my forehead met my hairline, I had an enormous bloody lump the size of an egg, the hair that normally grew in that spot completely missing. *Well, that's why my head is killing me. But what the fuck happened?*

Leaning forward, I studied the angry skin. I was sure I had a concussion—there was no way I didn't—and I may need stitches. My eyes fell and landed on a pile of towels on the bathroom floor that were soaked with blood. *Yeah, I'm sure I need stitches. But I can't afford to go to a doctor.* I shuffled from the sink toward the shower and turned on the water. As I waited for the water to warm, I remembered we were heading back that day.

Oh, fuck. Joe is going to lose his shit. Maybe I can hide it... After my shower, maybe I can find a way to part my hair that will cover it, at least until I feel like I can deal with the fallout from telling him.

After my shower, I did my best to cover the spot and worked harder than ever to get us inside people's homes for a demonstration; if I ended up having to go to the doctor for my head, we'd need money even more desperately. As I stood in the intense heat of the sun, struggling to remain conscious and to keep back the tears that continued to surface because of the pain I was in, I heard my coworkers' voices; they were laughing about how stupid I'd been, diving into the shallow end of the pool, but I had no memory of that. It made sense with the state of my head, but how had I been that fucking stupid? And not only that, but one of the guys hinted that I'd slept with several others, too. I'd denied it, though I had no memory of the night before, comforted only by the fact that those others also denied it. But the reality was that I had no idea.

God, I wish I hadn't woken back up.

late august 2003

"If we sell just about everything except our clothes, we can fit everything else into a tiny trailer, pay the money we owe for cancelling our lease, and should be able to buy enough gas to get us back," Joe said as we added up for what felt like the fiftieth time every single thing we thought we could sell quickly.

"Let's do it," I sighed.

I knew it was the only way we had a chance of saving our relationship, which had gone from bad to hellish since my work trip; in fact, we hadn't even spoken civilly to one another until we'd agreed I would quit my job and we'd leave the state. I also knew that if we didn't immediately dump all the bills associated with having an apartment, we'd end up being evicted and bankrupt. We'd cancelled our lease, having decided to spend the rest of my year off back in Virginia where it was less expensive to live, and were simply trying to figure out how to come up with the money needed to get our necessities across the country and not have anything we owed end up in collections.

Joe found someone to buy the furniture items, providing the cash we needed, and then I gave away everything else we didn't absolutely have to keep when the four-foot trailer and the back seat and trunk of our car couldn't fit what was left. We paid the remaining bills and hit the road to make the trek back to Virginia. I mentally waved good-bye to Macalester as we drove past St. Paul, promising silently that I'd be back in a year, even though I didn't feel in my gut that it was a promise I'd be able to keep.

til death do us part

"If there is someone in your life that you can't speak the truth to, and you walk on eggshells to avoid upsetting them, you are being controlled or manipulated."

-Anonymous

early september 2003

After the sudden and stressful departure from Minnesota, the exhaustion from driving over one thousand miles without stopping longer than it took to eat a meal, the worry over almost not making it to the tops of the mountains in West Virginia, and feeling our tiny Mazda Protégé struggle to tow the weight of the U-Haul trailer up the steep slopes, Joe and I had both been filled with a combination of relief and excitement as we pulled out of the last gas station to fill the tank before making it to his parents' house. The buoyancy of spirit, however, had gradually faded into trepidation as the final miles ticked by under the tires until there was nothing save a nauseous unsettling in the pit of both of our stomachs as we turned into the driveway.

The house itself was in a small valley between mountain peaks, where the houses were few and generally far between, and the structure was old and looked its age—and then some—inside and out. Dennis had bought it from his parents decades earlier and had done the bare minimum to maintain it—no more than necessary to keep the water running, electricity on, and toilets flushing.

When we'd walked in, we'd been assaulted by the smell of ammonia and cat feces mixed with stale woodsmoke and cigar smoke; all the smells had always been there but seemed to be more pungent than ever. Aside from Dennis smoking inside and Jan keeping a fire burning year-round, she now had fourteen cats, few of which had been neutered or were kept

343

up to date with shots, and many who preferred furniture, beds, and anywhere in the basement for relieving themselves over using the lone two litter boxes provided or the ample outdoor space.

It was a small three-bedroom house. Joe's parents, of course, occupied the master bedroom. Another bedroom served as storage for all the things Dennis had collected during his life, dating back to his childhood, so full you could barely crack the door open to reach in and add something to the pile. The last bedroom—the one that had been Joe's when I'd met him— held Jan's clothes that didn't fit in her own closet, a massage table, and a small futon. Our first week "home," Joe slept on the sofa in the living room while I slept on that futon next to the massage table.

The day after we'd arrived, Jan and Dennis had sat us down and told us that we would need to get married soon or I wouldn't be allowed to stay. At first, Joe and I had been speechless—they'd mentioned nothing about us having to get married to live there before we returned.

I had nowhere to go; I had no remaining friends from high school who'd be able to take me in, my foster mom and I weren't really speaking, and my sister—still in high school—was still living at home.

"We were going to get married anyway," Joe said with a shrug, taking a drag off his cigarette.

"I know, but... not right now!" I said, pacing as I smoked. "We were going to do it later."

He shrugged again. "But what does it really matter if we were going to get married anyway?"

"It matters a lot! There's the wedding itself, and the name change— how would that even work when I go back to Macalester? Everything is in my name now. And we can't afford a wedding. And you know Jean won't come."

"Who cares?"

"I do."

"You guys don't even talk."

My chest tightened as I thought back to the way I'd left things the year before. "I know," I said quietly, looking away into the woods behind the house. "But she's the only mom—the only *parent*—I have. I don't want to get married if she isn't going to be there."

"Just ask her, then."

"I can't do that."

"Why not?"

I shook my head, irritated. "Because she'll fucking say no!" I shouted.

"Then—"

"I don't want to talk about it anymore," I interrupted him as I tossed my cigarette butt into the can outside the front door and headed in. "Just leave me alone."

*****

"Hi," I said, trying to sound chipper and upbeat. A few hours after arguing with Joe about it, I was on the phone with my foster mom. "So... um... Joe and I..." I swallowed dryly as my vision narrowed and my heart raced. *Please just say yes.* "We're getting married and I'd like you to walk me down the aisle," I rushed out.

There was silence for several long seconds before she responded. "I don't think so, Katherine."

"Would you at least come? Please?" I asked, my voice cracking as tears spilled from my eyes.

I could hear her take a deep breath and sigh. "No. Weddings are supposed to be celebrations in support of the couple getting married, but I don't think you marrying him is something to celebrate, and I absolutely do not support it."

"I understand," I said through my tears. "I figured you would say no, anyway." I waited through several breaths, but when she still hadn't spoken, I hung up the phone.

late september

"I talked to Mom," Joe said one afternoon as we were splitting wood for his parents. "We're going to have a small ceremony here."

My stomach dropped. "No," I said through clenched teeth. "Absolutely not."

We had agreed when Jean said she wouldn't come that we would go to the courthouse—*alone*. I had already agreed to having the date be the same as his parents' and grandparents' anniversary, even though I was averse to the idea. But then he had promised his mother a few days before that she could come to the courthouse with us when she begged him. We'd fought for days because I didn't want her there—I didn't want *anyone* there if my foster mom wasn't there—and Joe had agreed. But he refused to tell his mom no, arguing that while he and I had agreed, he hadn't promised, but he *had* promised his mom.

"I already told her we could, Katherine."

"I don't give a fuck what you already told her," I seethed. "You promised me the other day that you wouldn't agree to anything else after you promised to let her come to the courthouse."

"You act like having a thing here at the house is bad."

"I don't want to do it!" I shouted. "I don't want to do this at all right now—especially without Jean. And you know that. You have to learn to tell your mom 'no' if we're going to get married, Joe. It's bad enough you let her talk you into promising she could come to the courthouse with us after we agreed no one would be there."

"Mom's just excited, you know—"

"I don't care!"

"Katherine—I already told her yes."

"Tell her you were wrong, then."

"I can't do that—she'd be so upset."

"*I'm* upset right now, Joe!" I screamed.

"I know, and I'm sorry, though I don't understand why it's such a big deal. But I won't go back on my word with Mom."

"What about your word with me, huh? You promised me that her coming to the courthouse was it."

"She's my mom, Katherine, you don't understand!"

I clenched my jaw as I fought back the tears that were surfacing. "I'm going to smoke a cigarette," I muttered.

*****

"Okay, Katherine, what are your favorite colors?" Jan asked. She said her wedding gift to us was going to be purchasing decorations for the ceremony and she was heading to the store.

Stuffing down my anger at even having a ceremony, I responded. "Fall colors. Browns and oranges and reds and deep pinks. Even yellows if they are orangey. But not bright yellows. And definitely not light pink or any shade of purple."

"No purples?" she shouted. "That's my favorite color."

No shit—half your clothes are purple, and your bedroom is painted purple. "I know," I said quietly.

"Okay—fall colors."

346

She hopped into her little red sports car and drove off. When she returned a few hours later, a spark of excitement for the wedding had me eagerly meeting her at her car to get a glimpse of what she'd selected. With each bag I pulled from her trunk, though, my heart sank, and anger flooded my veins.

"Um..." I started. "I'm a little confused. Everything in here is purple and yellow."

"Yeah," she said brightly with an enormous grin. "Those were the colors of my first wedding to Joe's father, and it was just so pretty."

"I thought... what happened to fall colors?"

She waved her hand dismissively. "I totally forgot what you said, so I got what I thought you liked."

Liar. "There's so much of it," I murmured, shocked by how many decorations there were for just the four of us plus the pastor who was going to conduct the ceremony.

"Well, I thought we should decorate inside some, too, since we're going to have so many people here."

My heart skipped. "What? People? I didn't think anyone was coming."

"Oh, Joe didn't tell you? Dennis's parents are coming and Justin—you haven't met him but he's a college buddy of Dennis's—and his girlfriend, and..."

Her voice faded under the ringing that started in my ears as I became dizzy.

*****

As soon as Joe got home from work, I started yelling at him about the decorations and the guests, but he only shrugged.

"Mom's just trying to make it nice the best way she knows how."

"By inviting people I don't know when no one was supposed to be here? By making everything the colors I said I didn't like?"

"She said she forgot—"

"That's bullshit and you know it!"

"She just wants it to be pretty, Katherine! She doesn't have a daughter and you're like her daughter now."

"I'm *not* her daughter. And she's *not* my mom," I bit out. "And I'm not going to get married with a bunch of strangers."

Joe laughed. "They're not strangers—"

"They are to me!"

"*I* know them."

I rolled my eyes. "Good for you. But that's not my point. We were supposed to be doing this alone at the courthouse. Hell, we shouldn't even be doing this at all right now! But if we have to and other people are here, I'm inviting some people I actually know."

"We can check with Mom."

"I don't give a fuck what your mom says. It's *my* wedding—not *hers*. So, I'm going to invite my sister and Ella and Janey."

october 2003

Gravel flew furiously behind the car as Jan swerved down the unpaved drive, going up on two tires as she turned at the bottom of the hill from the driveway onto the gravel road. My right hand clung tightly to the door handle, my left clutched the seat near my thigh, and my feet pressed impotently against the floorboards as if there was an invisible brake I could use to slow us down.

"Can you believe that fucking motherfucker piece of shit—FUCK!"

I had started to tune out Jan's screaming that had started before she'd gotten into the car, the painful ringing in my ears mixing with the whoosh of blood and the pounding of my heart as we went up on two wheels around the next curve and she screamed out as she struggled to maintain control of the car.

Please don't let us wreck. Please don't let us wreck. Please don't let us wreck.

I repeated the plea silently all the way over the mountain and into town where we were picking up my sister. It was my wedding day, and my sister was taking me to have my hair and make-up done as a wedding gift, and then coming back up the mountain with us for the remainder of the day. The ceremony was scheduled for early evening, intending to have it conclude at sunset, and it was only lunchtime. *If Jan doesn't calm down, though, we'll never make it back alive.*

I climbed out of the sports car to open the half-door to the back seat as my sister walked down the driveway toward us. As she climbed into the car, I opened my mouth to introduce her and Jan since they'd never met, but I didn't have a chance to speak before Jan did.

"Can you believe that motherfucking asshole I'm married to? Where the fuck does he think he gets off acting like that on our fucking anniversary?" she screamed at Laurel as if they were friends and Laurel had any idea what she was talking about.

My face was on fire and my stomach churned as I watched my sister try to conceal her shock and confusion. I shook my head and tears welled in my eyes. *I can't wait for today to be over.*

After getting my hair and makeup done to the sound of Jan going off about Dennis to everyone in the salon, we were finally headed back over the mountain. There wasn't much time left by the time we arrived, and I changed immediately into my dress, which I'd found and ordered online from a bargain shop for just under a hundred bucks. The dress was beautiful, with thin satin straps and a gauzy top material covered in intricately beaded designs. A simple cut, but that was all I'd ever wanted or needed. When I pulled it on, however, I needed help from my sister to get it zipped; I'd gained more weight since I'd bought it in Minnesota, and I could barely squeeze into it.

"Damn, sis," my sister laughed once I was zipped. "Can I have some of your cleavage?"

I looked down at where my breasts were about to burst out of the top of the dress and felt flames engulf my face—I wanted to put a t-shirt over myself. I knew as soon as I left that tiny room that my ample cleavage would draw my soon-to-be father-in-law's eyes.

"I need a cigarette," I muttered, desperate for something to take the edge off.

"Ew—then you'll smell like cigarette smoke while you're getting married."

"You think Joe won't?" I asked. "He's been chain-smoking since this morning, sure I'm going to back out." *As if I even have a choice.* "I really need to smoke. I don't care what I smell like. I just need a cigarette. Like, right now."

After my cigarette, the following hours flew by in a blur, including Dennis watching the bouncing of my breasts as he walked me down the makeshift aisle on their deck, careful to circumvent his beloved dog who was sleeping where I was supposed to walk and Dennis's dad with his beer in a cozy as we passed. Kissing and being pronounced man and wife, pushing play on the cassette player and having the tape I'd carefully recorded songs onto for the reception skip when it got to our song. My new mother-in-law clinking glasses with the pastor after giving a toast that urged us to have lots and lots of sex so she could have lots and lots of grandbabies. The sinking in my gut when I realized any child I had would have her for a grandmother. Standing with Janey and Ella and feeling awkward, like we were strangers, and realizing in that moment that the friendship I was trying to cling to with them was gone, that I had no one except my sister, who also felt more like a stranger, and my new husband.

I was grateful when the time came for everyone to leave.

Dennis's current job was a few hours' drive away, and he and Jan were planning to drive down there after the wedding so Joe and I could have a few days to ourselves. However, they changed their minds as everyone began to leave and decided to stay, offering instead to let us go stay in the motel room for the next few days. We threw some clothes into the back seat of the Mazda and got on the road in less than an hour. My ever-present tension eased as the miles piled up between us and them. I didn't care that we didn't have money to actually do anything; I was just excited to be away from my new in-laws for a couple of days.

*****

I bolted upright, instantly awake, my heart racing, with the first of a series of loud bangs coming from the door of the motel room. My eyes darted toward the nightstand and saw the neon numbers to indicate the time—it was 7:30 a.m. I reached out, shaking Joe to wake him as my gut twisted into knots. I *knew* what the sound meant now that I'd had a moment to process, though I wanted to be wrong. *There's simply no way. This can't be happening. I have to be wrong. I have to be.*

Joe sleepily rose and went to investigate. As the door cracked open, my suspicion was confirmed: Jan and Dennis were standing on the other side of the threshold.

"Good morning!" they shouted together.

"Mom? Dennis?" Joe asked, confused.

"Yeah," his mom responded, smiling. "We missed you guys, so we thought we'd come down, get another hotel room, and spend the weekend with you. We got up early and here we are."

"Huh?" Joe said, cocking his head to the side.

"Aren't you excited to get some extra time with us?"

I wanted to scream, to tell them the only thing I wanted was a break from them, but I felt a stab of guilt even as the thought took root. So instead, I smiled when they looked past Joe toward where I still sat in bed.

They were doing something kind for us, letting us stay in the hotel room, and it would be ungracious of me to voice what I was thinking; I should be grateful for what they were doing, and I should feel flattered they wanted to spend time with us.

never a home

"I hate this feeling like I am here, but I am not. Like someone cares, but they don't. Like I belong somewhere else, anywhere but here."

-Anonymous

november 2003

My eyes burned with unwanted tears and I clenched my jaw in effort to keep them at bay as I stood at the foot of our makeshift bed—an old, used futon mattress on the cold cement floor under the stairs in the basement. Jan and Dennis had told us we would need to make do with that small alcove—barely large enough for the futon mattress. When we asked if we could have Joe's old bedroom and move the massage table to the basement, we'd been called ungrateful and told we were getting a better deal. Even before we were sleeping down there, I didn't see how that was possible. The space was the about the same, but the washer and dryer as well as the two litter boxes were at the foot of the mattress. There was a cat door insert in the sliding doors that led from the unfinished and unheated basement to the outdoors that not only allowed the cats to come and go as they pleased, but insects and small animals as well.

But the worst part was that the cats thought our mattress and our pillows were extra litter boxes. We often had to strip everything and try to wash it—if the noise of the washer wasn't too loud for Joe's mom—because we came home to cat pee and poop all over our sheets and blankets and pillows. We'd tried using different Febreze sprays and tossing a different blanket over the top, but nothing deterred them.

Could this week get any worse? I thought. I was already feeling down after using gas we couldn't really afford to drive over the mountain that morning to the local free clinic so I could talk to a doctor about getting on birth control, only to be told the earliest appointment I could get would be in three months. Earlier in the week, I'd been excited to finally get hired on as a waitress at a small Italian restaurant over the mountain, but had made significantly less than we would need to pay our bills every month. Just the money we had to pay Jan and Dennis every month exceeded what Joe made at his job. And that didn't include our gas, car payment, car insurance, cell phone bill, or food. Jan insisted they were being generous, but I couldn't wrap my head around how that was possible.

Joe still paid Dennis as a punishment for a wrecked sportscar from years ago, except that Dennis had given Jan a new sports car when that happened, so Joe was actually paying for his mother's car now. We paid for a portion of the food Jan bought, as well as half of all the utilities, even though the area we lived in had no heat or air conditioning, half of the several cords of wood they bought yearly, as well as for most of the cat litter and cat food for Jan's sixteen cats, since she'd acquired two more over the last month. And we also had to pay rent, even though we did all the interior house cleaning, lawn mowing, weeding, bush and tree trimming, wood splitting, picked up their dog's poop from the yard, and cleaned the litter boxes daily in exchange for living there.

When we'd talked about it, Joe and I agreed that it seemed unfair how much we contributed, but when we tried to talk about it with Jan, she got angry. She called us ungrateful and said we had no idea how lucky we were, how good we really had it. When I tried to interject, she called me a bitch and kicked me out of the house and off the property. I'd found refuge at the neighbor's house for the next few hours until she allowed me to return.

How is this my life right now?

january 2004

I watched Jan walk out the door and listened for the sound of her tires on the gravel, the crunch receding as she progressed down the driveway. Finally, we were alone.

"Joe," I called into the living room from where I stood in the kitchen. We were inside to take a short break from chopping wood, something we'd been doing since Jan woke us up at 2:30 a.m. the night before, insisting we chop more immediately as if they didn't already have several cords chopped and stacked under tarps, insisting a snow storm that wasn't forecast was coming and that we would all freeze to death if Joe and I didn't immediately chop the rest of the last several cords they'd had delivered.

"Yeah," he responded, looking up from where his head had been resting in his hands, dark circles ringing his eyes. "I'm coming."

I shook my head. "Screw the wood right now. I need to tell you something."

His face hardened and his eyes widened. "What?"

My heart raced. The last time this had happened hadn't gone well and I was terrified of what might happen this time. But I couldn't *not* tell him.

"U-um," I started, stuttering as I struggled to exhale smoothly. "I'm pregnant."

He froze—he didn't move at all for a long moment as he stared at me. "Fuck."

I looked down, feeling guilty, like I was solely responsible for the predicament we were now in. "Yeah. Fuck."

"Well, I guess we need to tell Mom when she gets back."

My stomach clenched. "No," I said quickly. "We can't tell anyone."

"They'll figure it out, Katherine," Joe said condescendingly.

I rolled my eyes. "I'm going to get another abortion if we can find the money."

"Katherine—"

"No—don't start. I know what you're going to say, but I WILL NOT have a baby in this house. I'd rather fucking die."

He sighed heavily. "But—"

"Think about it! Where would we put a crib? In the basement? So our baby could sleep in cat shit and cat piss? Come on, be realistic. This is *not* a place we could have a baby. And your mom? What if the baby cried too loudly—would she kick us all out? Or throw something at it?"

Joe's jaw clenched and I could see the vein that ran along the side of his face pulsing with his heartbeat. "Fuck!" he shouted. "Damn it!" He slammed the side of his fist against the wall next to him. "No, you're right. We can't. But that means killing another baby."

"Jesus fucking Christ, Joe—it's not killing a baby!" I shouted. "Stop with that shit! Please. We have to figure out how we're going to do this."

"How much does it cost?"

I sighed. "Six hundred dollars, I think. We have to find a clinic, too."

"Fuuuuuck," he moaned.

"I know. We don't have even half of that."

He stared at the floor in silence for several minutes and I waited, unsure what to say. Finally, he looked up. "Okay, we'll tell Dennis the car needs some work and that it's going to cost six hundred dollars, so we'll be shorter than normal this month and have to add it to what we owe him."

february 2004

Something was off when I walked into the kitchen, half-asleep, heading toward the drawer with the drip pans for the electric coil stove, but I wasn't sure what. With a yawn, I opened the drawer to grab the shiny, pristine drip pans so I could swap them with the ones on the stove. We would normally have done it before going to bed, but we hadn't this time.

If anything—even water—spilled onto those drip pans when the coils were hot, they would stain, but having spots on those drip pans sent Jan into rages. So, Joe and I bought an extra set of the drip pans months ago and we simply swapped them out while we cooked. Then once the coils had cooled, we'd pull off the used ones with stains and put the brand-new drip pans back on. We'd discussed the plan with Jan, and she'd approved of our idea; anything that meant she had spotless drip pans was okay with her.

But the night before, we'd gotten home really late from work. We'd been half asleep as we cooked our boxed macaroni and cheese after swapping out every single drip pan for the used ones as we did every time we cooked, just in case a stray drop of water made its way to a pan under an unused burner. But we'd been so exhausted that we went to bed without waiting for the coils to cool so we could switch back to the brand-new drip pans, planning to swap them out first thing in the morning when we got up.

Closing the drawer, I turned to the stove to begin removing the coils and figured out what was off; all the coils and the used drip pans were missing. Confused, I opened the oven, wondering if they were in there for some reason—while I couldn't think of a single scenario in which that would make sense, that didn't mean I wouldn't find them there. Then I noticed that the racks from inside the oven were missing, too. *Did Jan say something about them getting a new stove?* Turning to check the time on the microwave that resided on the baker's rack, I encountered another surprise: the microwave was missing.

I went back downstairs after setting the pristine drip pans on the counter and woke Joe, telling him what I'd found and asking him if he had any idea what was happening. He shrugged and said he would ask his mom. We dressed and headed up the stairs to find his mom in the kitchen making herself a cup of coffee.

She looked up as we walked in, silent as she watched us.

"Good morning," I said.

She stared at me, expressionless and silent.

"Hey mom," Joe started. "What happened to the stove coils and the microwave?"

"You noticed, did you?" she said, her voice icy.

Joe's brow furrowed as he looked at her. "Yeah..."

"I told you guys there would be consequences if you kept staining my drip pans. You need to learn to respect other people."

Joe laughed. "Mom. We switch the pans out, remember? We just were tired last night and didn't switch them back. Katherine went to do it a little bit ago—there are the clean ones right there." He pointed to the shiny metal pans on the counter.

She shrugged and took a sip of her coffee. "You should have switched them last night. I woke up early this morning and came in here and had to look at those disgustingly stained pans on my stove because you were both too lazy and disrespectful to change them."

"Mom," Joe said again, angry this time. "We were exhausted from work. We weren't being lazy *or* disrespectful. The pans are right here. And we'll never go to sleep without changing them first again."

"Too late for that," she said lightly, her eyebrows raised. "You should have thought about that first."

"So, what, then?" I asked. "We have to ask you every time we cook or need to heat something up?"

She laughed loudly, her head shaking as she bent forward, setting her coffee on the counter. "You will not be cooking or heating anything up under this roof until I decide you've been punished long enough. That may be a few weeks or a few months. We'll see when I feel like being gracious enough to give your privileges back."

I balked, staring at her as my mouth hung open. *She's not kidding...*

"What the fuck, Mom!" Joe shouted. "We didn't do anything to your drip pans—that was the agreement!"

"Watch your tone, son!" she shouted back. "This is my house—"

"No," I interrupted, "this is fucking stupid! We can't afford to eat out all the time!"

"You should have thought about that before!"

"We didn't do anything wrong!" Joe roared.

"I can't believe this shit," I muttered.

Jan turned to me sharply, ignoring Joe for a moment. "You don't like it? Fine by me—get the fuck out of my house. Right now."

I rolled my eyes intentionally, knowing it would piss her off. "Right. This is getting old—you kicking me out every time you get mad like a toddler throwing a temper tantrum."

"Get the fuck out!" she screamed as Joe shouted at me to shut up.

Turning, I walked out the front door, slamming it behind me, and stomped next door barefoot. *At least the neighbors are early risers.*

april 2004

"Joe," Jan said as she walked into the living room carrying a large framed picture. "Can you hang this for me?"

Joe looked over and snorted. "No way. Dennis will lose his shit."

There was a running argument between Jan and Dennis about things she wanted to change about the house because Dennis wanted it to look the way his mom had it decorated when he was growing up. Even *I* knew better than to change anything in the house without Dennis's permission; it would instantly trigger his rage, charging the air with violence as his voice vibrated the walls.

"I'm your mother and I'm telling you to hang it," she said, her voice hard.

"No. I won't do it," Joe replied, shaking his head.

"I want it on the wall!"

"Uh-uh. No way. Dennis will be pissed."

"I talked to Dennis a few minutes ago and he said it was fine!" she shouted.

Joe snorted again and I shook my head. *I'm calling bullshit on that one.*

"I'm not hanging it, Mom."

"Are you telling me," she started, her voice rising to a scream, "that my own fucking son doesn't love me enough to hang a damn picture?"

"I love you, Mom, but—"

"If you love me, you'll hang it for me!"

They glared at each other for a long minute and then Joe sighed; he was going to cave.

"Don't do it," I said quickly.

"Stay out of it," Jan said. "This is none of your business, Katherine!"

I shook my head, silently imploring Joe to hold his ground.

"You swear you talked to Dennis?" Joe asked.

"I said I did," she replied.

Yeah, but you also said you're deathly allergic to tomatoes and then eat salsa, and you're deathly allergic to lettuce until you want to eat a salad, I thought as I raised my eyebrows at Joe in warning.

"You swear?" he asked again.

"Yes, Joe, I'm not going to lie to you! And I'd do it myself, but my hands don't work well, you know that."

Except they do when you want them to.

Joe sighed again. "Fine."

*****

We were all home in the living room when Dennis arrived for the weekend. He walked in the door, greeting everyone as he did, then froze when he stepped into the living room.

"What's that?" he asked, his voice nonchalant, though his body was rigid and tense.

My body flooded with electricity and I had an urge to run out the front door; I knew an explosion was imminent. Joe raised his hands in a gesture of surrender but said nothing.

"Hi, honey, how was your drive?" Jan asked, ignoring his question.

"Who hung that picture?" he asked slowly, punctuating each word as if it were its own sentence.

Not even enough time for a heartbeat passed before Jan responded, pointing her finger at Joe. "Joe did it. I told him not to, but he did it anyway."

My jaw dropped and hung there, limp for a moment. I'd figured out long ago that she was a serial liar. I'd realized that she was in some ways abusive. I'd even known how she'd twist facts to cast herself in a more positive light because I'd seen it happen enough times. I'd known all this and yet I was caught off guard by what just happened. In the second after my shock wore off, anger and indignation took its place, supplanting the instinctive fear I had of Dennis's temper that urged me to be as small and quiet as possible until what was about to happen was over.

"That's bullshit!" I shouted at her. "You're lying! I can't believe you're saying that! Joe said no, but you *swore* Dennis agreed to it, then made Joe do it for you!"

Dennis started yelling about people doing things to his house without his permission, his face mottled and red, at the same time Jan started toward me, her face twisted with hate as she screamed at me to get the fuck out of her house and never come back. She called me a liar and a bastard and a cunt and a whore and a slut and a bitch and every other name I'd ever heard of as she pursued me to the front door. The front of the house shook as Jan slammed the door behind me, the sound followed by the loud, dull *thunk* of the deadbolt. Joe's voice joined theirs as I walked shakily to the neighbor's house like I did every time she kicked me out. I knocked and our friend William was already at the door; his whole family could hear the screaming from inside their house, and he'd expected I'd end up over there. He walked out, handing me a jacket, and sat next to me on the steps of his porch. I started shouting, telling him about what happened, but my voice weakened as I spoke until my anger subsided and my words dissolved into sobs.

early august 2004

I stared at the cordless phone in my hand as I paced back and forth in the scorching sun in front of the house; I desperately didn't want to make this call. But it was my only hope of going back to college. Joe and I had told his parents that we would need to add extra money to the tab they kept of money we owed every month so we could hold onto the cash needed to get us back to Minnesota before my classes started at the end of the month and—for the first time—they'd said no. Without withholding some of the money they charged us every month, we couldn't even buy enough gas to drive the twelve-hundred miles. Breathing through the nausea and buzzing in my ears, I dialed.

My foster mom answered on the second ring and I wasted no time explaining our dire financial straits and asking her if I could borrow the money we needed to get to Minnesota and pay a deposit on housing for Joe, mentally crossing my fingers we could find another open spot in student housing since it was the least expensive option. She refused immediately and my heart dropped.

"I will give you gas money to go up there—*alone*," she said.

359

"I can't go without him," I said quickly, thinking about the situation I'd be leaving him in.

"You're blinded by infatuation!" she shouted angrily. "This is your education, Katherine!"

"I know!" I shouted back. "That's why I'm asking you for help. Do you think I'd ask if I had any other option?"

"But you do have options. You have the option to go back if you'll go by yourself. I'll happily help you if he's not with you."

"I can't do it without him," I reiterated, though more quietly. I didn't have to finish the conversation to know what was going to happen. I wanted to make her understand what it meant to leave him behind, what his parents were like, that I couldn't leave him alone to deal with them now that I had such intimate, first-hand knowledge of what it meant to live with them, but I didn't know how.

"I want to help you," she said. "But I can't do that until you're willing to do anything it takes, whatever it takes, to help yourself. When you figure that out, you can call me." And then she hung up.

I stared at the phone, crying for long minutes. I felt like the world was crumbling before my eyes. My ribs hurt from the strength of my cries as I watched my life disappear as if it was being rewound. *It sucks, but I can't do a thing about it. No point in being upset. Just forget you were ever there.* I resigned myself to a life more akin to that of my parents, shoving my emotions into my black hole until the tears stopped falling. Turning, I walked inside, still sniffling as I dug around in my folders of important papers to find my Macalester paperwork and pulled out the sheet with the contact information for the admissions office. Taking a deep breath, I dialed. And then I officially dropped out of college.

late september 2004

"Mom, Dennis," Joe started, his leg bouncing violently where he sat next to me on one sofa, his mom and stepdad seated opposite us on the other sofa. "Katherine and I want to move to Harrisonburg. We can afford it once we're there because we'll be able to work more hours without the commute. But we don't have the money to get moved. Would you be willing to loan it to us? We would need about eight hundred dollars, maybe a little more."

I held my breath, sure they would say no—they'd refused much less than that so we could drive to Minnesota.

"I think something could be arranged," Dennis said with a smile.

My shock and relief made my heart race even more than it already was and set off a throbbing in my face. "Fuck," I whispered, raising my hand to my forehead.

Joe turned sharply toward me. "Katherine?" he asked quickly. "Are you okay? What's wrong?"

I shook my head. "I'm fine, I just need more ibuprofen."

Joe let out a sigh as tension left him. "Okay. I'll get it for you."

"No," I said, already getting to my feet. "I can get it. You guys keep talking."

I walked out of the room, happy for a few minutes to myself, and headed to the bathroom. After tapping out some ibuprofen into my palm and swallowing them with a handful of water from the bathroom faucet, I sat down in the dark room and leaned my head back against the wall, hoping the pain would pass soon, but knowing it likely wouldn't. While it was nowhere near as bad as it had been right after the accident, it was still more pain than I could manage.

Only a few days after I'd dropped out of college, we'd had a week of steady rain from a hurricane that had made its way up the coast. Joe and I were driving over the mountain to go back to his parents' house late one night, both of us having found jobs in a city a little over an hour away. The rain had just tapered off a few hours before we'd started up the mountain. About halfway up, the earth keeping a massive roadside tree's roots stable and the trunk upright had eroded, and the tree had fallen across the road, blocking cars from being able to travel in either direction. The road was the only way over the mountain for many miles, and people filed out of their cars to see if they could do anything to help clear the road.

A man with a truck pulled some rope from inside his cab, and Joe and I helped him attach the rope to one branch at a time. The man would put his truck in drive and break the branch off, then move to the next one. He'd tried tying it around the main trunk first, but the tree was so waterlogged and heavy that he hadn't been able to move it. So, the goal was to remove enough weight by removing branches one at a time until the main trunk could be dragged to the side of the road. The other folks there worked together to dispose of the branches over the guardrail. Joe and I took a branch ourselves with a large secondary branch protruding from it, figuring we could stand the main branch up on the secondary one and just flip it over the guardrail. We got the unexpectedly heavy branch standing up as expected, counted to three, and pushed.

The next thing I knew, I was squatted down in the middle of the road, my hands near my face, an eerie wail filling the air that I suddenly realized was coming from me. Joe appeared and reached out, gingerly touching my face. *Crunch.*

"I think my nose is broken," I said, calm, though I was wondering how my nose could be broken when I wasn't in any pain. "What happened?"

"The branch hit your face," he replied, the tension in his voice betraying his worry and mounting panic.

I stood and Joe led me into the beam of someone's headlights so he could see the extent of the damage. I opened my eyes and looked toward my feet, but I had black spots in my vision and couldn't really see more than hazy light from my left eye.

"Is that blood?" I asked, confused. There seemed to be a thick liquid flowing from my face like someone pouring syrup.

"We're going to the emergency room NOW!" Joe shouted, starting to panic. He led me to our car, but I refused to get in.

"It's our only car, I can't bleed everywhere—it'll stain!" I shouted.

"Just get in the fucking car, Katherine!" he screamed back at me.

"No! The blood—"

"I don't fucking care—we need to go to the hospital right now!"

"NO!" I shouted again. "Find a towel or something first."

I could hear him cussing under his breath as he popped the trunk and began rummaging around until he shoved a small hand towel into my hands.

"Get in the fucking car, now," he said, running around to the driver's side.

I climbed in, needing help to buckle my seatbelt as I held the towel to my face. As soon as the seatbelt clicked, Joe was flying back down the mountain and speeding toward the hospital. The towel became completely saturated and the pain set in—I'd never felt pain like that. It was my nose, my eyes. My face. The back of my head, even, felt like I'd taken a hit from a sledgehammer and my neck ached. It was everything above my shoulders, pain that made it hard to breathe.

The first emergency room ran tests and cleared away some of the blood. My left cheekbone was shattered, and my nose was snapped with some of the bone splintering. I had a concussion, there were abrasions to my eyes which were still filled with dirt and bark from the tree, and I had a puncture wound at the corner of my left eye—a hole the size of the base of my pinky finger that went straight into my sinus cavity, the dislodged bone missing. They said that I was likely out of immediate danger of dying, that I had been extremely lucky; a millimeter to the left and the branch would likely have taken my left eye with it, a millimeter to the right and it would have punctured my brain and caused brain damage. However, they didn't have the expertise to address my injuries in that small rural hospital, so I was sent to another emergency room in a city about a forty-minute drive away. Against the hospital's recommendations, Joe drove me instead of us spending nearly three hours waiting for an ambulance that we couldn't afford anyway—we didn't even have health insurance.

By the time we arrived at hospital number two, the small dosage of painkillers hospital number one had given me having worn off long before, my left eye was completely swollen closed, leaving them unable to determine the extent of the damage to that eye from the tree debris. The doctor on call wriggled a long metal rod up my nose, shimmying it around the shards of splintered bone, before spending the longest ninety seconds of my life forcing the broken bits back into some semblance of being straight. He examined my eye and said they needed to call in a plastic surgeon to close the hole in the corner of my eye socket. The surgeon arrived some time later, telling me again how lucky I was, though this time because there was just enough shredded skin left after he trimmed it for him to sew the hole closed. Any less skin, he said, and I'd have needed a skin graft.

I was provided with paperwork indicating I couldn't work for a minimum of a week, that I would experience a lot of pain on the left side of my face for months—even years—and an appointment to follow up with the plastic surgeon about my left eye once the swelling had subsided and it was time to remove the stitches. After that, I was discharged. We headed home, the tree no longer blocking the road, and I cleaned up the best I could as the sun was rising for the next day.

I called the manager on duty at the Wal-Mart where I worked, explaining what had happened and that I had a note saying I couldn't work that I'd bring in the next week when I returned.

"You have to bring it in by the time your next scheduled shift starts, which is today," he said.

"I have an eye swollen shut and stitches in my face," I said, so drained from the night and in so much pain that I started crying. "I can't do that. Can my husband drop it off for me?"

"Hold on," he said. I waited, sniffling even though the pain through my cheekbone was excruciating each time I did so, until he returned to the line. "No, he can't. You have to drop it off personally."

"Fine," I said, defeated. Hanging up, I turned to Joe and relayed what I'd just heard.

"You've got to be fucking kidding me," he started. "That's bullshit, you're not—"

"Joe, honey," I said as soothingly as I could manage, my eyes closed against the throbbing in my face. "It may be bullshit, but I have to. We can't afford for me to lose my job."

So, instead of sleeping as he should have been before working later in the day, Joe drove me the hour to the Wal-Mart where I worked. He walked in with me, a hand around my waist to keep me from walking into things— aside from suddenly only having only one eye to see out of and my vision blurry from scratches in that eye, every step, every movement created a wave of pain so severe my vision blacked entirely, and I lost my breath; moving only feet left me panting and needing to take a break. I was angry with each step that I had to come in like that to hand them a note I could easily hand to them in a week or even have someone else drop off, but there was nothing I could do about it. So we hobbled to the back of the store and thrust it angrily toward the manager on duty, as he talked into a phone receiver and nodded at me distractedly.

I'd returned a week later, but work had been grueling and required frequent breaks; when the throbbing started in my face, my vision started to fade, and I'd have to sit somewhere dark and quiet for a while before it would come back. As the weeks passed, it happened less frequently, but I could still count on debilitating pain a few times a day.

I took a deep, slow breath, trying to will the throbbing to fade as I sat in the bathroom, listening to the muted sounds of Joe's voice mixing with those of his parents. Moving was going to suck, but I'd happily take the pain I knew I was going to suffer over staying even a moment longer than necessary where we were.

decking

"You wanna fly, you got to give up the shit that weighs you down."

-Toni Morrison

december 2004

We'd been living in our tiny apartment for about two months. When we moved, I'd had to rest often, allowing the pain radiating from the thinly-covered hole into my sinus cavity and my shattered cheekbone to fade back into the ever-present dull throbbing. There was nothing else I could do; the over-the-counter painkillers scarcely took the edge off. Joe wanted to help, but he'd been barely functional since we'd started the hunt for an apartment. I knew he'd moved a lot when he was little and I figured that had something to do with it, so I hadn't blamed him that the bulk of the preparation and packing and moving and unpacking had rested on my shoulders, but it certainly hadn't been easy. Even so, the physical pain was well worth escaping the situation we'd been in with his parents.

Shortly after we got settled, the medical bills had started rolling in. Hospital one included eighteen dollars for the bedpan I had to pee in once while I was waiting to be wheeled back for testing, although it was noticeably missing any charges from the doctor on call there who forfeited his fees because he knew we couldn't afford it. Hospital two had equally insane charges for things like slippers because my shoes and socks were soaked when I'd arrived. Then there was the bill from the plastic surgeon who was charging us eighteen percent interest for his emergency medical services. The final tally—even without the ambulance we'd been told would have cost somewhere between five and twenty thousand dollars—was a little over thirty thousand dollars.

We'd stared at each other and laughed like hyenas. *Thirty thousand dollars?* We could just barely afford to eat in our new living situation, and now we had minimum payments for medical bills totaling over five hundred dollars per month. Not only that, but the minimum payment for the plastic surgeon was less than the monthly interest charges, so our balance got larger every month.

We'd been picking up change we found on the ground and using coin machines to get a few dollars when we had enough; we knew the exact grace periods for every single bill we had and used them, and became intimately familiar with how many days we had between handing a check to someone and having the amount deducted from our bank account, often writing checks for funds we didn't yet have, counting on it not hitting our account a day early before the money was actually there. But with all the medical bills coming due and Dennis now charging us for all the money he'd tallied that we owed him from living there, we could no longer make ends meet at all—we weren't even close.

Joe was the first to get a second job, picking up an overnight shift at Wal-Mart. He begged me not to work any more than I was, keenly aware of the pain I was in every day, but we didn't have a choice. Shortly after he started his overnight shift, I switched my Wal-Mart shift to be overnight with him and then picked up a waitressing shift in the same restaurant where he worked as a line cook and assistant pastry chef.

But it still wasn't enough. With enough caffeine, I'd always been able to function on less sleep than Joe, so against his directive that he wouldn't allow it, I'd been on the hunt for a third job and had just found out that I'd gotten hired at Kohl's and would be starting in two days.

"I don't want you working any more—I don't even want you working as much as you are," Joe said with his jaw clenched.

"I know," I replied quietly. "But we need the money. We can't pay our bills if I don't do this."

"But you're in so much pain, Katherine—"

"It's okay. It's not as bad as it used to be."

"And you'll never sleep!"

I shrugged. "It'll be enough. I barely slept at Macalester and I made it through. I just have to make this work long enough for us to get a few things paid off."

"I don't like this!" he shouted as he started pacing.

I squeezed my knees together where I sat, wrapping my arms around my waist. *I don't like it either, but we have to suck it up.* "Even like this, it's better than it was," I said softly.

Joe's steps halted for a moment as his whole body shuddered. "Jesus Christ, yes."

april 2005

I now worked at Wal-Mart from about 3:00 or 4:00 p.m. until midnight for five days per week, at which point I went back to our apartment and slept for a few hours. At 3:30 a.m., I woke, had a cup of coffee, and then went over to Kohl's, where I worked from 4:00 a.m. until 6:30 a.m. or 10:30 a.m.—depending on my waitressing shift that day—unloading the truck and stocking the sales floor. I then worked waiting tables from whenever my Kohl's shift was over until 2:00 or 3:00 p.m. on the days I was at Wal-Mart and from 3:00 p.m. until around midnight on the days I wasn't. And whenever I had a moment to steal, I now had a dog to walk and—if it had been a long day with us gone—cleanup to do inside the apartment.

Jan had come to visit for a day right after Christmas. When she'd arrived, Joe had still been at work and we'd ended up at the local animal shelter for something to do. I longed for a dog, but knew we weren't really able to take care of one, let alone afford one, in our current situation. However, Jan said she was going to pay for us to adopt a dog as gift to us, and I went home that day with a skinny bundle of orange fur that looked like a fox, who we named Maggie. But then we had dog food and vet bills to add to our financial challenges, not to mention needing to find time to walk her.

And if that wasn't enough, I also had an unusual period to contend with. Since I'd gotten the abortion the year before, I'd tried every type of birth control on the market that was even remotely affordable with unmanageable side effects until we tried the shot. I had no odd side effects and it was easy—a shot every three months. My period had even stopped, meaning I didn't have to worry about spending money on menstrual products. But then something happened around Thanksgiving; I'd gotten a period. That alone wasn't the weird part, though.

What was strange was that my period had not yet stopped a few months later. We'd taken money we didn't have and I'd talked to a doctor, but I'd just been told I was worried for no reason, and that after I stopped the shot, my body would go back to normal. Only, I had already stopped getting the shot as soon as my period wouldn't go away, and I was still bleeding six months later.

As much as I tried to lie to myself, to convince myself that if I drank enough coffee and smoked enough cigarettes, I could will my way through it... I couldn't. The exhaustion and stress and never-ending worry over having enough money to pay our bills and eat, coupled with not understanding what was happening to my body and health, was becoming debilitating. Joe had already broken down under the pressure, leaving his job at Wal-Mart a few weeks earlier. I felt more pressure than ever to make three jobs work; with Joe working only one, the financial burden increased significantly.

But I'd reached my limit and knew I couldn't do it anymore. My eyes burning from the two hours of sleep I'd just had, I couldn't even get up, though I had less than half an hour to get to work at Kohl's. *How am I trying so damn hard and failing so horribly?* My chest felt like it was in a vice, and with a wail, I started sobbing, crying so hard I thought I might throw up the few bites of boxed macaroni I had in my stomach. I couldn't fathom going in or doing anything other than sleeping. I hated myself for being so weak, and I was ashamed to admit that I couldn't carry the load I needed to in order for us to survive.

It felt like the universe was telling me that I just wasn't trying hard enough. I told myself to give a two-week notice, but my body didn't move. I screamed at myself to get up, to get dressed and go in, but my limbs wouldn't obey. Instead, I curled into a ball and sobbed even harder as the minutes, then hours, ticked by. I saw the calls coming into my cell phone, but I couldn't move to answer them. What would I say? I knew everyone would be confused and worried because I was a hardworking and dependable employee; not showing up was completely out of character for me. But nothing could make my body climb off that filthy futon mattress to do anything—even answer the phone.

I'm a despicable human being.

late june 2005

As soon as I'd quit my job at Kohl's, I'd started tracking how much I was making (on average) each night I waited tables and comparing that to my income from Wal-Mart. Realizing I had significantly more earning potential waiting tables, I'd put in my two weeks' notice at Wal-Mart. I'd spoken to my managers at the restaurant and they gave me more shifts to fill the hours I suddenly had available. Soon, I was working there from before breakfast until after dinner.

Joe was struggling emotionally, however—he was passionate about cooking, but the environment in the kitchen where we both worked was toxic. Both the chef and the sous chef were some of the biggest assholes I'd ever met to everyone who worked there, but the other kitchen staff undeniably had it worse than any of us waitstaff did. I'd encouraged Joe to look for other cooking opportunities, his experience and the fact that he and his chef had won a cooking competition a significant boost to his application. Frankly, I didn't care what he did, as long as he was bringing in money and wasn't so unhappy. Seeing the misery on his face every day was more than I could stomach for much longer; he'd had enough shittiness in his life.

He reached his breaking point at the same time he received an offer to lead the kitchen somewhere else. The new cooking opportunity needed him to start right away and he agonized over what to do, knowing he should give a notice, that quitting without one went against everything we believed in and valued. Ultimately, he decided to leave without a notice, however, and I supported his decision—his emotional stability was more important to me than treating his chef with more respect and dignity than his chef gave him.

I hadn't been sure if anyone would ask me about Joe's sudden departure when I went into work—they obviously knew we were married—but no one did. I shrugged it off and figured it was because they realized we were two different people and that Joe leaving had no bearing on my own work, which our recent performance evaluations indicated was stellar. At the end of my shift, I went into the office for my turn to settle up and get my tips for the day as I normally did. But once that was done, the manager on duty asked me to stay another minute.

"Sure," I said, sitting back down and smiling through my exhaustion. Jeff was my favorite of all the managers there and I figured he was going to ask me about covering someone's shift the next day.

He glanced up at me, but then looked sideways at the wall as he sighed. "I've been asked to tell you not to come back."

My heart stopped. "What?" I whispered.

"You're being... let go," he said solemnly.

I stared at him in silence for a moment. *I was being fired?* "Let go? Like... I'm losing my job?"

"Yes."

"But... but *why*? What did I do?"

He glanced at me for a moment as he frowned. "I have no idea. I just had a note when I came in that I was to fire you after your shift today. I wasn't told anything else. I'm sorry."

I nodded as he shrugged apologetically; I could tell he felt bad, but there was nothing he could do. "It's okay," I said, though I had no idea how it would be.

july 2005

I don't have a choice, I reasoned with myself. I staunchly didn't want to do it, but I couldn't see any other option as I stared at it. We had no food, half a tank of gas, about thirty cents in the bank, a stack of bills due, and Joe wouldn't get his first paycheck at his new job for another two weeks.

I'd tried to file for unemployment the day after I was fired, but the restaurant stated that I'd been let go for chronic poor performance, so my claim had been denied. I'd called the unemployment office and explained that it wasn't true, that I'd been fired in retaliation, but without a copy of my performance evaluation to prove it, there was nothing that could be done. I'd also applied to everything that had an application—fast food, gas stations, pharmacies, retail, restaurants—but not one place called me back.

My hands shook as I reached forward and used both hands to gingerly lift my flute. Sitting down, I flipped the case open and gently ran my fingers over the keys. I remembered the day Jean had bought it for me, my shock that something so nice was mine, that someone would give me something of such value. I flashed through the concerts and competitions and lessons and performances and practices in which I'd played the instrument. My index finger smoothed over the pink on the keys where the finish had been worn off by the acids in my skin; when that happened to my peers' flutes, they'd replaced them. But while I'd considered it and could have saved enough money to do it after I'd started working when I was fourteen, I never came close to following through—I had been unable to part with the one I'd been given. I loved that flute as much as an object could be loved, and the thought of selling it felt like a piece of me was being ripped out.

But I have to.

With that thought, I flipped the lid down, locked it, and rushed out the door to the car. It had to be done and there was no point in delaying.

Despite my attempts to package my emotions and toss them into my black hole, I was crying when I walked into the local music shop. I tearfully asked the man behind the counter how much he could give me for it as I set it carefully on his counter, my hands lingering before I could make myself stop touching it. He examined my flute gently before replacing it and slowly closing the case.

"I can give you sixty dollars for it," he said quietly.

I stared into his aged and wrinkled face, his eyes reflecting some of the grief I felt, but it didn't dull the stab of pain his words gave me. I explained with a trembling jaw how special the instrument was to me, how intensely desperate I was, or I never would have even considered getting rid of it.

The man—the owner of the shop—was obviously moved by my emotional display. He explained kindly that he could give me eighty, but that was the most he could do; he'd be lucky to sell it for seventy, so he'd already be taking a loss.

I appreciated his honesty and his gesture of kindness; I'd noticed the dust when I walked in and knew his shop was likely barely afloat. I took the money, swearing I'd be back, though I couldn't figure out how, and drove back to our apartment.

I stared at those four twenty-dollar bills for a long time, thinking about how much money we needed and how that eighty dollars meant nothing, how it really wouldn't even help. I'd surrendered a possession that was so much more than a physical object to me for four measly pieces of paper and wasn't really in any better a position anyway. I fell onto my side on the futon and curled into the fetal position, squeezing my knees into my chest as I sobbed. I was utterly ashamed of myself, of where I'd managed to end up.

I'm just like my parents. I'm a worthless excuse for a human being.

I was disgusted; I wanted to stand up next to my own body and hit and kick and scream at myself for being so stupid, for being such a failure. I couldn't understand how I'd fucked up so badly or how I would ever escape the circumstances I found myself in now. There was a weight pulling both Joe and me down into an abyss, like having boulders tied to our feet and being pushed into the center of the ocean with instructions to swim to shore. There was an indomitable inertia toward the same extreme poverty and misery I'd been born into that it seemed we were simply powerless to battle, as if we'd shown up in a warzone with no weapons and no way to win. I knew if we didn't immediately figure out how to win anyway, we'd never again have a chance of escaping; I felt it deep in my core, in my soul. It was one of those things I couldn't articulate but I just *knew* with certainty.

As I cried, I heard my foster mom's voice in my head from the last phone call I'd had with her. "I want to help you," she'd said. "But I can't do that until you're willing to do anything it takes, whatever it takes, to help yourself. When you figure that out, you can call me."

Death sounded preferable to calling her and telling her that I needed help, admitting that I'd failed to succeed on my own. But it was the exact moment I had that thought cross my mind that I realized that if I *didn't* call her, I would actually die. An early, miserable death that would occur inside well before my body gave out. The light at the top of the hole I'd found myself in was nearly gone and I had exactly one chance to stop it from disappearing altogether.

"I need help," I said on a sob when she answered her phone. "I'll do anything."

"Okay," she said quietly, slowly, after a few excruciating seconds of silence. "Why don't you come over and we'll talk?"

rubber bands and pipe cleaners

"You will find society asking you for the happy ending, saying come back when you're better, when what you say can make us feel good, when you have something more uplifting, affirming. This ugliness was something I never asked for, it was dropped on me, and for a long time I worried it made me ugly, too."

- Chanel Miller

The day I pawned my flute and called my foster mom for help resides in a listing somewhere as one of the worst days of my life. I'd spent most of my days on Earth hating myself in various ways, for various reasons; I'd many times longed for death to provide relief from my pain. But I felt like I didn't *deserve* to be alive that day, to breathe air that someone else on the planet might need.

What kind of person fucked up so badly they pawned their most treasured possession, let alone for a paltry eighty bucks? *Only a complete and utter failure of a human being,* I thought. And making the call to my foster mom afterwards ensured that everyone else would finally see what I'd known about myself all along; that I was worthless and couldn't do anything right—at least not anything that mattered. They'd maybe gasp, shake their heads in pity and disappointment, then walk away for good. Saying aloud what I had done, giving voice to my desperation, would make my failure in life real because you can no longer lie to yourself once you've told someone else the truth. And that failure... it would mean that I had let down every single person I'd ever heard talk about my resilience over the years.

Starting not long after my sister and I were placed into foster care, we heard that word often. I knew what it meant, memorized the definition in the dictionary, understood it was a compliment, and I wore it like a badge of honor at first. My foster mom and social worker would talk, telling my sister and me to go play, but I couldn't help listening, sure some disaster lurked hidden in their conversation. They talked about many things: about how we would be fine if we had some stability in our lives, how we were only children, after all, and that children could bounce back from anything...

Whispers from memories wrapped around my brain like tendrils of fog. *It's not that easy to forget,* they said. I told them they were wrong, swiped my hands around to dispel their unwanted mist, and then swept it all down as deep as I could. *I'm resilient,* I thought. *I can do anything.*

My foster mom would be talking to her friends and they'd ask how my sister and I were doing. She'd tell them, her voice filled with pride and awe, about how well I was doing in school, how high my grades were. That it was simply amazing how resilient kids are, how resilient *I* was. *She's so proud of me because I'm resilient,* I thought. *I can keep this up. I have to keep this up.* I'd push and shove and twist and try to sever and trample and do *anything* I could think of to lock away any remnants of my past— far or more recent—that could threaten my success with being resilient. I screamed silently at the blackened sky at night, begging to just have those memories erased, simply carved out and lifted away; no memories would be a blissful experience, so much easier than trying to make them stay where I wanted them, locked up out of sight and out of mind.

My heart would break, losing a friend or beloved pet or floundering under a wave of longing for my parents. If I couldn't keep it hidden, I'd get sympathetic gazes, a warm hug or two if I asked for it. I'd be invited— sincerely—to talk about it if I liked. And then I was assured I'd be just fine, I just needed to "wait and see," because I was tough as nails, incredibly resilient. Hearing the word started to feel heavy, like a boulder on my back. I wanted to shake my head and hand it back—*thanks, but no thanks*—as if I'd never heard it, as if it had never been said. It got ever harder to lock everything away, and it never lasted as long. I'd think, *I don't want to be resilient anymore.*

Over time, the word took on a different meaning. Someone would say "resilient" and I'd hear "stop showing pain and weakness—that's not allowed." To be resilient was to be perfect, and that was where worthiness could be found. I had to be resilient to be worthy of love, to be worthy of pride, to be worthy of being treated well. Resilient meant doing well in school, never backing down from a challenge, but also never failing.

Resilient meant never making a mistake and pretending my past had no effect on me as if it had never even happened. Resilient meant smiling no matter how I felt inside so I wouldn't make those around me uncomfortable.

I became so adept at pretending my past was irrelevant that I started to believe it myself. To not be controlled by my past, I couldn't be impacted by it at all. And there was no way in hell my past had any control over me. I was better than that—I was resilient, damn it! And resilient meant that I could withstand shock without permanent damage, could recover easily from misfortune—at least, that's what the dictionary told me, and that definition seemed to be borne out in the expectations of those around me.

Shock without damage. Recover easily.

It's no wonder that asking for help and admitting mistakes was so difficult when this was the expectation weighing on my shoulders, the bar I was always measuring myself against. Resilience is used in other contexts in life aside from those provided by Merriam-Webster to refer to people who overcome the most extraordinarily difficult circumstances, and I think many people would be quick to interject here and explain that the dictionary definition isn't what they mean when they call someone resilient. And I would believe it—absolutely. But as my foster mom used to say often, the road to hell is paved with good intentions. The definitions are, in fact, what many people expect, even if they don't realize it.

Let me give you an example.

About a year and a half before the initial drafting of this book, my husband—the same man I married when I was barely nineteen—and I were arguing about his mom being invited to either a holiday or birthday. My husband had not yet made the decision to turn inward and start opening his own long-closed doors, so while he intellectually understood how abusive his mother was both then and years earlier, he shrugged it off and disconnected emotionally. I no longer had that luxury since I'd started my journey of healing, which created discord in our marriage on occasion, and this was one of those times. I was arguing—my heart racing and my body trembling, my hearing and vision distorted as they always are when I even think about his mother—and my husband asked me why I had such a problem with being around her. I balked, staring at him agape for a long minute, sure I'd misheard him, but his expression assured me I had not.

My eyes darted in the direction of my kids, who were happily playing in the next room, before returning to my husband. "You *know* why."

"You *used* to have a reason—that was a long time ago."

Understand that out of everyone who is or ever has been in my life aside from my therapist, no one had ever been more understanding or supportive of my decision to face my past and undertake the journey to heal than my husband. And he *still* said something so dismissive to me. Of course, there were things she'd done to or around our kids, but he was only thinking of what she'd done to me when I was myself a child. The message he was sending was, *Yeah, I know my mom abused you when you were a kid, but that was years ago, so what's the problem? Why are you so upset? You're an adult now, get over it.*

This is a common message survivors receive. *It's awful what happened, no one should go through something like that, but it's been a while since it happened, why haven't you moved on?* Or even, *The abuser loves you and didn't mean to hurt you, can't you see that? You owe them forgiveness, it's time to move on.*

More compassion is given to the abusers than to the survivors of their abuse. Survivors are told we *owe* it to the abusers to forgive them and give them what they want. We are told that our trauma and the way it impacts us has a shelf life, like a gallon of milk in the fridge. At first, it's fresh, palatable. As time passes, it smells a little unpleasant, the taste is stale and beginning to sour. And then it reaches that expiration date and it's lumpy and undigestible. Time for it to go! Toss it and be done with it—no one wants to see or smell soured milk, so get rid of it. Be finished with it, toss it like it was never even there, then just forget about it. Months later, if someone opens the fridge and that milk is still in there, they're indignant. *Why the hell is that milk still there? Toss it already!*

I'll tell you why: because we can't. That rotting milk is forever a part of us now.

Imagine you take two large and sturdy sticks, and you push them into the ground deep enough that they're stable and can withstand the pressure of pulling on them, but at least a few inches remain above the ground. Now, take a rubber band and stretch it out so that it's wrapped around the two sticks. Next, pinch the rubber band and pull it in a third direction. See how it's been deformed—changed—from its original shape? Instead of straight lines between two sticks, there's now a pointed shape, like two adjacent sides of a triangle. Now let go—what happens? It snaps instantly back into place, right? It has returned quickly and easily to its previous shape without any damage. The shape can still be changed, its elasticity is perfectly intact, and it looks exactly like it did right before the pinch-and-pull maneuver.

Remove the rubber band and instead imagine wrapping a pipe cleaner around the two sticks so that it's forming the same shape the rubber band had right before you pinched it—two parallel lines from one stick to the other. As you did with the rubber band, pinch the pipe cleaner and pull it to create the same pointed shape, deformed from how it was originally. Now let go. What happens this time? Nothing—the pipe cleaner remains exactly where it was when you let go, still deformed; it did not return to its previous shape. But is it destined to be that way forever?

Maybe. Maybe not. It depends entirely on what happens next.

If you use your fingers to pull it back toward where it started, spend the time patiently and gently smoothing it back out so the sides are again straight, you can get it back to something at least resembling the shape it started in. It likely wouldn't be perfect—those bends in the metal from the pressure that was applied aren't going to completely disappear, no matter how much effort you put into smoothing them back out and trying to make them look perfect and untouched. But it could again resemble its original state.

The first example using the rubber band is the dictionary definition of resilience, where the object returned freely and easily to its original shape and position on its own. The second example is a little bit murky. The pipe cleaner mostly returns to its original shape and position, but it's not perfect, and it required effort and patience from an external source. Technically, this falls outside Merriam-Webster's definition, but I'd argue this is also resilience.

After we've been through trauma—particularly trauma that is sustained for long periods or occurs when we're young—our natural elasticity fades and we become more and more like the pipe cleaner, less and less like the rubber band. But others expect of us—and, in turn, we expect of ourselves—that we're rubber bands; just pluck us from the situation where the trauma is occurring and plop us into a different one with an absence of trauma—or with less of it—and we'll be good as new in short order. And when it doesn't work that way, people around us are confused; *but we stopped the abuse, what's the problem?* We begin drowning in shame for our weakness, doing anything we can think of to hide it.

And the more people expect us to just flip a switch from traumatized to normal in an instant, to bounce back like that rubber band, the more we bury anything that may threaten to derail our ability to fulfill those expectations. This is akin to draping a picture of a rubber band over the entire area between the sticks to hide the bent pipe cleaner below and saying, "See? I'm a rubber band." If it's a good picture, it fools the people around us who expected that result anyway. And if it's a *really* good picture, we fool ourselves, too.

Then, when the picture inevitably begins to fade and weather over time, the paper thinning and holes appearing, the bent pipe cleaner underneath becomes visible. The people around us are shocked and indignant and don't understand what happened to that perfect rubber band they'd grown accustomed to seeing. We panic, and in our desperation to cover up the misshapen pipe cleaner underneath, we begin grasping frantically at the deteriorating picture of the rubber band, trying to hide the holes and reinforce the thin spots. In our reckless haste, all we can accomplish is ripping it to shreds.

Finally, we're left standing there with nothing left to hide behind, every sense of who we thought we were and what we thought we knew now scattered around us in tattered shreds of paper as everyone's eyes stare at our pipe cleaner, perplexed. *What happened to the rubber band?* We stare back, mouths hanging open because we can't find any words to explain away what they're seeing, only a single thought parading through our minds.

Oh, fuck. I'm not resilient after all. And now everyone else knows it, too.

no blame game here

"It's much easier to vilify than it is to deify. […] Real people fuck up."
-Rebekah Mallory

It's easy—especially in the blame culture we have today—to assign fault to someone for everything that happens, and I know at least a few well-meaning people who read this will be inclined to do so. It was the fault of social services or foster care or my social worker or my foster mom or my teacher... this list could go on for pages. It would be easy for me to say that *someone* should have noticed and that it's unfathomable to place some of these expectations on a child who's been abused, assaulted, neglected. Exposed to the types of things I was exposed to. Even when I shared things I'd never shared before with my foster mom prior to and during the writing of this book, I could see the shame sweep over her, physically transforming her features as she plopped the responsibility square onto her own shoulders, saying things like, "Jeez! Where the hell *was* I?" and "I had no idea."

But some things don't really have a specific cause or catalyst that can be pointed to; sometimes it's the result of small things in aggregate—a jar that is full of millions of tiny grains of sand. And for other things... we live in a different world today than the one I inhabited as a child. While I believe we still have a long way to go in the arena of understanding trauma, complex PTSD, and mental health, and a lot of work to do to improve social services and the foster care system, we have—truly—come a long way in the last few decades. People simply didn't understand then how certain things impacted children. When those lawyers and advocates were saying everything they could think of to persuade me to demonstrate how I'd been touched on that teddy bear, they were sincerely trying to help.

They had no idea it would haunt me for the next thirty years, possibly for the rest of my life. And while knowing that doesn't undo how traumatizing that experience was for me, blaming them for doing the best they could with what they knew doesn't accomplish anything either. People simply can't act on information they don't possess.

I don't blame anyone who missed my calls for help, and I don't blame the people who were only trying to help and didn't know they were making things worse. I don't blame social services for not understanding what children from my circumstances needed outside of a change in environment. I don't blame the friends—the *true* friends—who simply couldn't understand what I'd been through and be there in the way I needed.

I also don't blame myself, as others reading this may feel inclined to do. In the last chapter, I told a story about my husband thinking I no longer had a reason to be uncomfortable around his mother, but here I'll share the ending to that story.

After my husband dismissed my discomfort around his mother, I left the kitchen, muttering that I was going to shower and walked into my darkened bathroom, not even thinking to turn on the lights. I turned the knob to start the shower and mechanically stripped off my clothes. Opening the shower door, I climbed into the still-cold stream of water and my legs collapsed under me. My chest exploded into pain so acute that I couldn't breathe, my body straining but my muscles uncooperative. I thought I was honestly having a heart attack, but I couldn't move or call for help. *I very well may die in this shower.*

Suddenly, I was eight years old, begging my father to believe me that my cousin molested me. I was in my twenties when I found my father again, hearing him tell me I didn't remember things correctly when I brought that incident up, then being driven by him to that same cousin's house.

I was thirteen, begging to be believed that even though I hadn't physically fought back, I hadn't willingly had sex with my boyfriend's brothers, as my boyfriend ignored me, and my friend assaulted me.

I flashed through every memory of trying to explain what my mother-in-law did to me before I had the vocabulary or understanding of the abuse and having people brush me off, saying she was weird, but what could I *really* do about that?

It was over an hour later when I managed to climb out, not having used soap or shampoo—having done nothing save sit on the shower floor crying while stuck in other moments in time. I barely uttered more than a handful of words for the next few days before I even started to function again. I wrote a letter to my husband to explain what I'd been going through once I was able to form words again and handed it to him.

"You should have told me sooner!" he seethed moments later. "I didn't know—I figured you were just dealing with some stuff."

If you're nodding your head in agreement with his reaction, I'll tell you what I told him: it doesn't work that way.

It doesn't work that way.

For those days when I could barely make myself get out of bed, and almost couldn't shower? Those days when I couldn't make my eyes focus and my brain couldn't hold onto and make sense of words when people spoke to me, my eyes in a constant state of flooding with tears?

For those days, I was using every faculty I had just to do that much. I was stuck in a triggered state of psychological and emotional self-preservation and was doing the best I could.

Expecting anything more is unrealistic. Expecting survivors to understand, process, and clearly communicate what's happening during trauma? In the aftermath? When triggered years later? That's cruel. And unrealistic. Impossible, even.

And even if you can function, exposing yourself in that way to ask for help requires trust. Trust in those you confide in, yes, but also trust in yourself. Frequently we have neither. We *especially* don't trust ourselves, and we often don't understand what we're feeling or why or what we need. That expectation that we know these things as we're spinning and tumbling and trying to figure out what happened and which way is up is as common as it is impractical and unfair.

We're all doing the best we can, and we could all use a little more compassion and understanding.

not crazy, not stupid, and not alone

"Every single person you meet is repeating a cycle of generational trauma or carrying the burden of breaking cycles."

-Lindsay Braman

Several years ago, I was a few months into therapy with a new therapist. I'd been through several before finding her, but it had been worth it to keep searching; she was the therapist who restored my faith in therapy.

One day, early in our session, she asked, "Are you familiar with PTSD?"

"Post-Traumatic Stress Disorder?"

"Yeah. You're familiar with it?"

I was quiet for a moment as my mind sifted through everything I knew about PTSD before I responded. "I was going to say yes, but what I know of it wouldn't apply to me because I'm not a veteran and I haven't lived in a war-ravaged country, so I'm going to guess there's something I don't know."

She smiled at me and nodded. "You're right. We'll talk about it a little bit today and then I want you to do some research on your own before we meet next week, but before any of that, I would like to do a diagnostic questionnaire with you, if you're comfortable with that."

"Sure," I replied without hesitation, always eager for more information now that I'd found a safe place where I didn't feel so embarrassed for knowing so little about myself, and where at least one person seemed to understand me and made me feel less alone. Giving names to things I struggled with helped in some inexplicable way to give me power over them and begin to dismantle their control over my life. "Kind of like the one I did for anxiety?"

"Yes, exactly. Like that one, there isn't a specific score that means you have PTSD or you don't, but it's more a sliding scale for its severity. And, of course, it's possible none of this really applies to you, and then we'll know that PTSD isn't something we need to focus on."

I settled back into her deep sofa, kicking off my flip-flops and crossing my legs; I'm short, and when I sit all the way back on most sofas, my legs stick straight out like a child's. Reaching next to me, I slid over a big decorative pillow and situated it on my lap before closing my eyes and inhaling deeply, slowly. A brief hold at the top, and finally a gentle exhale.

"Okay, I'm ready," I said, opening my eyes.

"You'll answer on a scale to indicate severity over the last month, where a zero means it had no effect or didn't occur at all and a four is the most severe, completely disrupting your life."

"Got it," I replied.

"Have you experienced difficulty concentrating?"

I shifted uncomfortably. "Like at my job?"

"Yes. Or anything else you wanted or needed to concentrate on."

My eyes watched my fingers trace the herringbone pattern of stitches on the pillow. "A four?"

"Okay."

"I mean—wait—don't write that down yet. I can't concentrate, like at all, on anything. I go to take a quick shower and somehow thirty minutes or more passes. I find myself staring at my computer screen and realize an hour has disappeared without my knowledge. People talk, but I can't focus on the words long enough to process them. I feel like I'm going crazy, like I'm losing my grip on reality, you know?"

"Yeah," she murmured softly. When I glanced up, her eyes were warm and patient before they blurred.

"Shit—I mean shoot—I'm sorry, I don't know why I'm crying. I'm not a crier, I swear. I know I keep telling you that and then crying in here, but I really don't cry in front of people if I can help it. I'm not an emotional person, I swear." I felt desperate to justify myself, though I didn't understand why or even what exactly it was that I was trying to justify.

"It's okay to cry, to get upset. It's a normal and healthy expression of emotion. And you're safe here." The same words she offered after every time I apologized for tearing up, which I was starting to believe a little more each time I heard them.

I swiped the tears that started spilling over when she *didn't* also demand to know why I was crying like other people would if I let tears show. Sniffling loudly, I went back to what she'd asked me.

"So, I guess a three, not a four. Because no one else has really noticed yet. Well, my husband has, but he thinks I'm just preoccupied with work. But it can't be severe if it isn't yet impacting other people, right? Or maybe it should be a two—I'm probably just over-reacting. I mean, I'm sure I can try harder. If I tried harder, maybe I'd be able to make myself concentrate more. I thought I was trying as hard as I could, but maybe I'm not putting in enough effort, so maybe it should be a two? A one? I don't want to make things sound worse than they are. I mean, there are people who have it so much worse than I do."

I looked up at my therapist briefly, but I couldn't keep my eyes focused anymore—they started darting around the office.

"I'd like you to pick something and try to focus your eyes on it," she said gently. "Keep looking at it while we talk. It doesn't have to be me. It can be anything you want, just keep your eyes on it. And then I'd like you to actually scoot to the edge of the sofa and put your feet flat on the floor."

I flung the pillow to the side in my haste to do as I was told and it tumbled off the sofa. "Sorry," I mumbled as I picked it up and placed it more gently on the sofa. Scooching forward, I started to slide on my flip-flops.

"You don't need your shoes—your bare feet on the rug is fine."

I kicked my flip-flops to the side and focused on a picture frame over my therapist's left shoulder.

"Okay, breathe in slowly. As you breathe, feel the air expand your belly, the blood move through your veins to carry oxygen throughout your body. As the blood reaches your feet, notice your feet on the floor, grounded and stable. *You're here*, they're saying. *You're here. And you're safe.* When you're ready, exhale slowly."

"Okay, I'm alright now, we can continue. I'm sor—" I cut myself off with a short laugh; we'd talked about my propensity for apologizing in an earlier session, and I was working on not apologizing so often, but it was a deeply-ingrained habit that would take time to break.

She smiled at me. "It's fine. I know this is really hard. Take your time. You're doing great."

Great? By what standards? I can't even pick a number and I'm already crying and it's only the first question. I took a deep breath as I shook my head to rid myself of my negative self-talk and focus back on the task at hand. "Can I say three-slash-four?"

"Sure."

We continued with the assessment; some questions were easier than others. It was after the question about avoidance of activities or situations when I confessed that when I was driving alone or with my kids and my husband wasn't there, I would intentionally go the wrong direction out of a shopping center or at an intersection, extending my travel home by five, ten, even thirty minutes or more, to avoid a man or woman at the stoplight holding a sign indicating they were homeless. As soon as I saw the sign, I knew they'd be coming up to the car to ask for money and I panicked, terror and guilt invading every cell in my body. I couldn't see or think or breathe. I'd realize later tears were on my cheeks as I battled throwing up in my lap while I drove, barely managing to stay in my lane. My eyes left the picture frame and scanned relentlessly, my legs bounced violently, and I was drenched in sweat, stuttering my words.

That question got a four.

Right then, my therapist taught me Five Things to help me reground myself. In Five Things, you start with identifying five things you can see. Then four things you can touch, three things you could taste, two things you could hear, and one thing you could smell. The exercise forces you to focus on your senses and is an incredibly effective grounding technique that I still use regularly.

I completed the assessment and felt much the way I did when I completed a Tough Mudder, minus the self-pride: I was mentally and physically exhausted for days. I knew based on my responses—without having to wait for my formal score the following week that would confirm what I already knew—that PTSD was a significant piece of my puzzle.

Armed with that certainty in my gut, I devoured all the information I could find on PTSD over the next week. During that period of intense— borderline obsessive—research, I came across several medical articles and research findings that discussed the way both poverty and trauma, separately as well as in conjunction with one another, literally rewire how your brain functions. Different neural pathways are created based on the basic instinctive survival responses (think fight, flight, freeze, and fawn). The more extreme or the longer the exposure to those catalysts—poverty and / or trauma—the more deeply entrenched those new pathways become. After a certain point, removing the catalysts has no impact—those new survival pathways are now the brain's default pathways.

In addition to removal of the poverty and / or trauma catalysts, there must be *new* catalysts, including conscious intention, for the brain to begin to forge new, *non-survival* pathways. Not only that, but this must occur long enough for the new pathways to become the brain's default pathways and replace the survival pathways already entrenched.

Suddenly, so many things in my past made sense. Instead of continuing to buy into the criticism from others and myself that I'd made exceptionally stupid decisions intentionally, I now realized that making different choices had been nearly impossible under those circumstances. Really, the odds had been stacked against me from the moment I was born into my family, and trying to pretend those experiences never happened meant I was never able to forge those new, healthier pathways.

Were any of the decisions I'd made in the past any less detrimental—the questionable activities I engaged in and revealed in these pages, the equally-destructive but easier to hide behaviors in the years after that phone call to my foster mom for help (the years covered in my forthcoming memoir of addiction)? No. Of course not. I'm not suggesting that at all. The outcomes from what we do, what we've already done, of making a particular decision, will never change. Neither you nor I nor anyone else can undo something that's already been done. But I *was* now able to be gentler with myself, to arrest that immediate sinking feeling when I thought of my past, begin to banish the deep shame I carried for my decisions, and let go of the intense regret that consumed me for things I could never change. While I couldn't ever go back in time, this meant I had the power, and now the knowledge, to change those pathways over time, that I could influence my future to be something different, something better than my past.

Ultimately, I realized I wasn't crazy or stupid. That despite what I'd always told myself, I never *had* been. And then the most astounding revelation of all hit me. I remember the moment I connected the dots—it was like a neon flashing sign in front of my face just like in the movies. I looked up and stared through the window above my computer screen, at least thirty tabs open with various research, frozen as my heart flipped over in my chest. I'd discovered what I had because of published research findings. I put stock in those findings because there were so many of them. And if there were so many studies with large numbers of participants?

I'm not alone.

resilient

Writing this book was extraordinarily difficult. I brushed away thick dust and foreboding cobwebs, shouldered open reluctant doors, and shined a floodlight into some of the darkest places that reside in me. Some of those places I hesitated to enter. I cracked the door, peeked in through that sliver of space and thought to myself, *I don't need to go in here—this one can remain in the dark.* I knew I could just step back, softly close that door, padlock it anew, toss the key for good this time, then get back to working on forgetting it even existed. But then three words echoed in my ears, reminding me of what I'd discovered when I was researching PTSD.

You're not alone.

I took a deep breath, squared my shoulders and gritted my teeth, steeling myself the best I knew how. Then, with a firm grasp on the knob, I flung the doors open with everything I had, ensuring they opened so wide there wasn't a chance in hell they could ever swing back closed. Sometimes what was behind the door came bursting out like a tidal wave that had been contained within the room. Immediately—violently—I was swept off my feet and found myself tumbling as I tried desperately to figure out which direction would allow me to get my head above water long enough to take another breath. I wanted to pull the door closed again as a way to throttle how quickly the painful memories reached me, long enough to catch my breath and brace myself. And when I couldn't do that, I longed to turn and find an exit, to somehow run away; it was too much. So much harder than I'd expected. But I found my footing, got my chin above the waves, gulped in a quick breath and dove back into the flood, driven by that small voice inside me.

You're not alone.

Sometimes I peered through the crack as I slowly opened a door and thought there'd been a mistake. *There's nothing here,* I thought. I let the door swing fully open, stepped inside, and then I saw a little girl, scared, lost, and confused, with only herself to rely on. I watched as I realized I was seeing my younger self and my heart shattered into thousands of tiny pieces. I cried for her and wished I could go back in time and hold her tight, could use my body to shield her from all the things I knew were still to happen to her. I wanted to turn away when I could do nothing but watch, felt I could handle no more heartbreak and still have a functioning organ in my chest to keep me alive. But that quiet voice was growing ever stronger, ever steadier, and rose above the pain, the tears. The broken-heartedness.

You're not alone.

Sometimes what I discovered challenged all the progress I'd made to be forgiving and understanding of myself, everything I'd learned and been practicing in order to put an end to shame having control over my life. *How could I have done these things, allowed those other things to happen to me? In what world could I have believed that was a good idea?* I thought there was no way I could ever tell anyone some of what I discovered because... what would people think of me if they knew? But I reminded myself that what I was doing wasn't just about me—that it was about so much *more* than me—and that I needed to remember what I knew deep down.

You're. Not. Alone.

I opened doors and revisited rooms I'd already been to, made sure every inch of every room saw the brightness of the light, was free of dust and debris and cobwebs; anything left behind would flourish once I'd moved on to another room and I was determined to empty this mental house of horrors. I found myself on many occasions re-examining my life and my goals, questioning my desire—my ability—to continue. Was healing for myself and my family, was writing a book about those things I was healing from, important enough to justify what I was putting myself through? And I'll be honest, there were days when I was coming out of a three- or four- or five- or seven-day-long period of minimally functioning, of being ashamed that showering myself felt like an accomplishment akin to single-handedly winning a war of global proportions, when my answer was a tearful—but resounding—"no."

But then I remembered that I'm not alone, that there are so many of us survivors in the world. I imagined for a moment what I would have thought, what I would have felt, if I'd discovered a book like this one five years ago when I was struggling with my first therapist as an adult, feeling that her apathy was my fault because I was crazy. Stupid. Alone. Ten years ago, when I was battling myriad addictions to keep from caving under the pressure of being successful in order to redeem myself by doing what everyone else thought I should do and trying to bury anything that threatened my ability to do so. Twenty-five years ago, when I was hating myself more each day, trying to fit in with normal society and hide my oddities and my trauma, becoming more adept at pretending anything unpleasant in my past hadn't happened so I wouldn't feel so isolated and alone.

It would have changed my life. Reading about someone like me would have made me realize I wasn't alone. Reading about that person somehow making it through to the other side of the darkness, without shying away from all the messy, unhappy middle of that journey—without painting a rosy picture when it would have been a lie—would have been the life raft I was desperately searching for and never found.

My life likely would have unfolded differently and I'm confident I'd have made fewer self-destructive decisions. Maybe if I'd discovered it early enough, I wouldn't have turned to a suicide attempt, addictions, and self-harm to cope. Maybe I wouldn't have taken responsibility for other people's actions, *their* decisions. Maybe I wouldn't have blamed myself for being abused and molested and raped and sexually assaulted.

Of course, I *could* be wrong; perhaps it *wouldn't* have changed my life. Maybe I wouldn't have been receptive in the way I needed to be for it to have a profound impact. But just the *possibility* that it would have, coupled with knowing that I was desperately searching for something like this, means there is the potential for this book—for my life story—to positively impact someone else's life trajectory, to maybe spare them some pain, even if it's only the pain of feeling alone. And that "maybe" was good enough for me, so I staggered on.

And as I uncovered and sat with the darkness of my past, I noticed something else happening; my feelings toward the word "resilient" began to shift. While typing the word still causes a flutter in my stomach, my heart rate is only slightly elevated and no longer racing. I don't feel the visceral hatred for it that I've had for much of my life, that I had when I first wrote the introduction to this book.

The underlying issue driving my relationship with the word wasn't that I couldn't live up to societal expectations for resilience, but rather that those expectations weren't—and still aren't—aligned with reality.

I'm not a failure, I suddenly realized. *I'm a pipe cleaner.*

And I'm fucking resilient.

Wondering what happened after I called
my foster mom?

The next several years are the subject of
my memoir on addiction, expected in 2023.

acknowledgements

There are so many people to thank with any publication of a book, though I'm finding it most difficult to write this section for *this* book—my memoir. So many people have contributed in various ways throughout my life to help me become the woman I am, the woman who was ultimately able to write down my life's stories on the page for you to read. For you to find recognition and healing within.

There are two people I equally want to thank first because without them, my life story would have been so vastly different. Mom, thank you for not fighting to keep my sister and me with you when social services got involved. I know this may seem like a strange thing to say, but I believe you loved us enough to realize you were giving us the best gift you possibly could—a chance at a better life than you'd ever be able to provide. Yes, I spent much of my life feeling that was a sign you didn't love me, but I realize now it was the greatest act of love you could have bestowed upon us; I can only imagine how painful that was for you to do and I thank you from the bottom of my heart for doing it anyway. Equally, I want to thank my foster mom. Your generosity and kindness meant my sister and I had a stable home for the first time in our lives. You provided opportunities we never dreamed of and always encouraged us to do everything the best we could. Thank you for opening your heart and your home to us, and thank you for loving me and never giving up on me even when it was challenging to do so. I love you.

Sister of mine... thank you for being okay with me baring the parts of our history together I know you never wanted to see the light of day, for supporting me in my journey to heal and to write this book to help others heal. Thank you for giving me a reason when we were little to find the good in the world. Love ya, sis.

Thank you to my husband, Joe. We have a seriously rough history that continues well beyond where this book leaves off in time, but we stuck together through our trauma. Through all the noise in our lives, when it mattered most and no one else did, you always believed me. Ultimately, you have taught me what it is to truly love and find forgiveness as well as

393

be loved no matter what. Thank you for believing in me and in us even when I struggled to do the same—I love you.

Thank you to my two daughters, Marie and Grace. You came into my life many years after the time period in this book, but you were the catalyst for me to finally make the decision to face down my past and ensure you both had a better life, free of the kinds of experiences I lived through. Without you, I never would have healed the way I deserved and the way I needed to in order to write this book to help others. Thank you for being my inspiration, my heart, my reason. I love you both to the moon and back... and then some.

Janey—I miss you something fierce. I blamed you for a long time for abandoning our friendship, though I also understood it was complicated. I wish things could have evolved differently, but I am forever grateful for the time I had you in my life.

Thank you to everyone who read this book as a draft. To friends who cried as they read, but continued anyway. To the beta readers who were willing to take on not only a mammoth of a book, but one that was far from easy to read, filled with a myriad of triggers. A special thank you to Melissa and Olivia for being there when I just needed another soul to read the things I'd been through, for being a safe place for me. You'll never understand how much that meant to me or how grateful I am to you both. Just know you were critical to my healing as well as this book seeing the light of day.

Thank you to my therapists over the last few years. You all contributed in vital ways to my ability to heal and use my pain to help others. A special thanks to Shealyn for restoring my faith in therapy in full and for being exactly the therapist I needed when I called. Words cannot express my gratitude that I had you in my life for the short period I did.

Kayli and Olivia—you guys are the best editors anyone could ask for and my writing improves after every time I send something to you. Equally, I feel my life is better for knowing you both. Thank you from the bottom of my heart for not only taking on a project such as this with so much heart and care, but for your compassion and kindness regarding my experiences, and your tact with editing such personal content. You ladies are two of my favorite humans.

I can't thank you enough, Kathy Parker, for letting me use your beautiful words in another one of my books. Everything you've written, everything you continue to write, helps so many heal, including myself. Thank you for writing and thank you for letting me use that writing.

Shelly, thank you for the stunning custom artwork for my cover and interior—who knew that happening to cross paths on Twitter would lead to a collaboration like this one? I couldn't be happier with your work and I'm touched by your effort and care to use your considerable talent to make something so beautiful for me to use. And thank you to Murphy for (yet again!) designing a spectacular cover for my book baby; so glad to have you in my graphic design corner.

Thank you to Chanel Miller, K.L. Randis, and Rachael Brooks, among others, for telling your stories without cutting corners or adding a more positive spin on your experiences. Your courage has given me courage to do the same and I'll be eternally grateful. A special thank you to Rachael for your thoughtful, beautiful foreword to introduce my book; your words mean the world to me.

Finally, an enormous thank you to Brené Brown—your life's work and the books you've written based on that work have played a vital role in helping me heal and smooth my jagged edges.

resources

Below are a few resources that I've found helpful along my journey to heal from the trauma of my past, including organizations, websites, and books that can provide assistance, educate, and nourish the soul as it heals. There is a more comprehensive listing on my website at www.kturnerwrites.com/resources.

Organizations

RAINN
RAINN (Rape, Abuse, & Incest National Network) is the nation's largest anti-sexual violence organization.
www.rainn.org
800-656-HOPE (800-656-4673)

National Suicide Prevention Lifeline
National Suicide Prevention Lifeline provides free and confidential support for people in distress, prevention and crisis resources, and best practices for professionals.
www.suicidepreventionlifeline.org
800-273-TALK (800-273-8255)

ACA
ACA (Adult Children of Alcoholics World Service Organization) provides information and a safe environment to foster healing from growing up in dysfunctional homes with abuse, neglect, and trauma.
www.adultchildren.org

ADAA
ADAA (Anxiety and Depression Association of America) works to prevent, treat, and cure anxiety disorders and depression.
www.adaa.org

NIMH

NIMH (National Institute of Mental Health) is the lead federal agency for research on mental disorders and aims to transform understanding and treatment of mental illnesses.

www.nimh.nih.gov

NSVRC

NSVRC (National Sexual Violence Resource Center) provides leadership in preventing and responding to sexual violence.

www.nsvrc.org

Books

Know My Name by Chanel Miller

Beads: A Memoir about Falling Apart and Putting Yourself Back Together Again by Rachael Brooks

The Unravelled Heart by Kathy Parker

Braving the Wilderness by Brené Brown

The Gifts of Imperfection by Brené Brown

I Thought It Was Just Me (but it isn't) by Brené Brown

Spilled Milk by K.L. Randis

Healing Trauma by Peter Levine

Other

This Girl Unravelled (https://kathyparker.com.au/)

Brené Brown (http://www.brenebrown.com/)

about the author

Katherine Turner is an award-winning author, editor, and a life-long reader and writer. She grew up in foster care from the age of eight and is passionate about improving the world through literature, empathy, and understanding. In addition to writing books, Katherine blogs about mental health, trauma, and the need for compassion on her website www.kturnerwrites.com. She lives in northern Virginia with her husband and two children.

by katherine turner

Fiction

<u>Life Imperfect Series</u>

Finding Annie

Willow Wishes (2022)

Non-Fiction

moments of extraordinary courage

resilient: a memoir

Fantasies, Volume I: An Anthology (2022)

CPSIA information can be obtained
at www.ICGtesting.com
Printed in the USA
BVHW070356130821
613493BV00001B/8

9 781734 423075